D1807579

Capitalism in Transformation

Capitalism in Transformation

Movements and Countermovements in the 21st Century

Edited by

Roland Atzmüller

Johannes Kepler University, Austria

Brigitte Aulenbacher

Johannes Kepler University, Austria

Ulrich Brand

University of Vienna, Austria

Fabienne Décieux

Johannes Kepler University, Austria

Karin Fischer

Johannes Kepler University, Austria

Birgit Sauer

University of Vienna, Austria

Edward Elgar
PUBLISHING

Cheltenham, UK • Northampton, MA, USA

© Roland Atzmüller, Brigitte Aulenbacher, Ulrich Brand, Fabienne Décieux, Karin Fischer and Birgit Sauer 2019

All rights reserved. No part of this publication may be reproduced, stored in a retrieval system or transmitted in any form or by any means, electronic, mechanical or photocopying, recording, or otherwise without the prior permission of the publisher.

Published by
Edward Elgar Publishing Limited
The Lypiatts
15 Lansdown Road
Cheltenham
Glos GL50 2JA
UK

Edward Elgar Publishing, Inc.
William Pratt House
9 Dewey Court
Northampton
Massachusetts 01060
USA

A catalogue record for this book
is available from the British Library

Library of Congress Control Number: 2019949930

This book is available electronically in the **Elgar**online
Social and Political Science subject collection
DOI 10.4337/9781788974240

Printed on elemental chlorine free (ECF)
recycled paper containing 30% Post-Consumer Waste

ISBN 978 1 78897 423 3 (cased)
ISBN 978 1 78897 424 0 (eBook)

Printed and bound in the USA

Contents

Contributors

Roland Atzmüller is Associate Professor at the Department for the Theory of Society and Social Analyses, Institute of Sociology, Johannes Kepler University Linz, Austria. He works on critical social theories, transformation of (welfare) states, social policies and work. Recent publications include: *Krisenbearbeitung durch Subjektivierung: Kritische Theorie der Veränderung des Staates im Kontext humankapitalzentrierter Sozialpolitik*, Westfälisches Dampfboot 2019; *Empowering Young People in Disempowering Times: Fighting Inequality through Capability Oriented Policy*, Edward Elgar 2017 (co-edited with Hans-Uwe Otto, Valerie Egdell and Jean Michel Bonvin).

Brigitte Aulenbacher is Professor of Sociological Theory and Social Analysis, heads the Department for the Theory of Society and Social Analyses at the Institute of Sociology at the Johannes Kepler University Linz, Austria, and is vice-president of the International Karl Polanyi Society. She co-chairs (with Helma Lutz and Karin Schwiter) the project "Decent Care Work? Transnational Home Care Arrangements" and co-edits (with Klaus Dörre) *Global Dialogue – Magazine of the International Sociological Association.* Recent publications include: 'Global Sociology of Care and Care Work', *Current Sociology*, 66 (4) 2018 (co-edited with Helma Lutz and Birgit Riegraf); Special Issue: 'Care and Care Work: A Question of Economy, Justice and Democracy', *Equality, Diversity and Inclusion: An International Journal*, 37 (4) 2018 (co-edited with Birgit Riegraf); 'Karl Polanyi, "The Great Transformation", and Contemporary Capitalism', *Österreichische Zeitschrift für Soziologie*, 44 (2) 2019, 105–13 (co-edited with Richard Bärnthaler and Andreas Novy).

Richard Bärnthaler, MSc, works at the Institute for Multilevel Governance and Development (WU Vienna) and the Department of Development Studies (University of Vienna) on questions concerning philosophy of science, science studies, transdisciplinarity, and (Polanyi-related) transformation research. Recent publications include: 'The Fallacy of Naturalism as a Response to the Relativist', *Organon F: International Journal of Analytic Philosophy*, 25 (3) 2018, 316–38; 'Karl Polanyi, "The Great Transformation", and Contemporary Capitalism', *Österreichische Zeitschrift für Soziologie*, 44 (2) 2019, 105–13 (co-edited with Brigitte Aulenbacher and Andreas Novy).

Karina Becker is the scientific director of the Centre of Advanced Research "Post Growth Societies" at the Friedrich-Schiller-University of Jena (Germany). Her research areas include right-wing populism, care work, solidarity, and industrial relations. Recent publications include: 'Live-in and Burn-out? Migrantische Pflegekräfte in deutschen Haushalten', *Arbeit: Zeitschrift für Arbeitsforschung, Arbeitsgestaltung und Arbeitspolitik*, 25 (1–2) 2016, 21–46; *Arbeiterbewegung von rechts? Ungleichheit – Verteilungskämpfe – populistische Revolte*, Campus 2018 (co-edited with Klaus Dörre and Peter Reif-Spirek); 'Temporary Workforce Under Pressure: Poor Occupational Safety and Health (OSH) as a Dimension of Precarity?', *Management Revue*, 29 (1) 2018, 32–54 (co-authored with Thomas Engel).

Dorothee Bohle holds a Chair in Social and Political Change at the Department of Political and Social Sciences of the European University Institute, Florence. Her research is at the intersection of comparative politics and political economy with a special focus on East Central Europe. Her most recent book, *Capitalist Diversity on Europe's Periphery* (Cornell University Press 2012, co-authored with Béla Greskovits), won the Stein Rokkan Prize for Comparative Social Science Research. Her publications have also appeared in *Comparative Politics, Studies in Comparative International Development, West European Politics, Journal of Democracy, European Journal of Sociology*, and *Review of International Political Economy*. Recent publications include: 'European Integration, Capitalist Diversity and Crises Trajectories on Europe's Eastern Periphery', *New Political Economy*, 23 (2) 2018, 239–53.

Ulrich Brand is since 2007 Professor of International Politics at the University of Vienna. Since 2017 he is member of the Scientific Advisory Board of the Institute for Advanced Sustainability Studies (IASS) in Potsdam. His research areas are: imperial mode of living, multiple crises of liberal globalization, social-ecological transformation, political ecology, state and regulation theory, and Latin America. Recent publications include: *The Limits to Capitalist Nature: Theorizing and Overcoming the Imperial Mode of Living*, Rowman & Littlefield 2018 (co-edited with Markus Wissen); 'The Double Materiality of Democracy in Capitalist Societies: Challenges for Social-Ecological Transformations', *Environmental Politics* (online), 2018 (co-authored with Melanie Pichler and Christoph Görg); 'Growth and Domination: Shortcomings of the (De-)Growth Debate', in Stefan G. Jacobsen (ed.), *Climate Justice and the Economy: Social Mobilization, Knowledge and the Political*, Routledge 2018, 148–67.

Michael Brie, Dr. habil., is senior fellow at the Institute for Critical Social Analysis of the Rosa Luxemburg Foundation in Berlin in the field of history and theory of socialism and communism. He is chief-editor of the series

Contribution to Critical Transformation Research. His most recent books are: *Das Kommunistische: Oder: Ein Gespenst kommt nicht zur Ruhe*, VSA 2016 (edited with Lutz Brangsch); *Karl Polanyi in Dialogue: A Socialist Thinker for our Time*, Black Rose Books 2017; *Lenin neu entdecken: das hellblaue Bändchen zur Dialektik der Revolution & Metaphysik der Herrschaft*, VSA 2017; *Karl Polanyi's Vision of a Socialist Transformation*, Black Rose Books 2018 (co-edited with Claus Thomasberger); *Rosa Luxemburg neu entdecken: ein hellblaues Bändchen zu "Freiheit für den Feind! Demokratie und Sozialismus"*, VSA 2019.

Ayşe Buğra is Emerita Professor at Bogazici University and an affiliate of the Bogazici University Research Center Social Policy Forum which she co-founded in 2004. She has taught and published in the areas of development studies, social policy, state–business relations, and the socio-economic history of modern Turkey. She is currently working on questions of equality and politics of social policy. Recent publications include: *New Capitalism in Turkey: The Relationship between Politics, Religion and Business*, Edward Elgar 2014 (co-authored with Osman Savaskan); 'Revisiting "Freedom in a Complex Society": A View from the Periphery', in Michael Brie and Claus Thomasberger (eds), *Karl Polanyi's Vision of a Socialist Transformation*, Black Rose Books 2018. She is the translator of Karl Polanyi's *The Great Transformation* into Turkish (*Büyük Dönüşüm*, Alan Yayıncılık 1986).

Michele Cangiani is Associate Professor of Economic Sociology; he has taught at the Università di Bologna and Università Ca' Foscari Venezia. He is a member of the Board of Directors of the Karl Polanyi Institute (Montréal) and of the Editorial Board of the *Forum for Social Economics*. His main fields of research are: the history and method of economic theories and political philosophy. Recent publications include: 'Economic Knowledge and Value Judgements', in Monika Poettinger and Gianfranco Tusset (eds), *Economic Thought and History: An Unresolved Relationship*, Routledge 2016, 58–72; '"Social Freedom" in the Twenty-First Century: Rereading Polanyi', *Journal of Economic Issues*, 51 (4) 2017, 915–38; *Karl Polanyi, Economy and Society: Selected Writings*, Polity Press 2018 (co-edited with Claus Thomasberger).

Fabienne Décieux is a PhD candidate at the Department for the Theory of Society and Social Analyses, Institute of Sociology, Johannes Kepler University Linz, Austria. Her fields of interest and research are: critical social theories, gender studies, sociology of work and research on care. Recent publications include: 'The Economic Shift and Beyond: Care as a Contested Terrain in Contemporary Capitalism', *Current Sociology*, 66 (4) 2018, 517–30 (co-authored with Brigitte Aulenbacher and Birgit Riegraf); 'Capitalism Goes Care: Elder and Child Care between Market, State, Profession, and Family and Questions of Justice and Inequality', *Equality, Diversity and Inclusion: An International Journal*, 37 (4) 2018, 347–60 (co-authored with Brigitte Aulenbacher and Birgit Riegraf).

Christoph Deutschmann is Professor (emeritus) of Sociology at the University of Tübingen, Germany. His research interests and publications are in the fields of economic sociology, the sociology of work, and social theory. Recent publications include: *Disembedded Markets: Economic Theology and Global Capitalism*, Routledge 2019; 'Disembedded Markets as a Mirror of Society: Blind Spots of Social Theory', *European Journal of Social Theory*, 18 (4) 2015, 368–89; 'Entzauberung des Geldes: Max Weber und der heutige Finanzmarkt-Kapitalismus', in Thomas Schwinn and Gert Albert (eds), *Alte Begriffe – Neue Probleme: Max Webers Soziologie im Lichte aktueller Problemstellungen*, Mohr Siebeck 2016, 149–70.

Klaus Dörre is Professor of Sociology at the Friedrich-Schiller-University of Jena (Germany) where he chairs the Department of Labour, Industrial and Economic Sociology. His areas of research include the theory of capitalism, flexible and precarious employment, and labour relations, among others. He is spokesman of the German Research Foundation (DFG) research group "Post-Growth Societies" (with Hartmut Rosa), research associate at the Society, Work and Development Institute (SWOP) at the University of the Witwatersrand, Johannesburg, and co-editor (with Brigitte Aulenbacher) of *Global Dialogue – Magazine of the International Sociological Association*. Recent publications include: *Capitalism and Labor: Towards Critical Perspectives*, Campus 2018 (co-edited with Nicole Mayer-Ahuja, Dieter Sauer and Volker Wittke); 'Social Capitalism is a Thing of the Past: Competition-driven "Landnahme" and the Metamorphosis of the German Model', in Paolo Chiocchetti and Frédéric Allemand (eds), *Competitiveness and Solidarity in the European Union: Interdisciplinary Perspectives*, Routledge 2019, 149–81; 'A Right-Wing Workers' Movement? Impressions from Germany', *Global Labour Journal*, 9 (3) 2018, 339–47.

Karin Fischer is Senior Lecturer and teaches global sociology at the Institute of Sociology at Johannes Kepler University Linz, Austria. Her research focuses on neoliberal transformation, global commodity chains and uneven development in historical and transnational perspective. Recent publications include: *Handbuch Entwicklungsforschung*, Springer 2016 (co-edited with Gerhard Hauck and Manuela Boatcă); *Clases dominantes y desarrollo desigual: Chile entre 1830 y 2010*, Ediciones Universidad Alberto Hurtado 2017; *Globale Ungleichheit* (co-edited with Margarete Grandner), Mandelbaum 2019. She coordinated the section on Neoliberal Think Tank Networks in *Global*

Dialogue – Magazine of the International Sociological Association (online), 8 (2) 2018.

Christoph Görg is since 2015 Professor of Social Ecology at the Institute of Social Ecology at the University of Natural Resources and Life Sciences, Vienna. His research areas are: critical theory of societal nature relations, social-ecological transformation, political and social ecology, state theory, and landscape governance. Recent publications include: 'Challenges for Social-Ecological Transformations: Contributions from Social and Political Ecology', *Sustainability*, 9 (7) 2017, 1–21 (co-authored with Ulrich Brand, Helmut Haberl, Diana Hummel, Thomas Jahn and Stefan Liehr); 'Die Historisierung der Staatsform: Regulationstheorie, radikaler Reformismus und die Herausforderungen einer Großen Transformation', in Ulrich Brand and Christoph Görg (eds), *Zur Aktualität der Staatsform: Die Materialistische Staatstheorie von Joachim Hirsch*, Nomos 2018, 21–38; 'The Double Materiality of Democracy in Capitalist Societies: Challenges for Social-Ecological Transformations', *Environmental Politics* (online), 2018, 1–21 (co-authored with Melanie Pichler and Ulrich Brand).

Béla Greskovits is University Professor at the Department of International Relations at Central European University, Budapest. His research interests are the political economy of East-Central European capitalism, comparative economic development, social movements, and democratization. His articles appeared in *Studies in Comparative and International Development, Labor History, Orbis, West European Politics, Competition and Change, Journal of Democracy, European Journal of Sociology, Global Policy*, and *Transfer – European Review of Labor and Research*. Recent publications include: 'Politicising Embedded Neoliberalism: Continuity and Change in Hungary's Development Model', *West European Politics* (online), 2018, 1–25 (co-authored with Dorothee Bohle); 'Civic Activism, Economic Nationalism, and Welfare for the Better Off: Pillars of Hungary's Illiberal State', in Michael Ignatieff and Stephan Roch (eds), *Rethinking Open Society: New Adversaries and New Opportunities*, Central European University Press 2018, 295–310.

Bob Jessop is Distinguished Professor of Sociology at Lancaster University, UK. He is best known for his contributions to state theory, critical political economy, critical social theory, and critical governance studies. Recent publications include: *Towards a Cultural Political Economy: Putting Culture in its Place in Political Economy*, Edward Elgar 2013 (with Ngai-Ling Sum); *The State: Past, Present, Future*, Polity Press 2015. An extended research project on financial crises and crises of crisis-management led to two co-edited volumes: *Financial Cultures and Crisis Dynamics*, Routledge 2014 (co-edited with Brigitte Young and Christoph Scherrer); *The Pedagogy of Economic,*

Political and Social Crises: Dynamics, Construals, and Lessons, Routledge 2018 (co-edited with Karim Knio). He is currently writing a new monograph on *Civil Society as a Mode of Governance: Between Self-Emancipation and Self-Responsibilization* (forthcoming 2020).

Ernst Langthaler is Professor and the head of the Department of Social and Economic History at Johannes Kepler University Linz and of the Institute of Rural History in St. Pölten, Austria. His current research focuses on commodity history in the age of globalization. Recent publications include: *Agro-Food Studies: eine Einführung*, Böhlau 2018 (co-edited with Ulrich Ermann, Marianne Penker and Markus Schermer); 'The Soy Paradox: The Western Nutrition Transition Revisited, 1950–2010', *Global Environment*, 11 (1) 2018, 79–104; 'Food Regimes and their Trade Links: A Socio-ecological Perspective', *Ecological Economics*, 160 (June) 2019, 87–95 (co-authored with Fridolin Krausmann).

Michael Leiblfinger is a researcher within the project "Decent Care Work? Transnational Home Care Arrangements" at the Department of the Theory of the Society and Social Analyses at Johannes Kepler University Linz, Austria. Recent publications are: 'Völlig legal!? Rechtliche Rahmung und Legalitätsnarrative in der 24h-Betreuung in Deutschland, Österreich und der Schweiz', *Österreichische Zeitschrift für Soziologie*, 44 (1) 2019, 1–19 (co-authored with Jennifer Steiner, Veronika Prieler and Aranka Benazha); *Elf Jahre 24-Stunden-Betreuung in Österreich: Eine Policy- und Regime-Analyse*, KU Linz 2018 (with Veronika Prieler).

Maria Markantonatou is an Assistant Professor in Political Sociology at the Department of Sociology of the University of the Aegean in Lesvos, Greece. She was a fellow at the Kolleg Postwachstumsgesellschaften (Research Group on Post-Growth Societies) at the Friedrich-Schiller-University Jena, Germany. Her research interests focus on the transformations of democracy under neoliberalism and especially in the framework of the crisis in Greece. Her recent publications on the Greek crisis include: 'State-Imposed Austerity in Greece', *Global Dialogue – Magazine of the International Sociological Association* (online), 6 (4) 2016; 'The "Politics of Fulfillment" as Preliminary for the Making of a Precarious State in Greece', in Vassilis K. Fouskas and Constantine Dimoulas (eds), *Greece in the 21st Century: The Politics and Economics of a Crisis*, Routledge 2018, 142–62. She is also working on Karl Polanyi and she is currently co-editing a book on Polanyi together with Gareth Dale and Christopher Holmes: *Karl Polanyi's Political and Economic Thought*, Agenda Publications 2019.

Andreas Novy is Associate Professor and head of the Institute for Multi-Level Governance and Development at the Department of Socioeconomics at WU

Vienna and president of the International Karl Polanyi Society. He works in the field of urban development, international political economy, social innovation and social-ecological transformation. Recent publications include: 'Karl Polanyi, "The Great Transformation", and Contemporary Capitalism', *Österreichische Zeitschrift für Soziologie*, 44 (2) 2019, 105–13 (co-edited with Brigitte Aulenbacher and Richard Bärnthaler); *Die Finanzialisierung der Welt: Karl Polanyi und die neoliberale Transformation der Weltwirtschaft*, Beltz Juventa 2019 (authored by Karl Polanyi-Levitt, co-edited with Claus Thomasberger and Michael Brie); *Local Social Innovation to Combat Poverty and Exclusion: A Critical Appraisal*, Policy Press 2019 (together with Stijn Oosterlynck and Yuri Kazepov).

Antonino Palumbo is an Associate Professor in Political Philosophy at Palermo University (Italy). His research is on globalization, the transformation of governance and the implications of changes in state steering for modern representative democracies. His most recent works in English are: *Situating Governance: Context, Content, Critique*, ECPR Press 2015; *Remaking Market Society: A Critique of Social Theory and Political Economy in Neoliberal Times*, Routledge 2018 (co-authored with Alan Scott). He is also co-editor of the *Routledge Library of Contemporary Essays in Political Theory and Public Policy*.

Kari Polanyi-Levitt is Emerita Professor at McGill University, Montreal, and Honorary PhD of the University of the West Indies, Jamaica; recipient of the Order of Canada. She is the author and editor of (amongst others) *Silent Surrender: The Multinational Corporation in Canada*, Macmillan 1970; *The Life and Work of Karl Polanyi: A Celebration*, Black Rose Books 1990; *Karl Polanyi in Vienna: The Contemporary Significance of "The Great Transformation"*, Black Rose Books 2000 (co-edited with Kenneth McRobbie), *Reclaiming Development: Independent Thought and Caribbean Community*, Ian Randle 2005; *Essays on the Theory of Plantation Economy: A Historical and Institutional Approach to Caribbean Economic Development*, University of the West Indies Press 2009 (co-edited with Lloyd Best); *From the Great Transformation to the Great Financialization: On Karl Polanyi and Other Essays*, Fernwood 2013.

Vishwas Satgar is Associate Professor in the Department of International Relations at the University of the Witwatersrand (Johannesburg) and chairperson on the board of the Cooperative and Policy Alternative Centre (COPAC). He is the principal investigator for the Emancipatory Futures Studies project at Wits and is a board member of the Wits Food Sovereignty Centre. He is the series editor of the *Democratic Marxism* series (Wits University Press) and has published widely on systemic alternatives, Africa's political economy, South African politics, and Marxism. Recent publications include: *Racisms after Apartheid: Challenges for Marxism and Anti-Racism*, Wits University Press 2019; *Climate Crisis: South African and Global Democratic Eco-Socialist Alternatives*, Wits University Press 2018; *Capitalism's Crises: Class Struggles in South Africa and the World*, Wits University Press 2015; *The Solidarity Economy Alternative: Emerging Theory and Practice*, University of KwaZulu-Natal Press 2014; *Marxisms in the 21st Century: Crisis, Critique & Struggle*, Wits University Press 2013 (co-edited with Michelle Williams).

Birgit Sauer is since 2006 Professor at the Department of Political Science at the University of Vienna. She has published on gender, governance and democracy, on gender equality policies, on gender and right-wing populism and on affective labour and state transformation. Recent publications include: 'Intersections and Inconsistencies: Framing Gender in Right-Wing Populist Discourses in Austria', *NORA: Nordic Journal of Feminist and Gender Research*, 22 (4) 2014, 250–266 (together with Edma Ajanovic and Stefanie Mayer); *Unaccompanied Children in European Migration and Asylum Practices: In Whose Best Interests?*, Routledge 2017 (co-edited with Mateja Sedmak and Barbara Gornik); *Populism and the Web: Communicative Practices of Parties and Movements in Europe*, Routledge 2017 (co-edited with Mojca Pajnik).

Alan Scott is Professor of Sociology in the School of Humanities, Arts and Social Sciences, University of New England (Australia) and an adjunct in the School of Social and Political Sciences, University of Innsbruck (Austria). His research interests are in political sociology and social theory. He is co-author – with Antonino Palumbo – of *Remaking Market Society: A Critique of Social Theory and Political Economy in Neoliberal Times*, Routledge 2018; '(Plebiscitary) Leader Democracy: The Return of an Illusion?', *Thesis Eleven*, 148 (1) 2018, 3–20; 'Shifting Repertoires of Populism and Neo-Nationalism: Austria and Brexit Britain', in Bligh J. Grant, Tod W. Moore and Tony Lynch, *The Rise of Right-Populism*, Springer 2019, 217–35.

Beverly J. Silver is Professor of Sociology and Director of the Arrighi Center for Global Studies at the Johns Hopkins University (USA). Her best-known book is *Forces of Labor: Workers' Movements and Globalization since 1870*, Cambridge University Press 2003. Her ongoing research focuses on the historical dynamics of global capitalism, including a revisiting of the arguments put forward in *Chaos and Governance in the Modern World System*, University of Minnesota Press 1999 (co-authored with Giovanni Arrighi) in light of the current period of systemic chaos.

Basil Stadelmann, MSc, is a research assistant at the Institute for Multilevel Governance and Development at the Department of Socioeconomics at WU

Vienna. His research topics are housing, gentrification, financialization, and urban development. He recently graduated from the interdisciplinary Master Programme Socio-Ecological Economics and Policy with a thesis on the financialization of housing in Vienna.

Claus Thomasberger is Professor (emeritus) at the University of Applied Sciences, Berlin, Germany. His research interests are: European integration, history of economic thought, economic history, and political philosophy. He is the author and editor of numerous books, including: *Chronik der großen Transformation* (3 vols), Metropolis 2002–2005 (co-edited with Michele Cangiani); *From Crisis to Growth? The Challenge of Debt and Imbalances*, Metropolis 2012 (co-edited with Hansjörg Herr and Torsten Niechoj); *Das neoliberale Credo: Ursprünge, Entwicklung und Kritik*, Metropolis 2012; *Auf der Suche nach dem Ökonomischen – Karl Marx zum 200. Geburtstag*, Metropolis 2018 (co-edited with Rainer Lucas and Reinhard Pfriem); *Karl Polanyi's Vision of a Socialist Transformation*, Black Rose Books 2018 (co-edited with Michael Brie); *Economy and Society: Selected Writings*, Polity Press 2018 (co-edited with Michele Cangiani).

Hans-Jürgen Urban, Dr. phil. habil., is a member of the Executive Committee IG Metall, lecturer at the Friedrich-Schiller-University Jena, and Permanent Fellow at the Kolleg Postwachstumsgesellschaften (Research Group on Post-Growth Societies) at the Friedrich-Schiller-University Jena. His research interests are: theory of capitalism, political economy of the welfare state, union revitalization, and labour policy. Recent publications include: 'Ausbruch aus dem Gehäuse der European Governance: Überlegungen zu einer Soziologie der Wirtschaftsdemokratie in transformatorischer Absicht', *Berliner Journal für Soziologie*, 28 (1–2) 2018, 91–122; 'Social Critique and Trade Unions – Outlines of a Troubled Relationship', in Klaus Dörre, Nicole Mayer-Ahuja, Dieter Sauer and Volker Wittke (eds), *Capitalism and Labor: Towards Critical Perspectives*, Campus 2018, 378–99; 'Ökologie der Arbeit: Ein noch offenes Feld der Gewerkschaften?', in Lothar Schröder and Hans-Jürgen Urban (eds), *Gute Arbeit: Ökologie der Arbeit – Impulse für einen nachhaltigen Umbau*, Bund Verlag 2018, 329–49.

Bernhard Weicht, Dr. habil, works at the Department of Sociology at the University of Innsbruck. He has studied economics in Vienna and social policy in Nottingham. He holds a PhD from the University of Nottingham where he researched the construction of care. Prior to joining the University of Innsbruck he held positions at Utrecht University and Leiden University College. Bernhard has published on ageing, care, dependency, migrant care workers and the intersection of regimes. He is the author of *The Meaning of Care: The Social Construction of Care for Elderly People*, Palgrave

Macmillan 2015; *The Commonalities of Global Crises: Markets, Communities and Nostalgia*, Palgrave Macmillan 2016 (co-edited with Christian Karner).

Michelle Williams is Professor of Sociology at the University of the Witwatersrand (Wits) in Johannesburg. She is chairperson of the Global Labour University Programme (GLU) at Wits (2010 to present), chairperson of the International GLU Steering Committee (2017–18), and a member of the board of the Wits Development Studies programme. She has published widely on democracy, development, Marxism, gender, and South–South comparisons. Her publications include: *The Roots of Participatory Democracy: Democratic Communists in South Africa and Kerala, India*, Palgrave Macmillan 2008; *Building Alternatives: The Story of India's Oldest Construction Workers' Cooperative*, LeftWord 2017 (co-authored with Thomas Isaac); *South Africa and India: Shaping the Global South*, Wits University Press 2011 (co-edited with Isabel Hofmeyr); *Labour in the Global South: Challenges and Alternatives for Workers*, International Labour Office 2012 (co-edited with Sarah Mosoetsa); *Marxisms in the 21st Century: Crisis, Critique, and Struggle*, Wits University Press 2013 (co-edited with Vishwas Satgar); *The End of the Developmental State?*, Routledge 2014.

Markus Wissen works since 2012 as Professor for Social Sciences at the Berlin School of Economics and Law (HWR). Since 2014 he is a member of the editorial board of *PROKLA: Zeitschrift für kritische Sozialwissenschaft.* His research areas are: imperial mode of living, social-ecological transformation, (auto)mobility, labour and ecology. Recent publications include: *The Limits to Capitalist Nature: Theorizing and Overcoming the Imperial Mode of Living*, Rowman & Littlefield 2018 (co-edited with Ulrich Brand); *Imperiale Lebensweise: Zur Ausbeutung von Mensch und Natur im globalen Kapitalismus*, Oekom 2017 (co-edited with Ulrich Brand); 'Territory and Historicity: Time and Space in Nicos Poulantzas's State Theory', in Lars Bretthauer, Alexander Gallas, John Kannankulam and Ingo Stützle (eds), *Reading Poulantzas*, Merlin Press 2011, 186–200.

1. Polanyian perspectives on the movements and countermovements of "our time": an introduction

Roland Atzmüller, Brigitte Aulenbacher, Ulrich Brand, Fabienne Décieux, Karin Fischer and Birgit Sauer

> The countermove against economic liberalism and laissez-faire possessed all the unmistakable characteristics of a spontaneous reaction. At innumerable disconnected points it set in without any traceable links between the interests directly affected or any ideological conformity between them. (Polanyi 2001, p. 156)

> Social history in the nineteenth century was [. . .] the result of a double movement: the extension of the market organization in respect to genuine commodities was accompanied by its restriction in respect to fictitious ones. While on the one hand markets spread all over the face of the globe and the amount of goods involved grew to unbelievable proportions, on the other hand a network of measures and policies was integrated into powerful institutions designed to check the action of the market relative to labour, land, and money. (Polanyi 2001, p. 79)

For five decades we have been witnessing deep and far reaching changes of capitalism and society. A vast array of analyses and diagnoses of these developments depict their dynamics from different angles: the erosion of the post-war order understood as the end of Fordism and the beginning of an alleged post-Fordist era since the 1970s; the increasing economic liberalisation politically imposed and accompanied by neoliberal governance since the 1980s; the collapse of state socialism after 1989 and the new phase of globalisation along with the consolidation of capitalism; the finance driven economic development culminating in the 2008/9 crisis and subsequent austerity schemes; digitalisation; labour disputes, and primarily new forms of progressive social protest, the increasing influence of right-wing movements and the (re-)emergence of illiberal democracies and authoritarian regimes (e.g. Burawoy 2015, 2017; Campani and Sauer 2017; Della Porta 2017; Fabry 2019; Markantonatou 2014; Streeck 2014).

1

The outlined changes have proved to be fundamental as they affect the relations of economy and society, economy and politics, market and democracy, production and reproduction, society and nature and the contradictory and crisis prone effects of economic, ecological, social and political developments. Thus, debates have emerged in the social sciences, which have begun to discuss these ruptures in terms of a caesura or the end of an epoch, the uncertain future of capitalism or its transformation (Block 2018; Brie 2014; Wallerstein et al. 2013).

In this context scholars from different disciplines and research fields around the globe have rediscovered and re-read Karl Polanyi's economic and cultural history of capitalism for today, as Marguerite Mendell (2019) reconstructs the enduring legacy of and global interest in his work (Block and Somers 2014; Polanyi-Levitt 2013). His oeuvre has become a crucial point of reference for the scientific investigation of and socio-political debates about the changes of capitalism and society. There are many remarkable strands of the renaissance of Polanyi's oeuvre which contribute to a sensitive debate about how to deal with it in a broad and inspiring international, systematic reflection and application of Polanyian perspectives to investigate contemporary capitalism (compare Aulenbacher et al. 2019; Block 2018; Block and Somers 2014; Blyth 2002; Buğra and Ağartan 2007; Deutschmann 2019; Hann and Hart 2009; Kuttner 2018; Palumbo and Scott 2017).

Karl Polanyi's view on recent changes and ruptures of contemporary capitalism might help us to understand whether we live in an era of another great transformation. Although our book does not strive – and would not be able – to answer this question, it builds on the Polanyian approach and the debates about it and makes use of his perspectives to investigate some of the before mentioned developments. Therefore, we emphasise the concepts which are relevant for this book and which inspired our re-reading of Polanyi's work for today.

1.   READING POLANYI FOR TODAY

Building on earlier reflections concerning important influences on his work and life (McRobbie and Polanyi-Levitt 2005; Polanyi-Levitt 1990), biographical research has been conducted to historicise and contextualise Polanyi's thought. It includes impressive reconstructions of his life and of core ideas of his oeuvre, which have opened new perspectives. In particular Gareth Dale's (2010, 2016a, 2016b) meticulous historical reconstruction of Karl Polanyi's life and work contextualises his thoughts in early twentieth-century debates and shows how "his analysis of the pathogenesis and malign consequences of free market globalization" (Dale 2010, p. 206) became a very promising reference of the analysis and critique of neoliberalism and market fundamentalism.

"Despite being much less well known than other major economic thinkers, Karl Polanyi provides us with the most incisive intellectual apparatus available to understand the actual workings and consequences of market economies", as Fred Block and Margaret R. Somers (2014, p. 218) state.

A lot of work examining the contemporary relevance of Polanyi's approach has been done already. Apart from the systematic re-reading of Polanyi's oeuvre by Fred Block and Margaret R. Somers (2014) a few pathbreaking studies have to be mentioned here. Mark Blyth (2002) investigates the "double movement" of the 1920s and 1930s and the development initiated by the economic downturn in the 1970s showing how economic ideas influence institutional changes. Ayşe Buğra and Kaan Ağartan (2007) organise their collection around Polanyi's perspectives on the disembedding of the market and the "commodity fiction" (Polanyi 2001, p. 76). Michael Burawoy (2015) applies the concept of the "double movement" to analyse the new "wave" of "marketization" since the 1970s and new forms of social protests after the 2008/9 crisis. A growing number of scholars use Polanyian concepts to investigate how globalisation and the (finance driven) market economy affect the relations between capitalism and democracy, the latter being the target of contemporary neoliberal, populist and fascist movements (Bieling 2017; Brie and Thomasberger 2018; Dörre 2019; Kuttner 2018). These examples show the enduring strength of Polanyi's approach as it allows to reflect upon capitalism in transformation which realises itself through the contestation of market driven development. The effects of these dynamics are often described as a multiple ecological, economic, social and political crisis (Brand 2016; Demirović et al. 2011; Jessop 2013) which we can better understand by making use of Polanyi's perspectives. Just to give one example, the concept of three "fictitious commodities" – land, labour and money – has inspired Nancy Fraser (2018) to reconceptualise the ecological, economic, social and political dimension of the crises. In this spirit systematic reconstructions of Polanyi's core arguments and theoretical concepts reflect on and contribute to their actualisation.

For the recent research about and with Polanyi it was in particular *The Great Transformation* – published in 1944 and being an example of the intellectual examination of fascism by exiled scientists – which has become an indispensable point of reference for contemporary debates about the future of capitalism.[1]

---

[1]   This is not to deny that the status which Polanyi's work has gained recently does not necessarily stem from its systematic and well developed account of the dynamics of capitalist market societies. As for many other eminent intellectuals of the early twentieth century this was hindered by the biographical consequences he (and his family) had to endure in a time of fascist usurpation of many European countries leading up to the Second World War (Dale 2016a). Rather, recent debates have highlighted that – similar

This includes the question of whether we are witnessing a deep transformation and which attempts to reorder society can be identified, not least from a global perspective and focusing on the pressing questions of economy and democracy as discussed by Fred Block (2018), Christopher Holmes (2018) and Robert Kuttner (2018) (see also Block and Somers 2014; Buğra and Ağartan 2007; Hann and Hart 2009).

The Great Transformation ([1944] 2001), which is a main reference for our book too, was influenced by the Wall Street crash of 1929 and its effects on societies, the Great Depression, the fascist and socialist attempts to reorder society, the New Deal, and the Second World War. Notwithstanding some empirical similarities between those developments and our times, which certainly pushes the continuing interest in Polanyi's work, its far-reaching conceptualisation of societal dynamics offers an important reason for its contemporary significance (Block and Somers 2014; Brie and Thomasberger 2018). Karl Polanyi's attempt to understand the history of capitalism as result of a "double movement" remains an important analytical tool for the investigation of societal developments and change.

Polanyi's (2001, pp. 138 ff.) analysis of the "double movement" identifies the dialectical interplay of two antithetical organising principles: the "principle of economic liberalism" and the "principle of social protection" (Polanyi 2001, p. 138). However, the theoretical value of this conceptualisation must not be interpreted as a deterministic understanding of the development of capitalist societies as a swing of the pendulum (Polanyi 2001, p. 275) between more or less stable phases of market expansion and stable phases of social protection which result from a great transformation (Dörre 2016; Fraser 2013; Harvey et al. 2007; Sparsam et al. 2014). Rather, it refers to a fundamental dialectic of capitalist market dynamics and their destructive effects on societies which might lead to the often forceful and contradictory emergence of contested and conflictive reactions of society. These may or may not bring about a great transformation, which may or may not lead to a re-embedding of the economy. The ambiguous and contradictory character of the concept of "double movement", which at the same time refers to its enduring strength, becomes obvious in Polanyi's difficulties to adequately assess and differentiate the character and prospects of "countermovements" in his times. As different as they are, Polanyi described socialism, the New Deal and fascism not only as a protective countermovement to the expansion of market processes but also as a move(-ment) to a "reform of market economy" (Polanyi 2001, p. 245). Thus, given its ambiguous and contradictory character, and notwithstanding the critical

---

to e.g. Antonio Gramsci – the importance of his work arose despite or maybe because of its fractured, open, unfinished and transgressive character (Hodgson 2016; Peck 2013).

remarks and revisions, the concept of the "double movement" remains, in our view, a powerful analytical tool for examining neoliberal globalisation and the extension of the market since the 1970s. Indeed, it is the vision of the persistent tensions between the two sides of the "double movement" that makes Polanyi's historical analysis heuristically valuable. It serves as a powerful and persuasive concept to analyse the conflictive and crisis prone dynamics of contemporary capitalism and society.

Apart from his understanding of the history of capitalist market societies as a double movement the vivid debates on Polanyi's work have focused on a range of other concepts and notions which have turned out to be of specific relevance. The enduring strength of Polanyi's substantivist economic thinking (Polanyi 1977, pp. 19–21, 31–43), as pointed out by Jamie Peck (2013), seems to emerge from a peculiar historical reconstruction of "industrial capitalism" (Polanyi 2001, pp. 13, 87, 107, 188) and the critique of the idea of the "self-regulating market" (Gemici 2008; Polanyi 2001, pp. 44–5). The idea of a self-regulating market launched, as Polanyi states, a "movement" in which the market as a "specific institution" began to dominate the economy, impacting massively on "the whole organization of society" and leading to the "running of society as an adjunct to the market" (Polanyi 2001, p. 60). Through this expansion of market mechanisms the "market system" took hold of wider society, turning it into a "market society" (Polanyi 2001, pp. 44, 60). For Polanyi, the establishment of a (capitalist) economy based on self-interest affected the organisational principles of the economy as a whole, among which he enumerated not only "exchange" through market patterns (Polanyi 2001, pp. 59 ff.) but also "redistribution", "reciprocity" (Polanyi 2001, pp. 49–50) and "householding" (Polanyi 2001, p. 56).

This is an important point because it leads to another crucial concept Polanyi's approach has to offer. The three economic principles – redistribution, reciprocity and householding – are defined by the "interaction between man and his surroundings" (Polanyi 1977, p. 32) and the "institutionalization of that process" (Polanyi 1977, p. 31). These interactions cause economic activities that are more strongly embedded (Hodgson 2016; Polanyi 1977, pp. 35–42; 2001, pp. 44 ff.) or "instituted" (Harvey et al. 2007; Polanyi et al. 1957, pp. 157, 239–70) in contrast to the increasingly dominant market "exchange" (Polanyi 2001, pp. 59 ff.). The demolition of the non-economic foundations of economic activities and social reproduction by subordinating society to the market shows, according to Polanyi, the "deleterious" effects of market expansion. In the same process the three "essential elements of industrial life" – land, labour and money – are transformed into commodities. In other words, they are priced and subjected to the market with the "supply-and-demand mechanism" (Polanyi 2001, p. 75). But Polanyi points out that their character as goods is merely "fictitious" as they are "not produced for sale" and therefore are put at risk of being destroyed (Polanyi 2001, pp. 74–6). Against the "movements" of expanding commodification and marketisation "countermovements" can emerge (Polanyi 2001, pp. 87, 136, 138). They constitute various opposing reactions through which society seeks "protection" from market dynamics and their effects – i.e. countermovements. A countermovement can take the form of state interventions, political or legal regulations – not least as a result of workers' movements which aim at reigning in market forces – but also of other social movements, progressive and regressive, left- and right-wing, like those we have witnessed post-1968, through the 1970s and post-2008/9 until today (Bieling 2017; Brand and Wissen 2018; Burawoy 2015; Della Porta 2017).

In current debates, the concept of "fictitious commodities" is not simply rediscovered, but also revised and applied considering other "elements" which are commodified in the contemporary movements of market expansion since the 1970s. On the one hand this analytical tool allows to investigate recent and changing commodifications of land (nature), labour and money. On the other hand it allows to ask whether new "fictitious commodities" are emerging in "our time" or whether other "fictitious commodities", which have not been of the same relevance or have not been recognised in the same way in Polanyi's time, are becoming more important. Thus, against the background of current technological and social developments, knowledge (Burawoy 2015; Irzik 2007; Jessop 2007; Palumbo and Scott 2017) and care are debated as new "fictitious commodities" (Aulenbacher et al. 2018; Fraser 2012; Lutz 2017).

Notwithstanding their strengths, any contemporary use of Polanyian concepts and analytical tools, however, must recognise and thoroughly address their historical limitations and weaknesses. Thus, some points of criticism have to be mentioned. Although Polanyi's (2001, pp. 25 ff.) "substantivist" (Peck 2013) understanding addresses economy's historically shifting position in the societal structure, more specific study is necessary on the embedding and disembedding of the market, i.e. the economy as an "instituted process" (Polanyi et al. 1957, p. 250; Polanyi 1977, pp. 35–42) and the significance of the state (Burawoy 2003; Gemici 2008; Hann and Hart 2009; Harvey et al. 2007; Hodgson 2016). Polanyi's concept of the "double movement" is criticised for not adequately capturing inequality and dominance based on gender, race, class and emancipatory movements beyond marketisation and protection (Fraser 2012, 2016, 2018). Attention is drawn to questions of exploitation and accumulation driven dynamics of capitalism (Dörre 2016; Holmwood 2016; Rogan 2017). Such criticism has been the starting point for many attempts to combine Polanyian perspectives with those of Gramsci, Marx and others (Burawoy 2003; Fraser 2018; Silver 2003) or with other strands of theoretical reflection on contemporary capitalism like regulation theory, cultural political economy, new institutionalism and feminist theory (e.g. Aulenbacher et al. 2018; Bohle and Greskovits 2012; Djelic 2006; Sum and Jessop 2013).

Apart from the critical debates about Polanyi's approach and its limitations, the current renaissance of his thinking also includes attempts to discover the unfulfilled aspects of his thought. These attempts refer firstly to yet undiscovered theoretical and analytical dimensions of his work and secondly to the peculiarities of his political perspectives. Here, Polanyi suggests a societal order which is based on an economy not dominated by self-interest and which allows for the expansion of freedom and democracy (Block and Somers 2014, pp. 218–40; Brie and Thomasberger 2018). Scholars identify such moments in different aspects of his work. For example, Polanyi combines his economic analysis with a cultural critique of industrial capitalism arguing that the permanent "dislocation" associated with market dynamics endangers human relationships and the natural "habitat" (Polanyi 2001, p. 44). But in case of the liberation of "industrial society" from the dynamics of the "market economy" through "regulation and control", society "can achieve freedom not only for the few, but for all. [. . .] Such a society can afford to be both just and free" (Polanyi 2001, p. 265).

Polanyi's concept of "improvement" and "habitation" (Polanyi 2001, p. 35) leads to fundamental questions that have gained importance at the beginning of the twenty-first century: how can humankind survive industrial civilisation? How can justice and freedom be achieved in the "machine age" (Polanyi 2018, p. 197)? What could be a pluralist socialist vision of "freedom in a complex society" (Polanyi 2001, p. 268; Brie and Thomasberger 2018; Cangiani 2012; Holmes 2018)? Such debates are of crucial importance. Besides nostalgia and right-wing visions of how to reorder society (Becker et al. 2018; Karner and Weicht 2016; Kuttner 2018), we are currently witnessing growing debates about emancipatory or progressive visions of a fundamental reform of capitalism or its transformation into a post-capitalist society (Brie 2014; Dörre 2016; Honneth 2015; Winker 2015; Wright 2010).

We have summarised core perspectives of Polanyi's approach and the enduring and growing interest in his work, because they are of crucial importance for our book. The book aims at contributing to the critical analysis of the crisis prone and at the same time contested ecological, economic, social and political developments of our time. These result, we contend, from the socially destructive effects of the commodification of land, labour and money, but also of knowledge and care. At the same time the concepts of "double movement" and "fictitious commodities" are of crucial relevance to understand societies' attempts to seek protection. Furthermore, Polanyi's four economic principles as well as his analyses of "dislocation" and "habitation" enrich contemporary debates about the growing significance of additional fictitious commodities which complement land, labour and money.

However, the renaissance of Polanyi's approach is not confined to debates that remain within these limits. Rather, his work has also been (re)discovered by scholars from different strands of theories of society or capitalism. This broad reception is an effect of Karl Polanyi's theoretical approaches, empirical analyses and evolving research strategies covering economics, social sciences, history and social anthropology (Peck 2013) and therefore may enrich different theoretical and methodological approaches. This strength of Polanyi's work also holds true for many contributions in our book.

This book strives to take up many of the outlined debates and tries to advance a Polanyian analysis of contemporary capitalism. It re-reads and revises his perspectives and applies them to the analyses of ecological, economic, social and political challenges of our time. By confronting Polanyi's approach with competing approaches or adding complementary ones, the chapters seek to build up profound theoretical and empirical approaches which help to better understand the transformation of capitalism since the 1970s up to the first decades of the twenty-first century. To move these debates forward the chapters of the book are organised around the following lines of reflection.

## 2.	ANALYSING THE TRANSFORMATION OF CONTEMPORARY CAPITALISM

The first section of this book – **Historical and theoretical reflections: Karl Polanyi, capitalism and society** – starts with a biographical contextualisation of Polanyi's theoretical and methodological approach. The following chapters contribute to debates which aim at reconstructing and reformulating Polanyi's theoretical achievements and most significant concepts and research strategies in the light of current developments of capitalism and capitalist market societies.

An adequate understanding of Polanyi's work needs to explore the times in which he lived. Therefore, the book starts with an interview with **Kari Polanyi-Levitt** conducted by **Michael Brie** and **Claus Thomasberger**. The interview is as much a foreword to the book as it is a forceful reminder on the prospective and forward-looking strengths of Karl Polanyi's thinking. If there is anyone who can describe in detail the continuities, but also the ruptures in the life and work of Karl Polanyi, it is his daughter, the renowned political economist Kari Polanyi-Levitt. The interview focuses on the leitmotif of Polanyi's lifelong (re)search process, the problem of freedom in a complex society. Kari Polanyi-Levitt reveals the Central European roots of his thinking, traces the different questions he had to face in Red Vienna after his emigration and discusses Polanyi's work in England and in the United States, his concern about the future of civilisation and the dangers that the machine age poses to personal freedom. The interview ends with a brief look at his final project, the magazine *Co-Existence*.

Beverly J. Silver presents a first theoretical reflection on Polanyi's work. She argues that it is necessary to complement his analysis with an adequate theory of capitalism. Silver conceptualises capitalism as a world-historical system beset by a fundamental contradiction between profitability and social legitimacy, the only way, she contends, to understand the project of creating self-regulating markets (and its limits). She further argues that this contradiction led to an alternation between crises of profitability and legitimacy, and to successive pendulum swings between periods when the predominant tendency is towards protecting "fictitious commodities" (e.g. in the era of Keynesianism and developmentalism), and when the predominant tendency is toward stripping them of protections (e.g. in the neoliberal era). Silver identifies four crises of the long twentieth century and links them to this pendulum swing as well as to the establishment and limits of successive world hegemonies. Her chapter concludes by asking why the world's ruling class (then and now) failed to shift course in time to avert a global slide into systemic chaos.

In the following chapter **Michele Cangiani** argues that the current crisis asks for a reflection on the most general aspects of our society and its history. Karl Polanyi's theoretical achievements provide relevant suggestions for this purpose. The fundamental characteristics of the market-capitalist society reproduce themselves under different "institutional arrangements" or "transformations" which result from major crises. Thus, for him Polanyi's analysis of the "great transformation" from liberal to corporative capitalism can be inspiring for explaining the crisis of the 1970s and the neoliberal transformation. For Cangiani, Polanyi's writings, and also those of a few other scholars of both his time and ours, prove not only the depth of his thought but also its topicality.

Christoph Deutschmann's take on Polanyi starts from the observation that his concept of the "double movement" shows an analytical asymmetry: Polanyi puts all his emphasis on explaining why a regime of self-regulated markets, once established, cannot sustain, and will provoke political and social countermovements aiming at protecting societies against the risks of unlimited market exposure. He paid, however, comparatively little attention to the prior disembedding process of markets itself. According to Deutschmann Polanyi's analysis is inclined to mix up the levels of socio-historical analysis with that of economic model construction and to economistically misunderstand the liberal message, which is focused one-sidedly on the utilitarian and social Darwinist sidelines of liberal thought. The chapter shows how a revised version of Polanyi's theorem could open up an encompassing view on the socially disruptive and ecologically destructive consequences of disembedded markets.

The historical and theoretical section is concluded with an article by **Bob Jessop**. Jessop starts from the assumption that Polanyi's analysis invites reconsideration for the neoliberal age. Comparing Marx's and Polanyi's views on land, money and labour, Jessop notes that Polanyi was unaware of their overlap nor did he exploit his own distinctions between money, money as credit, and money as capital. This limits the heuristic power of Polanyi's approach when applied to contemporary developments in capitalism. This also holds true for the double movement which appears less effective against neoliberalism compared with historical liberalism. Jessop concludes that it is necessary to go beyond his account of money if a Polanyian analysis of neoliberalism and its double movement should make sense. Polanyi's broad understanding of the relation between the market economy and market society, however, has to be retained.

The second section of the book – **Contemporary developments of society and capitalism in Europe and beyond** – includes chapters which apply Polanyian concepts to a critique of current global capitalism. The crisis prone movements of contemporary capitalist market societies and the emerging forms of crisis management, which are dominated by austerity, and their effects on democracy are pivotal for this section. A particular focus is put on the countermovements emerging in different shapes in distinct historical, societal and country-specific contexts.

Dorothee Bohle and **Béla Greskovits** focus on capitalisms after state socialism and present cornerstones of a Polanyi-inspired analytical framework of the varied paths of post-socialist capitalism in good times and bad. Instead of looking for complete similarities, the authors consider Polanyi's work as a rich source of reference points, analogies and contrasts to better understand the birth, stabilisation, and recent turbulences of the nascent market societies. Therefore they follow the trajectories of East Central European capitalisms through three phases: the early-to-mid-1990s, marked by what they term a "neoliberal moment" and the transformational recession; the new social orders' "democratic moment" and brief golden age roughly from the late 1990s to the mid-2000s; and the return of hard times after 2008 with the global financial crisis and Great Recession, heralding what seems to be a "nationalist moment".

In her analysis of today's crisis in Greece and the Eurozone, **Maria Markantonatou** draws on Polanyi's analysis of the tension between economy and democracy. First, Markantonatou discusses some of the economic and social effects of the Greek austerity programme. She does so with reference to Polanyi's observations on liberal international interventionism in the inter-war period. Secondly, she looks at the ways in which democratic outcomes (elections, referenda, parliamentarian decisions) in Greece and elsewhere were put aside in favour of market discipline and austerity doctrines. In her conclusion, Markantonatou argues that Polanyi's thesis on the "mutual incompatibility" between capitalism and democracy – the core of what he termed the "anti-democratic virus" – is crucial for understanding today's crisis and crisis management in the framework of the Eurozone's liberalism.

Ayşe Buğra investigates the rise of political Islam as a "reactionary countermovement" in Turkey after the country's integration into the global market economy. Political Islam presents a society-specific response to the social disruptions associated with market expansion. In line with Polanyi's discussion of different political forms that countermovements can take on, political Islam seems to be an inevitable reaction of the society to the tensions inherent in the market economy. Buğra argues that the recent trajectory of political Islam in Turkey was shaped by both domestic factors and certain characteristics of the global context which enabled reactionary political currents to appear as viable channels in which the feelings of insecurity caused by the market-led socio-economic transformations could be expressed.

The connections between the recent crisis of capitalist market societies and the upsurge of right-wing populist movements and parties are at the core of **Roland Atzmüller** and **Fabienne Décieux**'s chapter. It is the first in a row of three chapters that analyse contemporary right-wing countermovements in core countries of the Global North/the European Union. Atzmüller and Décieux show that for Polanyi the emergence of far-right, fascist countermovements was not simply an answer to the crisis of unfettered market expansion but also to the post-First World War expansion of democracy and welfare policies and the stalemate the unresolved tensions between these developments created. In his papers about fascism of the 1930s as well as in *The Great Transformation* Polanyi identified three elements of fascist philosophy that build the core of its political strategy to "save capitalism": a full-scale attack on democracy; the rejection of equality; and an attack on freedom in all social spheres. By focusing on emerging aporias of neoliberal welfare reforms (retrenchment of democratic participation of e.g. unions; expansion of inequality; enforced commodification at the expense of individual autonomy) the authors explore whether and how fascism and/or right-wing populism constitutes itself as a social alternative to tackle not only the crisis of neoliberal market expansion but also to overcome the (fractured) continuities of a welfarist embedding of the economy.

Karina Becker and **Klaus Dörre**'s chapter argues that the current rise of right-wing populist formations represents a caesura in the political system of many early industrialised countries. Although populist parties generally recruit their voters from all classes and strata of society, it is undeniable that they enjoy above-average approval and support from male production workers. This is particularly true for Germany. As their study on Germany reveals, right-wing populist orientations are hardening even among active members of works councils and trade unions. The contribution examines right-wing populist formations as movements of a Polanyian type which are successfully ethnicising the social question. Becker and Dörre interpret these Polanyian type movements as a kind of imaginary, conformist revolt in opposition to excessive market control of gainful employment. In contrast to the implications of Marxian class universalism, levelling market powers can reinforce an endemic tendency among wage-earners towards demarcating non-class-specific boundaries as a basis for claims for protection from the "maelstrom of the market" and market competition. As the chapter demonstrates, right-populism is currently achieving just that.

The section is completed by **Birgit Sauer** who argues that right-wing parties across Europe seem to have one single issue: they mobilise against immigration. Sauer's gender perspective reveals, however, that behind this surface another project becomes visible, i.e. the fundamental transformation of liberal democracies. To deepen the analysis of this development the chapter re-reads the Polanyian notions of commodification and "double movement" in a gender perspective. Right-wing movements against the disembedding of markets turn the frustration over neoliberal restructuring against immigrants, but also against emancipatory movements of the 1960s and 1970s such as the feminist movement, evoking a "crisis of masculinity". Sauer shows that the radical right claims to resolve the losses of the working class by reinterpreting class issues as issues of migrants and of gender equality policies. Thus, recent right-wing mobilisation must be seen as (male) identity politics against liberal democracy. Moreover, anti-gender mobilisation is used to modulate new hegemonic constellations and to forge new alliances with conservatives, with the Catholic Church as well as with liberals.

The third section of the book debates the forward-looking significance of Polanyian concepts and expands and advances their scope to the analysis of **"Fictitious commodities" and the challenges of "our time".** In particular, the articles in this section focus on fundamental problems and tensions of contemporary capitalism and capitalist market societies which result from the still unresolved and increasingly global contradictions and crisis that emerge from the ever expanding marketisation and commodification of more and more spheres of nature and society.

Ulrich Brand, **Christoph Görg** and **Markus Wissen** show that manifold ways to deal with the ecological crisis are subsumed under the header "transition/transformation to sustainability" or even "Great" transformation in recent years. Their chapter critically discusses the current debate from the perspective of a Polanyian understanding of *The Great Transformation*. Brand, Görg and Wissen argue that the debate suffers from a narrow analytical approach to transformation ignoring the dynamics of global capitalism and the power relations involved. Thus, a "new critical orthodoxy" of knowledge about transformation is emerging which runs the danger of contributing to ecologising capitalism while ignoring the root causes of the social-ecological crises. Against this the authors distinguish between three types of transformation – based on Polanyi, but also on regulation theory – which focus either on an adaptation of the current institutional systems or on a new phase of green capitalism. Beside these two types, they state, a post-capitalist Great Transformation however requires more profound structural changes and exceeds the accumulation imperative as much as other structural constraints of capitalist development.

In the following chapter the analysis of the ecological crisis is continued by **Vishwas Satgar** and **Michelle Williams** who focus on Polanyi's rich conceptual thinking about nature and the international in *The Great Transformation*. For the authors this helps to understand contemporary dimensions of ecological crises and the link between imperialism, ecology and historical capitalism. Building on Polanyi's conceptions of nature, they argue that capitalism's deleterious relation to nature has been there from the beginning – since its emergence in the European centre and in its relations with peripheries. In other words, capitalism is grounded in particular forms of imperial ecocide that lie at the centre of its functioning. Extending Polanyi's analysis in this way Satgar and Williams examine contemporary capitalism's domination of nature and ecological crises and the challenges for resistance in this field.

Karin Fischer and **Ernst Langthaler** continue the debate of ecological problems and take the marketisation of land and food as a starting point. They focus on movements and countermovements around the expansion of soy production in three countries of South America, namely Argentina, Brazil and Bolivia. The authors use Polanyi's concept of the double movement and place it in dialogue with critical state theory adapted for (semi-)peripheral contexts. They investigate both the drivers of marketisation in the agro-food sector as well as protective countermovements, i.e. state action of the respective progressive governments and rural social movements. From a historical and comparative perspective, Fischer and Langthaler analyse how rural social movements became disarticulated (Brazil), demobilised (Argentina) and fractured (Bolivia) precisely during the administration of left-wing governments. The results of their study call for a realistic assessment of countermovements, taking into account both the room for manoeuvre and the limits of protective countermovements.

The chapters on ecological crises are followed by a historical analysis of the connections between commodification and decommodification of land and social reproduction by **Andreas Novy**, **Richard Bärnthaler** and **Basil Stadelmann.** By taking up the Polanyian dialectics between "improvement" and "habitation" they investigate the history of housing and urban infrastructure in Vienna (Austria). In particular the authors discuss countermovements seeking for habitation in five historical periods: an anti-liberal countermovement (Vienna before 1918), a social-democratic countermovement (Red Vienna, 1919–34), fascist countermovements (1934–45), the institutionalisation of the social-democratic countermovement (1945–89), and its erosion (1989 onwards). Through the historical analysis Novy, Bärnthaler and Stadelmann demonstrate the ambivalence of anti-market countermovements, as they are not unconditionally promoting holistic forms of social cohesion, peaceful communal life, and emancipation. "Improvement" is not always destructive and "habitation" not always unifying. Their outcomes depend on their specific form of implementation and framing. The chapter ends with a reflection on how to navigate between "improvement" and "habitation" today.

The following chapter by **Brigitte Aulenbacher** and **Michael Leiblfinger** continues the focus on social reproduction and the significance of Polanyian concepts for in-depth analyses of emerging social problems and tensions in this field. Their chapter starts from the rise of new care markets which raise the question whether societies of the Global North are experiencing a commodification of care. They argue – by referring to the international sociology of care and care work – that the forced commodification and marketisation of care has to be seen as interrelated with new forms of governance and changing welfare regimes as well as the transnationalisation of labour, politics and policies in contemporary capitalisms. To exemplify this, the authors discuss the 24-hour care provided by home care agencies. Combining the Polanyian with a neo-institutionalist perspective Aulenbacher and Leiblfinger show that care has become a "fictitious commodity", how the 24-hour care market in Austria is embedded in the care regime and how the brokering of care workers and the sale of care tend to destroy the always difficult reciprocity of caring, although care arrangements are the results of a complex interplay of the logics of the market, state, family and profession.

The analysis of care through Polanyian concepts is further deepened in the following chapter. **Bernhard Weicht** shows that informal care gaps and widespread resistance to institutional care settings have fostered a system in Austria in which live-in migrant care workers substitute the idealised family carer in people's households. As a consequence, an ever-increasing market has been established on which predominantly women from other countries seek and find employment opportunities. Drawing on Fraser's utilisation of Polanyi's concept of the double (triple) movement, Weicht seeks to demonstrate that due to different national systemic conditions, both increasing marketisation (in the care workers' countries of origin) and resistance to market and state logics in care (in Austria) meet in generating a unique transnational market of care. In this, moral resistance to both an increasing marketisation and an extension of the state, as well as moral longing for informal care need to be seen as part of the process that has generated and boosted the development of self-marketisation of Eastern European care workers.

After these analyses which investigates the question whether care is becoming a "fictitious commodity" and what this process means for the reproduction of "livelihood" the next chapter by **Antonino Palumbo** and **Alan Scott** focuses on another crucial aspect of contemporary capitalist market societies which has experienced new forms of commodification and marketisation over the last decades – knowledge. The authors offer a close reading of *The Great Transformation* that emphasises the recursive nature of the double movement which is, in their view, consistent with the logic of Polanyi's own account of British nineteenth-century history. The authors argue that rather than creating a settled state – embodied in embedded liberalism – protectionist counter-movements are inducing further disruptive strains. The resultant crisis then instigates a new pro-market coalition that takes the crisis as an opportunity to commodify further areas of human activity. In the wake of the global financial crisis 2008/9, knowledge is the most likely candidate to follow land, labour and money as a further fictitious commodity. Palumbo and Scott argue that in this context, a drive towards digital Taylorism is couched in terms of the imperatives of the "knowledge economy". The welfare settlement created a commons beyond commerce and outside lines of direct state control which has now become ripe both for commodification by the market *and* greater political control.

The final chapter by **Hans Jürgen Urban** focuses on the disembedding of capitalist markets from state regulation which is observed in the transition from welfare-state capitalism to global financial-market capitalism. The author asks what role the digitalisation of work plays in this process and shows that digitalisation is driving a new surge of marketisation and rationalisation which promotes a double transformation: the transformation of labour in the sense of a restructuring of work processes and organisation; and concurrently, the transformation of the institutional setting of social rights on which the previously attained degree of decommodification of labour power in the welfare state depended. The author uses the digitalisation of industrial added value (*"Industry 4.0"*) as an example to illustrate that conflicts in the sphere of interest politics are the place of decision-making on the developmental path of digitalisation, and that special significance attaches to the democratisation of economic decisions as a prerequisite for labour and social policy successes.

Acknowledgements

The editors want to thank Jakob Kapeller, head of the Institute for Comprehensive Analysis of the Economy (ICAE) at Johannes Kepler University Linz, Austria, Klaus Dörre, spokesman of the Research Group on Post-Growth Societies ("Kolleg Postwachstumsgesellschaften") at the Friedrich-Schiller-University of Jena, Germany, and Andreas Novy, head of the Institute for Multi-Level

Governance and Development at the Department of Socioeconomics, Vienna University of Economics and Business, Austria. We benefited greatly from lively debates with them on the topics of the book. Special thanks go to Anita Winkler, the ever-patient secretary of the Institute of Sociology at Johannes Kepler University Linz, for the editorial assistance. With due care and thoroughness she guided us through the production process of the book. Last but not least, Kari Polanyi-Levitt deserves a special mention. Without the energy and visionary of Kari Polanyi-Levitt this book and many other related activities would never have come about.

REFERENCES

Aulenbacher, B., R. Bärnthaler and A. Novy (eds) (2019), *Karl Polanyi: "The Great Transformation" and contemporary capitalism* (Special Issue of *Österreichische Zeitschrift für Soziologie*, 44 (2)).

Aulenbacher, B., F. Décieux and B. Riegraf (2018), 'Capitalism goes care', *Equality, Diversity and Inclusion: An International Journal*, 37 (4), 347–60.

Becker, K., K. Dörre and P. Reif-Spirek (eds) (2018), *Arbeiterbewegung von rechts: Ungleichheit – Verteilungskämpfe – populistische Revolte*, Frankfurt/Main and New York: Campus.

Bieling, H.-J. (2017), 'Aufstieg des Rechtspopulismus im heutigen Europa: Umrisse einer gesellschaftstheoretischen Erklärung', *WSI Mitteilungen*, 8, 557–65.

Block, F.L. (2018), *Capitalism: The future of an illusion*, Berkeley: University of California Press.

Block, F.L. and M.R. Somers (2014), *The power of market fundamentalism: Karl Polanyi's critique*, Cambridge, MA: Harvard University Press.

Blyth, M. (2002), *Great transformations: Economic ideas and institutional change in the twentieth century*, Cambridge: Cambridge University Press.

Bohle, D. and B. Greskovits (2012), *Capitalist diversity on Europe's periphery*, New York: Cornell University Press.

Brand, U. (2016), 'How to get out of the multiple crisis? Contours of a critical theory of social-ecological transformation', *Environmental Values*, 25 (5), 503–25.

Brand, U. and M. Wissen (2018), *The limits to capitalist nature: Theorizing and overcoming the imperial mode of living*, London: Rowman & Littlefield.

Brie, M. (ed.) (2014), *Futuring: Perspektiven der Transformation im Kapitalismus über ihn hinaus*, Münster: Westfälisches Dampfboot.

Brie, M. and C. Thomasberger (eds) (2018), *Karl Polanyi's vision of a socialist transformation*, Montréal: Black Rose.

Buğra, A. and K. Ağartan (eds) (2007), *Reading Karl Polanyi for the twenty-first century: Market economy as a political project*, New York: Palgrave Macmillan.

Burawoy, M. (2003), 'For a sociological Marxism: The complementary convergence of Antonio Gramsci and Karl Polanyi', *Politics & Society*, 31 (2), 193–261.

Burawoy, M. (2015), 'Facing an unequal world', *Current Sociology*, 63 (1), 5–34.

Burawoy, M. (2017), 'Social movements in the neoliberal age', in M. Paret, C. Runciman and L. Sinwell (eds), *Southern resistance in critical perspective: The politics of protest in South Africa's contentious democracy*, London and New York: Routledge, pp. 21–35.

Campani, G. and B. Sauer (2017), 'The neo-fascist and neo-nazi constellations', in G. Lazaridis and G. Campani (eds), *Understanding the populist shift: Othering in a Europe in crisis*, London and New York: Routledge, pp. 31–49.

Cangiani, M. (2012), 'Freedom in a complex society', *International Journal of Political Economy*, 41 (4), 34–53.

Dale, G. (2010), *Karl Polanyi: The limits of the market*, Oxford: Wiley.

Dale, G. (2016a), *Karl Polanyi: A life on the left*, New York: Columbia University Press.

Dale, G. (2016b), *Reconstructing Karl Polanyi: Excavation and critique*, London: Pluto Press.

Della Porta, D. (2017), 'Political economy and social movement studies: The class basis of anti-austerity protests', *Anthropological Theory*, 17 (4), 453–73.

Demirović, A., J. Dück, F. Becker and P. Bader (eds) (2011), *VielfachKrise: Im finanzmarktdominierten Kapitalismus*, Hamburg: VSA.

Deutschmann, C. (2019), *Disembedded markets: Economic theology and global capitalism*, New York: Routledge.

Djelic, M.-L. (2006), 'Marketization: From intellectual agenda to global policy-making', in M.-L. Djelic and K. Sahlin-Andersson (eds), *Transnational governance: Institutional dynamics of regulation*, Cambridge: Cambridge University Press, pp. 53–73.

Dörre, K. (2016), 'Grenzen der Landnahme: Der Kapitalismus stirbt nicht von allein, doch wir können ihn überwinden', in A. Tauss (ed.), *Sozial-ökologische Transformationen: Das Ende des Kapitalismus denken*, Hamburg: VSA, pp. 52–109.

Dörre, K. (2019), '"Take back control!": Marx, Polanyi and right-wing populist revolt', in B. Aulenbacher, R. Bärnthaler and A. Novy (eds), *Karl Polanyi: "The Great Transformation" and contemporary capitalism* (Special Issue of *Österreichische Zeitschrift für Soziologie*, 44 (2)), 225–43.

Fabry, A. (2019), 'Neoliberalism, crisis and authoritarian–ethnicist reaction: The ascendancy of the Orbán regime', *Competition & Change*, 23 (2), 165–91.

Fraser, N. (2012), 'Can society be commodities all the way down? Polanyian reflections on capitalist crisis', accessed 10 April 2019 at https://halshs .archives-ouvertes.fr/halshs-00725060/document.

Fraser, N. (2013), 'A triple movement', *New Left Review*, 81, 119–32.

Fraser, N. (2016), 'Contradictions of capital and care', *New Left Review*, 100, 99–117.

Fraser, N. (2018), 'Krise, Kritik und Kapitalismus: Eine Orientierungshilfe für das 21. Jahrhundert', in A. Scheele and S. Wöhl (eds), *Feminismus und Marxismus*, Weinheim and Basel: Beltz Juventa, pp. 40–58.

Gemici, K. (2008), 'Karl Polanyi and the antinomies of embeddedness', *Socio-Economic Review*, 6 (1), 5–33.

Hann, C. and K. Hart (eds) (2009), *Market and society: The great transformation today*, Cambridge: Cambridge University Press.

Harvey, M., R. Ramlogan and S. Randles (eds) (2007), *Karl Polanyi: New perspectives on the place of the economy in society*, Manchester: Manchester University Press.

Hodgson, G.M. (2016), 'Karl Polanyi on economy and society: A critical analysis of core concepts', *Review of Social Economy*, 75 (1), 1–25.

Holmes, C. (2018), *Polanyi in times of populism: Vision and contradiction in the history of economic ideas*, Abingdon: Routledge.

Holmwood, J. (2016), 'From political economy to moral economy: Provincialising Polanyi', in C. Karner and B. Weicht (eds), *The commonalities of global crises: Markets, communities and nostalgia*, London: Palgrave Macmillan.

Honneth, A. (2015), *Axel Honneth – Die Idee des Sozialismus: Versuch einer Aktualisierung*, Berlin: Suhrkamp.

Irzik, G. (2007), 'Commercialization of science in a neoliberal world', in A. Buğra and K. Ağartan (eds), *Reading Karl Polanyi for the twenty-first century: Market economy as a political project*, New York: Palgrave Macmillan, pp. 135–53.

Jessop, B. (2007), 'Knowledge as a fictitious commodity: Insights and limits of a Polanyian perspective', in A. Buğra and K. Ağartan (eds), *Reading Karl Polanyi for the twenty-first century: Market economy as a political project*, New York: Palgrave Macmillan, pp. 115–34.

Jessop, B. (2013), 'The North Atlantic financial crisis and varieties of capitalism: A Minsky and/or Marx moment: And perhaps Max Weber too', in S. Fadda and P. Tridico (eds), *Financial crisis, labour markets and institutions*, London and New York: Routledge, pp. 40–59.

Karner, C. and B. Weicht (eds) (2016), *The commonalities of global crises: Markets, communities and nostalgia*, London: Palgrave Macmillan.

Kuttner, R.L. (2018), *Can democracy survive global capitalism?*, New York: W. W. Norton & Company.

Lutz, H. (2017), 'Care as a fictitious commodity: Reflections on the intersections of migration, gender and care regimes', *Migration Studies*, 5 (3), 356–68.

Markantonatou, M. (2014), 'Social resistance to austerity: Polanyi's "double movement" in the context of the crisis in Greece', *Journal für Entwicklungspolitik*, 30 (1), 67–87.

McRobbie, K. and K. Polanyi-Levitt (eds) (2005), *Karl Polanyi in Vienna: The contemporary significance of "The Great Transformation"*, Montréal: Black Rose.

Mendell, M. (2019), 'Karl Polanyi and his enduring legacy: An interview', in B. Aulenbacher, R. Bärnthaler and A. Novy (eds), *Karl Polanyi: "The Great Transformation" and contemporary capitalism* (Special Issue of *Österreichische Zeitschrift für Soziologie*, 44 (2)).

Palumbo, A. and A. Scott (eds) (2017), *Remaking market society: A critique of social theory and political economy in neoliberal times*, London: Routledge.

Peck, J. (2013), 'For Polanyian economic geographies', *Environment and Planning A: Economy and Space*, 45 (7), 1545–68.

Polanyi, K. (1977), *The livelihood of man*, New York: Academic Press.

Polanyi, K. (2001), *The great transformation: The political and economic origins of our time*, Boston: Beacon Press.

Polanyi, K. (2018), *Economy and society: Selected writings*, Cambridge: Polity Press.

Polanyi, K., C.M. Arensberg and H. Pearson (eds) (1957), *Trade and market in the early empires: Economies in history and theory*, Glencoe: Free Press.

Polanyi-Levitt, K. (ed.) (1990), *The life and work of Karl Polanyi: A celebration*, Montréal: Black Rose.

Polanyi-Levitt, K. (2013), *From the great transformation to the great financialization: On Karl Polanyi and other essays*, Halifax: Fernwood.

Rogan, T. (2017), *The moral economists: R. H. Tawney, Karl Polanyi, E. P. Thompson, and the critic of capitalism*, Princeton: Princeton University Press.

Silver, B. (2003), *Forces of labor: Workers' movements and globalization since 1870*, Cambridge: Cambridge University Press.

Sparsam, J., D. Eversberg, T. Haubner, D. Mader, B. Muraca and H. Pahl (2014), 'The renewal of a critical theory of capitalism and crisis: A comment on Nancy Fraser's interpretation of Polanyi's works', Working Paper 7, Jena: DFG-KollegforscherInnengruppe Postwachstumsgesellschaften.

Streeck, W. (2014), *Buying time: The delayed crisis of democratic capitalism*, London and New York: Verso.

Sum, N.-L. and B. Jessop (2013), *Towards a cultural political economy: Putting culture in its place in political economy*, Cheltenham, UK and Northampton, MA, USA: Edward Elgar Publishing.

Wallerstein, I.M., R. Collins, M. Mann, G.M. Derluguian and C.J. Calhoun (2013), *Does capitalism have a future?*, Oxford: Oxford University Press.

Winker, G. (2015), *Care Revolution*, Bielefeld: Transcript.

Wright, E.O. (2010), *Envisioning real utopias*, London: Verso.

PART I

Historical and theoretical reflections: Karl
Polanyi, capitalism and society

2. A life-long search for freedom. From Budapest to America and back: a journey through Karl Polanyi's life

Kari Polanyi-Levitt, interviewed by Michael Brie and Claus Thomasberger

Karl Polanyi is regarded as one of the most influential intellectuals of the twentieth century. Too often, however, the reception of his work is reduced to his most famous book *The Great Transformation* and categories such as "embeddedness", "double movement" and "fictitious commodities". By concentrating on his masterpiece, the question of what was the driving force of his thinking and the leitmotif of his lifelong search process – the problem of freedom in a complex society – and the variety of issues he dealt with have been lost from view. The interview attempts to highlight these lesser-known aspects of his oeuvre and thus contribute to overcoming some of the shortcomings of current Polanyi reception. The interview took place in Vienna, November 2017.

1. CENTRAL EUROPEAN ROOTS: FREEDOM TO LIVE A MEANINGFUL LIFE

Q. Karl Polanyi's life was, as he wrote in a letter, a "'world'-life". Although born in Vienna, his formative years were Hungarian. In 1919, at the age of 33, he left Budapest for Vienna. Emigration from Vienna to London took place when he was 47 years old. In his mid-fifties, Polanyi moved to North America. How did all these reorientations influence his work?

A. Wherever he lived, he was concerned with the issues of the day, both local and relating to international affairs. He was not the kind of intellectual with an "idée fixe" which he imposes on every situation he encounters. Polanyi did not do that. He lived in many different places, but wherever he lived, he engaged with the local environment according to context and circumstance.

Q. Nonetheless, isn't there also continuity? How can we describe the underlying, more permanent aspects of his work?

A. I think the continuity is the *search for freedom.* Imagine the world he lived in, the world of the late nineteenth, early twentieth century in Russia and East Europe. Polanyi identified with Bakunin, because he was courageous and broke out of so many prisons. He admired the courage of people who resisted the *ancient régimes* of the era. In Hungary, freedom meant freedom from the rule of feudal landowners, the Catholic Church, and the Hungarian gentry, for whom he had no respect whatsoever. Socialism in those times was about freedom. The battle cry of the socialist parties was "Freiheit!" – Freedom.

Q. Let us first get back to the time before the First World War. In the Hungarian writings of Polanyi, we find a very special understanding of freedom closely related to the anarchists, the Narodniki. He understands freedom not in a restrictive liberal sense.

A. I think you are quite right. The struggle of the Narodniki and other populist or socialist oppositions in the tsarist time were not very different from those in Hungary. How did they struggle? It was mostly by assassination. That was what they did. It was not by parliamentary action. The social democratic party did the parliamentary thing, but my father was not very interested in it. Because of the semi-feudal type of social structure there was not much difference between socialist and anarchist opponents of the *ancient régime.*

Q. Thus, the understanding of freedom in this tradition was much more linked to the struggles of the popular classes and to the longing of a meaningful life in communes.

A. Right, not to parliamentary struggles! Samuel Klatchko[1] was a Russian family friend and mentor of my father. When he was young, he and others founded a utopian commune in Kansas, named after Tchaikovsky. It fell apart eventually. Forming communes was part of the political culture.

Q. It seems that in Karl Polanyi's understanding of freedom different currents merged in a contradictory way. He had a multidimensional understanding of freedom, combining the ideas of negative and positive freedom of Isaiah Berlin with the search for a meaningful life and the responsibility to be in solidarity with the weaker parts of society. Is it true that he sometimes used the term liberal socialist in order to define himself?

---

[1]   Samuel Klatchko (1851–1914) was a Russian revolutionary, and a close friend of the Polanyi family. In 1875, he participated in the foundation of a Utopian community in Kansas (together with Nicolai Tchaikovsky and others). When the community failed, he and his wife settled in Vienna (1880). Here he became a non-party envoy of illegal parties and movements that existed in tsarist Russia at the time. Among his friends were many Russian revolutionaries, including Plekhanov and Trotsky.

A. What you say is correct, because he insisted on the right to dissent, the right to free speech, the right to free ideas. These rights should be constitutionally guaranteed; that is what he meant by liberal socialism but I do not know if he ever used the term liberal socialist to describe himself. The freedom to live a meaningful life is the freedom from involvement in meaningless economic activities to produce things that we do not need. It is the freedom from engagement in this market, an engagement that uses so much of our time, takes over our lives.

Q. In Polanyi's understanding there is a strong link between freedom and responsibility. Responsible action is more than simply positive or negative freedom.

A. It is a wish to live in a society that is socialist – each cares for all. That is why he said, "as in a family". But that is not possible, we know. It is not possible in a society which is divided by class, by race. This is in contradiction with our desire and our need to live in a socially supportive society. To live in such a society is freedom. Responsibility is part of that, but when you are speaking about responsibility as Polanyi is doing in his lecture 'On Freedom' [Polanyi 2018a] it is difficult for people to understand what that means. I think it is our wish to be mutually responsible for each other.

2.   THE GREAT WAR: THE DEFINING EVENT OF POLANYI'S LIFE

Q. Let us go back again. What was the impact of World War I? He was an officer. Why was he so depressed? It seems like an existential crisis.

A. It was a form of serious mental illness. It was to a large degree personal. The loss of his father was a terrible blow. It affected his young adult life, at least for two decades or three. Therefore, it is a mixture of a personal loss and the larger societal crisis. Family influences played an important role. Aspects of Russian culture came through his mother, Cecile Wohl, which manifested in the idealisation of Russian revolutionaries, especially the Social Revolutionary Party, and women like Vera Zasulich[2] and other students, as well as Russian literature, particularly Dostoevsky and Tolstoy. And then the father he adored. The father was an anglophile and believed in all the good liberal values that came at this time from England. These are the two contradictory sides – on the

---

2   Vera Zasulich (1849–1919) was a Russian writer and revolutionary. She became famous for the "Trepov incident" when in 1878 she seriously injured the governor of St Petersburg, Fyodor Trepov, with a revolver.

hand the anarchism and the revolutionaries and on the other hand the respect for the liberal values, for responsibility, and civic duty. What was plainly absent was anything Hungarian. No respect, the opposite of respect – disdain. He shared it with my mother. She rejected her own aristocratic ancestry.

The death of his father was a terrible blow to Karl. In addition, he felt the weight of responsibility of providing for his mother and the family. He gave classes and earned money by tutoring. The eldest brother Adolph had departed for Japan, leaving Karl as the eldest son. That was the personal side of the depression. Then of course, he studied law. It was expected that he would join his wealthy uncle Károly Pollacsek's legal chamber. My father was briefly engaged there, but he did not wish to pursue the profession. He wanted to be free. My cousin Eva once described him as a "dropout". He wanted to drop out of that bourgeois life. He didn't want to be lawyer. Frankly speaking, he once told me he didn't want to be married. He wanted to be free!

Q. For sure, this is an important dimension. Nevertheless, his participation in the war also created some kind of inner tension.

A. I don't know. Why did Karl Polanyi volunteer? Why did he not refuse? This is interesting, because somehow he felt he had a duty to serve in the war. You didn't really have a choice. You could not speak for your people if you were not prepared to serve in the war.

Q. In his essay on Hamlet [Polanyi 1954, reprinted in 2018b], Karl Polanyi is referring to his time as an officer and he poses the problem Hamlet was facing in the following way: There was no good choice for Hamlet. To kill the king, the murderer of his father, would mean he himself would become king. But he did not want to be king. He disliked the life at the court to the utmost. Not to kill the king would mean he would forsake the oath he had given to his father. Thus, not until he was mortally wounded could he fulfil the oath he had given his father. It seems to me no accident that Karl Polanyi starts this essay with a reference to his time in the war. To join the war or not to join the war – both were bad choices. You have to fulfil your duty and take part in the war; but whatever you are doing in the war is a terrible and senseless thing.

A. Yes, Karl wrote a lot about the war. The war was terrible, the loss of all these lives; it didn't settle anything, nobody knew what it was about. Was it about the Serbs? Was it about the Belgians? Was it about Germany which wanted to have colonies? The capitalists made a lot of money. It is an example that there is no good solution. But I do think the Hamlet story is about his life, about the question which role he should play. My mother put pressure on him to be more active, more politically engaged, to give political leadership. Yet that was not what he wished to do.

Q. Before and immediately after the war he was quite close to politics, not as a leading figure, but as an adviser.

A. In 1918 he was close to Jászi and the Radical Bourgeois Party.[3] He wrote for Jászi's journal. At the same time, he supported the socialists who wanted to make the peace and the republic. The only time he participated in a political party were the two years with Jászi. In Austria, he was nominally a member of the Austrian Social Democratic Party. But that was entirely nominal. He did not play any role other than in education. He gave classes at the *Volkshochschule*. He was an educator and a social philosopher, not a politician. I don't think he ever gave any advice to the Austrian Social Democratic Party. In England, where he had close connections with the Labour Party, he might have become more engaged if he had not left in 1947 to take up the appointment at Columbia University in New York. Many years later, the year before he died, Ilona and Karl visited Budapest and met some former members of the Galilei Circle.[4] My father was described by one of them as a prophet: "He could see far into the future, we loved him. He was the man for us." Political leadership was not given to him. Karl and Ilona rest together in a Budapest cemetary.

3.   RED VIENNA AND ENGLAND: FROM THE SOCIALIST ACCOUNTING DEBATE TO MARX'S CRITIQUE OF ALIENATION

Q. Let's return to the problem of freedom and responsibility. It seems that in the 1920s your father found a way to deal with this problem. In the early 1920s, he was drawn to guild socialism[5] [see Polanyi 2016a, 2016b], a system whereby different associations represent the different functions of society (producers, consumers, local life etc.) and deal with the problems of complex societies. However, later he said that he had wasted time because there was

---

[3]   Oszkar Jászi was the editor of the journal *Twentieth Century* (*Hszadik Század*), leader of the Radical Bourgeois Party (Országos Radikális Párt) and Minister of the first Hungarian Republic in 1918. Polanyi was elected to the party secretariat. His friendship and cooperation with Oszkar Jászi continued after their emigration to Vienna.

[4]   The Galilei Circle (Galilei Kör) was a non-partisan student initiative established in 1908 in Budapest: it organised thousands of courses for adults and numerous debates, to which speakers such as György Lukács, Karl Mannheim, Sandor Férenczi, Werner Sombart, Max Adler and Eduard Bernstein were invited. Karl Polanyi was the founding president of the circle.

[5]   The leading protagonist of Guild Socialism was G.D.H. Cole. In the 1920s Polanyi elaborated the idea in his contributions to the "Socialist Accounting Debate" and published several articles on the issue.

no solution to this economic model. Why was he so critical of his own work of this time?

A. Because he worked for years on the construction of an economic model with Schafer[6] and other economists. Following the exchange with Mises in 1922, they all tried to become economists and follow the methodology of economics. They spent a lot of time with that and it didn't work. In a letter Schafer later wrote to Ilona and myself, he says, quite correctly, that they couldn't solve the problem. I'm not surprised, because when I tried to translate to English the famous article on socialist accounting, 'Rechnungslegung' [cf. Polanyi-Levitt 2018, originally published in German: Polanyi 1924], I thought that there were a lot of loose ends in the model and a lot of open questions: the role that money would play and so on. Schafer concluded that Polanyi solved that problem later in *The Great Transformation*, where he expressed his ideas in terms of social and economic history.

Karl Polanyi's background of economics was Austrian economics. He and his colleagues did not reject markets. He did not believe in what was then called "the natural economy", the moneyless economy [cf. Neurath 1919]. Prices were important, but should not be negotiated individually but between associations representing workers and producers, cooperatives or other associations representing consumers and municipalities representing local communities.

Q. The insight of the impossibility to find a satisfying solution opened up a new search process which led to The Great Transformation. *Already in the accounting debate, Polanyi was aware of the fact that we can never go beyond the complexity of modern societies. This opened up the discussion in direction of history, of concrete embedded institutions and the cultural context.*

A. Very important for Karl Polanyi was the introduction of institutions, because of the variety of institutions which can be observed in societies of roughly similar technological development. In a list of economic institutions, from the corporation down to the corner store, we note the range and variety of economic enterprise. Karl Polanyi often said that important things are discovered by accident. Some institution may have a greater significance than is generally accorded to it. That is quite true. Today, we have a fashion for social innovation. It is an interesting idea because of the variety of institutions that can play a role in the economy and because of their hybrid nature – part coop-

---

[6]   Felix Schafer was a lifelong friend of Karl Polanyi. He published some of the results of their joint discussions in two articles (Schafer 1937, 1939). Extracts from a long memoir about their cooperation in Vienna have been published in Schafer (2006).

erative, part equity, and part voluntary employment. You can make all kinds of mixtures. That is different from the textbook economic approach. We are now developing varieties of economic institutions out of necessity.

Q. What is changing in Karl Polanyi's thinking with the Great Depression and the uprising of fascism in the late 1920s? There seems to be a new shift in the work of your father. Also with regard to his work in Great Britain in the 1930s. How is he reformulating the conflict between freedom and industrial capitalism?

A. First, if we are looking at the English period, it is clear that the Grants,[7] the English family that he had known in Vienna and with whom had become personal friends, introduced him to the Christian circles. Polanyi's link to England partly came through the works of G.D.H. Cole and Tawney.[8] Then there was the Christian socialist connection that came through the Grants. When Karl first came to England he lived with John and Betty McMurray. John was a Christian socialist philosopher.[9] Karl was nominally a Protestant of the Calvinist sect. He had no knowledge of Catholic liberation theology. The Protestant Christian socialists provided him with a social support system in England.

When the two Landshut-Mayer volumes – I remember what they looked like – arrived in England in 1933 or 1934,[10] there was a third encounter of Karl Polanyi with Marx. Given the background (fascism), it spoke to him very much – the alienation, the inhumanity of capitalism. Polanyi discovered the English class system and the cultural degradation of the working class. The economic conditions were very bad in Vienna, but the social and cultural life was on a higher level. He began to study that which he had never studied before – English social and economic history. He read the same things that Marx had 80 years earlier: Adam Smith, Malthus, David Ricardo – all the English classical economists of the time of the poor-law reform and before. I believe that my father discovered industrial capitalism in England. In Austria,

---

[7]   Polanyi had met Irene and Donald Grant in the 1920s. Already in Vienna they had taken part in discussions of the "Lega of the Religious Socialists of Austria". In England, Irene Grant was the principal organising spirit of the Christian Left Group.

[8]   Richard Henry Tawney (1880–1962) was an English economic historian, social critic and Christian socialist. From 1928 until 1944, he was President of the Workers' Educational Association.

[9]   John McMurray (1891–1976) was Grote Professor of Philosophy at London University (from 1928 to 1944). He was part of the editorial board which published the book Lewis et al. (1935).

[10]   Kari refers to the Landshut-Mayer edition of Marx's early writings (Marx et al. 1932), which Karl Polanyi introduced, discussed and (in part) translated for the "Christian Left Study Circle".

there was poverty, but it was not as dismal as some working-class areas of England at that time. It was not that massive degradation, both human and natural. It shocked him, it shocked me, and I was ten years old! I thought I had landed in the most awful place in the world – grey houses and chimney pots and not a tree to be seen anywhere. I remembered the big demonstrations of May Day in Vienna – these were workers of the railway and public transport, not of industry. So for Polanyi, there was the encounter with the circumstances of the industrial revolution and the establishment of the free labour market which features so big in *The Great Transformation*. Those things he only learned about in England.

4. ENGLAND: CAPITALISM AND INDUSTRIAL CIVILIZATION – THE CHALLENGES OF THE MACHINE AGE

Q. In discussions with the Christian socialists, Polanyi, as opposed to McMurray and some others, stressed the fact that society can never be reduced to community, it will always stay complex. One can never go back or forward and dissolve society into community again.

A. I don't think he ever had illusions that community can become more than a voluntary association of people. He rejected the idea that the state could ever be one community, as he explained in the last chapter of *The Great Transformation*, which is a strong statement on the necessary role of the state to generate an essential minimum of social consensus. A modern society requires a state to create the consensus necessary for the social cohesion of a modern complex society.

Most people who comment on Polanyi have not read much of what he wrote. Polanyi was concerned throughout his time in England and, certainly, from the time he wrote *The Great Transformation*, with civilisational future and the question of whether humanity could truly deal with the Machine Age. Reflecting on the dropping of the atomic bomb in an article published in 1947, he called it "scientific barbarism". I myself found that the questions raised by Leontieff in the 1980s, regarding the revolution of information technology and the dystopia of a world where 20 per cent of people are highly educated and well paid and can produce everything we need, while 80 per cent of workers are simply redundant, is crucial [see Leontief 1983]. We now know a lot more about artificial intelligence. It raises many very serious problems.

We have to take into account the way technologies have affected the three categories of fictitious commodities – land, labour and money. Polanyi would not have hesitated to point out that we are facing civilisational choices regarding environmental degradation, technological unemployment and the financialisation of daily life.

The tendency for society to approach the dystopia I have just described raises a question of socialism. Marx considered that when the machines could produce everything with only minimal human supervision, there would be no more need for capitalism. But this is where the problems start. Polanyi's argument against economism is largely an argument against economic growth per se. Today, it seems we require economic growth as a means of providing employment for young people entering the labour market rather than the additional material goods produced. We do not seem to know how to transform an economic system which is environmentally destructive, wasteful and which cannot, and should not, be replicated globally.

Q. Peter Drucker[11] wrote several books about technology and its influence on modern civilisation. Do you know if in the 1950s there was any discussion between Peter Drucker and your father about the issue?

A. Very possibly! There is a goldmine to be researched. There also are the discussions with Abraham Rotstein.[12] All this is in the archive and nobody has looked at it to this day. Polanyi's last concerns were precisely about technology. There was a proposal to write a book with Abraham on the subject. Peter Drucker was a close friend of my father's. I do not know if Drucker visited my father in Canada. I don't think so. There is a lot of correspondence which nobody has looked into.

Q. You started with the problem of decommodification and then addressed the problem of technology that goes much deeper. It is directly related to the whole mode of production and its civilisational basis. This would mean creating societies of culture where we are able to discuss and decide how we want to live, to produce, to exchange. Until now, we do not have civilisations able to steer the economic and technological developments. Maybe this is what is meant when Polanyi discusses the problem of machine age.

A. Well, absolutely! If we need Polanyi, it is because he addressed this issue. This goes back to the late 1940s. Some people think this is only about capitalism; but it is not, it is about industrial civilisation. The problem of technology

---

[11]   Peter Drucker (1909–2005), "the founder of modern management", was a friend of Karl Polanyi. They met in Vienna. Later he was instrumental in helping Polanyi get the appointment to Bennington College.

[12]   Abraham Rotstein (1929–2015), a former student and friend of Karl Polanyi, kept notes of numerous meetings with Polanyi on at least twenty weekends between 1956 and 1958. The "Weekend Notes" are available in the Karl Polanyi Archive, Con 45 Fol 02 to Con 45 Fol 20 [www.concordia.ca/research/polanyi/archive.html].

haunted my father. It was the dropping of the bomb and atomic energy, and this is why I wrote the piece about Einstein's consciousness and responsibility [Polanyi-Levitt 2013, pp. 107–12]. Einstein made the statement that we have a moral responsibility. He said that the creations of our mind – in other words ideas and things we invent – shall be a blessing and not a curse to humanity. Einstein said that every scientist must be guided by consciousness that what we do is morally good, that is much in line with the thinking of Polanyi. You see, Einstein's close friend, Leo Szilard, was a close friend of the Polanyi family. Szilard is responsible for the family story that Einstein said at the end of his life: "The Chinese sages were right: it is best to do nothing."

There is a belief in scientific progress and that you cannot stop it. My father would have been absolutely opposed to that. To my mind, if we want to follow these thoughts of Polanyi, it leads one to the conclusion that we are in a civilisational crisis. Information technology can be part of the solution, but it is certainly part of the danger.

Q. That's why we have to stress the problem of freedom "for what"? What are the aims of freedom? How are we making use of it? Today, the smartphone is used by young people on average 200 minutes per day! And concerning the living standard: a lot of people are living in societies of material abundance. The time people are employed is now shorter than the periods before and afterwards. This goes much beyond the problem of decommodification.

A. That's true. We must keep in mind that a further, very important contradiction Polanyi is dealing with, is the relation between science and religion, if one takes religion in a broader sense – I call it belief systems. They are part of human nature and human society. Fundamentalist secularism has a problem with this. It rejects belief systems. This is an invitation to reactions of a kind we have seen – religious, nationalistic and cultural – because people need belief systems. This is part of our humanity. If you go back to the so-called primitive societies, they had their own constructs of the meaning of life. Without a meaning of life, you are going to kill yourself. Polanyi dealt with this problem when he tackled the relation of science and religion and the wrong idea that only science is valid and religion is not. The same is true for the relation between the reality of complex societies and freedom. Both are valid.

Another of these contradictions Polanyi is referring to is the contradiction between humanity and efficiency. Polanyi said that we are rich enough to be inefficient. Efficiency belongs to the world of the engineer. That makes sense. The engineer must be efficient. You must economize the input of energy etc. If we follow economics, at least how it is defined by Robbins [1932] and neoclassical economists – that economics is about the allocation of scarce resources and alternative uses – it means treating the inputs as if they were technical inputs. However, the inputs are human beings; and life is not more or less scarce. This is no way to deal with it. Ultimately, efficiency in a capitalist society is just about how cheap it can be and how costs can be reduced. This of course leads to a lot of costs which don't belong to the market economy. It is about environment, etc. When we look into information technology, people say: It is so wonderful, you can do so many things! This is true, but what is the cost? What does it do to people's brains in the long run, to the conception of how we live?

5.   BACK TO THE ROOTS

Q. Let us come to the last years of your father's life. On the one hand, it was a return to Hungary with the book The Plough and the Pen *[Duczynska and Polanyi 1963] that your mother and he edited and on the other, they started the journal* Co-Existence. *What did this mean to the tension between the search for freedom and the reality of a technological society Polanyi was dealing with his whole life?*

A. *The Plough and the Pen* is a collection of poetry by Hungarian populist writers, selected by Karl and Ilona and translated to English with the assistance of established Canadian poets. The book is an homage to the folk wisdom of the peasantry (*das Volk*) and the dissident writers who chose to remain after the revolution of 1956. The publication is related to the idea in Polanyi's talk on Rousseau and the wisdom of the common people [Polanyi 2018d]. Polanyi liked the term "the common people". It was used by the socialist historian G.D.H. Cole. Historically inclusive from ancient to modern society, it is the source of vernacular culture in all modern societies. The term working class has a connotation of industrial work; but the common people encompasses the peasantry and everybody else.

The revolution of 1956 was a people-led protest against the ruling communist bureaucracy. My father was very strongly supportive. It was characterised as counterrevolutionary by the communist establishment. A lot of people left Hungary. It was a huge emigration. For Ilona and Karl, *The Plough and the Pen* was a statement on their belief in the possible regeneration of Hungary, and of socialism in Hungary.

Q. And the journal Co-Existence *as the second project your father started at this time?*

A. The project of the journal *Co-Existence* goes back to my father's belief and hope in the possibility of a world of post-war peaceful coexistence between the United States, the Soviet Union, and Great Britain with its Commonwealth connections, together with India, China, and other regional blocs, as expressed in his article of 1945 'Universal Capitalism or Regional Planning' [Polanyi 1945, reprinted in Polanyi 2018c]. In the late 1950s and early 1960s, when the journal started, coexistence really meant the relationship between the US and the Soviet Union. Forget Great Britain. The first post-war objective of the US was to destroy the British preferential system and the Sterling Bloc. And they did that in short order. This was off the table already. Concerning the journal, a lot of progress was made to contact interested intellectuals: Joan Robinson, who was already a friend of my parents and mine too, Kenneth Muir, who was a friend from the Christian Left; Adam Schaff was also a friend. However, a number of the others, particularly the economists, were brought on board by one of my father's students at Columbia University, Paul Medow, whose family was of Russian origin. They included Ragnar Frisch, Oskar Lange, P.C. Mahalanobis, Gunnar Myrdal, Rudolf Schlesinger, Hans Thirring, Jan Tinbergen, Shigeto Tsuru. On a visit to the Soviet Union, he reached out to eminent Russian intellectuals, but regrettably they were not in a position to accept the invitation.

I believe that coexistence has to live on. It could become my father's most enduring legacy. Financialised rentier capitalism is destroying societies and the natural environment. Regarding the civilisational challenge of information technology, we repeat Einstein's warning that the creations of our mind shall be a blessing not a curse to humanity. Coexistence is the celebration of the collective wisdom of the common people in all variety of languages, cultures, and religions. It is a plea for the conservation and protection of the richness of human and natural life in the hope of a civilisational rejection of the destruction of life on Earth by the commodification of everything.

REFERENCES

Duczynska, I. and K. Polanyi (1963), *The plough and the pen: Writings from Hungary 1930–1956*, Toronto: McClelland and Stewart.

Leontief, W. (1983), 'National perspective: The definition of problems and opportunities', in National Academy of Engineering Symposium (ed.), *Long-term impact of technology on employment and unemployment*, Washington, DC: National Academy Press, pp. 3–7.

Lewis, J., K. Polanyi and D.K. Kitchin (eds) (1935), *Christianity and the social revolution*, London: Victor Gollancz.

Marx, K., S. Landshut and J.P. Mayer (eds) (1932), *Der historische Materialismus: Die Frühschriften*, Leipzig: Kröner.

Neurath, O. (1919), *Durch die Kriegswirtschaft zur Naturalwirtschaft*, München: G.D.W. Callwey.

Polanyi, K. (1924), 'Die funktionelle Theorie der Gesellschaft und das Problem der sozialistischen Rechnungslegung', *Archiv für Sozialwissenschaft und Sozialpolitik*, 52 (1), 218–27.

Polanyi, K. (1945), 'Universal capitalism or regional planning?', *The London Quarterly of World Affairs*, 10 (3), 86–91.

Polanyi, K. (1954), 'Hamlet', *Yale Review*, 43 (3), 336–50.

Polanyi, K. (2016a), 'Guild socialism', in K. Polanyi, *The Hungarian writings*, ed. G. Dale, Manchester: Manchester University Press, pp. 118–20.

Polanyi, K. (2016b), 'Guild and state', in K. Polanyi, *The Hungarian writings*, ed. G. Dale, Manchester: Manchester University Press, pp. 121–2.

Polanyi, K. (2018a), 'On freedom', in M. Brie and C. Thomasberger (eds), *Karl Polanyi's vision of a socialist transformation*, Montréal: Black Rose, pp. 298–319.

Polanyi, K. (2018b), 'Hamlet', in K. Polanyi, M. Cangiani and C. Thomasberger (eds), *Economy and society: Selected writings*, Cambridge: Polity Press, pp. 301–13.

Polanyi, K. (2018c), 'Universal capitalism or regional planning?', in K. Polanyi, M. Cangiani and C. Thomasberger (eds), *Economy and society: Selected writings*, Cambridge: Polity Press, pp. 231–40.

Polanyi, K. (2018d), 'Jean-Jacques Rousseau, or is a free society possible?', in K. Polanyi, M. Cangiani and C. Thomasberger (eds), *Economy and society: Selected writings*, Cambridge: Polity Press, pp. 167–76.

Polanyi-Levitt, K. (2013), *From the great transformation to the great financialization*, London: Zed Books.

Polanyi-Levitt, K. (2018), 'The functionalist theory of society and the problem of socialist economic accounting', in K. Polanyi, M. Cangiani and C. Thomasberger (eds), *Economy and society: Selected writings*, Cambridge: Polity Press, pp. 41–50.

Robbins, L. (1932), *An essay on the nature and significance of economics*, London: Macmillan.

Schafer, F. (1937), 'Reine Rechtslehre und Reine Wirtschaftstheorie', *Internationale Zeitschrift für die Theorie des Rechts*, 11, 203–14.

Schafer, F. (1939), 'Rechtliche und wirtschaftliche Zurechnung', *Internationale Zeitschrift für die Theorie des Rechts*, 13, 162–76.

Schafer, F. (2006), 'Vorgartenstrasse 203', in K. McRobbie and K. Polanyi-Levitt (eds), *Karl Polanyi in Vienna*, Montréal: Black Rose, pp. 328–46.

3. "Plunges into utter destruction" and the limits of historical capitalism

Beverly J. Silver

1. THE RESURGENCE OF MARKET FUNDAMENTALISM AND THE DYNAMICS OF HISTORICAL CAPITALISM

Writing in the midst of the Second World War, Karl Polanyi expresses hope that humanity had been taught an enduring lesson from the great catastrophes of the first half of the twentieth century. He posits that "our age will be credited with having seen the end of self-regulating markets" ([1944] 2001, p. 148). Indeed, in the decades immediately following the Second World War, "self-regulating markets" appeared to be dead and buried. With an almost universal move toward some combination of state regulation of markets and planning (albeit in different forms and to varying degrees), it was possible to read Polanyi's statement – that "our age will be credited with having seen the end of self-regulating markets" – as an accurate prediction.

But economic liberalism – on the defensive for decades – was not in fact dead. It returned with a vengeance less than four decades after Polanyi's *magnum opus* was published and a decade after Nixon declared "we are all Keynesians now". One obvious question that emerges from a reading of *The Great Transformation* is "why was there a resurgence of economic liberalism (in the form of neoliberalism) in the final decades of the twentieth century"? I will argue that in order to answer this question, we need to supplement Polanyi's analysis – which focuses on the role of ideology and industrial society – with an explicit theory of historical capitalism that brings the pursuit of profits and power to centre stage.[1]

While Polanyi does not discuss, much less predict, a resurgence of economic liberalism, he did express concern that it was a powerful ideology that was far

---

[1]   The author wishes to thank Ricardo Jacobs and Corey Payne for their very helpful comments and suggestions.

from dead. Polanyi argued that the persistence of economic liberalism – even in the wake of the catastrophes of the first half of the twentieth century – was rooted in the fact that it had become a quasi-religious worldview, formulated in a way that was difficult, if not impossible, to falsify. According to purveyors of "the liberal creed", the failure of liberalism was due to "interference with the market". But as Polanyi notes, adherents of the liberal creed will always be able to point to evidence of the imperfect application of the principles of economic liberalism, *precisely because* the effort to establish "self-regulating markets" is a "utopian endeavor" that inevitably calls forth a protective counter-movement ([1944] 2001, pp. 150–151).

Polanyi worried that the advocates of "self-regulating markets" would "continue to hold the floor in the contest of arguments" – with disastrous results for humanity – unless their core claims were unquestionably refuted ([1944] 2001, p. 151). Thus, in *The Great Transformation*, Polanyi set himself the task of falsifying "the liberal creed" by demonstrating that the cataclysm of the first half of the twentieth century – fascism, depression, world wars – is unambiguously traceable, in the first instance, to "the utopian endeavor [. . .] to set up a self-regulating market system" ([1944] 2001, p. 31). Polanyi does a masterful job of falsifying the liberal creed.

Although Polanyi's emphasis on ideology has some utility in explaining the *persistence* of economic liberalism in the face of mounting human catastrophes in both his and our own time, it is not plausible as an explanation for the re-emergence of that project in the late twentieth century.[2] For one thing, the defeat of economic liberalism (as ideology and policy) was so thorough and "taken for granted" in the post-war decades, that few people read *The Great Transformation*; its critique and cautionary tale (so relevant today) seemed superfluous. Indeed, Nixon's 1971 quip that "we are all Keynesians now" was an admission that even his conservative administration would look toward Keynesian tools to solve the crisis.

Likewise, the second element in Polanyi's explanation for the rise of self-regulating markets – the use of complex machines for production in industrial societies – does not help us understand the return to economic liberalism in the 1980s. While Polanyi makes scattered use of the term "capitalism", the concept of capitalism as a historical social system with contradictions plays no role in his analysis. Rather, at the centre of Polanyi's analysis is a theory of *industrial society*, whose key contradiction is between the requirements of

---

2   For a critique of Polanyi's over-emphasis on the role of ideology – "the evangelical fervor" of British political economists – in explaining the origins of the nineteenth-century project to construct self-regulating global markets, and his discounting of the role played by the pursuit of profits and power, see Silver and Arrighi (2003).

machine-based mass production, on the one hand, and the physical and cultural well-being of humankind, on the other hand. According to Polanyi, "unless all factors involved [in production] are available in the needed quantities", undertaking "production with the help of specialized machines is too risky [. . .] both from the point of view of the [entrepreneur] [. . .] and of the community as a whole" ([1944] 2001, p. 43). The "solution" – creating "self-regulating markets" for all inputs, including the fictitious commodities of land, labour and money – inevitably led to a series of human catastrophes. Thus, Polanyi maintained that the only stable solution to the contradiction faced by industrial societies is the pursuit of regulated markets and planning ([1944] 2001, pp. 264–6). Armed with Polanyi's theory of the contradictions of industrial society we are still left without a plausible explanation for the resurgence of economic liberalism starting in the 1980s – i.e. we cannot answer the question, "why neoliberalism?", rather than, say, a further consolidation of regulation and planning.

To make sense of both the shift away from "self-regulating markets" in the 1930s and 1940s, *and* the eventual return to economic liberalism in the 1980s and beyond, we need to make central to our analysis a theory of capitalism as a world-historical system beset by a *fundamental contradiction between the pursuit of profitability and maintenance of social legitimacy* (Silver 2003).[3] This inherent contradiction between profitability and legitimacy has led to an alternation over time between crises of profitability and crises of legitimacy. One type of crisis can only be resolved by measures that eventually bring about the other type of crisis. Thus, historical capitalism has been characterised by successive pendulum swings between periods when the predominant tendency is towards protecting Polanyi's fictitious commodities, and periods when the predominant tendency is towards stripping them of protections.

The period that Polanyi focuses on in *The Great Transformation* was a deep crisis of legitimacy for capitalism. By the 1930s and 1940s, capitalism was widely seen as having failed to guarantee minimum livelihoods and physical

---

[3]   Polanyi and Marx take different paths to the same conclusion about the tendency of capitalism to produce a deep crisis of legitimacy; but Marx's analysis also put the problem of profitability at the centre. In *The Communist Manifesto*, for example, Marx and Engels (1848) implicitly point to the tension between profitability and legitimacy. They write: "it becomes evident, that the bourgeoisie is unfit any longer to be the ruling class in society [. . .] It is unfit to rule because it is incompetent to assure an existence to its slave within his slavery, because it cannot help letting him sink into such a state, that it has to feed him, instead of being fed by him. Society can no longer live under this bourgeoisie, in other words, its existence is no longer compatible with society." The phrase – *it has to feed him, instead of being fed by him* – recognises (already in 1848) the incompatibility of a system of capital accumulation based on the profit motivation with the generalisation (in geographical space and time) of the welfare state.

security to the mass of the population. When crises of legitimacy deepen to the point that they become dysfunctional even for political and economic elites – that is, when elites are either faced with such a lack of security that they cannot conduct business, or they are faced with such anger from below that they risk revolutions – they *attempt* to shift gears (Arrighi and Silver 1999, pp. 151–216). Such was the case in the mid-twentieth century as welfare and developmental states (and multilateral institutions) implemented policies that – by promoting full employment, extending workplace rights to labour, and reining in financial speculation – in essence, recognised that labour and money are "fictitious commodities".[4]

However, these post-war social compacts were founded on the (implicit or explicit) presumption that there was no fundamental contradiction between guaranteeing profitability and guaranteeing livelihoods. While these measures resolved the crisis of legitimacy, leading to the Golden Age of Capitalism in the decades following the Second World War, they eventually contributed to a squeeze on returns to capital, provoking a crisis of profitability. When the squeeze on profits first emerged in the 1970s, the initial reaction was to double-down on the Keynesian solution. But the profitability crisis intensified further in the late 1970s, and *without a clear commitment to put livelihoods over profits* (if/when the two came into conflict), Keynesianism was abandoned, and the Reagan–Thatcher counter-revolution took hold in the 1980s. Political and economic elites began to extol the virtues of self-regulating markets as they pursued policies that deregulated money and stripped protections from labour.

These policies eventually resolved the crisis of profitability by making it easier for capital to profit from financial speculation and from the exploitation of labour and nature. Indeed, by the time of the 2008 financial crisis, the squeeze on profits was long resolved. But, in the process, the pendulum swung back to a deep crisis of legitimacy for capitalism.

These pendulum swings map onto two important tendencies within historical capitalism. The first relates to the alternation between periods of financial expansion and periods of material expansion (cf. Arrighi 2010). It is no coincidence that both the late nineteenth-century and late twentieth-century moves toward global self-regulating markets for "money" were periods in

---

[4]   I have purposely left "land" out of the list of protected "fictitious commodities", because one of the main characteristics of the mass production/mass consumption/ developmentalist project of the post-Second World War decades was the "externalisation of the costs of reproduction" of non-renewable resources and nature. Put differently, while the protection of labour and money were built into the post-Second World War social compacts, their failure to recognise and provide for the protection of nature was even more extreme than in the nineteenth and early twentieth centuries.

which finance capital came to dominate the world capitalist system. Financial expansions – periods during which money capital is increasingly channelled into economic speculation divorced from trade and production – played an important role in the resolution of crises of profitability. In contrast, material expansions – periods during which capital predominantly flows into trade and production – played an important role in the resolution of crises of legitimacy (Silver 2003, pp. 124–67).

This brings us to the second important (and interrelated) tendency – the alternation between periods of rising and declining class inequality. Various empirical studies of long-term trends in class inequality have found a U-shaped curve over the past century – that is, class inequality in most countries was high and rising in the decades leading up to the 1930s crisis, it declined steadily from the crisis of the 1930s to the crisis of the 1970s, and then rose dramatically once again in the decades leading up to (and beyond) the 2008 crisis, reaching unprecedented heights today (see, e.g., Piketty 2013; Saez 2017). This U-shaped curve parallels the pendulum swing between crises of profitability and crises of legitimacy. This happens for several reasons. The most straightforward reason is the alternation between labour-friendly and capital-friendly policies; that is, between periods in which the trend is toward the protection of labour (in response to crises of legitimacy) and periods in which the trend is toward stripping those protections (in response to crises of profitability). Less directly, the rise of finance itself has a negative impact on equality because the FIRE sector tends to create fewer jobs and absorb less labour than trade and manufacturing (Krippner 2011, pp. 1–26; Phillips 1993, p. 197). Finally, financialisation of the economy tends to promote a regressive redistribution of income – the rich get richer – as the wealthy are better placed to profit from the game of financial speculation.

2.   THE FOUR CRISES OF CAPITALISM IN THE LONG TWENTIETH CENTURY

Figure 3.1 presents a graphic summary of the four capitalist crises of the "long twentieth century". Writing in the midst of the crisis of the 1970s, Giovanni Arrighi (1978) argued that not all capitalist crises are the same, and that the crisis of the 1970s (and 1870s) was different from that of the 1930s. The 1870s and 1970s crises were fundamentally characterised by a squeeze on profits, while the 1930s crisis was fundamentally characterised by an excessive squeeze on labour. Following Arrighi's logic, but using the "Polanyian" terminology introduced above, Figure 3.1 classifies the crises of the 1870s and 1970s as ones in which the "protection of fictitious commodities" is "too high", and the crisis of the 1930s as one in which the "protection of fictitious commodities" is "too low" – that is, "too low" even from the long-term point of view of capital. Extending Arrighi's logic to the present, the current crisis of capitalism is classified as one in which the root of the crisis is the insufficient protection of the fictitious commodities labour, land and money.

	PROTECTION OF FICTITIOUS COMMODITIES	
	"TOO LOW"	**"TOO HIGH"**
	(Legitimacy Crisis)	(Profitability Crisis)
RESOLUTION 4		
CRISIS 4 (2001/2008–?)	*Terminal Crisis 2001/2008–?*	
RESOLUTION 3	Redistribution to Capital – Financial Expansion (CM) (Reagan/Thatcher counter-revolution)	
CRISIS 3 (1968/73–1980)		*Signal Crisis 1968/1973–1980*
RESOLUTION 2	Redistribution to Labour – Material Expansion (MC) ("Global New Deal")	
CRISIS 2 (1929–1945)	*Terminal Crisis 1929–1945*	
RESOLUTION 1	Redistribution to Capital – Financial Expansion (CM) ("Monopoly Capital")	
CRISIS 1 (1873–1896)		*Signal Crisis 1873–1896*

Figure 3.1   Four capitalist crises of the long twentieth century and "Polanyian" pendulum swings

The "utopian endeavour" to construct a *global* self-regulating market chronicled in *The Great Transformation* stretches from the period leading up to crisis #1 through crisis #2 in Figure 3.1. Polanyi's hopes for an end to self-regulating markets found their greatest validation in the period labelled "resolution #2" – the post-war "Global New Deal"; but those hopes were dashed with the "Reagan–Thatcher counter-revolution" (resolution #3). Four decades of neoliberal policies have brought us to where we are today – in the midst of crisis

#4, a deep crisis of legitimacy for capitalism, rooted in the failure to protect land, labour and money.

In the aftermath of the 2008 financial crisis, we might have expected political and economic elites to "shift gears" and move toward policies that, in essence, recognise the fictitious nature of the commodities land, labour and money. Put differently, we might have expected a swing of the pendulum toward greater protection – that is, a "resolution #4" analogous to "resolution #2" (see Figure 3.1). Instead of a course correction, however, we have witnessed the continued movement by the world's elites down a path that is taking us toward a widening and deepening human catastrophe. Mushrooming class inequality, the proliferation of wars without end, the explosion of the refugee crisis, and the rise of xenophobic, neo-fascist and far right movements are among the symptoms that we have entered a period of systemic chaos analogous to the great catastrophe of the first half of the twentieth century (cf. Silver and Arrighi 2010).

3.   "A PLUNGE INTO UTTER DESTRUCTION"

Unless the alternative to the social set up is a plunge into utter destruction, no crudely selfish class can maintain itself in the lead. (Polanyi [1944] 2001, p. 163)

Why have the world's economic and political elites not heeded the warnings coming from the growing number of Cassandras who have come forward since the 1990s – many of them inspired by *The Great Transformation* – to warn of the urgent need to shift course away from neoliberal globalisation?

This failure is puzzling from several points of view. For one thing, while there is a sense of *déjà vu* about current trends, it is important to note that Polanyi did not think that the human catastrophes of the first half of the twentieth century were inevitable. Rather he argued that, "if not for the stubborn and impassioned insistence of economic liberals on their fallacies," both the world's leaders and the mass of the population "would have been better equipped for the ordeal of the age and *might perhaps even have been able to avoid it altogether*" (Polanyi [1944] 2001, p. 149, emphasis added). To be sure, today's neoliberals are also guilty of "stubborn and impassioned insistence on their fallacies", and they deserve their share of the blame for the mounting human catastrophes.[5] Nevertheless, following Polanyi, there is no reason to presume that the current slide into systemic chaos was somehow pre-ordained.

---

[5]   Among the many examples, the failure of the European Union to break away from austerity policies, notwithstanding the mounting evidence of their disastrous results on all fronts (political, social and economic).

Indeed, Polanyi gives us reasons to expect that a "course correction" could have come sooner and with greater ease than has been the case. Operating with an organic (solidaristic) conceptualisation of society, Polanyi sees "self-regulating markets" as posing a challenge to "society as a whole". Because "the social interests of different cross sections of the population [are] threatened by the market, persons belonging to various economic strata unconsciously [join] forces to meet the danger" (Polanyi [1944] 2001, pp. 161–2). Moreover, Polanyi maintains that the capacity of a group or class to lead depends on "the breadth and variety of the interests, other than its own, which it is able to serve". As such, "no policy of narrow class interest can safeguard even that interest well" (Polanyi [1944] 2001, p. 163; cf. Gramsci 1971). Working with this conceptualisation of leadership, we would expect ruling groups and classes to mobilise for the "self-protection of society" as a whole, including groups and classes lacking the power to protect themselves.

While the above passages from *The Great Transformation* suggest that it is "normal" for ruling groups and classes to protect the interests of society as a whole, in Polanyi's historical account, what is "normal" is not what is common or prevalent. This distinction, which might at first appear odd, is analogous to the way in which Durkheim's ([1893] 2014) "normal" form of the division of labour (organic solidarity) was quite rare in "actually-existing" capitalist societies, whereas his "abnormal forms" (anomic and forced)[6] were actually quite common. Polanyi makes a similar move. Whereas he argues that there are "few exceptions" to the rule that "no crudely selfish class can maintain itself in the lead" (Polanyi [1944] 2001, p. 163), he actually provides us with a wide range of exceptions – both theoretical and historical.[7]

Thus, while Polanyi points to the "vital function" played by "enlightened reactionaries" among the landlord class in fighting for protections for the emergent (still voiceless) British working class in the early and mid-nineteenth centuries as an example of a ruling group protecting broader social interests,[8]

---

6   It is these abnormal – yet prevalent – forms of the division of labour that, according to Durkheim, accounted for the prevalence of social conflict (rather than social cohesion and solidarity) in his own time.

7   It might make sense to understand Polanyi's "normal" as meaning "prevalent" if the temporal scope of his statement includes all human history and not just "industrial society".

8   "By interest and inclination, it fell to the landlords of England to protect the lives of the common people from the onrush of the Industrial Revolution [. . .] Their resistance [. . .] averted ruin for several generations and allowed time for almost complete readjustment. Over a critical span of forty years it retarded economic progress, and when, in 1834, the Reform Parliament abolished Speenhamland, the landlords shifted their resistance to the factory laws [. . .] The Ten Hours Bill of 1847, which Karl

he also argued that the triumphant British bourgeoisie lacked the capacity to perform the task of social protection.

> [The triumphant bourgeoisie] *had no organ to sense the dangers* involved in the exploitation of the physical strength of the worker, the destruction of family life, the devastation of neighborhoods, the denudation of forests, the pollution of rivers, the deterioration of craft standards, the disruption of folkways, and the general degradation of existence including housing and arts, as well as the innumerable forms of private and public life that do not affect profits [. . .] [Their] all but sacramental belief in the universal beneficence of profits [. . .] disqualified them as the keepers of other interests as vital to a good life as the furtherance of production. (Polanyi [1944] 2001, p. 139)

Likewise, in explaining the catastrophe that befell colonised peoples, Polanyi argued that the protection which "the organized states of Europe" could secure for themselves was out of reach for those who lacked sovereign governments and for those whose sovereign states were relatively weak (Polanyi [1944] 2001, pp. 192, 216–17). Not only did the European colonisers have "no organ to sense the dangers" to colonised societies; equally important, the "self-protection of European societies" and the devastation of colonial societies were often two sides of the same coin (Silver and Arrighi 2003).[9]

As such, it is not inevitable that ruling groups and classes rise to the challenge and take on the "vital function" of protecting the broader interests of society. At the same time, if "a crudely selfish class" maintains itself in the lead, then "a plunge into utter destruction" in the form of a long period of systemic chaos is, sooner or later, inevitable (Arrighi and Silver 1999). A long period of systemic crisis on world scale characterised crisis #2 (1929–45) and the odds are increasing that with crisis #4 (the contemporary crisis of capitalism) we have entered another long period of global systemic chaos (see Figure 3.1).[10]

In the twentieth century, it was only with the rise of mass workers' movements and the force of anti-imperialist revolts – that is, with the threat of revolution from below – that ruling groups and classes awakened to the dangers

---

Marx hailed as the first victory of socialism, was the work of enlightened reactionaries" (Polanyi [1944] 2001, pp. 173–4).

[9]   These two illustrations point to two types of failure that are both relevant to today's predicament. One is a failure of dominant classes to protect subordinate groups within a given state; the other is the failure of strong states to facilitate, or at least not impede, the "self-protection of society" in weaker states.

[10]   Both crisis #2 and crisis #4 are conceptualised as terminal crises of a cycle of hegemony in Figure 3.1 – UK (crisis #2) and US (crisis #4). This is an important part of the story, but beyond the scope of this chapter (cf. Silver and Arrighi 2010; Arrighi and Silver 1999).

inherent in the project of a global self-regulating market. This sense of danger was kept alive in the 1950s and 1960s by ongoing anti-imperialist struggles in the Third World and the active Cold War rivalry between East and West. It is in this context that the United States (as the world hegemonic state) used its power to implement policies that helped swing the pendulum back toward the self-protection of society at the local and global levels (Figure 3.1, resolution #2). But it took a depression, the rise and spread of fascism, and two world wars for it to become clear that, if capitalism were to survive, a change of course was essential.

Why have today's economic and political elites been so slow to sense the danger? To be sure, the Trump presidency marks a change of course in the sense that his administration openly proclaims the end of US adherence to global "free trade" policies.[11] But this project involves *stripping* the remaining protections from fictitious commodities in order to further enrich the super-wealthy, rather than a swing of the pendulum back toward protection of the general interests of society (nationally or globally). As such, it is one more step down the road of systemic chaos.

Perhaps the *après moi le deluge* attitude of today's ruling groups is not much different than their counterparts a century ago. Yet, one would have hoped today's ruling groups would have learned some lessons from the disastrous experience of their counterparts, if not from reading *The Great Transformation*. It is worth pondering – in another context – whether we have seen an evolution in historical capitalism that has produced especially venal ruling groups. Might, for example, the growing surplus population on a world scale – that is, surplus to the needs of capital – help explain the shocking level of disregard for the dangers to the physical and cultural well-being of the majority of the world's population exhibited by today's ruling groups? Might the stratospheric wealth of today's super-rich be deluding them into thinking they can immunise themselves from the effects of the systemic chaos – be it wars, social revolution or societal breakdown – by setting themselves up with luxury bunkers in remote locations? Might their wealth in combination with an abundant faith in science and technology, make them think that they can keep safe from rising seas and otherwise protect themselves from the devastation of nature even as the majority suffer and die?[12] But even more palpable than these dystopic plans and visions are the growing movements proposing a vision that

---

[11]   As we argue in Silver and Arrighi (2003), although the United States adopted a free trade rhetoric beginning in the 1980s, it never actually adopted free trade policies.

[12]   A spate of articles have appeared in the press in recent years with titles such as 'The super rich of Silicon Valley have a doomsday escape plan', 'Inside billionaires bunkers where richest plan to sit out apocalypse', and 'Survival of the richest'. For the latter see Osnos (2017).

moves us beyond the contradictions of historical capitalism to a world that unequivocally chooses to place the protection of humans and nature over the pursuit of profits.

REFERENCES

Arrighi, G. (1978), 'Towards a theory of capitalist crisis', *New Left Review*, 1 (111), 3–24.

Arrighi, G. (2010), *The long twentieth century: Money, power and the origin of our time (New and updated edn)*, London: Verso.

Arrighi, G. and B.J. Silver (1999), *Chaos and governance in the modern world system*, Minneapolis: University of Minnesota Press.

Durkheim, E. ([1893] 2014), *The division of labor in society*, New York: Free Press.

Gramsci, A. (1971), *Selections from the prison notebooks*, New York: International Publishers.

Krippner, G. (2011), *Capitalizing on crisis*, Cambridge, MA: Harvard University Press.

Marx, K. and F. Engels (1848), *Manifesto of the Communist Party*, Moscow: Foreign Languages Publishing House.

Osnos, E. (2017), 'Survival of the richest: Why some of America's wealthiest people are prepping for disaster', *The New Yorker*, 30 January, 36–45.

Phillips, K. (1993), *Boiling point: Democrats, Republicans, and the decline of middle-class prosperity*, New York: Random House.

Piketty, T. (2013), *Capital in the twenty-first century*, Cambridge, MA: Harvard University Press.

Polanyi, K. ([1944] 2001), *The great transformation: The political and economic origins of our time*, Boston: Beacon Press.

Saez, E. (2017), 'Income and wealth inequality: Evidence and policy implications', *Contemporary Economic Policy*, 35 (1), 7–25.

Silver, B.J. (2003), *Forces of labor: Workers' movements and globalization since 1870*, Cambridge, MA: Cambridge University Press.

Silver, B.J. and G. Arrighi (2003), 'Polanyi's "double movement": The *belle époques* of British and U.S. hegemony compared', *Politics & Society*, 31 (2), 325–55.

Silver, B.J. and G. Arrighi (2010), 'The end of the long twentieth century', in C. Calhoun and G. Derluguian (eds), *Business as usual: The roots of the global financial meltdown*, New York and London: New York University Press, pp. 53–68.

4. Crises and transformations: suggestions from Karl Polanyi's works

Michele Cangiani

Neoliberal policies showed themselves to be a counterproductive attempt to face the structural crisis of capitalist accumulation beginning in the 1970s; moreover, they have had distressing consequences on human beings, society and natural environment. We are then compelled to reflect, not only on the neoliberal age and the present crisis, but on the most general traits of our society, its basic dynamics and transformations.

Karl Polanyi's theory offers a clue on this subject. Section 1 synthetically deals with that theory at its most abstract level regarding the market capitalist society in general. Section 2 shows that such general conception is the ground on which more specific Polanyi's analyses of the "great transformation" rest. Section 3 suggests that Polanyi's approach – at both its levels, the more and the less general – is consistent with some radical explanations of the neoliberal transformation. Such correspondence, in turn, confirms Polanyi's theory – as interpreted in the previous sections.[1]

1.   BASIC PRINCIPLES OF POLANYI'S THEORY

Polanyi connotes the market capitalist society[2] at the most general, wide-comparative theoretical level. The way production is instituted, then factors of production combined, characterises each economic system. In the market capitalist society, he maintains (1977, p. 9), the factors of production – labour and land – are combined "into industrial units under the command of private persons mainly engaged in buying and selling for profit". The two fundamental institutions of this form of society, distinguishing it from any

---

[1]   A more detailed version of this interpretation, together with a criticism of different interpretations, can be found in Cangiani (2011) and (2017).
[2]   Ron Stanfield (1977) adopts this expression with reference to Polanyi's conception.

other, are, in fact, the market system and capitalist relations of production. The exchange, based on the market system, becomes the dominant "form of integration", while preceding economic systems were basically "integrated" (i.e. organised) by "reciprocity" and "redistribution"; correspondingly, also labour, land and money become commodities. Like Max Weber, Polanyi points out that only in this society "hunger and gain" are the motives of economic activities and relationships. Being "economically" organised, autonomous, "disembedded" ("rational" and differentiated, according to Weber), the economy constrains the social system as a whole, which results, then, "embedded in the mechanism of its own economy" (Polanyi 1977, p. 9).

Polanyi's concept of "self-regulation" applies to the autonomy of the economic system, and not merely to the functioning of more or less competitive markets. The economic system tends to be autonomous because it is organised by the market in view of profit, that is – Polanyi points out in a manuscript of 1940 ([n.d.] 2014, pp. 216–17) – by "a blind mechanism removed by its very nature from the needs of the living community embodied in every human society". This is the deepest meaning of the "separation of the political and the economic sphere", being a "unique peculiarity" of capitalism ([n.d.] 2014, pp. 216–17), implying the need to recover the "integration" of society, on a modern basis of individual freedom and democratic politics. But any attempt in this direction requires struggles by the working class and provokes reactions by the ruling class. As a result, the functioning of the system is damaged. Society is, then, "caught on the horns of a dilemma: either to continue on the path of a utopia bound for destruction, or to halt on this path" ([n.d.] 2014, p. 217), thereby undermining the functioning of the system.

The relevance of the class conflict clearly results both from Polanyi's articles – for example in his essay on the crisis (1933), where conflicting claims on the national product are highlighted – and *The Great Transformation*, where he writes that "the conflict of class forces entered decisively" in the "final phase" of the crisis of the nineteenth-century capitalism ([1944] 2001, p. 228).

Partial political interventions for the "defence" of society against the damages due to the autonomy of the economic system are inevitable, but, sooner or later, they lead to an "impasse" revealing the "dilemma". There are strict limits to reforms: the system never allows them to reach the necessary extent, because, at this point, they would be non-reformist, that is, steps toward a different social organisation. As he will further explain in *The Great Transformation*, in the manuscript of 1940 Polanyi affirms that the "counter-movement" attempting at "the integration of society" – that is, at a political democratic control on the economy – though partial and provisional as it could have been, "*merely increased the strain on the social system*" ([n.d.] 2014, p. 218; Polanyi's italics). The working class fought for protection; "the leaders of business, on their part, made use of industrial property and finance to weaken political democracy" ([n.d.] 2014, p. 218). As a result, society found itself in an impasse.

After the First World War, when "the separation of economics and politics developed into a catastrophic internal situation", Polanyi points out ([n.d.] 2014, pp. 218–19), "the need for a reintegration of society was apparent", but opposed directions could be followed: "the alternative was between an integration of society through political power, on a democratic basis, or, if democracy proved too weak, an integration on an authoritarian basis, at the price of the sacrifice of democracy". Although specifically addressed to the interwar period, Polanyi's reflection holds a general meaning. After the Second World War, two tendencies were again confronting each other. The first one – Polanyi maintains ([1947b] 2018, pp. 210–11) – leads to "a truly democratic society", where the economy would be organised "through the planned intervention of the producers and consumers themselves". The second tendency leads to a society "more intimately adjusted to the economic system", whose basic institutions (the market, the capitalist relations of production) will remain "unchanged". The alternative between these two tendencies is rooted in the fundamental features and dynamics of capitalist society, and becomes evident whenever systemic crises occur.

2.   FROM LIBERAL TO CORPORATIVE CAPITALISM

This section is dedicated to some aspects of Polanyi's analysis of the "transformation", consistently based on his general theory of capitalism. The term "transformation" implies a subject that is transformed, whose fundamental traits persist under different "institutional arrangements" and must be considered for explaining the different phases of an irreversible historical development. In *The Great Transformation*, in effect, the analysis of the market society is carried on at two levels: in the general sense of capitalist society, within a wide-range comparison with preceding societies, and at a less general level, in the sense of liberal or "Victorian" capitalism, whose systemic crisis gave rise to diverse varieties of corporative capitalism.

With the Poor Law Reform of 1834 instituting the labour market, Polanyi writes ([1944] 2001, pp. 86–7), "industrial capitalism as a social system" came into existence; the effects on labourers and on society as a whole were "deleterious [. . .] until in the 1870s the recognition of the trade unions offered sufficient protection". The novelty and the progressive-democratic meaning of the "defence" of society by the working class is represented by the extension of modern citizenship rights analysed by Thomas Marshall (1950).[3] The social struggle aimed at that extension met difficulties and defeats. It was partially successful, especially in the "golden" phase of capitalist development after the Second World War. In our times we have witnessed the neoliberal turnabout. The goal of equality and democracy has inevitably remained a horizon, since the motive of gain and the correlative class division constitute the ultimate constraint, an insuperable limit all along the history of the market capitalist society. Polanyi – like Marshall, who probably noticed this theme in *The Great Transformation*, which he cites with the title of the British edition of 1945, *Origins of our Times* – points out the gap of several decades between the Reform of 1834 and the achievement of workers' political citizenship with the right of suffrage. This gap reveals the relevance of class division. The universal suffrage threatened the rule of capital, thereby importantly contributing to the decline of the "the liberal state".

Even the possibility of moderate reforms by "popular governments" was, in fact, so worrying as to give rise to more or less anti-democratic reactions. The defeat of the socialist alternative and the institutional transformation allowed the survival of capitalism. To this purpose, according to Charles Maier (1987, p. 263), various strategies of "stabilization" were carried out, involving various social forces and motives in view of removing "divisive issues from political determination", that is, of stabilising social hierarchies, together with the market capitalist system. Already in the 1920s and 1930s, in his articles for *Der Österreichische Volkswirt*, Polanyi comments on the corporatist transformation, differently shaping in different countries and times. His reflection is addressed to "Capitalism in its non-Liberal, i.e. corporative, forms", allowing it to continue "its existence unscathed under a new alias" (Polanyi [1935] 2018, p. 87).

A good part of Polanyi's articles of the 1920s deals with British events: the workers' movement and its organisations, the question of the coal mines, the struggles culminating with the 1926 General Strike. His conclusion is that possibilities of a radical change, if any, ceased very early after the war. As early as 1928 he analyses the corporative reorganisation proposed by the report published on behalf of the left wing of the Liberal Party by the Liberal Industrial Enquiry, on which John M. Keynes collaborated. Polanyi points out that forms of economic coordination and class collaboration are not necessarily signs of a move beyond "a society whose substance is the cash-nexus". Even if wage work would cease to be "a mere contractual relation by acquiring a legally guaranteed position with clear social status", the managerial power

---

[3]   See also the fundamental historical analysis by Robert Castel (1995).

of employers could grow and private property get stronger (Polanyi [1928a] 2002, [1928b] 2002).

Several articles of 1934 concern the reorganisation of British industry, the government intervention, and the collaboration by trade unions and the Labour Party to the corporative transformation. Little was left of social struggles of the first quarter of the twentieth century, Polanyi notes. While even Conservatives seemed to share the planning mood, trade unions no longer represented a "socialist tendency", but only "the corporative interests of individual categories of workers" (Polanyi [1934a] 2002, [1934b] 2002) within the limits set by so-called technical managerial choices and the need to make profit.

In *The Great Transformation* Polanyi explains that the crisis was also a consequence of the refusal of necessary reforms by the ruling class, supported by free-market ideologies. The same class, ironically relying on the same ideologies, claimed a "stronger state", protectionism and an exclusive control on political decisions about the quality and extent of reforms needed to face the crisis (Polanyi [1944] 2001, p. 236): actually counter-reforms – like neoliberal ones. Anti-democratic and anti-liberal attitudes spread. Polanyi interprets in this sense the "fascist situation" of the 1930s; in his opinion, the "fascist virus" is endemic in the market society,[4] and awakens when necessary.

The anti-democratic reaction can also assume softer forms, such as the British National Government of 1931, a coalition government whose Prime Minister, Ramsay MacDonald, had occupied the same charge in the resigning Labour Government. In this case, Polanyi comments ([1931] 2002), Labour statesmen espoused the reasons of the City ("of the markets", we currently say): they sacrificed the interests of the working class – for the salvation of the pound, they claimed – and caused a damage to democracy by suspending the two-party system.

Many scholars of Polanyi's time adopted a similar approach to the crisis of nineteenth-century capitalism. Like him, they were capable both of distinguishing the two levels of conceptual generality – capitalist society and its different historical forms – and of linking them to one another.

An exemplary case is that of Thorstein Veblen, who achieves a deep and detailed analysis of the new forms of business organisation, showing their growingly parasitic relationship with a technologically developed industry. Then he explains the non-coincidence, to say the least, between profitability and "serviceability for society at large" as an inherent, general tendency of the market-capitalist productive system (Veblen [1901] 1994). The "investment for a profit", in particular that of "business enterprises", is presented by Veblen

---

[4]   'The Fascist Virus' is the title of two manuscripts of the second half of the 1930s (Karl Polanyi Archive, file 18–08, n.d.). Reprinted in Polanyi (2018).

in the first page of his *Theory of Business Enterprise* (1904) as the "directing force" of the "Capitalistic System". Polanyi ([1944] 2001, p. 178) similarly mentions "the principle of gain and profit as the organising force in society".

The First World War solicited a greater attention to the crisis and transformation of liberal capitalism. John Hobson points to the control that "strong business organisations" have acquired over government, with a view to turning internal and external policies to their own advantage, thus compromising both the interest and freedom of the majority of citizens and of the nation as a whole. The overcoming of such class supremacy seems to Hobson the condition for establishing a really democratic government, founded on the development of "intelligent co-operation" with a view to "clearly defined ends". However, it seems likely to him that capitalism will be able to persist, in a new, corporative shape, where state control and intervention, and the management of public opinion, would be "consistent with the largest liberty and opportunity of private profiteering" (Hobson 1919, pp. 75, 87, 143, 200).

Richard Tawney ([1926] 1947, p. 59) speaks of the twentieth-century new kind of capitalism characterised by the "control of industry by business and of both by finance".

In March 1918 Antonio Gramsci envisages a future "organization of freedoms" as being more "mature" than bourgeois individualism: indeed, as the only way to achieve modern freedom.[5] Shortly after, he warns against the opposite tendency emerging in the proposal, made in particular by the nationalist daily *L'Idea Nazionale*, to form a government from technical experts, in fact businessmen. A "professional state, a kind of capitalistic unionism", a *"régime* of association" achieve, he maintains, a regressive caesura in the evolution of modern society (Gramsci 1994, pp. 19–20). The following year he affirms that "the War has destroyed all the attainments of liberal ideology", both in internal and international politics. Politics is no longer separate from economic processes: monopolistic capitalism increases in strength, together with bureaucracy and militarism, and the state "distributes wealth to private capitalists" (Gramsci 1994, p. 21).

These examples of early reflections on the transformation from liberal to corporative capitalism parallel Polanyi's approach,[6] particularly his idea that a reintegration of society can be achieved in opposite ways.

---

[5]   For a convincing parallel between Gramsci's and Polanyi's political philosophy cf. Burawoy (2003).

[6]   An approach confirmed by Charles Maier's research (1975) on the origin of corporative mentality and practice at the time of the First World War.

3.   FROM THE CRISIS OF THE 1970S TO THE NEOLIBERAL TRANSFORMATION

Polanyi's analysis of the events of the interwar period, insofar as it reveals more general tendencies, is also illuminating concerning our neoliberal epoch.[7] There is continuity beyond the historical change. Systemic crises and transformations resulting in diverse institutional arrangements must be explained by referring them to the general features of the market capitalist society, of its dynamics and contradictions.

Crises sharpen conflicts and open alternatives: this is the theme of the last two pages of the nineteenth chapter of *The Great Transformation*, where socialism is defined as a break "with the attempt to make private money gains the general incentive to productive activities" and a tendency toward such an extended democratic control over the economy as to make it cease to be autonomous (Polanyi [1944] 2001, p. 242).

Immediately after the Second World War, Polanyi renewed the hopes he shared with Austrian socialists after the First World War. He wonders, for instance, if the British Labour Government could be an opportunity to attempt the construction of a radically different social organisation, in the direction of socialism (cf. Polanyi [1945] 2018, [1947a] 2018). However, his hopes were balanced by a realistic analysis of facts, like in the interwar period, when he supported the minority, defeated positions of the Independent Labour Party and the Socialist League.

In fact, the continuity of the market-capitalist social organisation and world order has been safeguarded through the second of the two tendencies Polanyi opposes to one another (see above, end of section 1). Even if we consider the most notable achievements of post-liberal capitalism after the Second World War – such as the pluralistic interest representation and the welfare state – society was still based on the "cash nexus" and labour remained a commodity. Yet, as Polanyi points out concerning the interwar period, limited democratic reforms and moderate popular governments were so worrisome as to contribute to starting a period of crisis in the 1970s. The crisis required the reversal of economic and democratic protections conquered by the working classes; at the same time, it was – as usual – instrumentally employed to make that reaction easier. Besides, the attack against democratic institutions, attitudes and practice, being both a preliminary condition and an effect of the neoliberal transfor-

---

[7]   An interesting analysis on this point can be found in Polanyi-Levitt (2013), particularly in Chapter 5, 'Keynes and Polanyi: The 1920s and the 1990s'.

mation, started in that decade.[8] This is the normal effect of the crisis, Polanyi explains in *The Great Transformation*. And in 'The Essence of Fascism' he alludes to "the mutual incompatibility of Democracy and Capitalism [. . .] as the background of the social crisis" ([1935] 2018, p. 135).

Joan Robinson, interviewed by Bertram Silverman (1980) on the British welfare state crisis, raises fundamental issues about the neoliberal turn. How effective can be Keynesian fiscal and monetary policies in a world "dominated by large transnational corporations" (p. 28), troubled by the crises of the 1970s and bewildered in the face of stagflation? In the interview, reference is made to the post-Keynesian approach. According to the latter, governmental functions should include social equity, promotion and quality of investments, control of large corporations, full employment, and the system of international relations. Besides, an effective planning requires a democracy made real through broad and informed public participation. Instead, monetarism, cuts in public spending and privatisations were carried on, initiatives and forces of the working class were harnessed, and democracy depleted, as a reaction, Polanyi would say, to the possibility of reforms that could be decided and implemented under the influence of the working class.

The Labour Party and trade unions "didn't take advantage of the prosperity to make a socialist policy", Robinson maintains; they were merely "trying to get [their] stick into the cake" (Silverman 1980, p. 30). A similar metaphor is employed by C.B. Macpherson (1987, p. 128) in his analysis of the crisis of the Fordist-Keynesian-neo-corporative institutional setup: each union, he says, seeks "to maintain its slice of pie, but does not question the methods of the bakery" (cf., in this regard, Polanyi's criticism to the trade unions and the Labour Party recalled above, section 2).

Macpherson's essay, like the interview conducted by Silverman, deals with the transition to a new phase, fully launched by Margaret Thatcher in 1979 and Ronald Reagan in 1980. Important precedents were the economic liberalisation promoted by Deng Xiaoping in 1978, while the Chinese regime did not cease to be illiberal, and the adoption of the Chicago School economic policy by the Pinochet government in Chile, after the coup d'état of 1973.

According to Macpherson, the historical evolution of capitalism has unmasked the illusion of the theoreticians of liberal democracy that pluralism had swallowed and metabolised class antagonism. When the era of develop-

---

[8]   Cf. e.g. the Report of the Trilateral Commission (Crozier et al. 1975). A continuity can be noted with a recent report, directly coming from a great financial corporation: it recommends amending "Constitutions [that] tend to show a strong socialist influence", and avoiding "weak executives, [. . .] constitutional protection of labour rights, [. . .] and the right to protest if unwelcome changes are made to the political status quo" (J.P.Morgan 2013, p. 12).

ment came to an end, it seemed no longer possible to redistribute, partly at least, the benefits of the increases in productivity and, in general, to satisfy the need for equality and well-being. An institutional transformation was necessary to overcome the crisis – but what kind of transformation? In its most radical terms, the alternative was the usual one – similarly indicated by Polanyi (1947b), as we have seen – between "more participatory democratic institutions", demanded by "popular movements", and the dismantling of democracy in the direction of "some kind of corporatist plebiscitarian state" (Macpherson 1987, p. 127). The latter proved to be the dominant trend in the new, neoliberal phase.

Robinson interprets the crisis of the 1970s and its neoliberal solution as "almost a conscious class war of the rich against the poor" (Silverman 1980, p. 30).[9] Flagging growth produced inflation by increasing competition on resources among different social categories and, basically, between classes. Polanyi (1933) similarly regards that competition as a cause of the crisis. He also considers the need to reduce wages as a motive of the above-mentioned (section 2) substitution of the Labour Government with the National Government of 1931. Robinson also recalls the transfer of resources from welfare to armaments, with particular reference to Reagan's policy; armaments have the advantage of being directly a source of profits, while taxes to pay for them are only partially loaded on profits. In fact, another aspect of the Reagan policy has become a guideline of neoliberal policies: the reduction of the progressivity of taxation. Governmental policies further contribute to increasing inequality with their interventions on the labour market, the reduction of welfare expenditure and, in general, a "supply-side" orientation.

Robinson defends the cause of a productive expansion policy and income redistribution – against monetarism – also in order to ward off inflation, while government spending on welfare should increase. The state should be the employer of last resort; a floor for wages would thus be warranted and the problem of poverty solved, through full employment and fair wages. Such theoretical and political attitude typically belongs to the radical reformist tendency of the last years of the post-war boom. It inspires, for example, Hyman Minsky's writings between the end of the 1960s and the first half of the 1970s (Minsky 2013). The definition and achievement of the "public purpose" – which inevitably clashes with the "planning system" carried out by private corporations supported by the "technostructure" – is a crucial requirement for John K. Galbraith (1973). James O'Connor's analysis (1973) of the crisis

---

[9]   A quarter century later, the outstanding American financier Warren Buffet declares: "There's class warfare, all right, but it's my class, the rich class, that's making war, and we're winning" (Stein 2006).

of the post-war "Fordist" development is less confident in the possibility of a reformist way out.

In those times, it still seemed possible that a world could be built "where social and civil progress would not represent a by-product of economic development, but a consciously pursued objective" (Caffè 1977, p. 42). Polanyi's above-mentioned idea of "reintegration" of society indicates the same direction. An alternative seemed still plausible. However, Polanyi is aware that serious reformist policies go beyond the limits capitalism tolerates. This is, according to him, a basic factor of the "dilemma" the market capitalist society has inevitably to confront, and of the "alternative" it is faced with (cf. section 1) when (inevitably) systemic crises occur.

Neoliberalism is the attempt to end the crisis of capitalist accumulation in ways consistent with its essential characteristics – that Polanyi points out, as we have seen – and, in particular, with dominant financial interests, even at the expense of the so-called competitive sector of small and medium entrepreneurs. The rate of profit is to be increased with the collaboration of governments, through an enhanced exploitation of labour force, natural resources, common goods and "social capital". Greater and greater amounts of "social costs" are shifted to the human and natural environment (Kapp 1950). New fields for investment are looked for, preferably endowed with rent positions. But the tendency to the crisis is not defeated – in spite, indeed *because* of all these strategies.

Economic interventions by governments and international organisations have not decreased, on the contrary: but certain goals are pursued at the expense of others. Market freedom – "reduced to a fiction by the hard reality of giant trusts and princely monopolies" (Polanyi [1944] 2001, p. 265) – is now supported, more than in Polanyi's times, by national and international political institutions, which are increasingly "privatized", that is, directly influenced and even occupied by the economic-financial oligarchy. "Economic" reasons – corresponding to the interest of that oligarchy – have excluded the reasons of democratic policy aimed at citizens' happiness. Thence policy in its authentic meaning disappears, Polanyi would say. This is, in his view, a tendency thoroughly accomplished by fascism: contrary to appearances, in "the Fascist solution", if its corporative setup would be fully achieved, not politics, but the economy would dominate. In fascism, he maintains, "after abolition of the democratic political sphere only economic life remains; capitalism as organised in the different branches of industry becomes the whole of society" (Polanyi [1935] 2018, p. 106). We could say that the need Polanyi upholds to recover the "integration" of the economy in society is realised by fascism (also understood as a permanent tendency in capitalist societies) in a perverse form – opposed to the form Polanyi wished: "the extension of the democratic principle from politics to economics" ([1935] 2018, p. 105).

Even moderate Keynesian reforms are at present not merely rejected by the dominant ideology, but practically unrealisable in the current economic and political situation. More radical reforms, like those supported by post-Keynesian economics, are unfeasible for a better reason. In fact, in the present systemic crisis, differently from that of the 1970s, the social forces supporting an alternative solution have almost disappeared. Reforms being then excluded, capitalism survives by increasing the exploitation of labour, sucking up the savings of the middle classes, containing as much as possible public regulation and the welfare state, favouring big tax evaders and avoiders, condemning weak countries to failure,[10] and diffusing disorder, famine and war around the world.

Our socio-economic organisation reveals to be counter-adaptive. The economic system is dramatically inefficient, if its effects on its human, social and natural environment are accounted, beyond the closed playground of conventional economics. As Polanyi maintains (1977, p. XLIII), in order to avoid the risk of an entropic drift and to restore society's "freedom of creative adjustment", the problem of the economy has to be "totally reconsidered". We are thus led to a demanding conception of *positive freedom*, understood as the ability of human beings to democratically adapt social institutions in view of a growing well-being, obviously implying an intelligent, non-destructive relationship of the social system, of its economic organisation in the first place, with its environment.

Such conception of freedom and democracy constitutes the core of Polanyi's political philosophy (Cangiani 2012); it is grounded on his theoretical achievements, which, as I have tried to show, can supply precious suggestions for understanding the nature and history of our society, and also its current crisis, both in its resemblance to previous crises and its diversity from them.

REFERENCES

Burawoy, M. (2003), 'For a sociological Marxism: The complementary convergence of Antonio Gramsci and Karl Polanyi', *Politics & Society*, 31 (2), 193–261.

Caffè, F. (1977), 'Intervista', in A. Esposito and M. Tiberi (eds), *Federico Caffè: Realtà e critica del capitalismo storico*, Catanzaro: Meridiana Libri, pp. 36–42.

Cangiani, M. (2011), 'Karl Polanyi's institutional theory: Market society and its "disembedded" economy', *Journal of Economic Issues*, 45 (1), 177–97.

---

[10] On the absurdity of such policy concerning Greece see for example Stiglitz (2015).

Cangiani, M. (2012), '"Freedom in a complex society": The relevance of Karl Polanyi's political philosophy in the neoliberal age', *International Journal of Political Economy*, 41 (4), 34–53.

Cangiani, M. (2017), '"Social freedom" in the twenty-first century: Rereading Polanyi', *Journal of Economic Issues*, 51 (4), 915–38.

Castel, R. (1995), *Les métamorphoses de la question sociale*, Paris: Fayard.

Crozier, M., S.P. Huntington and J. Watanuki (1975), *The crisis of democracy: Report on the governability of democracies to the Trilateral Commission*, New York: New York University Press.

Galbraith, J.K. (1973), *Economics and the public purpose*, Boston: Houghton Mifflin.

Gramsci, A. (1994), *Scritti di economia politica*, ed. G. Lunghini, Turin: Bollati Boringhieri.

Hobson, J.A. (1919), *Democracy after the war*, London and New York: George Allen & Unwin.

J.P.Morgan (2013), 'The Euro area adjustment: About halfway there', *Europe Economic Research*, 28 (May), 1–16.

Kapp, W.K. (1950), *The social costs of private enterprise*, Cambridge, MA: Harvard University Press.

Liberal Industrial Enquiry (1928), *Britain's industrial future*, London: E. Benn.

Macpherson, C.B. (1987), *The rise and fall of economic justice*, London: Oxford University Press.

Maier, C.S. (1975), *Recasting bourgeois Europe*, Princeton: Princeton University Press.

Maier, C.S. (1987), *In search of stability*, Cambridge: Cambridge University Press.

Marshall, T.H. (1950), *Citizenship and social class*, Cambridge: Cambridge University Press.

Minsky, H. (2013), *Ending poverty: Jobs, not welfare*, Annandale-on-Hudson, NY: Bard College Publication.

O'Connor, J. (1973), *The fiscal crisis of the state*, New York: St. Martin's Press.

Polanyi, K. ([n.d.] 2014), 'The trend toward an integrated society', in K. Polanyi, *For a new west*, ed. G. Resta and M. Catanzariti, Cambridge: Polity Press, pp. 214–19.

Polanyi, K. ([1928a] 2002), 'Liberale Wirtschaftsreformen in England', in K. Polanyi, *Chronik der großen Transformation: Band 1*, ed. M. Cangiani and C. Thomasberger, Marburg: Metropolis, pp. 90–94.

Polanyi, K. ([1928b] 2002), 'Liberale Sozialreformer in England', in K. Polanyi, *Chronik der großen Transformation: Band 1*, ed. M. Cangiani and C. Thomasberger, Marburg: Metropolis, pp. 95–103.

Polanyi, K. ([1931] 2002), 'Demokratie und Währung in England', in K. Polanyi, *Chronik der großen Transformation: Band 1*, ed. M. Cangiani and C. Thomasberger, Marburg: Metropolis, pp. 120–128.

Polanyi, K. (1933), 'Der Mechanismus der Weltwirtschaftskrise', *Der Österreichische Volkswirt*, Sonderbeilage, pp. 2–9.

Polanyi, K. ([1934a] 2002), 'Labour und die Eisenindustrie', in K. Polanyi, *Chronik der großen Transformation: Band 1*, ed. M. Cangiani and C. Thomasberger, Marburg: Metropolis, pp. 251–2.

Polanyi, K. ([1934b] 2002), 'Labour in Southport', in K. Polanyi, *Chronik der großen Transformation: Band 1*, ed. M. Cangiani and C. Thomasberger, Marburg: Metropolis, pp. 256–8.

Polanyi, K. ([1935] 2018), 'The essence of fascism', in K. Polanyi, *Economy and Society: Selected Writings*, (eds) M. Cangiani and C. Thomasberger, Cambridge: Polity Press, pp. 81–107.

Polanyi, K. ([1944] 2001), *The great transformation*, Boston: Beacon Press.

Polanyi, K. ([1945] 2018), 'Universal capitalism or regional planning?', in K. Polanyi, *Economy and society: Selected writings*, (eds) M. Cangiani and C. Thomasberger, Cambridge: Polity Press, pp. 231–40.

Polanyi, K. ([1947a] 2018), 'British Labour and American New Dealers', in K. Polanyi, *Economy and society: Selected writings*, (eds) M. Cangiani and C. Thomasberger, Cambridge: Polity Press, pp. 226–30.

Polanyi, K. ([1947b] 2018), 'Our obsolete market mentality', in K. Polanyi, *Economy and society: Selected writings*, (eds) M. Cangiani and C. Thomasberger, Cambridge: Polity Press, pp. 197–211.

Polanyi, K. (1977), *The livelihood of man*. New York: Academic Press.

Polanyi, K. (2002), *Chronik der großen Transformation: Band 1*, ed. M. Cangiani and C. Thomasberger, Marburg: Metropolis.

Polanyi, K. (2014), *For a new west*, ed. G. Resta and M. Catanzariti, Cambridge: Polity Press.

Polanyi, K. (2018), *Economy and society: Selected writings*, (eds) M. Cangiani and C. Thomasberger, Cambridge: Polity Press.

Polanyi-Levitt, K. (2013), *From the great transformation to the great financialization*, Black Point, Nova Scotia: Fernwood, and London: Zed Books.

Silverman, B. (1980), 'The crisis of the British welfare state', *Challenge*, 23 (4), 28–39.

Stanfield, J.R. (1977), 'Institutional economics and the crises of capitalism', *Journal of Economic Issues*, 11 (2), 449–60.

Stein, B. (2006), 'In class warfare, guess which class is winning', *The New York Times*, 26 November.

Stiglitz, J. (2015), 'Greece, the sacrificial lamb', *The New York Times*, 25 July.

Tawney, R. ([1926] 1947), *Religion and the rise of capitalism*, New York: Mentor Books.

Veblen, T. ([1901] 1994), 'Industrial and pecuniary employments', in *The place of science in modern civilisation*, London: Routledge.

Veblen, T. (1904), *The theory of business enterprise*, New York: Scribner's.

5. Karl Polanyi as a theorist of disembedded markets

Christoph Deutschmann

1. POLANYI'S MESSAGE

At the time of its first publication – 1944 – Karl Polanyi's book *The Great Transformation* did not garner much attention. It was not until the late 1970s that Polanyi's work began to achieve larger resonance among political economists and social theorists, and was translated into several languages. Obviously, the new attractiveness of Polanyi's ideas had to do with the global political and economic changes of the time. The breakdown of the Bretton Woods order of global finance and trade between 1971 and 1973 became the starting point of lasting moves to deregulate and liberalize markets. Foreign exchange rates were allowed to "float", nationally based capital controls were removed, allowing capital to move freely across borders. As a consequence of rising tax competition between national states, corporate taxes and taxes on high incomes fell markedly. The erosion of tax revenues forced governments to cut social expenditures and public investments and to downsize public sector personnel. Due to the depressing impact of public austerity policies and high interest rates, unemployment rose and real wages stagnated or even declined in many OECD countries since the 1980s. Many authors diagnosed an end of the social compromise that had shaped the development of Western democracies during the first decades after the Second World War. With rising social inequality, economic crises and class conflicts revived too (Eichengreen 1996; Streeck 2013).

Polanyi's analysis – of course – reflected the historical experience of *his* time. It had been focused on the spread of the free market movement in the nineteenth century, and the subsequent crises and world wars in the twentieth century – a development which, in Polanyi's view, was extremely unlikely to be repeated.[1] With the rise of global financial capitalism in the last decades of the twentieth century, things – nevertheless – appeared as if history would repeat itself, giving new and unexpected actuality to Polanyi's interpretations. There were at least four developments after 1973 that seemed to be perfectly in line with Polanyi's model: *First*, the resurging public and political influence of liberal market ideologies. While the liberal creed of the nineteenth century was represented by authors such as Adam Smith, David Ricardo, Jeremy Bentham, John Stuart Mill, or Thomas Malthus, neoliberalism in the late twentieth century was largely associated with the name of Polanyi's Viennese colleague Friedrich von Hayek. *Second*, the rising political influence of neoliberalism resulted in a liberalization and deregulation of markets, which contributed to, and was reinforced by, the fall of the socialist system. The former socialist countries subsequently were integrated into the world market. The trend towards globalization did not confine itself to finance and capital markets, but evolved in product and service markets too, e.g. in the GATT and WTO agreements, and the project of the European single market; moreover, transnational companies and firm networks grew significantly. *Third*, just as in the "great transformation" of the nineteenth and early twentieth century, the transition towards global self-regulation of markets had a disruptive impact on the fabric of society; with the dismantling of national welfare states, unemployment, social instability and class conflicts intensified too. *Fourth*, as a consequence of mounting social instability and inequality, political counter-movements to protect the underprivileged against the forces of self-regulated markets emerged, just as Polanyi predicted. Until the late 1990s, these coun-termovements partly took the form of militant anti-globalist activism, culmi-nating in campaigns such as for a "Tobin tax" on financial market transactions (Helleiner 2006); partly the countermovements manifested themselves also in electoral successes of social democratic and social liberal parties. After the 9/11 terrorist attacks, and particularly after the global financial crisis of 2007–2009, however, the countermovements increasingly took a nationalistic and right-wing turn. This became evident not only in the election of Donald Trump for president in the USA, and in the Brexit decision, but also in the rise of right-wing, nationalist parties in many other European countries. To some degree, the trend towards the political right was due to the fact that many of the social democratic parties had accommodated to the neoliberal *Zeitgeist* under the etiquette of the "third way", and lost their credibility as defenders of the interests of the poor.

---

[1] "In retrospect our age will be credited with having seen the end of the self-regulating market" (Polanyi 1944, p. 142).

However, Polanyi's work would not have become so influential, if it had done no more than making these – still limited – historical analogies apparent. The crucial point, rather, was Polanyi's theoretical message, i.e. his critique of market liberalism that he tried to substantiate by his historical analyses. Following Block and Somers, this critique can be summarized in three points:

First, "while markets are necessary, they are also fundamentally threatening to human freedom and the collective good" (Block and Somers 2014, p. 8). As Polanyi emphasizes, markets have existed at almost all times throughout human civilization; they have proved indispensable even under the regime of real socialism. Not all kinds of markets, however, are beneficial for society; a critical distinction for Polanyi is that between markets for goods, products and services, and markets for the material and human conditions of production, i.e. land, industrial means of production, labour, money. Whereas the first kind of markets always had been vital for the decentral organization of society, the spread of the second kind of markets gives rise to serious social and ecological problems. Polanyi goes so far as to characterize them as "fictitious", as land, money and labour constitute basic conditions for human life, which cannot be treated as commodities. As Polanyi argued, the commodification of land and labour, if continued for a long time, would annihilate "the human and natural substance of society" (Polanyi 1944, p. 3) – a thesis which he illustrated by accounts of the ecological devastations and the misery of the working class in England during the industrial revolution. The extension of the market system to the entire circuit of human reproduction, as it evolved in the "great transformation" of the nineteenth century, "means no less than the running of society as an adjunct of the market. Instead of the economy being embedded in social relations, social relations are embedded into the economic system" (Polanyi 1944, p. 60). Such a system of "self-regulating" markets is unique from a broad historical and anthropological view, as in pre-modern societies markets never had been so dominant. Moreover, it is extremely unlikely to be sustained, as the idea of self-regulating markets, as it is put into practice, will mobilize political and social countermovements aiming to restore the control of society over the material and human conditions of life.

The *second* point of Polanyi's message, if we follow Block and Somers further, is that "the free market celebrated by economists and political libertarians has never – and cannot ever – actually exist" (Block and Somers 2014, p. 9). Political regulations and interventions from local and national political authorities have always been essential to secure the functioning of markets. This does not apply only to pre-capitalist markets, but also to capitalist ones, where contract terms, rules of competition, social and ecological standards and many other issues are subject to detailed legal regulations. Paradoxically, even the "deregulation" of markets itself had to be orchestrated by intense state intervention, and, hence, did not mean to abolish the rule setting power of states as such, but only meant to replace existing rules by new ones. This does not apply only, as shown by Polanyi, to the "great transformation" of the nineteenth century, but also to the actual "deregulation" of the financial sector in the USA: "In place of an older set of rules that were designed to protect the public from fraud and excessive risk-taking by financial institutions, politicians established a new set of rules that provided government protection for the financial sector to engage in predatory lending and a huge expansion in dangerous speculation" (Block and Somers 2014, pp. 9–10). The idea of markets regulating simply "themselves", which guided nineteenth-century liberal reform movements as well as contemporary neoliberalism, thus, was far removed from reality.

This leads to the *third* point of Polanyi's message, "that in a complex society we cannot escape the necessity of politics and governmental coordination of economic and social life" (Block and Somers 2014, p. 11). Liberalism as well as contemporary neoliberalism are *political* movements, aiming not at a reduction of the role of government in the economy, but at a re-direction of politics favouring the interests of those who will benefit from an expansion of the market sphere. This must provoke countermovements of social groups who suffer from the consequences of such policies. In this sense, society has no chance to escape the political struggle between the social forces promoting the expansion of markets and those opposing it, which Polanyi circumscribes with his concept of the "double movement" (Polanyi 1944, pp. 136 f.). Polanyi's concept of "countermovements" is different from the Marxian concept of class struggle, as it does not focus solely on the conflict between the bourgeoisie and the proletariat, but refers to a larger variety of social coalitions and conflicts. While it includes trade union movements and left-wing political parties (ranging from social democracy to communism), it also includes industrial and agrarian business organizations, and even right-wing and fascist political movements, insofar as they are fighting for nationally based political restrictions of markets, and protectionist interventions.

2.   AMBIGUITIES IN POLANYI'S CONCEPTS

Polanyi's approach, without doubt, has proved fruitful and stimulating for a variety of disciplines in the social sciences, including social anthropology, sociology, economic sociology and political economy. However, what Polanyi has left behind, is not a systematic theory but an analysis of capitalism that is open for very different interpretations; the controversies between the interpreters are continuing (e.g. Lie 1991; Krippner et al. 2004; Beckert 2007; Hann and Hart 2009; Go 2012). I will confine myself here to discussing the inherent ambiguities in the above mentioned key concepts of market "self-regulation" and "double movement".

As we have seen, Polanyi views modern capitalism as a society governed by "self-regulating" markets, with markets no longer being embedded into social institutions, but vice versa. Self-regulating markets, in other words, are *disembedded markets* developing a life of their own beyond the coordinating and socially integrative role of political institutions. What does this mean precisely? When examining Polanyi's notion of "disembeddedness", we have to distinguish between the historical phenomena Polanyi is referring to, and the scientific reconstruction of the same phenomena by neoclassical economics, which is the focus of Polanyi's anthropologically based critique. As I am going to argue, with Lie (1991), many of the ambiguities in Polanyi's account go back to his inclination to mix up these two heuristic levels.

From a historical point of view, Polanyi's analysis points to two trends of the economic development in the nineteenth century. The first trend is the *territorial disembedding* of markets, i.e. the growth of transnational markets, resulting in a historically unprecedented upswing of world trade, and a parallel erosion of the self-sufficiency of local and national economies, which was promoted politically by the free trade movement. The second trend is the extension of the market nexus from products and services to the material and human conditions of production, which was the result of the land and craft reforms, and the "liberation" of the peasantry. As a consequence, the markets for the "fictitious commodities" of land, industrial technology, labour and money, though not completely absent in the pre-modern era, expanded significantly. The commodification of land and labour worked to deprive the peasantry of the natural bases of their subsistence, to undermine family production in agriculture and small crafts, and to subject the working population to the regime of the labour market. Markets, thus, expanded in the *social* dimension, as the commodity form now began to permeate social relationships *within a given territory*. The entire circle of human reproduction, including production, distribution and consumption, became reorganized by the principle of commodity production. Moreover, with the commodification of land, means of production, labour and money, the scope of the *possible objects* to be appropriated and produced via money expanded spectacularly. Mobilizing the creative capacities of labour became a key challenge for capitalist entrepreneurs and managers. As a consequence, the stationary logic of traditional economies gave way to a dynamic pattern, characterized by ever new innovations, "industrial revolutions" and continuous "growth". Thus, the social disembedding of the economy was associated with a process of *material disembedding*, resulting in an incessant stream of new products, services and technologies available at the market. Last, but not least, disembedding also had a temporal dimension, as the dynamic nature of capitalism meant a thorough restructuring of *social time.* Instead of the cyclical and organic pattern characteristic of pre-modern time, time now became experienced as a linear, future-orientated flow, to be filled with ever new "visions" and "imaginations" (Beckert 2016). While daily life came under permanent pressure for acceleration and efficiency enhancement (Rosa 2005), the social esteem of experience and tradition declined; learning, adaptation and flexibility became top virtues.

Without doubt, Polanyi has rightly emphasized the historical uniqueness of these transformations, which I have recalled here very briefly. Moreover, he was fully justified, when stressing the revolutionary impact of the "great transformation" on the structure of society. What raises questions, however, is Polanyi's characterization of disembedded markets as an "a-social" system, driven by nothing but the "egoistic" motives of hunger and profit (Polanyi 1979, pp. 129 f.). According to Polanyi, the "great transformation" had the effect of locating markets "outside" society, which, in its turn became subject to the extremely "artificial" regime of self-regulating markets. Contrary to such contentions, Fred Block has insisted that markets are always "embedded" into society in some sense and never can be completely "non-embedded". Indeed, even the disembedded markets of modern, global capitalism are clearly a *social* system, not a quasi-technical mechanism governed solely by rational egoisms. They are unthinkable without the social institution of private property; they are governed by the social norm of exchange; they depend on money as a medium to represent and transfer private property rights. Though opening a vast arena for the pursuit of individual gain, the social logic of markets should be distinguished clearly from that of brute egoism (which would be force or fraud).

Nevertheless, Block's concept of the always embedded economy is encountering severe difficulties too, when it is applied to global capitalist markets. For Block and Somers, "embeddedness" is an essentially *political* concept, focusing on the national state as the key agency to institute the legal and regulatory framework of markets.[2] However, the transnational markets of contemporary capitalism are not subject to an overarching political authority. Although markets did not develop in a political vacuum, and political power was an important factor shaping the capitalist world economy, politics became efficient only in an anarchic and uncoordinated way. Rival national interests were bridged only fragmentarily by bi- and multilateral agreements. Binding political and legal regulations of the economy are largely confined to the national, or, as in the case of the EU, to the regional level. By contrast, capitalist markets, including not only product-, but also capital-, finance- and labour markets, today have reached a historically unprecedented level of

---

[2]   "Economic arrangements are neither natural nor autonomous, but they are deeply embedded within the state's exercise of power and authority" (Block and Somers 2014, p. 37).

global interconnectedness. As a globalized nexus, they represent a social system of a higher order, which, as it transcends the reach of national sovereignty and economic policies, indeed is regulated by nothing except itself in the last instance. As Wolfgang Streeck has put it: "While politics may operate as a countermovement to the capitalist market, and sometimes even as a successful one, the market moves on its own generating the movement to which the countermovement must respond" (Streeck 2012, p. 315). In this sense, the idea of market self-regulation cannot simply be dismissed as a fiction, as Block does.

In contrast to Block, Polanyi himself was convinced that self-regulated markets did exist.[3] At a closer view, however, Polanyi's own analysis does not really help further at this point either. The challenge would have been to go into a deeper analysis of the contradictions of a system that is *socially* integrated by markets at the global level, while being embedded *politically* only at a national one. Instead of following such an empirical line of analysis, Polanyi switches to the level of economic model construction. Drawing on the findings of his anthropological research, Polanyi engages in an extended critique of the "fictitious" character of the assumptions underlying economic models. When securing the needs of their material reproduction, people in pre-modern societies neither acted as isolated individuals, nor were their actions governed by the motive of material gain, as Polanyi's well-known argument goes. Rather, economic actions were "submerged" (Polanyi 1944, p. 46) into non-economic relationships securing social order, cohesion and trust. The neoclassical model of "economic" man, guided by the principle of maximum individual utility, hence, is at odds with basic anthropological insights. Though this is hardly deniable, Polanyi here seems to misunderstand the neoclassical model as an empirically oriented analysis, which it never could claim to be. Polanyi's anthropological considerations are not relevant for a critique of neoclassical economics as an *analytical* model of the market consciously starting from fictitious and simplified premises. Nor do they – despite the undeniable influence of neoclassical models on political decisions – have an immediate impact on the empirical analysis of globalized markets. The self-regulation of the capitalist world market as a *historical* phenomenon should not be mixed up with the neoclassical *model* of the market, as Polanyi seems to do.

---

[3]   Kari Polanyi-Levitt, too, criticized Block in this point. In her view, Block's "always embedded economy" thesis meant to move Polanyi "into the mainstream of socioeconomic discourse", and to obscure "the radical implications of the existential contradiction between a market economy and a viable society" (Polanyi-Levitt 2013, p. 102). In a recent publication, she goes even further, speaking of a "trivial interpretation of Polanyi's concept of embeddedness" (Polanyi-Levitt 2018, p. 33).

Even beyond these methodological issues, a basic problem in Polanyi's analysis is obvious: Given the strong anthropological foundations of economic embeddedness, and given the extreme "artificiality" of the liberal model, which Polanyi is insisting upon, how does he explain the historical emergence of the self-regulated market economy of modern capitalism out of the context of formerly "embedded" economies? Polanyi tries to give an answer by his concept of the "double movement"; here we enter into the second step of our review of Polanyi's concepts. Polanyi conceptualizes the rise of the liberal market society and the subsequent countermovements to protect society from the destructive consequences of disembedded markets as a political struggle between pro-market and anti-market orientated social groups. However, as it appears, the design of Polanyi's double-movement concept is highly asymmetric and biased in favour of the second sequence, the reaction of society to the unfettering of market forces. Polanyi puts all his emphasis on demonstrating why a system of self-regulating markets, once established, cannot sustain and must provoke social and political countermovements. However, what about the first sequence, i.e. the rise of the market economy itself? What Polanyi is offering here are ad hoc hypotheses, at best. Sometimes, he seems to explain the rise of the market economy from the ideological influence of the laissez-faire doctrine. He characterizes the economic liberalism of the 1830s as a "militant creed" (Polanyi 1944, p. 137) that took possession of the minds of the political and economic elites. Here, Polanyi suddenly seems to switch from the perspective of social anthropology to that of the sociology of knowledge, without any attempt to justify and elaborate this turn. In other passages of the text, Polanyi insinuates the idea that the invention of industrial machinery could have stimulated the rise of the self-regulating market. "We do not intend to assert that the machine caused that which happened, but we insist that once elaborate machines and plant were used for production in a commercial society, the idea of a self-regulating market was bound to take shape" (Polanyi 1944, p. 40). Again, there is no attempt to elaborate this hypothesis further – a hypothesis, which in the light of contemporary sociological critique of technological determinism appears extremely doubtful and seems to mix up causes and consequences of the commodification of industrial labour. As it appears, Polanyi interpreted the rise of self-regulated markets as a kind of historical "accident"; consequently he ruled out – prematurely, as we know today – that market liberalism would come back again. Polanyi's theory suffers from his failure to give a convincing explanation as to why the extremely "artificial" doctrine of laissez-faire could be so overwhelmingly successful in the nineteenth century – a problem which comes to the fore even more, if one tries to apply Polanyi's theory to contemporary neoliberalism. The revival of liberal ideas in the last decades of the twentieth century certainly cannot again be brushed aside as a historical "accident".

A problem with Polanyi's reception of liberalism is his one-sided focus on the Social Darwinist sidelines of liberal thought. Certainly, liberalism does not exhaust itself in the travesty of the "economic man", driven by the instincts of hunger and profit; Polanyi also imputes it falsely to Marx, thereby mixing up later, Engelsian versions of popularized Marxism with the original. The liberal movement, at least if one sticks to its original versions emerging in the context of the Scottish moral philosophy of the eighteenth century, had much more to offer than such a mechanistic worldview. Considering Adam Smith, the inter- preters today agree that Smith's *Wealth of Nations* and his earlier great work on the *Theory of Moral Sentiments*, where he pioneered basic insights of later sociological theory and symbolic interactionism, must be considered as a unity (Skinner 1999; Lenger 2018, pp. 49 f.). The liberal narrative created by Smith did not simply offer a blueprint for the market as an *economic* system. Rather, it contained a vision of a free *society*, based on private contract, which consti- tuted one of the main currents of European enlightenment, and which found vast resonance among contemporaries. In a nutshell, the narrative consisted of three points: *First*, the market is conceived as a model to construct not only the economy, but *society* in a decentralized, bottom-up way. Born free and equal, individuals are able to settle their affairs among themselves, via free contracts, and without the intervention of an external or divine authority. Though the state is required as a rule setting and supervising agency, it is not the state, but free individuals concluding private contracts, that constitute society. *Second*, free market exchange will not only maximize the welfare of the immediate participants, but the collective too. Collective welfare is the outcome not of political intervention but of spontaneous market forces, as the famous concept of the "invisible hand" contends. *Third*, the message of a free market society (a "commercial" society, as Smith called it) is a *universal* one, addressing itself to the entirety of mankind, irrespective of religion, nationality, race or sex.

Polanyi was well aware of the paradoxes and blind spots of the liberal narrative, which he characterized as a "stark utopia" (Dale 2018). His understanding of personal freedom, which he explicated in particular in his writings of fascism, however, is shaped by his commitment to Christian ethics, and shows little sense for the *sociological* interconnectedness between free markets and personal autonomy. Due to his economistic misinterpretation of Smith's theory, Polanyi underestimated the visionary power of the liberal narrative, which nourished itself from the very European legacy of enlight- enment Polanyi himself is subscribing to. Even today, it seems still far away from having exhausted itself completely. Starting from strong "anthropolog- ical" assumptions, Polanyi ruled out the possibility of markets becoming the core of a new, global society, transcending the religious, national and ethnic particularisms of traditional societies. Viewed from today, it seems to be this hypothesis, not Polanyi's own assumption of a re-embedding of markets into nationally and culturally bounded "societies", which materialized since the late twentieth century. Self-regulated global markets experienced a powerful revival and helped to create a level of transnational economic and social inter-connectedness that is unprecedented despite severe economic and political crises. In the social sciences, this development was echoed, as is well known, in "world society" concepts, and a vast debate on the phenomenon of "globalization" (for an overview see Axford 2013).

3.   AN ALTERNATIVE INTERPRETATION

Needless to say, the global capitalist society of today, which the liberal market narrative has helped to create, is far away from the peaceful and prosperous one that the fathers of liberalism anticipated. The liberal narrative, like any great social vision, cannot be expected to materialize one to one, when becoming a force of real transformation. In the course of its practical implementation, the market narrative did not generate only beneficial, but also unintended and socially disruptive outcomes, which became the target of a vast variety of anti-capitalist countermovements (see also Mishra 2017). This is the context, where a revised version Polanyi's "double movement" theorem, which I can outline only briefly here, could find its proper place too (cf. Deutschmann 2015, 2019).

Obviously, the "double movement" has to do with the unplanned and socially antagonizing consequences of the historical implementation of the liberal narrative (Thomasberger 2018). What the liberal narrative represents is indeed a utopia of the strongest possible kind: individual freedom *within a global society*. Individualism and cosmopolitanism are two sides of the same coin. The fascination of such promises does not confine itself to the wealthy and transnationally mobile classes of today,[4] but extends to the entire society. Money-based lifestyles have a deep impact on consumption cultures even of the working poor; thus it is not simply the political pressure of the capitalists that promotes the expansion of markets. Rather, at least under conditions of economic prosperity, the political advocates of liberalization could count on meeting broad public support. This may provide a first answer to a key question left open by Polanyi: Why could pro-market movements become so powerful under particular circumstances and at certain times? The answer lies in the iconic power of money and in the cosmopolitan and consumerist idols of individual freedom inspired by it, whose relevance today perhaps is even more obvious than it was in Polanyi's time.

---

[4]   Ironically, Craig Calhoun (2002) spoke of a "class of frequent flyers".

However, the promises of money, of course, have their reverse sides. First of all, the double character of money as a claim of myself against others, *and of others against myself* should not be forgotten. Money does not only represent a claim, but also a debt, and with the capitalist expansion of promises the debts expanded accordingly. As a consequence of the extension of the market nexus to the conditions of production, the debts became allocated to the working class, while the claims and promises were reserved to the capital owners. The liberal vision of a society of free and equal individuals ended up, as Marx had shown, in a class society, whose internal antagonisms produced the proletarian countermovement.

As we have seen, Polanyi's analysis is not at odds with this well-known Marxian conception; however, it takes a larger perspective, which makes up the originality of Polanyi's approach. The reverse side of the promises of money neither exhausts itself in its debt character, nor in the "alienation" of social relations due to their commodification, which Marx had emphasized in his theory of commodity fetishism. Polanyi's point, rather, is that people – even the most wealthy – simply cannot live in a world that is governed by the market and money nexus *alone*. Humans are not born as ready-made capitalist entrepreneurs; only in the course of complex primary and secondary socialization processes, taking place outside the market in families and schools, do they acquire the personal qualifications required to participate productively in markets. Moreover, the market itself as an institution does not fall from heaven. The state and the political solidarity of citizens are required to set up and to maintain the rules of the market, and to settle social conflicts. The welfare state and public social security systems are indispensable to prevent people from falling into extreme poverty in cases of sickness, unemployment, or old age. It is beyond controversy that a liberal market society can develop its productive capacities only under the condition of being *more* than a mere market society, of being embedded into an institutional infrastructure providing different forms of extra-market solidarities.

However, non-market solidarities are mostly confined to local or national contexts and, thus, are falling back behind the universality of markets, as I have noted above. As reciprocity becomes more binding and encompassing, it is taking a more exclusive and personal character. While markets are transnational, and firms are operating globally, the social infrastructure of capitalism is largely bound to the national state, to political and professional organizations, to local communities, or families. Thus, not only are markets "embedded" into non-market institutions, but the latter are in their turn "embedded" into the more encompassing system of self-regulating markets, as Polanyi had emphasized. This relationship of bilateral "embeddedness" is anything but a stable and harmonious one; rather it is prone to conflicts and in-built vicious circles. The locally and nationally based social infrastructures of capitalism are vulnerable to the forces of transnational competition, as globally mobile investors, though relying on the stability of the local infrastructures themselves, always are free to opt for exit. The functional coexistence between capitalist markets and the political and social institutions embedding them is characterized by parasitic traits; Wolfgang Streeck (2009) has described this as a vicious circle between "Durkheimian" and "Williamsonian" institutions. The hollowing out of non-market solidarities may give rise to political countermovements, aiming to restore the exclusive character of national or local identities; eventually, such countermovements could endanger the transnational market nexus itself.

If reinterpreted in this way, Polanyi's double-movement theorem could contribute to analyse present-day changes of political conflicts. Some authors have introduced the keywords "cosmopolitanism" vs. "communitarianism" to denote a new line of political conflict, which they deem central for contemporary advanced capitalist societies (Zürn and de Wilde 2016; Merkel 2017). The term "cosmopolitanism" circumscribes political orientations of actors and social groups supporting liberal market and migration regimes, the primacy of supranational political regulations over national ones, and the priority of general human rights over local collective identities. The "communitarians", on the other hand, are voting against open markets and free immigration; they are supporting a strong national state and the primacy of collective goods over individual rights. As the authors are arguing, it is this conflict which tends to become predominant in Western democracies and has largely superseded the traditional confrontation between the "left" and the "right".

A revised version of Polanyi's double-movement theorem could shed more light into these still unfinished debates (cf. also Deutschmann 2018). It could help to clarify where the true political challenge of today lies: restructuring private property rights in a way that allows transnational markets to develop, while no longer endangering the social infrastructure of society. Contrary to orthodox Marxism, which, after the disastrous experiences with real socialism, has largely lost its credibility today, Polanyi's approach does not culminate in a *general* critique of markets and private property. Rather, it focuses on *different designs of markets and private property rights*, and their compatibility with overall social and ecological concerns. Beyond the neoclassical standard plea for transnational markets, it allows, for example, a more balanced view about the economic and ecological advantages of local markets. Moreover, Polanyi's approach opens a critical perspective on the social disembedding of markets, which is advancing at many fronts in contemporary society, and has reached a new level with the commercialization of private relationships via digital networks (Sandel 2012). How could the interfaces between markets and non-market subsystems be rearranged in order to make them interact productively, instead of generating vicious circles? Last, but not least, Polanyi's approach allows to raise the issue of production control in a way that avoids the abstract dichotomy of markets and central planning. Following the rich traditions of non-orthodox socialism, Polanyi's approach gives room for cooperatively oriented concepts of production, aiming to reintegrate property rights over the human and the material conditions of production (Dale 2018). Given the disastrous experiences with capital ownership in the last financial crisis, cooperative models, in combination perhaps with an extension of public control over land and money, appear more realistic than ever. Can we still "afford" the rich, as Andrew Sayer (2016) has put it? In short, Polanyi's approach could pave the way for new political ideas about how to reconcile the universality of markets with the need to preserve the inevitably particularistic foundations of social life.

REFERENCES

Axford, B. (2013), *Theories of globalization*, Cambridge: Polity Press.

Beckert, J. (2007), *The great transformation of embeddedness: Karl Polanyi and the new economic sociology*, Köln: Max Planck-Institute for the Study of Societies.

Beckert, J. (2016), *Imagined futures: Fictional expectations and capitalist dynamics*, Cambridge, MA: Harvard University Press.

Block, F. and M.R. Somers (2014), *The power of market fundamentalism: Karl Polanyi's critique*, Cambridge, MA: Harvard University Press.

Calhoun, C.J. (2002), 'The class consciousness of frequent travelers: Toward a critique of actually existing cosmopolitanism', *The South Atlantic Quarterly*, 101 (4), 869–97.

Dale, G. (2018), 'Karl Polanyi and the paradoxes of freedom', in M. Brie and C. Thomasberger (eds), *Karl Polanyi's vision of a socialist transformation*, Montréal: Black Rose, pp. 126–40.

Deutschmann, C. (2015), 'Disembedded markets as a mirror of society: Blind spots of social theory', *European Journal of Social Theory*, 18 (4), 368–89.

Deutschmann, C. (2018), 'Geld und "individuelle Freiheit"', in R. Lautmann and H. Wienold (eds), *Georg Simmel und das Leben in der Gegenwart*, Wiesbaden: Springer, pp. 29–47.

Deutschmann, C. (2019), *Disembedded markets: Economic theology and global capitalism*, London: Routledge.

Eichengreen, B. (1996), *Globalizing capital: A history of the international monetary system*, Princeton, NJ: Princeton University Press.

Go, J. (ed.) (2012), *Political power and social theory*, Bingley: Emerald Group.

Hann, C. and K. Hart (eds) (2009), *Market and society: The great transformation today*, Cambridge: Cambridge University Press.

Helleiner, E. (2006), 'Globalization and *haute finance – déjà vu?*', in K. McRobbie and K. Polanyi-Levitt (eds), *Karl Polanyi in Vienna: The contemporary significance of the great transformation*, London: Black Rose, pp. 12–31.

Krippner, G. et al. (2004), 'Polanyi symposium: A conversation on embeddedness', *Socio-Economic Review*, 2 (1), 109–35.

Lenger, F. (2018), *Globalen Kapitalismus denken: Historiographie-, theorie-, und wirtschaftsgeschichtliche Studien*, Tübingen: Mohr Siebeck.

Lie, J. (1991), 'Embedding Polanyi's market society', *Sociological Perspectives*, 34 (2), 219–35.

Merkel, W. (2017), 'Kosmopolitismus versus Kommunitarismus: Ein neuer Konflikt in der Demokratie', in P. Harftst, I. Kubbe and T. Poguntke (eds), *Parties, governments and elites: The comparative study of democracy*, Wiesbaden: Springer, pp. 9–24.

Mishra, P. (2017), *Age of anger: A history of the present*, London: Allen Lane.

Polanyi, K. (1944), *The great transformation: The political and economic origins of our time*, Boston: Beacon Press.

Polanyi, K. (1979), *Ökonomie und Gesellschaft*, Frankfurt/Main: Suhrkamp.

Polanyi-Levitt, K. (2013), *From the great transformation to the great financialization: On Karl Polanyi and other essays*, Halifax: Fernwood Publishing.

Polanyi-Levitt, K. (2018), 'Freedom of action and freedom of thought', in M. Brie and C. Thomasberger (eds), *Karl Polanyi's vision of a socialist transformation*, Montréal: Black Rose, pp. 18–51.

Rosa, H. (2005), *Beschleunigung: Die Veränderung sozialer Zeitstrukturen in der Moderne*, Frankfurt/Main: Suhrkamp.

Sandel, M. (2012), *What money can't buy: The moral limits of markets*, New York: Farrar, Straus & Giroux.

Sayer, A. (2016), *Why we can't afford the rich*, Bristol: Polity Press.

Skinner, A. (1999), *Analytical introduction to Adam Smith, The Wealth of Nations, Books I–III*, London: Penguin.

Streeck, W. (2009), *Re-forming capitalism: Institutional change in the German political economy*, Oxford: Oxford University Press.

Streeck, W. (2012), 'On Fred Block, varieties of what? Should we still be using the concept of capitalism', in J. Go (ed.), *Political power and social theory*, Bingley: Emerald, pp. 311–21.

Streeck, W. (2013), *Gekaufte Zeit: Die vertagte Krise des demokratischen Kapitalismus*, Berlin: Suhrkamp.

Thomasberger, C. (2018), 'Freedom, responsibility and the recognition of the reality of society', in M. Brie and C. Thomasberger (eds), *Karl Polanyi's vision of a socialist transformation*, Montréal: Black Rose, pp. 52–66.

Zürn, M. and P. de Wilde (2016), 'Debating globalization: Cosmopolitanism and communitarianism as political ideologies', *Journal of Political Ideologies*, 21 (3), 280–301.

6. A Polanyian paradox: money and credit as fictitious commodities, financialization, finance-dominated accumulation, and financial crises

Bob Jessop

One of Polanyi's key contributions to the social sciences was his claim that land, labour and money are fictitious commodities. They were essentially inputs into production rather than commodities whose production could be regulated through the price mechanism. Indeed, "[t]he postulate that they are produced for sale is emphatically untrue" (Polanyi 2001, p. 75). Nonetheless, the liberal propensity to treat them *as if* they were real commodities had real effects that damaged society and prompted diverse social forces to fight back against the resulting environmental, economic and social harms. In this sense, Polanyi developed a critique of the *moral* as well as *economic* dimensions of the market economy and market society and of the *moral* as well as *economic* bases of the double movement, in which society fights back against the fictitious commodification of three key inputs into capitalist production. Polanyi was commenting on the epoch of commercial, industrial and financial capitalism, when land, labour and capital (comprising, one might add, money as money, money as capital, and physical capital) were regarded as the three main "factors of production", each of which had its corresponding form of revenue. Today, one might add knowledge as an ever more important fourth fictitious commodity whose enclosure is intensifying the tragedy of the anti-commons (Jessop 2007). Here, however, I focus on changes in financialization and its crisis tendencies that invite a return to Polanyi's original conceptual schema and the associated historical analysis and, in this context, to the question of whether Polanyi's general approach is adequate to the task of analysing these more recent developments and the blowback that they have prompted from the turn of the century onwards.

1.   SOME BASIC CONCEPTS

The significance of fictitious commodification is grounded in six key Polanyian concepts: substantive economy, the economistic fallacy, dis- and re-embedding, market society, and double movement. The substantive economy comprises "an instituted process of interaction between man and his environment, which results in a continuous supply of want satisfying material means" (1957b, p. 248).[1] This need not (and for millennia did not) involve major economic roles for money, let alone "all-purpose money" (1957b, pp. 264–6; 1977, pp. 97–122). All-purpose or general money is a late development in economic history and, according to Polanyi, did not generate a self-regulating domestic or international monetary system until the mid-to-late nineteenth century. This coincided with the rise of market economies based on the generalization of exchange relations to "all elements of industry, including land, labour, and money" (2001, p. 72; cf. 1957b, p. 247). Nor were the relevant substantive want-satisfying activities much motivated by "economic" goals, i.e. undertaken for gain or fear of hunger for lack of employment, as occurs in capitalist market economies (1977, pp. 11–12, 47). Rather, production and distribution were embedded in social activities and institutions, such as kinship, state, magic and religion, wherein other individual motives or social purposes were primary. Thus, the economic theory of the market did not apply to periods or situations when the production and circulation of goods occurred through householding, reciprocity or redistribution (1957b, pp. 251–6; 1977, pp. 36–42).

> Labor is only another name for a human activity which goes with life itself, which in its turn is not produced for sale but for entirely different reasons, nor can that activity be detached from the rest of life, be stored or mobilized; land is only another name for nature, which is not produced by man; actual money, finally, is merely a token of purchasing power which, as a rule, is not produced at all, but comes into being through the mechanism of banking or state finance. (2001, pp. 75–6; cf. 1977, pp. 10–11)

Nonetheless, once they are integrated into exchange relations, these elements acquire "market prices": In other words, the disembedding of self-regulating

---

[1]   Material means may include services where these satisfy physiological wants, such as food or shelter, or involve logistical movements in circulating and administering goods (Polanyi 1957b, p. 248).

markets from socially embedded economic activities "takes its start from the widespread use of money as a means of exchange" (1957a, p. 68).

> Man under the name of labor, nature under the name of land, were made available for sale; the use of labor power could be universally bought and sold at a price called wages, and the use of land could be negotiated for a price called rent. There was a market in labor as well as in land, and supply and demand in either was regulated by the height of wages and rents, respectively; the fiction that labor and land were produced for sale was consistently upheld. (2001, pp. 136–7; cf. 1977, p. 10)

Likewise, for money, argued Polanyi, the price is interest payments (2001, p. 72). As with the prices of labour power and land, the rate and volume of interest "serves industrial and mercantile capitals even as a prerequisite and a factor in the calculation of their operations" (Marx 1998, p. 365). While all three prices may be illusory, insane categories (as Marx put it), they influence "motivations and valuations", leading to "the marketing mind" (Polanyi 1977, p. 10; cf. 1957a, p. 68) and self-regulating market (2001, pp. 71–2) and thereby have real effects on the movement and relations of money, credit and capital and, in turn, on the distribution of social wealth (1977, pp. 12–13).

The fictitious commodification of these three factors of production is the rational basis of the "economistic fallacy", which occurs when the specific properties and dynamics of pre- and non-capitalist economies are disregarded and treated as if they were the same as those of market economies (1977, pp. 5–17; cf. 2001, p. 74). A special case of this fallacy occurs when the market economy is considered as an autonomous, *sui generis* sphere with its own logic, separate from its articulation with wider sets of social relations (1977, p. 6). It is in this context that Polanyi was wont to criticize classical Marxism for economic determinism (e.g. 2016, pp. 86–9, 102, 107, 115, 182, 206). Instead, he stressed the social embeddedness of economic activities: disembedding was only a temporary phase, perhaps repeated if lessons about its effects were ignored or forgotten, that was followed by their re-embedding in new or hybrid forms.

The historical precondition of the development of the economistic fallacy is the disembedding of profit-oriented, market-mediated economic activities from other sets of social relations. In particular, fictitious commodification deprives resources of all but economic value; we see the emergence of *homo economicus*, the bare economic individual. This provided the material basis in turn for the ideological retrojection of economic motives and their economizing logic back into pre-capitalist social formations. However, once this disembedding has emerged it sooner or later encounters the reality and consequences of (self-regulating) market failure. Thus, Polanyi noted, the tendential disjunction between the logic of markets in land and labour and their respective reproduction requirements; and further noted the damaging effects of dissociating monetary circulation from the satisfaction of human needs. This led him to argue that markets in land, labour and money cannot be self-regulating without generating failures – they must depend in the medium-to-long-term on their integration into an ensemble of formally and substantively adequate institutions that provide a stable, calculable framework for their pursuit. In short, the market economy must be re-embedded – into a market society. This does not occur automatically. Instead market failures sooner or later trigger the "double movement" as social forces organize to defend their interests and/or demand state intervention to protect them against the allegedly self-regulating but often destructive market. Consequently, "the extension of the market organization in relation to genuine commodities was accompanied by its restriction in relation to fictitious ones" (2001, p. 79).

2.   MARX AND POLANYI ON MONEY

This chapter is not the place to undertake a detailed, point-by-point comparison between Marx's critique of political economy (including pre-capitalist as well as capitalist social formations) and Polanyi's critical moral economy of the market economy. Table 6.1 summarizes some of the key differences between their initial questions and their approach to answering them. Here I want to focus on some key differences between their views on money, credit and capital as a basis for exploring the extent to which Polanyi's arguments about the disembedding of the market economy from traditional society and the double movement can be productively applied to neoliberalism or, more precisely, to the nature of neoliberal finance-dominated accumulation. This is where money, credit and capital rather than land, labour or knowledge become the central categories of fictitious capital – although, as I suggest below, the rise of more rarefied forms of fictitious commodification of money, credit and capital also have major repercussions on these other fictitious commodities.

Polanyi's views on Marx's critique of political economy fluctuated (partly influenced by his opinions on contemporary political movements claiming inspiration from Marx) (Dale 2016; Polanyi 2016). More generally, I suspect that he did not realize the extent to which Marx also regarded labour power, money and land as fictitious commodities, in part because Polanyi saw Marx as adopting a value theory of labour (treating it, therefore, as a commodity like any other), a commodity theory of money (tied in the initial discussion in the first volume of *Capital* to gold or silver as commodities that had later acquired the form and functions of money as money),[2] and regarding land as a commod-

---

[2]   Polanyi: "Das Kapital implied the commodity theory of money, in its Ricardian Form" (2001, p. 26). Likewise, he mentions Marx's too close adherence to Ricardo and

Table 6.1   *Problematic and method in Marx and Polanyi*

	Karl Marx	**Karl Polanyi**
Theoretical focus	Modes of production, focusing on capitalist mode (CMP) plus minor interest in pre-capitalist formations	Modes of resource distribution or societal integration (householding, redistribution, reciprocity, markets)
Critical focus	Critique of political economy, i.e. the categories that organize CMP as organic totality and their impact on dynamics	Critique of market liberalism, i.e. the belief in (disembedded) free markets as efficient mechanism of *distribution*
Analytical focus	Form-analysis of capital relation: includes effects of generalizing commodity form to labour power, money, land, and general intellect (their fictitious commodification)	Substantive economics (with formal economics regarded as ideological aberration that distorts economic analysis and undermines working of a self-protecting market society)
Ultimate analytical horizon	World market as historical presupposition of capital accumulation; and subsequent integration of world market as unity of all contradictions	Disembedding of markets from the integument of pre-modern society and their (partial) re-embedding into a functioning market society
Magnum opus	*Das Kapital* (incomplete: three or four missing books from Marx's projected "six-book plan")	*Great Transformation: The Political and Economic Origins of Our Times* (has a rushed ending)
Opening problem of this work	Why wealth in social formations dominated by capital takes the form of a huge mass of commodities	The collapse of nineteenth-century civilization (focusing on the four pillars of a self-regulating market economy)
Starting point for this work	The commodity as the economic "cell form" of the capital relation and its wider societal implications	Market fundamentalism as a liberal movement and the rise and scope of countermovements

Source: own elaboration.

ity (Marx did not discuss the complexities of land and rent until volume three). In fact, as Marx relaxes his initial assumptions concerning all three kinds of social relation, he increasingly treated them as fictitious commodities. This can be seen in Marx's analysis of labour power as a living subject rather than passive victim of capitalist exploitation, capitalist credit creation as the key to accumulation and, later in *Capital*, of fictive capital (e.g. capital as property rather than functioning capital), and his analysis of land in terms of absolute

the traditions of liberal economics (2001, p. 131); and that Marx followed Ricardo in defining classes in economic terms (2001, p. 158). These judgements seem to anticipate Paul Samuelson's remark that Marx was "a minor post-Ricardian" (1957, p. 911).

and differential rent based, respectively, on monopolistic titles to land as property, its location, and its differential productivity.[3]

The dead hand of official, scholastic Marxism (historical materialism and dialectical materialism) might well have influenced Polanyi's reading of Marx, especially as he was critical of the labour theory of value, the immiseration thesis, the tenets of accumulation and concentration, the panurgy of material interests, the dominance of manual over intellectual labour, the primacy of class struggle to the exclusion of potential solidarities between classes, and the *Zusammenbruchstheorie* (a theory of the eventual collapse of capitalism under the weight of its own contradictions) (see Polanyi 2016, pp. 86–9, 91, 107, 115, 184; on crude class theory and narrow sectional interests, see also 2001, p. 158). But another, and certainly more important, factor was the influence of Ferdinand Tönnies's distinction between *Gesellschaft* and *Gemeinschaft* on Polanyi's historical institutionalist approach to political economy (1957a, pp. 69–70; 1977, pp. 48–9; cf. Dale 2016, pp. 25–9). This inclined him, one might say, to critique the *moral economy of bourgeois society* rather than engage in a critique of *the political economy* of capitalist social formations based on the specific economic, juridico-political, and social forms of the capital relation.

This is reflected in Polanyi's distinctive approach to Marx's *Capital*, which, according to Gareth Dale's incisive analysis:

> Cleaves its critique of capitalism into a sociology and an economics. In effect, Polanyi 'sociologised' *Capital* by extracting its heart, the theory of commodity fetishism, while discarding the remaining body as 'Ricardian economics'. In contrast to Marx, the weight of explanation in Polanyi's writings falls upon patterns of 'economic integration' and rarely, if ever, upon the exercise of control over productive property and the systematic relationships of inclusion and exclusion that flow from it. Hence, where for Marx generalised commodity exchange and large-scale proletarianisation are two sides of the same coin, *The Great Transformation* roots the socio-cultural corrosion of nineteenth-century capitalism not in the commodification of labour-power and nature *and* exploitation and domination, but solely in the former. (Dale 2016, p. 52)

Dale further notes that this was associated with a peculiar combination of a Marx-influenced sociology of capitalism and a marginalist-inspired economic theory. Certainly, Polanyi endorsed Carl Menger, the Austrian marginalist, and his subjective theory of value (1977, pp. 21–34); and he lamented that Bentham failed to discover that value derives from utility (2001, p. 124).

---

[3]   For alternative views on their fictitious nature, based on close reading of Marx, see Elson (1979) and Lebowitz (2003) on labour-power; Jessop on money as money and money as capital (2013); and Foster on nature (land) and the metabolic rift (2013).

Marginalism also mattered to Polanyi ethically because "it places human decision-making at its centre, in contrast to the 'mechanistic' and 'objective' value theory of Locke-Ricardo-Marx" (Dale 2016, pp. 48–9).

One consequence of Polanyi's historical institutionalist and marginalist analysis of substantive economics is that, in *The Great Transformation* and his contributions to *Trade and Market in the Early Empires*, he discussed money as money but did not explicitly consider money as capital. This seems strange in the light of his observation that Aristotle did not discuss "the uses of money as credit and capital" (2001, p. 57). This neglect may reflect Polanyi's focus on modes of distribution and sources of revenue rather than modes of production and the valorization of capital. Yet, while several kinds of money and monetary functions (such as usury and credit) are long-established, they are all transformed by capitalist development (Polanyi 1977, pp. xl–xli; Marx 1996, pp. 112, 527; 1998, pp. 325–37; 1972, pp. 468–70, 485–92). In general, Polanyi's account of special-purpose monies and all-purpose money is concerned with their four conventional functions as money (store of value, hoard or treasure; means of circulation or exchange; means of deferred payment or credit; and measure of price) (1977, pp. 117–19; 1957b, pp. 264–6; for a critique of Polanyi on money, see Melitz 1970). He also highlighted its early role in foreign trade and, later, in currency regimes; and he discussed interest as the price of money and analysed the fetishistic operation of the international gold standard. Yet he did not consider the distinction between money as money, money as functioning capital, and capital in its role as property rather than functioning capital. Likewise, he focused on the institutions in which money as money is embedded historically and, later, when disembedded, is re-embedded and reregulated through central banks and international monetary systems. Money as capital figures mostly in relation to capital as a factor of production (investment capital); as loan capital, including foreign loans, especially in the context of banking activities and financial intermediation; and as finance capital (often depicted as an agent, especially in the context of haute finance). It also figures, of course, as the purchaser of labour in the self-regulating labour market (there is little discussion of the labour process and none of the self-valorization of capital in production). Finally, capital as property figures mostly in the context of the commodification of land.

Marx showed that, in a fully-developed capitalist system, money can no longer take a commodity form (the principal exception is bullion as world money) but develops as increasingly complex forms of credit. He distinguished (a) real from fictitious commodities; (b) real, or commodity, money from fictitious money (symbolic tokens, fiat money); and (c) real capital – or functioning capital – from fictitious capital (e.g. state bonds). The third distinction overlaps those between money as functioning capital and interest-bearing capital as property and between credit advanced for consumption (usury) or state activities (public debt). In Polanyian terms, money's role as functioning capital facilitates and reinforces the transition from social production based on householding, political redistribution, or simple exchange relations into a capitalist economy. Moreover, in this role, for Marx, it expresses the power of capital to organize and control labour power in production.

In short, in contrast to Marx, who took great pains to differentiate money and capital, Polanyi did not, and, without this and related distinctions, tended to conflate them. This limited his theoretical capacity, regardless of his historical acuity, to deal with emerging features of the capitalist credit system, including the development of fictitious credit and fictitious capital. Thus, his approach to credit creation focused on the traditional functions of financial intermediation or the rise of finance capital rather than the scope for financial capital and institutions to dominate the circuits of capital. And, just as he adopted an orthodox view of the functions of money as money, he analysed the gold standard in terms similar to those advanced by its proponents, whether from the perspective of the bullionist, banking, or currency schools, namely, as a means of establishing self-regulating money markets free from state interference both nationally and internationally (see Kubik 1992). Finally, apart from a reference to freight insurance (e.g. 2001, p. 56), there is no discussion of hedging; even vis-à-vis risky foreign bonds, or the early role of derivatives in agriculture or commercial trade. Yet, as we shall see, derivatives are now a crucial device, as Polanyi would describe them, in the process of financialization and rise of finance-dominated capitalism.

3.   MORE ON COMMODITIES AND FICTITIOUS COMMODITIES

Building on Polanyi's discussion of substantive economies and the rise of failure-prone self-regulating markets in fictitious commodities, I suggest seven stages of commodification, beginning with the rise of an exchange economy and culminating in finance-dominated accumulation. However, given his limited account of money as capital and capital as property, Polanyi is not directly useful for later stages. I therefore draw on Marx's critique of money as a fictitious commodity, fictitious credit and fictitious capital to illuminate these. This is crucial to better understand neoliberalism and finance-dominated accumulation. The starting point would be the same for both Marx and Polanyi. Specifically, commodification presupposes actual or potential use-values that have not yet become exchange-values. Not all use-values are offered for sale, let alone produced for sale. This is the point of Polanyi's discussion of four ideal-typical modes of distribution: householding, reciprocity, redistribution and market exchange. It is also evident in Marx's analysis of the organizing role of community, polity and politics in pre-capitalist economic formations. Starting from this point, seven stages can be distinguished.

First, a simple *commodity* is a good or service offered for sale, whether through direct bartering, incurring a debt, or using a medium of exchange. These goods and services can arise from peasant, petty commodity, state, or cooperative production as well as from capitalist enterprises. The variety of such potential producers led Schaniel and Neale, the latter of whom was a collaborator in Polanyi's project on *Trade and Markets in the Early Empires*) to distinguish between *simple* and *full* commodities. Whereas the former may just be surplus to the immediate needs of households, reciprocal networks, and redistributive communities and sold to secure needed goods and services or raise revenue (Polanyi 1957b), the latter are produced in factory-like ways for sale on a commercial market (Schaniel and Neale 1999, p. 96).

Second, building on this distinction, a full *capitalist* commodity is one that is produced in a labour process in which all inputs take the form of commodities and which is organized by capital to maximize surplus-value (Polanyi would say gain) and is subject to competition to reduce the socially necessary labour-time for its production and socially necessary turnover time for its circulation and eventual sale. While this stage and the next two stages are defined in Marxian terms (in order to make subsequent stages consistent with the analysis of the first four stages), they are compatible with Polanyi's views on the development of the market economy.

Third, as a corollary, a *capitalist economy* develops when all four core inputs into production acquire market prices: land, labour power, money and knowledge (cf. Marx 1963; Polanyi 2001; Jessop 2007). These are, of course, fictitious commodities. They have the form of a commodity (can be bought and sold) but are not produced *in order to be sold*. Moreover, none has inherent qualities that require it to be exchanged for money in corresponding markets in the form of rents, wages, interest or royalties. Production of a money commodity, such as gold, for profit is an exception. However, even here, once it circulates primarily as money (Polanyi's all-purpose money, Marx's universal commodity) rather than as just another commodity, it acquires important fictitious aspects (Stemmet 1996). It then has two kinds of price – interest rates and exchange rates as currencies (both discussed by Polanyi 2001).

Fourth, treating land, labour, money and knowledge *as if* they were commodities can transform them into *quasi-commodities* as each gets integrated into the wider cash nexus of a market society. This occurs when economic agents aim to increase the price, as opposed to value, of such inputs, through appropriate forms of "investment". Examples include: investments of capital and labour to improve "land" (reflected in changes in absolute and differential rent); efforts to reskill labour power (considered as marketable "human capital") and/or increase its scarcity (e.g. through artificial barriers to labour market entry); actions to ensure the credibility of money by linking it to real assets (e.g. backing the new German mark in the Weimar Republic by linking it to land values); or investing in new knowledge or new uses of knowledge and making access dependent on payments for use of this private intellectual property. Such actions reflect and reinforce the "economistic fallacy" and commodity fetishism, which, *pace* Polanyi's claim that Marx discussed only in relation to ordinary commodities (2001, p. 76), he also discussed in relation to gold, labour power, and interest-bearing capital (Marx 1996, pp. 81–94, 144; 1998, p. 396).

A fifth step is the creation of *fictitious capital*, that is, tradable commodities whose price depends on calculation about discounted future revenues driven by the power of abstraction inherent in capital accumulation. Thus, land and intellectual property could be securitized in terms of future flows of absolute and differential rent, royalties, etc.; and money could be traded in futures markets and/or in increasingly rarefied derivative markets. Analogously, one can calculate the future earnings of labour power considered as human capital. This occurs theoretically in neoclassical economics, practically in legal compensation or insurance systems, and, increasingly, in workers' own calculations as self-responsibilized, entrepreneurial subjects about the discounted returns to "investment" in their own "human capital". As fictive capital, these *quasi-commodities* can be assimilated to the category of interest-bearing capital when it assumes the form of money *as property* rather than money *as functioning capital*. These developments are all consistent with Polanyi's account of the economistic fallacy and the penetration of economic calculation into all spheres of society.

Sixth, a *competitive financialized economy* develops when production, distribution and exchange based on the generalization of the commodity form to land, labour power, money and knowledge are closely articulated with, even subordinated to, the circuits of capitalist credit-money. This intensifies competition by: (a) enhancing the equalization of profit rates across the entire market economy as finance capital *qua* functioning capital is reallocated among competing profit-generating investments; and (b) promoting the equalization of interest rates – or equivalent returns in the form of future rents, wages and royalties where present or anticipated interest rates serve as the discount rate for calculation – as finance capital *qua* property, i.e. fictitious capital, is re-allocated among alternative asset classes (e.g. real estate, student loan asset-based securities, government bonds, and securitized royalties).

Seventh, a *finance-dominated capitalist economy* emerges as the world market becomes more tightly integrated in real time, with the use of ever more rarefied forms of fictitious capital (including, notably, derivatives in ever more complex forms), and with growing use of debt leverage in the search for super-profits. This reinforces the dominance of finance capital *qua* property rather than as functioning capital and works to universalize competition for gain, thereby intensifying capital's contradictions.

4. FINANCIALIZATION AND FINANCE-DOMINATED ACCUMULATION

For Marx, money as functioning capital can be considered as profit-generating capital. This comprises all capitals involved in the production and realization of surplus-value. Interest-bearing capital belongs here insofar as it is lent to profit-generating capital in the expectation that the loan will lead to the production and sale of goods or services at a price that enables repayment of capital and interest. This cannot be guaranteed. In this context, then, interest-bearing capital is subordinate to profit-generating capital. It nonetheless participates in the redistribution of surplus-value via interest payments just as productive "land" (broadly defined) receives rents and capitalist firms receive profits of enterprise.

The rise of finance-dominated accumulation leads, however, to major changes in the circuits of capital as interest-bearing capital comes to dominate the overall circuit of capital and forms closer ties to the state apparatus. Its activities are less concerned with financial intermediation and risk-management and focus more on rent extraction through financial arbitrage and innovation. As financialization proceeds, so does financial innovation and this, in turn, increases the leverage of interest-bearing capital and leads to increasing household, corporate, and public debt – further facilitated by lenders' new ability to securitize loans and offload their risks onto those who purchase these securities. Among other harmful effects, these securities multiply the volume of opaque, highly leveraged, largely unregulated financial transactions. This overwhelms central banks' capacity to act as lender of last resort and has prompted the transformation of private Ponzi debt into public and/or sovereign debt. This is even harder when financial markets work through shadow banking activities, dark pools, and/or offshore. This is not exactly how Polanyi perceived the role of central banks in seeking to re-regulate and re-embed the market economy in market society. On the contrary, unregulated financial innovation now plays a pro-cyclical, heavily destabilizing role via financial speculation and risk-taking by highly leveraged financial institutions (Haldane and Alessandri 2009). Indeed, as more financial scandals emerge, it seems that super-profits derive in part from predatory and, indeed, criminal activities that were enabled by deregulatory measures implemented in exchange for campaign funds or other forms of political corruption (Will et al. 2013; Black 2015).

More generally, as financialization expands and penetrates deeper into the social and natural world, it transforms the micro-, meso- and macro-dynamics of capitalist economies. First, as Polanyi would have expected, financialization alters the calculations and behaviour of non-financial firms. This is apparent in the rise of shareholder value as a coercive discourse, technology of governance, and vector of competition and leads *non-financial* firms to engage in financial activities that are not directly tied to their main profit-generating pursuits in trade and commodity production. Examples include treasury functions, financial intermediation, using retained profits for share buybacks and/or acquisition or expansion of financial subsidiaries (Krippner 2005; Lapavitsas 2013). Second, it boosts the size and influence of the financial sector as it focuses on fee-producing and risk-taking activities over financial intermediation and risk management. Third, as successive crises from the mid-1970s show, financialization makes the economy more prone to recession and, in severe cases, more liable to the downward spiral of debt-deflation-default dynamics (Rasmus 2010).

Fourth, most types of money tend to lack intrinsic value apart from inherently useful objects, commodity money and bullion (Polanyi 1977, pp. 264–7; Marx 1998, pp. 316–18). This holds for interest-bearing capital and, especially, derivatives in the finance-dominated era. Their development generalizes and intensifies competition in relation to means of production, money capital, specific capitals as units of competition, and social capital. In this sense, the spread of derivatives has similar effects to the world market integration and operation of the gold standard that had so interested Polanyi.

> By the fourth quarter of the nineteenth century, world commodity prices were the central reality in the lives of millions of Continental peasants; the repercussions of the London money market were daily noted by businessmen all over the world; and governments discussed plans for the future in light of the situation on the world capital markets. (Polanyi 2001, p. 11)

But derivatives operate very differently. They are the most generalized form of representing claims on assets and revenue streams. Derivatives reinforce the separation between the general movement of capital based on valorization and the fluctuation of money prices and profit and, in this way, facilitate financialization and the rise of finance-dominated accumulation. Thus, based on the calculation of value at risk, they help to commensurate all investment opportunities and every single risk in the world market (Bryan and Rafferty 2006). In extending and deepening the basis for hedging and financial speculation, derivatives help to complete the world market in transforming future income streams (profit, dividend or interest) into tradable assets and change the dynamics of global competition. They mark a step change in the commodification and monetization of world society.

5.   SOCIETY FIGHTS BACK

The financialization promoted by neoliberalism facilitates the rise of finance-dominated accumulation and leads to growing inequalities in income and wealth due to deregulation, liberalization and the interpenetration of economic – especially financial – and political power. It is also associated with political capitalism (Weber 1968) where profits depend on predatory political profits, including kleptocracy and primitive accumulation based on dispossession, profit on the market from force and domination, including use of state power to impose neoliberal rules, institutions and practices on other accumulation regimes and open up new fields of accumulation, or "unusual deals with political authorities" – such as financial contributions for special legislative, administrative, judicial, fisco-financial or commercial decisions that privilege particular capitals and fall well outside the normal working of the rule of law. This prompts diverse social forces to fight back in different ways: the Occupy movement sought to polarize opposition around the populist slogan of the 99 per cent against the 1 per cent, a more specific variant of Main Street vs. Wall Street – with its equivalent antagonism in the United Kingdom between the industrial heartlands and the City of London; right-wing populist resistance is reflected in Trump's promise to "drain the swamp" or in more general opposition to "banksters", "fat cats", and so on; the promotion of the Green New Deal as a solution to the triple crisis (environmental, financial and social); the rise of the indignados and the "squares" movements; more modest but still radical demands to re-regulate finance, limit the size of "too big to fail" and/or systemically important banks, and impose a Tobin tax on financial transactions; and so on.

This said, in contrast with the period about which Polanyi wrote and the first years of post-war reconstruction, there is less evidence of an *effective* double movement. For, while resistance has developed, the political conjuncture is less favourable to serious constraints on the one-sided neoliberal treatment of fictitious commodities in terms of their contribution to the profitability of capital. This is reflected in the treatment of land as a source of rents rather than a substantive free gift of nature to be safeguarded for future generations; of labour power as a cost of production to be substituted by other factors where this proves profitable rather than as a source of demand or specific set of skills; of capital as a sum of mobile money for profitable investment anywhere in the world, including in speculation and derivatives, rather than as a stock of assets to be valorized in particular times and places; and of knowledge as a source of intellectual property rents rather than as part of the intellectual commons. This shift in the political conjuncture is related to globalization, which limits the territorial and temporal sovereignty of states; the development of authoritarian statism and the functional decline of democratic institutions; the new constitutionalism that consolidates the power of capital; and the increasing integration of interest-bearing capital into the legislative and administrative apparatuses. This limits the capacity of society to fight back by demanding social protection against unregulated free markets. It also fuels the rise of right-wing populism.

6. CONCLUSIONS

I have advanced four main arguments in this chapter. First, Polanyi performed major theoretical and political services in distinguishing between substantive economies and formal economics, between embedded economic activities and self-regulating markets, and between commodities and fictitious commodities. Second, he was unaware of the overlap between his analyses and those of Marx in regard to all three of these contributions. Third, for diverse reasons, he did not build on a distinction that he recognized between money, money as credit, and money as capital. In this regard, Marx offered the more incisive and powerful categories for exploring the effects of extending market forces into the operation of the economy and wider society. Fourth, I demonstrated this by extending a Polanyian analysis of commodification, and monetization that drew on Marx's work to explore some features of neoliberalism and society's capacity to fight back comparable to Polanyi's analysis of liberalism and the double movement. This leads to a fifth conclusion, hinted at in my title. For this analysis indicates the paradox that, in order to apply a Polanyian analysis to neoliberalism and its double movement, we need to go beyond the conceptual and theoretical scope of Polanyi's account of money even as we retain his broader understanding of the relation between the market economy and market society.

REFERENCES

Black, W.K. (2015), 'Now the Justice Department admits it got it wrong', *New Economic Perspectives*, accessed 15 March 2019 at http://neweconomicperspectives.org/2015/09/now-the-doj-admits-they-got-it-wrong.html.

Bryan, D. and M. Rafferty (2006), *Capitalism with derivatives: A political economy of financial derivatives*, Basingstoke: Palgrave Macmillan.

Dale, G. (2016), *Polanyi: A life on the left*. New York Columbia University Press.

Elson, D. (1979), 'The value theory of labour', in D. Elson (ed.), *Value: The representation of labour in capitalism*, London: CSE Books, pp. 115–80.

Foster, J.B. (2013), 'Marx and the rift in the universal metabolism of nature', *Monthly Review*, 65 (7), 1–19.

Haldane, A.G. and P. Alessandri (2009), 'Banking on the state', *Bank of International Settlements*, accessed 15 March 2019 at www.bis.org/review/r091111e.pdf.

Jessop, B. (2007), 'Knowledge as a fictitious commodity', in A. Buğra and K. Ağartan (eds), *Reading Karl Polanyi for the 21st century*, Basingstoke: Palgrave Macmillan, pp. 115–34.

Jessop, B. (2013), 'Credit money, fiat money and currency pyramids', in G. Harcourt and J. Pixley (eds), *Financial crises and the nature of capitalist money*, Basingstoke: Palgrave Macmillan, pp. 248–72.

Krippner, G.R. (2005), 'The financialization of the American economy', *Socio-Economic Review*, 3, 173–208.

Kubik, P.J. (1992), 'A re-examination of the great transformation: The establishment of money as a fictitious commodity in the United States', *Social Science Journal*, 29 (1), 53–63.

Lapavitsas, C. (2013), *Profiting without producing: How finance exploits all*, London: Verso.

Lebowitz, M.A. (2003), *Beyond capital: Marx's political economy of the working class*, Basingstoke: Palgrave Macmillan.

Marx, K. (1963), *Theories of surplus value: Part I*, London: Lawrence & Wishart.

Marx, K. (1972), *Theories of surplus value: Part III*, London: Lawrence & Wishart.

Marx, K. (1996), *Capital: Vol. 1*, London: Lawrence & Wishart.

Marx, K. (1998), *Capital: Vol. 3*, London: Lawrence & Wishart.

Melitz, J. (1970), 'The Polanyi school of anthropology on money: An economist's view', *American Anthropologist*, 72 (5), 1020–1040.

Polanyi, K. ([1944] 2001), *The great transformation: The political and economic origins of our time*, Boston: Beacon Press.

Polanyi, K. (1957a), 'Aristotle discovers the economy', in K. Polanyi, C.M. Arensberg and H.W. Pearson (eds), *Trade and market in the early empires: Economies in history and theory*, Glencoe, IL: Free Press, pp. 64–94.

Polanyi, K. (1957b), 'The economy as instituted process', in K. Polanyi, C.M. Arensberg and H.W. Pearson (eds), *Trade and market in the early empires: Economies in history and theory*, Glencoe, IL: Free Press, pp. 243–69.

Polanyi, K. (1977), *The livelihood of man*, New York: Academic Press.

Polanyi, K. (2016), *Karl Polanyi: The Hungarian writings*, Manchester: Manchester University Press.

Rasmus, J. (2010), *Epic recession*, London: Pluto.

Samuelson, P.A. (1957), 'Wages and interest: A modern dissection of Marxian economic models', *American Economic Review*, 47 (6), 884–912.

Schaniel, W.C. and W.C. Neale (1999), 'Quasi-commodities in the first and third worlds', *Journal of Economic Issues*, 33 (1), 95–115.

Stemmet, F. (1996), *The golden contradiction: A Marxist theory of gold*, Aldershot: Ashgate.

Weber, M. (1968), *Economy and society*, New York: Bedminster Press.

Will, S., S. Handelman and D. Brotherton (eds) (2013), *How they got away with it: White collar criminals and the financial meltdown*, New York: Columbia University Press.

PART II

Contemporary developments of society and capitalism in Europe and beyond

7. Polanyian perspectives on capitalisms after socialism

Dorothee Bohle and Béla Greskovits

Although the region is hardly ever mentioned in *The Great Transformation* (Polanyi [1944] 1957), perhaps nowhere is this grand vision of greater comparative relevance than in contemporary East Central Europe.[1] After the breakdown of the socialist system, neoliberalism scored a major victory in the region. As in nineteenth-century England, the utopia of self-regulating markets guided state elites in their efforts to put in place the institutions of market society. The very intellectuals Karl Polanyi was so much polemicizing against became the acclaimed heroes of reformers. Even if the uncontested neoliberal moment was brief, its socio-economic consequences were so striking that talking about a "new great transformation" does not seem to be exaggerated.

Against this background, this chapter highlights some of the ways in which Polanyi's theory complements alternative understandings of the new great transformation. Drawing on our earlier study (Bohle and Greskovits 2012), we specifically hone in on Polanyi's theory of the double movement, and discuss how it has played out in the varied paths of post-socialist capitalism. Instead of looking for total similarities, we consider Polanyi's work as a rich source of reference points, analogies and contrasts.

Polanyi's conceptual historical analysis is framed by two turning points: the triumph of market society dated to the passing of England's new Poor Law of 1834 that effectively transformed labour into a commodity; and the systemic crisis of the interwar period that paved the way to fascism and the Second World War. In between stretches a whole century of capitalism's global expansion and gradual democratization. Although post-socialist capitalism came into existence only three decades ago, we structure the chapter to mimic the Polanyian cycle, in order to make it easier to identify aspects that are common and those that differ. Accordingly, we follow the trajectories of East Central

---

[1] By East Central Europe we mean the former socialist member states of the EU: the Baltic states of Estonia, Latvia and Lithuania, the Visegrád states of the Czech and Slovak republics, Hungary and Poland, and Bulgaria, Croatia, Romania and Slovenia.

European capitalism through three phases: the early to mid-1990s, marked by what we term a "neoliberal moment" and the transformational recession; the new social orders' "democratic moment" and brief golden age roughly from the late 1990s to the mid-2000s; and the return of hard times after 2008, with the global financial crisis and Great Recession, heralding what seems to be a "nationalist moment".[2]

1. THE NEOLIBERAL MOMENT: EARLY TO MID-1990S

Analysing the region's policies of economic liberalization, privatization and deregulation, Peter Murrell concluded that "taken as a whole, this is the most dramatic episode of liberalization in economic history" (Murrell 1996, p. 31). The drama was staged in hard times. Often compared to the Great Depression of 1929–33, a long and deep recession erupted from the agony of socialism and the birth of capitalism. Neither the front-runners nor the laggards of transformation were spared from its impact. However, as to the political consequences, the interwar analogy proved less than perfect, because no similar magnitude of disruptive class conflicts could be observed during the transformational recession. Indeed, with some country-specific variation, in the 1990s the overall strike intensity of East Central European workers lagged far behind the militancy of their counterparts in other European regions (Vandaele 2011). Why was there so limited an occurrence of "Polanyi-type labour unrest", which Beverly Silver defined as "the backlash resistances to the spread of a global self-regulating market particularly by working classes that are being unmade by global economic transformations as well as by those workers who had benefited from established social compacts that are being abandoned from above" (Silver 2003, p. 20)?

According to Leszek Balcerowicz, the architect of Poland's economic transformation, the limited resistance to the extraordinary economic measures is explained by the "extraordinary politics" of the time. In his view, "liberation from foreign domination and domestic political liberalization produce a special state of mass psychology and corresponding political opportunities:

---

[2]   These dates are only indicative rather than carved in stone, and do not apply in the same way in each country. For instance, both the neoliberal and the democratic moments arrived only much later to Bulgaria, Romania and Croatia than to the Visegrád countries or the Baltic states, while radical neoliberalism was never really adopted in Slovenia. Similarly, the economic and political turbulences of Hungary, leading to the country's nationalist moment, started before the global financial crisis struck, while the Polish economy did not have a recession in the critical years. See for the country-specific details Bohle and Greskovits (2012).

the new political structure is fluid and the older political elite is discredited. Both leaders and ordinary citizens feel a stronger-than-normal tendency to think and act in terms of the common good" (Balcerowicz 1995, p. 161).

Other analysts, interested more specifically in why workers remained passive in the face of measures threatening them with lower wages, worse work conditions, unemployment and great uncertainty, put the blame on the legacy of communist "workers' states" (Crowley and Ost 2001). One of the early formulations of this thesis drew on Polanyi's analysis of the English poor-relief system instituted by the Speenhamland Act of 1795, which undermined labour's resistance to commodification under the new Poor Law of 1834 (Glasman 1994).

Discussing this legislation, which granted a "living wage" subsidy not only to the unemployed but even those in employment but poorly paid, Polanyi could not have been more vigorous a critic of ill-conceived income protection. He found the reason for the social catastrophe caused by Speenhamland in that – combined with a ban on labour organization – the system prevented the English working class from forming. It had done so by undermining labour's working morals, dignity and self-respect, and thus denying workers a status that would have distinguished them from paupers. In Polanyi's own words: "As long as a man had a status to hold on, a pattern set by his kin or fellows, he could fight for it, and regain his soul. But in the case of the labourer this could happen only in one way: by his constituting himself the member of a new class. Unless he was able to make a living by his own labour, he was not a worker but a pauper. To reduce him artificially to such a condition was the supreme abomination of Speenhamland" (Polanyi [1944] 1957, p. 99).

In Polanyi's footsteps, Maurice Glasman argued that, like the Speenhamland system, the paternalist welfare state of Polish (and more generally Soviet-type) socialism undermined its beneficiaries' skill, will and morals to resist after 1989 the "shock therapy" and the ensuing transformation of labour into commodity. "The effects of paternalism on the 'substance' of the common culture were so devastating that anything seemed better in comparison" (Glasman 1994, p. 66). To translate this claim to Silver's language, after the fall of Soviet-type socialism there was limited Polanyi-type labour unrest because the system neither allowed the formation of a working class worth the name, nor did it leave behind an established social compact worth a defence. "Authoritarian protectionism has done the work of Speenhamland on a European scale" (Glasman 1994, p. 69).

The argument that the memory of state paternalism fuelled deep distrust of public intervention and thus paved the way to acquiescence to or even support of radical marketization, cannot be dismissed. Nevertheless, there exist opinion polls and anthropological research findings which suggest that workers' shared sentiments about the past system were not merely negative.

Thus, individuals interviewed for a recent volume on working-class populism expressed nostalgia about their respected status based on their employment (often in line with family traditions) in skilled occupations in socialist flagship firms (Kalb and Halmai 2011). These workers also recalled experiences of community life, which question the assumption that social compacts were altogether absent in socialism. Reading their recollections of cultural and holiday events at the communal centre, rooting with friends and colleagues for the company's soccer team, or organizing family vacations in the trade union's summer camp or holiday home, makes it difficult to view these people merely as "socially homeless" paupers. Indeed, we shall argue that such memories and attachments became no less politically consequential for the features of nascent capitalism than the welcome of liberation from repressive state control.

2. THE DEMOCRATIC MOMENT: LATE 1990S TO MID-2000S

With the transformational recession over, the new social order has taken more solid shape. Large inflows of foreign capital, fast expanding foreign and domestic demand for its products, rising GDP and modestly improving living standards signalled that East Central Europe entered what could have become its post-socialist golden age. As a further sign of stabilization, extraordinary politics gave way "to the more mundane politics of contending parties and interest groups" (Balcerowicz 1995, p. 161). Finally, preparation for EU enlargement, which for most countries brought about full membership in 2004, contributed to the spread of optimistic assessments of future perspectives. Transnational capitalism, which fostered deep integration into the global and European economy through flows of goods, capital and ideas, as well as through institutions, seemed to function fairly well in the region until the late 2000s when it was shaken worldwide.

These developments were largely unforeseen. Over the 1990s, many observers retained pessimism about the new system's future either on the grounds that the "Leninist legacy" was inimical to capitalist democracy, or because they thought that building markets, democracies and nations simultaneously were mutually incompatible tasks (Jowitt 1991; Offe 1991). Others, like Michael Burawoy, worried that the West exported to the East not "the 20th-century mixed economy of advanced capitalism but an early 19th-century market utopianism" replete with "barbaric tendencies", which these "naive and expectant nations" would not be able to contain any time soon. "After all, how many advanced capitalisms can there be in the world?" (Burawoy 2001, p. 1118). While the former socialist latecomers still fall short of the advanced status, below we argue that they *did* establish their own sort of mixed economy after all, and adapting Polanyi's terms and concepts to the post-socialist conditions helps to understand why and how this happened.

As is well known, capitalism's mechanisms of fuelling and containing its "barbaric tendencies", and the related risks and opportunities of system reproduction, are central to Polanyi's theory. Perhaps his most frequently cited notion is that "the idea of a self-adjusting market implied a stark utopia. Such an institution could not exist for any length of time without annihilating the human and natural substance of society; it would have physically destroyed man and transformed his surroundings into a wilderness. Inevitably, society took measures to protect itself" (Polanyi [1944] 1957, p. 8).

A paradoxical argument follows from this: without its victims and adversaries, who resisted and corrected its excesses, capitalism could not have reproduced itself but would have fast perished due to its deleterious impact on "the social fabric" and the habitat. At the same time, Polanyi does not leave us with an idyllic picture of society's self-defence either. Rather, similar to the "movement" of unregulated market expansion, the "countermovement" of (ill-conceived) social protection could also undermine the reproduction of society, because it "impaired the self-regulation of the market, disorganised industrial life, and thus endangered society in yet another way" (Polanyi [1944] 1957, p. 8). Hence the significance of the political sphere for *viable* capitalism. Polanyi considered functioning political institutions to be crucially important both as arenas for the agents of the double movement to fight out their conflicts, and as organs coordinating, checking, and possibly moderating their struggles (Block and Somers 1984, p. 68). That is why we read his notion as a *political* theory of capitalism, according to which the coordination capacity of the political sphere is key to the system's rise, reproduction and demise.

Adopting the Polanyian triad of capitalism's key institutions, namely those of the market, social protection, and the political sphere, helped us identify and empirically substantiate several post-socialist types of capitalism (Bohle and Greskovits 2012). From the viewpoint of this chapter, one of our more interesting findings is the contrast between the pure "neoliberal" Baltic countries, which have combined the region's most radical marketization strategies with minimalist social protection measures; and the "embedded neoliberal" Visegrád states, in which losers of relatively less radical marketization programmes have been compensated by more generous welfare states. Polanyi provides an intellectual toolkit to grasp *how* the new system and its varied models have come about. Nevertheless, his original terms and concepts cannot be directly applied but must be adjusted to fit the circumstances of the new great transformation.

One of the key questions of post-socialist capitalism's dynamics is: which actors keep the double movement in motion and how do they pursue their objectives? For the period covered by his analysis, Polanyi's answer is straightforward. The main agents of the movement were "trading classes" whose quest for market expansion was motivated not merely by material greed but also by liberal ideology. In turn, the countermovement was formed by members of "the working and landed classes" who, driven by the communitarian spirit of socialism or nationalism tried to defend society by "protective legislation, restrictive associations, and other means of intervention" (Polanyi [1944] 1957, pp. 132 ff.).

The post-socialist situation differed in respect to both, the movement and the countermovement. As to the forces of movement, Gil Eyal, Iván Szelényi and Eleanor Townsley have convincingly argued that in contrast to "the classical, West European path of 'capitalists *before* capitalism'", in East Central Europe a "capitalism without capitalists" emerged in the sense that instituting the market economy outpaced the creation of a private propertied class (Eyal et al. 1998, pp. 16, 4–5). Although eventually foreign capitalists acquired dominance within the new grand bourgeoisie, their influence became important mainly *after* the varied coalitions of technocrats, bureaucrats and former dissidents turned politicians used state power to lay the new order's foundations.

Yet, elite class formation, while lagging behind institutional transformation, still outpaced the emergence of a new working class with all that it would entail: shared identity, revitalized trade unions, and left parties. Although from the late 1990s the relocation of capitalist production from Europe's core has brought about economic expansion in some sectors and adversity in others, strike intensity in the region has declined further (Vandaele 2011). To use Silver's term, there was little evidence of "Marx-type labour unrest", that is, "struggles of newly emerging working classes that are successively made and strengthened" by inflows of foreign capital (Silver 2003, p. 20). How then should we make sense of the fact that despite the absence of a robust labour-based countermovement, from the late 1990s to mid-2000s some of the post-socialist countries maintained or even expanded (even if others retrenched) their welfare states? Are we faced with instances of concessions to absent countermovements?

For an answer, we take on board Kurt Vandaele's argument that a low level of strike activity "does not imply that workers in CEE countries have not reacted" to commodification, because "strike action is far not the only or even main form in which workers' resistance to being treated as a commodity is expressed" (Vandaele 2011, p. 10). As to the possible alternative forms of labour resistance, Antonina Gentile and Sidney Tarrow proposed that globalization – rather than undermining workers' protest across the board – leads to its diverse manifestations in different varieties of capitalism (Gentile and Tarrow 2009).

They argued that in countries of large organized labour forces with institutionalized inclusion in policy making via collective bargaining or social pacts (as in Nordic Europe) organized workers tend to protest by strikes at the work-place and count on the solidarity of other trade unions. Conversely, in countries lacking such organizations and institutions – as in their case the USA, but in our view also post-socialist East Central Europe – workers tend to define the injustice they suffer from with reference to their rights as democratic citizens (rather than as workers). They will likelier respond to grievances by demonstrations, rallies or signing petitions, and seek the support of non-labour-based organizations, such as social movements and NGOs. Even more important, workers will use their political rights and vote for or against parties depending on whether they perceive them acting in or against their interests.

Hence the specificity of the post-socialist double movement, and our reason for calling the period of consolidation the "democratic moment": while the movement was mainly driven by technocratic, bureaucratic and partisan political, rather than propertied capitalist, agents and logics, the countermovement was primarily electoral and civic in terms of its agents, methods and spirit. It would, however, be erroneous to believe that all these actors had clear and full-fledged political identities. On the one hand, the ambiguity of electoral preferences was noted early on by the economic adviser to the Polish government, Jeffrey Sachs, who – witnessing that East European electorates brought back to power communist successor parties, which increased social outlays but typically did not stop market reforms – noted: "Generally speaking, most East Europeans want both a market economy and the security of an extensive social security net" (Sachs 1995, p. 1).

On the other hand, in the context of still not settled political institutions, the ambiguous demands of the electorate were met (or not) by the ambiguous supply of political elites. Eyal and his collaborators were not alone in recognizing that in some countries the "Communist Party now views itself as a Social Democratic Party but implements the cruellest anti-labour policies . . . Former anti-communist intellectuals claiming to have formed neoliberal parties often find themselves advocating the causes of the oppressed and the exploited. The notions of Left and Right, conservative and liberal, are still being negotiated" (Eyal et al. 1998, p. 189). It follows that the actual members, ideologies and aims of the movement and countermovement were still under construction as well. Importantly, by being present in both camps, the EU and its bodies contributed to blurring the boundaries between movement and countermovement. Thus, James Caporaso and Sidney Tarrow saw *"supranational embedded liberal compromises"* emerging from the decisions of the European Court of Justice on decommodifying migrant labour (Caporaso and Tarrow 2009). In turn, more critical approaches lamented the dominant impact of the Single Market over that of the European Social Model.

Let us finally point out that in most cases the social protection provided by the transformative elite was meant to *pre-empt*, rather than respond to, contention. This leads to the question: how was it that in the Baltic states consistently less social protection was needed to pre-empt resistance to marketization than in the Visegrád states? Our answer is that, while the Visegrád states' relatively generous welfare benefits tried to tame the countermovements through recognition of attachment to social status acquired in the past regime, the sentiment of "collective commitment to nationhood . . . and independence" (Landes 1991, p. 49) had for historical reasons wider resonance among the Baltic states' citizenry, and opened more room for mobilizing consent to painful economic measures by nationalist identity politics. The other side of the coin is that through restrictive citizenship laws Estonia and Latvia effectively disenfranchised their large ethnic Russian minorities, who were also disproportionately suffering from radical marketization.

Consequently, the fully enfranchised worker-citizens of the Visegrád states meant a stronger constraint on the power holders than their only partially enfranchised Baltic counterparts – hence one key factor of the asymmetric transformation strategies. These differences have not evaporated but remained politically consequential even for the types of adjustment to the new hard times after 2008, bringing about the region's nationalist moment.

3.   THE NATIONALIST MOMENT: SINCE 2008

Soon after the EU enlargement, the new capitalist democracies started to show signs of vulnerability. As the editors of a special issue of *Journal of Democracy*, reflecting on the dire state of East Central European democracies, wrote: "Whatever danger remained of their reverting to authoritarianism seemed to be removed by their entry into the European Union ... Yet today, all are beset by sharp political conflict, and there is growing concern about the solidity of their democracies" (Plattner and Diamond 2007, p. 5).

Starting in 2008, the Great Recession brought more trouble: most countries in the region were plagued by the temporary drying up of international finance, collapse of their export markets, economic stagnation or contraction. This time, the economic hardship was not without political consequences. The relatively balanced "political economy of protest and patience" (Greskovits 1998), which during the run-up to EU enlargement had allowed the simultaneous expansion of markets and democracy, became a thing of the past. Rather, public sector employees and other losers of austerity responded by disruptive demonstrations, work stoppages and economic violence (Beissinger and Sasse 2012). As a lasting consequence, the combination of street protest with voting against the incumbents at referenda and elections increased the influence or even brought to power leaders with illiberal nationalist political agendas.

Thus, we conclude asking how far the politics of these new crises can be analysed through analogies with the Polanyian account of the interwar period. Concretely, we try to use this comparison to better understand why it is that right-wingers, albeit this time not fascists but nationalists, rather than reinvigorated political liberals or socialists, have emerged as winners from the "impasses" and battles at the international and national levels of political economy.

The defeat of political liberals may not be all that surprising given that their economic ideology is mostly neoliberal, which, similar to the 1930s, makes them easy targets as promoters of globalization responsible for the economic uncertainty and inequality exacerbated by the recent downturn. Nevertheless, a peculiar feature of the aftermath of the new crisis is that the inequality traced to the free market vision is not the only "sin" liberals are blamed for. Rather, liberalism is also under attack, and often by the same right-wing adversaries, for its efforts to educate citizens to be willing to recognize and accept their societies' diversity. Clearly, interwar fascism had been savagely anti-liberal in political terms as well. Still, the novelty of anti-liberalism of our times is in its determination to undo the achievements of the post-war "silent revolution" of values (Inglehart and Norris 2016), and reverse the resulting emancipation of women, sexual and ethnic minorities and non-whites, and the protection of "the habitat" – all issues of impressive progress, which Polanyi surely would embrace.

Polanyi had considered a "socialist solution" of the economic problems of the interwar period, namely "transcending the self-regulating market by consciously subordinating it to a democratic society". However, in the 1930s when "normal methods were insufficient, abnormal ones would be tried . . . which were socialistic . . . the very hint would suffice to throw markets into confusion and start a universal panic" (Polanyi [1944] 1957, pp. 234–5). By its ill-timed and/or "overdone" countermovement, then, the interwar left seems to have itself contributed to the impasse between democratic and market forces, and to its own coming misfortunes. In contrast, the left of the new millennium in East Central Europe and beyond appears to suffer from a very different problem, namely the loss of political support due to its close association with the movement of economic neoliberals, and its neglect of workers and their civic organizations.

While in varied ways though the left was part of the problem, and the right brought about "perverse" solutions in the aftermath of both crises, we can find as many differences as similarities between the victorious right-wing camps in the interwar period and the new millennium. Polanyi defines the "fascist situation" as a moment of "easy and complete fascist victories", when "*minute fascist forces would brush aside what seemed until then the overwhelming strength of democratic governments, parties, trade unions*" (Polanyi [1944] 1957, p. 239, italics added). In contrast, by the time of the Great Recession, East Central European democracy was far from being "overwhelmingly strong". Rather, its stability was undermined by country-specific combinations of hollowing and backsliding. Further, in the critical Hungarian case, where by now democracy is largely abandoned, the political triumph of the right was for long prepared by its conquest of civil society (Greskovits 2015).

A no less important difference is that, unlike in the 1930s, in the aftermath of the Great Recession economic neoliberalism is still pursued in East Central Europe, but increasingly by illiberal nationalist governments. As pointed out above, the fact that in the Baltic states nation builders and neoliberals had joined forces early on, is well established. In turn, it is less well understood that a variant of nationalist neoliberalism is now being championed in Hungary (and lately Poland) as well, even if earlier in these countries' nation (re)building was perceived a less urgent task, and the political agenda was dominated by modernization with welfare and through Westernization.

A cursory comparison of the crisis trajectories of Hungary and Latvia points to some of the reasons (Bohle 2018). Different as they were in terms of the specificities of their capitalist models, both states had been among the first "hot spots" to be hit hard by the global financial crisis. Under the combined pressures of large current account deficits, currency and banking crises, and plummeting exports, both countries had to rely on the bailout packages of the IMF and EU, conditional on the implementation of draconic austerity measures in the face of angry populations.

Mobilizing consent for painful measures through appeals to national identity and the need for solidarity in hard times was nothing new in Latvian politics, especially given that an increasingly assertive Russia was again perceived as a major threat to the country's security and independence. Also, Latvia's economic institutions reflected the perceived need to break away from the socialist past as radically as possible. Fusing identity politics with radical neoliberalism allowed Latvia to comply easily with the conditions of its international creditors and reinforce its earlier strategy of accommodating global neoliberalism.

The Hungarian case is different. Here, from the moment that embedding neoliberalism in socially protective arrangements had become untenable due to financial constraints, democratic politics lost balance, and stabilization occurred only via larger doses of identity politics leading ultimately to the loss of democracy. Yet, using the opportunity opened by the crisis also required the skill and will of the Hungarian right. That its leader Viktor Orbán possessed both, is attested by the resilience of his illiberal state, which politicized dependency by using militant anti-Western and anti-EU rhetorics but maintained some key features of the country's "embedded neoliberalism" by being cautious and selective in actual economic nationalist measures.

4.   CONCLUSIONS

In this chapter we have argued that Polanyi-inspired debates about the progress capitalism can bring about, but also about its vulnerabilities, are helpful in understanding post-socialist trajectories after 1989. Even if Eastern Europe's new great transformation differs from the earlier great transformation in terms of the strength of both movement and countermovement, these movements' agents, and the degree and forms of embeddedness that can be achieved under the conditions of global neoliberalism, a double movement dynamic is also discernible in Europe's East. There is another parallel: similar to the Great Depression, the Great Recession has also brought about a radical nationalist and anti-democratic moment. While a decade ago capitalist liberal democracy was "the only game in town", recently we have witnessed a defunct international economy, blockages of democratic government, and their "solutions" by nationalist leaders at the cost of democracy's backsliding. Are we then back to the 1930s? Three differences stand out. First, unlike in the 1930s, current autocrats cannot cement their rule through stable mass movements and fascist corporatism. Rather, they have to put up with fickle voters, which might be a reason for hope. However, a second difference is that these voters are not being offered a convincing socialist alternative, which could effectively challenge the reactionary forces of our time. And third, while the 1920s heralded the emergence of democratic rule, and the post-war compromise of embedded liberalism led to its consolidation, in the new millennium democracy seems exhausted. None of this bodes well for the future of a robust emancipatory countermovement.

REFERENCES

Balcerowicz, L. (1995), *Socialism, capitalism, transformation*, Budapest: Central European University Press.

Beissinger, M. and G. Sasse (2012), 'An end to "patience"? The great recession and economic protest in Eastern Europe', in N. Bermeo and L.M. Bartels (eds), *Mass politics in tough times: Opinions, votes, and protest in the great recession*. Oxford: Oxford University Press, pp. 334–70.

Block, F. and M.R. Somers (1984), 'Beyond the economistic fallacy: The holistic social science of Karl Polanyi', in T. Skocpol (ed.), *Vision and method in historical sociology*, Cambridge: Cambridge University Press, pp. 47–84.

Bohle, D. (2018), 'Capitalism and democracy in East Central Europe: A sequence of crises', in M. Ignatieff and S. Roch (eds), *Rethinking open society: New adversaries and new opportunities*, Budapest and New York: Central European University Press, pp. 281–94.

Bohle, D. and B. Greskovits (2012), *Capitalist diversity on Europe's periphery*, Ithaca and London: Cornell University Press.

Burawoy, M. (2001), 'Neoclassical sociology: From the end of communism to the end of classes', *American Journal of Sociology*, 106 (4), 1099–1120.

Caporaso, J.A. and S. Tarrow (2009), 'Polanyi in Brussels: Supranational institutions and the transnational embedding of markets', *International Organization*, 63, 593–620.

Crowley, S. and D. Ost (eds) (2001), *Workers after workers' states: Labor and politics in postcommunist Eastern Europe*, Lanham, MD: Rowman & Littlefield.

Eyal, G., I. Szelényi and E. Townsley (1998), *Making capitalism without capitalists: The new ruling elites in Eastern Europe*, London: Verso.

Gentile A. and S. Tarrow (2009), 'Charles Tilly, globalization, and labor's citizen rights', *European Political Science Review*, 1 (3), 465–93.

Glasman, M. (1994), 'Polanyi, Poland, and the terrors of planned spontaneity', *New Left Review*, 1 (205), 59–86.

Greskovits, B. (1998), *The political economy of protest and patience: East European and Latin American transformations compared*, Budapest: Central European University Press.

Greskovits, B. (2015), 'The hollowing and backsliding of democracy in East Central Europe', *Global Policy*, 6 (1), 28–37.

Inglehart, R.F. and P. Norris (2016), *Trump, Brexit, and the rise of populism: Economic have-nots and cultural backlash*, Cambridge, MA: Harvard Kennedy School.

Jowitt, K. (1991), 'The new world disorder', *Journal of Democracy*, 2 (1), 11–20.

Kalb, D. and G. Halmai (eds) (2011), *Headlines of nation, subtexts of class: Working class populism and the return of the repressed in neoliberal Europe*, Oxford and New York: Berghahn.

Landes, D. (1991), 'Does it pay to be late?', in J. Batou (ed.), *Between development and underdevelopment*, Geneva: Publications du Centre d'Histoire Économique Internationale de l'Université de Genève, pp. 43–62.

Murrell, P. (1996), 'How far has the transition progressed?', *Journal of Economic Perpsectives*, 10 (2), 25–44.

Offe, C. (1991), 'Capitalism by democratic design? Democratic theory facing the triple transition in East Central Europe', *Social Research*, 58 (4), 649–84.

Plattner, M.F. and L. Diamond (2007), 'Is East-Central Europe backsliding?', *Journal of Democracy*, 18 (4), 5–6.

Polanyi, K. ([1944] 1957), *The great transformation: The political and economic origins of our time*, Boston: Beacon Press.

Sachs, J. (1995), 'Postcommunist parties and the politics of entitlements', *Beyond Transition: The Newsletter about Reforming Economies*, accessed 20 February 2009 at www.worldbank.org/html/prddr/trans/mar95/pgs1-4 .htm.

Silver, B. (2003), *Forces of labor: Workers' movements and globalization since 1870*, Cambridge: Cambridge University Press.

Vandaele, K. (2011), *Sustaining or abandoning 'social peace'? Strike development and trends in Europe since the 1990s*, ETUI Working Paper 2011/5, Brussels: ETUI.

8. Economy–society tensions in the Eurozone: the "anti-democratic virus" revived

Maria Markantonatou

1. INTRODUCTION

Polanyi's (2001, p. 3) diagnosis already in the first line of *The Great Transformation* that liberalism had once and for all collapsed after the Second World War was not verified in the next decades, and this has been a justifiable point of critique. According to Burawoy (2014, p. 38), Polanyi's "false optimism" was related to his stance towards Marxism and his failure to capture capital's "recurrent deployment of market fundamentalism as a strategy for overcoming its internal contradictions". A different, but equally justifiable critique point is raised by Fraser (2017, p. 4) concerning Polanyi's loose concept of "society", which ends up a "catch-all" term that "mixes together everything that is not the 'economy', conflating important distinctions between, for example, states and civil society". These two shortcomings, however, do not downplay the importance of his analysis regarding what he described as the "mutual incompatibility" between capitalism and democracy, leading to the birth of the "anti-democratic" or "fascist virus", terms which he used alternately.

In his text *The Fascist Virus*, Polanyi (n.d. [a]) considers the period "from the introduction of universal suffrage to the outbreak of the Great War", in which "capitalism and democracy seemed to flourish side by side", as a "period of false security" followed by crisis. With the rise of fascism, "the dilemma of a democracy versus capitalism emerged in the most acute form". Fascism was, however, *not* the only form, but "merely the most recent and most virulent outburst of the anti-democratic virus" (Polanyi n.d. [a]). The virus itself was present in various contexts, and Polanyi devoted a great part of his work to deconstructing "anti-democratic" thinking and politics, and thus, various endeavours, both theoretical and political, undertaken in different historical conjunctures that had, however, one common aim: to insulate economy from society and move away or minimize the influence of the working class in political decision making. He thus recognized the "anti-democratic virus" in various circumstances.

He criticized the strong opposition to universal suffrage of English thinkers such as Burke, Malthus and Martineau and their idea that economic stability could only be secured when the inferior classes accepted their social position and the belief that poverty was natural (Polanyi n.d. [a]). Polanyi (n.d. [b]) criticized Hegel's defence of guilds under the regime of Prussian monarchy and compared this system to the twentieth century's fascist corporatism. Hegel anticipated the "anomaly" that the separation of economic from political life would cause but failed to recognize the need for real democratization, whereas the young Marx opposed absolutism and the pseudo-constitutions of some German Estates based on traditional power (Polanyi n.d. [b]). Polanyi (1935), further, sharply criticized Othmar Spann's vision of the "corporatist state" (*Ständestaat*), in which class differentiations gave their place to a pseudo-pacified social totality rooted in the Middle Ages' political Christianity and an urge for the restoration of traditional hierarchies. He also criticized Pope Pius XI's Encyclical *Quadragesimo Anno* (1931), because it "maintained the sole rule of the capitalist class over State and industry" (Polanyi n.d. [b]). While the Encyclical *Rerum Novarum* (The Holy See 1891) by Pope Leo XIII had argued in favour of workers' rights, wealth redistribution, the strike right etc., the *Quadragesimo Anno* (The Holy See 1931) pursued the repression of trade unions and socialist movements – proposals strongly rejected by Polanyi.

This heterogeneity of cases means that the "anti-democratic virus" cannot be confined to 1930s fascism but should be understood in a broader sense, as the result of the "hostility of capitalism to popular government" (Polanyi n.d. [a]). In that regard, Polanyi's analysis offers important tools to the understanding of current tensions under Eurozone's liberalism and its current crisis, which worst hit Greece. In the following section, we discuss some of the effects of the Greek austerity programme with reference to Polanyi's observations on liberal international interventionism in the interwar period, and then we look at recent revivals of the "anti-democratic virus" in the Eurozone.

2.   THE REQUIREMENT OF SOUND BUDGETS

The repayment of foreign loans and the return to stable currencies were recognized as the touchstone of rationality in politics; and no private suffering, no restriction of sovereignty, was deemed too great a sacrifice for the recovery of monetary integrity. The privations of the unemployed made jobless by deflation; the destitution of public servants dismissed without a pittance [...] were judged a fair price to pay for the fulfillment of the requirement of sound budgets. (Polanyi 2001, p. 148)

Were the author's name in the above quote hidden, one could assume that it might be referring to present-day Greece. Since 2010, deflationary policies have been implemented in the framework of the "Memoranda of Understanding", three complex loan agreements concluded between the so-called "Troika" (European Commission, European Central Bank, International Monetary Fund) and a series of Greek governments of various ideological guises (social democratic, right-wing, left-wing in different but equally controversial coalitions). The conditions for the provision of loan tranches include the implementation of specific measures. They are related to sound budgets, privatizations, liberalization of domestic markets, public administration reforms, restructuring of the tax, wage, pension and social benefits system, and the deregulation of welfare services. Cutting down public expenditure, reduction of personnel in the public sector, slashing social incomes, and the dismantling of the pre-crisis institutions of labour protection have been the fundamental aims underlying a barrage of measures since 2010. After three austerity packages, it is concluded by the European Stability Mechanism (ESM 2018) that "the Greek economy has improved its competitiveness by reducing unit labour costs. The improvement can be seen in the falling current account deficit [...]. Greece is the best performing economy in terms of implementing OECD recommendations on structural reforms".

However, this view focuses on specific indices while putting aside others, and hardly looks at the socio-economic effects. Within nearly a decade of austerity, Greek GDP was reduced by more than 25 per cent and public debt skyrocketed from 110 per cent of GDP in 2008 to 180 per cent in 2017 (Greek Institute of Labour 2018). Living standards deteriorated severely as wages and pensions were cut by 20 per cent to 50 per cent. Total unemployment rose from 7.8 per cent in 2008 to 27.5 per cent in 2013, and although it was reduced to 20.2 per cent in 2017 (Greek Institute of Labour 2018), it remains at the highest in the EU. From 2009 to 2017, full time recruitments were reduced by more than half (Greek Institute of Labour 2018, p. 17) and precariousness and in-work poverty increased for all categories of workers. Trade unions were attacked and the institutions of collective bargaining were gradually deregulated.

The political effects of the crisis management were equally significant. Support for the Social Democratic Party (PASOK), which was the first to impose austerity policies, fell from 43.92 per cent in 2009 to a mere 6.29 per cent in September 2015. A large share of its voters moved to the Coalition of the Radical Left (SYRIZA), which managed to articulate an electorally successful anti-austerity campaign and rose from 4.6 per cent of the vote to 35.46 per cent in September 2015. This electoral shift crystallized the Greek version of the "double movement",[1] but it was not its sole dimension. If SYRIZA's rise was unimaginable in the pre-crisis era, this is true also for the neo-fascist Golden Dawn, support for which rose from 0.29 per cent in 2009 to 7 per cent in September 2015 (for all electoral results, Greek Ministry of Interior 2018). What dominated was a deep representation crisis, evident in the electoral earthquakes since 2010, the abrupt changes in electoral preferences, the shifts of relatively stable electoral groups to other parties, the increase of "anti-establishment" and protest votes, and the emergence of various new parties. Some of these parties failed to ever enter the Parliament, but others managed to participate as minority parties in coalition governments. Seven different governments were formed from 2009 to 2015 (including a "techno-cratic" and two "operational" ones).

When the government of SYRIZA surrendered to the creditors' demands after the referendum in 2015, the experiment of the left-wing government in Greece was over and one more austerity package was imposed. SYRIZA's orientations gradually yielded to the political mainstream: promises of growth after the measures' implementation, appeals to investors to invest in Greece, and reassurances to foreign leaders that Greece now offered the right legal framework for entrepreneurialism.[2] Given that the continuum of austerity politics at the behest of creditors was, finally, not challenged by SYRIZA's rise to power, Greece remains committed to the aims of sound budgets and debt repayment. Creditors' dictates became not just a vital part, but, actually, the ultimate measure of Greek politics. With reference to the interwar period, Polanyi (2001, p. 14) described this kind of devotion to creditors' demands as the politics of "good behavior":

> Loans, and the renewal of loans, hinged upon credit, and credit upon good behavior. Since under constitutional government [...] behavior is reflected in the budget and the external value of the currency cannot be detached from the appreciation of the budget, debtor governments were well advised to watch their exchanges carefully and to avoid policies which might reflect upon the soundness of the budgetary position.

Interwar structural adjustment programmes such as Austria's (Polanyi 2001, p. 237) are comparable to the ones in Greece. In addition, the Eurozone is comparable to the gold standard, with parallels including the imbalances

---

[1]   With this well-known concept, Polanyi described the practices and ways of social resistance to marketization, commodification and liberalization, namely how society, already since the nineteenth century, "protected itself against the perils inherent in a self-regulating market system" (Polanyi 2001, p. 80).

[2]   Such a "reassurance" was, for instance, provided to Donald Trump (see The White House 2017).

between increasingly interdependent economies, deflationary policies, punishments for debtor countries, loss of governments' control of exchange rates and the absence of a central bank accountable to the state (Pettifor 2015). Non-intervention demands were the first to be sacrificed during the interwar period, as various countries were forced by creditors and the League of Nations to reintroduce the gold standard, stabilize the economy in a market-friendly way, and restore liberal principles. As we learn from Polanyi (2001, p. 242):

> [...] in the course of these vain deflationary efforts free markets had not been restored though free governments had been sacrificed. Though opposed in theory to interventionism and inflation alike, economic liberals had chosen between the two and set the sound-currency ideal above that of nonintervention. In so doing they followed the logic inherent in a self-regulating economy.

International interventionism dominated in Greece too, and the country became a case of systematic assessment by creditors, international organizations, rating agencies and banking groups. What Polanyi characterizes above as the "logic inherent in the self-regulating economy" was followed in the Greek case in two ways. First, the programme required an extended political intervention and was fostered as a state and interstate project. This is of course, not new, as explained by Polanyi, who stressed that liberalization was mainly a state intervention result, rather than a spontaneously created social order. The fact that "the economic liberal" would "without any inconsistency call upon the state to use the force of law" (2001, p. 155) was for him anything but coincidental. It showed that the idea the state ought not to intervene in the market system (the theory of the economy–society separation) was different than its actual implementation.[3] This is confirmed in the Greek case, as shown by the legislation related to liberalization, privatization and internal devaluation. Recent studies emphasize too the political dimension of the Eurozone's economic governance. Bruff (2014, p. 117) speaks of an "authoritarian neoliberalism" through the constitutionalization of austerity. Oberndorfer (2015, p. 185) radicalizes the concept of "new constitutionalism" (Gill) and describes a shift to "authoritarian competitive statism". Jessop (2016, pp. 234–6) speaks of an "austerity state" which tends to institutionalize permanent austerity and is differentiated from "conjunctural austerity policies" and the "enduring politics of austerity".

---

[3]   As Polanyi (1939) put it "the State was supposed to keep strictly to political matters and to govern as little as possible; the industrial system on the other hand, was allegedly controlled by laws of its own – the sacred laws of competitive prices. So long as the State did not interfere with these prices, they provided the greatest possible yield of commodities. Such was the theory; but of course these conditions of affairs never existed in actual fact".

Second, the "logic inherent in the self-regulating economy" was followed, provided that the Greek programme's proponents attributed its failure to opposing groups' resistance by blaming or demonizing trade unions and caricaturing those dependent on welfare services as selfish rent-seekers who consciously blocked reform (Markantonatou 2013). This is the kind of ideology criticized by Polanyi: if liberalism failed, the reason was never its internal mechanisms, but its social opponents. For liberals, as Polanyi (2001, p. 157) depicted their view, "shortsighted trade unionists, Marxist intellectuals, greedy manufacturers, and reactionary landlords" were made responsible for the crisis – and similar views dominated in the Greek case. Indeed, several EU officials blamed Greece for "living beyond its means", and Greek governments, in their turn, blamed specific class groups for asking too much social protection, too many working privileges, etc. Contrary to views such as Hayek's (1976, p. 101), that the Great Depression "was wholly due to mismanagement of money by government", Polanyi (2001, n.d. [a]) perceived crises as being the result of an economy–democracy tension and the weakening or even abandonment of democracy as a tendency incubated in liberalism. Before we return to this thesis at the end of the chapter, in the following section, we look at some recent economy–democracy tensions.

3.   ECONOMY–DEMOCRACY TENSIONS IN THE EUROZONE

In his book *Come un Incubo e come un Sogno* ("Like a Nightmare and like a Dream"), the Italian economist Paolo Savona (2018, p. 215) characterized some aspects of the process of what, in the pre-crisis period, was triumphantly called "European integration" as the "clearest manifestations of the most unjust and dangerous political philosophy". Citizens were not allowed to have a say when the monetary union was decided, but their leaders proceeded with such important decisions, Savona explained, further arguing that "Italy has slipped into a new colonial condition, the same one experienced by Greece" (2018, p. 215). In the same book, Savona expressed various views about the Euro: it befits the economies of the European North rather than the South; it has reduced the Italians' purchasing power; without a Plan B, Italy will end up like Greece. Savona, a former Minister of Industry and president of various banking think tanks and organizations, is no Marxist whatsoever, but a Euro critic. His views on the Euro were, however, enough to make the Italian President Sergio Mattarella veto the decision of the new Five Star/Lega government to appoint Savona as Finance Minister. In his speech, Mattarella resorted to the "economic" argument:

> I shared and accepted all the proposals made for the ministers, except the one for the Minister of the Economy. The designation of the Minister of the Economy always constitutes an immediate message of confidence or alarm for economic and financial players. [...] A representative who [...] may not be seen as the promoter of a line of reasoning [...] could probably, or even inevitably, provoke Italy's exit from the Euro. (Presidenza Della Republica 2018)

This episode made many speak of a "post-democracy" in Italy and raised the question: "Mattarella did not specify how the verdict of the markets can be established. Should we look at the volatile stock exchange, productivity, trade, investment, or growth? And who is in the position to speak on behalf of the markets? The rating agencies? The IMF? The President himself?" (Zielonka 2018). Such questions and controversies are, of course, nothing new for Greece. Likewise, statements like that of the European Budget Commissioner, Günther Öttinger, that "the markets will teach Italians how to vote" (see Wishart 2018), or the Director of the Walter Eucken Institute, Lars Feld (2018), that "Italy, after the elections, is developing to Europe's problematic child" are in the same spirit as the dictates towards Greece by Troika representatives.

According to Polanyi (n.d. [a]), this kind of political devotion to the principles of market economy was "anti-democratic" in nature, reflecting the idea that "the laws of market economy prohibit any intervention in economic life in the part of the working people". What is reminiscent of the crisis episodes in Greece and Italy regarding the efforts to remove undesired politicians, political parties and governments is his description of how "the mere possibility of [popular parties'] disregarding the sanctity of titles to property in an emergency, would throw security markets into a panic and governments out of office". A "crisis of confidence" had the result that "the political forces responsible for the messes were promptly made to disappear from the scene" (n.d. [a]).

One of the first forces to be "made to disappear" during the Eurozone crisis was the government of PASOK in 2011. When Prime Minister George Papandreou mentioned in front of an international audience the possibility of a referendum on the austerity package proposed by creditors, his government rapidly fell due to forceful national and international reactions. In its place, an unelected so-called "technocratic government" was appointed, with an international banker, Lucas Papademos, as Prime Minister (a similar development took place in Italy the same year with the appointment of Mario Monti).

In 2015, when the government of SYRIZA announced a referendum on the so-called "Juncker Plan" (another austerity package), it was interpreted, as the Eurogroup's President, Jeroen Dijsselbloem put it, as "a sad decision for

Greece", which meant that the government had "closed the door on further talks" and had "broken off the process" (see Kanter and Yardley 2015). As in the previous loan agreements, "the process" could continue only if it excluded the involvement of voters and social majorities. In between economic panic and political tension, the electorate was divided between the "Yes" (supported by pro-austerity domestic parties, Eurozone and IMF officials, Greek industrialists and Greek owners of private television channels and newspapers) and the "No" (trade unions, lower economic strata, small entrepreneurs, wage-earners, the unemployed and precariously working young people). Despite the pro-"Yes" hysterical mass media campaigns and blackmailing by both national and international elites, the outcome was 61.31 per cent for Yes and 38.69 per cent for No. This outcome had a clear class orientation,[4] constituting the peak of the anti-austerity countermovement and a victory of the "democratic sphere", in the Polanyian sense.

On the other hand, the "economic sphere" used its own weapons. During the phase of euphemistically called "negotiations" between the newly elected government of SYRIZA and the creditors, the latter's pressures led to a complete drying up of liquidity and the default of Greece's payment to the IMF in June 2015, making the country "the first in the EU to default on its creditors" (Traynor and Rankin 2016). After the announcement of the referendum in July 2015, the Eurogroup adjourned financial assistance. The ECB (2015) decided not to increase liquidity for the Greek banks through the Emergency Liquidity Assistance (ELA), despite increased needs caused by an extended bank run. It also excluded Greece from the "Quantitative Easing" programme, while it offered this lending option to all other Eurozone member states. As noted by De Grauwe (2016), contrary to the ECB's claims, this exclusion was "not the result of some unsurmountable technical problem", but the result of "discrimination against Greece" and "a political decision that aims at punishing a country that has misbehaved".

These kinds of tensions in the Eurozone countries between national electorates (especially Greek but also Italian and other) on the one hand, and the

---

[4]   For instance, in Perama, a working-class municipality in Pireus faced with extreme poverty, "No" scored 76.64 per cent of the vote. Perama's inhabitants are mainly workers in the shipbuilding industry, which, however, declined heavily over the last decades due to global competition, which left the Greek shipbuilding sector behind such countries as Taiwan and Turkey. As a result, in that socially and environmentally degraded area, unemployment has skyrocketed at more than double the national average. On the contrary, in Ekali, an upper-class small area at North Athens, the Yes vote dominated with 84.62 per cent. Ekali's population consists of Greek elites, mainly industrialists, ship owners and high status managers, and the area's houses are the most expensive in the country.

(national or international) supporters of the Eurozone's liberalism on the other, take us to Polanyi's (2001, p. 74) descriptions of the pressures exercised on democracy in the interwar period by international liberalism's demands and priorities. They apply to Greece too, given that since 2010, a series of heterogeneous governmental parties have to conform to austerity programmes, *regardless* of their pre-electoral campaigns or the social effects their policies cause. As a result, whatever the vote, authoritarian neoliberalism remains unaltered. After the referendum in 2015, Greece has lost, for an indeterminate period of time, the chance to defend itself against the Eurozone's liberal pressures. As for Italy, it "now resembles Greece, in that it can neither hope to recover on its own nor to be saved by others" (Streeck 2018, p. 185). Notably, demands for "modernization" in the sense of fiscal and constitutional reform for the shrinking of democratic rights concern not only Greece, but the European South in general. According, for instance, to a J.P. Morgan (2013) report:

> Constitutions [in the periphery] tend to show a strong socialist influence [...]. Political systems around the periphery typically display several of the following features: weak executives; weak central states relative to regions; constitutional protection of labor rights; consensus building systems which foster political clientalism; and the right to protest if unwelcome changes are made to the political status quo. [...] Countries around the periphery have only been partially successful in producing fiscal and economic reform agendas, with governments constrained by constitutions (Portugal), powerful regions (Spain), and the rise of populist parties (Italy and Greece).

This mentality that heterogeneous democratic specificities within different national contexts have to be restructured so as to conform to market norms is expressed by Eurozone leaders too. The "Five Presidents' Report" (Junker et al. 2015) is one out of many examples of the plans for the Eurozone's future architecture. The report calls for "economic convergence", which, as it is stressed, should mean common liberalization rather than "income equalization". It asks for more "sharing" of national sovereignty in order to promote "sound policies" and supports investments, which, however, should neither "equalize incomes between Member States", nor "undermine the incentives [...] to address national structural weaknesses" (Junker et al. 2015, p. 15). Given that the Euro regime has become "a gigantic, and indeed hubristic, gamble of technocratic social engineering" (Scharpf 2016, p. 23), this is in the name of a "convergence" to competitiveness and neoliberal restructuring.

4. FINAL REMARKS

In the interwar period, Polanyi experienced the rise of policies of economic self-sufficiency and nationalism triggered by financial and currency crises.

Although he did not advocate economic self-sufficiency, he was critical of the League of Nations' efforts to reintroduce the gold standard, the austerity programmes it imposed and what he described as the "identification of inter-nationalism with the international gold standard" (Polanyi 1937–8). This is alarming for a similar identification today, expressed for instance not only by Angela Merkel's motto "if the Euro fails, then Europe fails" (Deutscher Bundestag 2010), but also by many of the Greek Memoranda supporters and advocates of this idea.

As for the causes of the 1930s crisis, Polanyi (1933, p. 11) did not share the mainstream view which blamed the USA for limiting money supply, but shared "the opposite criticism, that American policies of [...] mindless capital exports were responsible for the crisis". Topical today, he further believed that the US should have forgiven the debt of the countries defeated in the First World War instead of pressing them for a total repayment, while at the same time injecting new loans to them. He was in favour of "political solutions" (Polanyi 1933, p. 11) to debt impasses, but he also emphasized these were not desired in liberalism – and this is confirmed regarding the Eurozone's stance towards the Greek public debt. Most importantly, reliance on loans, as is the case in today's debt and financialization economies, was for Polanyi a method to just *postpone* a total crisis: "Europe is witnessing the dire economic consequences of the postponement of the crisis by artificially enhanced consumption, and excess dependence on credit by debtors and creditors, alike" (Polanyi 1933, p. 12).

Polanyi's argument on the "postponement of the crisis" (and, in a similar spirit, Streeck's 2014 analysis of post-war democratic capitalism "buying time") understands the coexistence of capitalism and democracy as an "illusion of harmony" (Polanyi n.d. [a]), and, thus, takes for granted that the various endeavours to bridge them can neither always be successful nor aspire to be permanent. The crack in this fragile "harmony" deepens in crisis times, as happened after 2010. Fears still haven't melted away today, as those expressed at the beginning of the Eurozone crisis by the IMF chief back then, Christine Lagarde, of a "1930s moment", namely "a moment where trust and cooperation break down and countries turn inward" (BBC News 2012). Just when the threat of a "1930s moment" is thought over, a new source of threat for international markets re-emerges in another country, by another triggering event. National crises are "resolved" by means of international pressure and former Eurozone doubters are forced to conform to stability policies, hoping for a change in the international power articulation at some point in the future. Various neo-fascist parties struggle for electoral gains, speculating on an increasing social resentment caused by the unprecedented attack on social income, the shrinking of welfare services and a deepening gap between the electorate's will and the implemented, actual economic policies. As put by Streeck (2018, p. 186, original emphasis), these impasses have resulted in an "emerging *société bloquée* of Europe", while politics "continues to deteriorate into ritualistic symbolism, following the hard-won insight of power holders [...] that politics cannot oppose global markets and therefore should not even try to do so".

Today, there are suggestions of "bringing back Polanyi to Brussels" (Huebner 2014) and remarks that "if policymakers in Athens, Brussels, and Berlin want to avoid risking the uncontrolled disintegration of the European economic space, it's time to take a cautionary look back at The Great Transformation" (Fuller 2015). Such suggestions do not imply an uncritical espousal of Polanyi's interpretative schemes, but rather serve as reminders that today's blind devotion to hard currency policies, deflation, and the neglect of the social effects of economic policy are along similar lines to the policies followed in the interwar period, and can, thus, lead to similar social and political outcomes as those described by Polanyi.

REFERENCES

BBC News (2012), 'IMF's Christine Lagarde warns of "1930s moment"', 27 January, accessed 3 July 2018 at www.bbc.co.uk/news/business-16689211.

Bruff, I. (2014), 'The rise of authoritarian neoliberalism', *Rethinking Marxism*, 26 (1), 113–29.

Burawoy, M. (2014), 'Marxism after Polanyi', in M. Williams and V. Satgar (eds), *Marxisms in the 21st century: Crisis, critique and struggle*, Johannesburg: Wits University Press, pp. 34–52.

De Grauwe, P. (2016), 'The ECB grants debt relief to all Eurozone nations except Greece', *Greece@LSE*, London School of Economics Blog, 14 June, accessed 4 July 2018 at http://blogs.lse.ac.uk/greeceatlse/2016/06/14/the-ecb-grants-debt-relief-to-all-eurozone-nations-except-greece/.

Deutscher Bundestag (2010), 'Scheitert der Euro, dann scheitert Europa', accessed 3 July 2018 at www.bundestag.de/dokumente/textarchiv/2010/29826227_kw20_de_stabilisierungsmechanismus/201760.

European Central Bank (2015), 'ELA to Greek banks maintained at its current level', 28 June, accessed 2 July 2018 at www.ecb.europa.eu/press/pr/date/2015/html/pr150628.en.html.

European Stability Mechanism (2018), 'Greece: Ongoing Program ESM/EFSF, Explainer', accessed 5 April 2018 at www.esm.europa.eu/assistance/greece#explainer.

Feld, L. (2018), Interview [in Greek]. *Nea*, 10 March, accessed 3 April 2018 at www.tanea.gr/interview/article/5525526/h-ellada-xreiazetai-prolhptikh-grammh-pistwshs/.

Fraser, N. (2017), *Why two Karls are better than one: Integrating Polanyi and Marx in a critical theory of the current crisis*, Working Paper der DFG-Kolleg 'Post-Growth Societies', Jena: DFG-Kollegforscher_innengruppe.

Fuller, G. (2015), 'Polanyi's lesson for Europe', *EurActiv*, accessed 12 May 2018 at www.euractiv.com/sections/elections/polanyis-lesson-europe -311525.

Greek Institute of Labour (INE/GSEE) (2018), *Greek economy and employment: Annual report 2018*, accessed 20 June 2018 at www.inegsee.gr/ ekdosi/etisia-ekthesi-2018-ine-gsee-i-elliniki-ikonomia-ke-i-apascholisi/.

Greek Ministry of Interior (2018), *Election results*, accessed 10 May 2018 at http://ekloges-prev.singularlogic.eu/v2009/pages/index.html.

Hayek, F. (1976), *Denationalisation of money*, London: Institute of Economic Affairs.

Huebner, K. (2014), 'Why Brussels needs to read Karl Polanyi', *Social Europe*, 28 November, accessed 24 June 2018 at www.socialeurope.eu/karl-polanyi.

Jessop, B. (2016), *The state: Past, present, future*, Cambridge: Polity Press.

J.P. Morgan (2013), 'The Euro area adjustment: About halfway there', *Europe Economic Research*, accessed 20 July 2018 at https://culturaliberta. files.wordpress.com/2013/06/jpm-the-euro-area-adjustment-about-halfway -there.

Juncker, J.-C., D. Tusk, J. Dijsselbloem, M. Draghi and M. Schulz (2015), 'Completing Europe's economic and monetary union', European Commission, accessed 20 July 2018 at http://ec.europa.eu/priorities/ economic-monetary-union/docs/5-presidents-report_en.pdf.

Kanter, J. and J. Yardley (2015), 'Greek debt crisis intensifies as extension request is denied', *New York Times*, 27 June, accessed 2 May 2018 at www .nytimes.com/2015/06/28/world/europe/for-eurozone-a-day-of-dueling -agendas-on-greek-debt.html.

Markantonatou, M. (2013), 'Fiscal discipline through internal devaluation and discourses of rent-seeking: The case of the crisis in Greece', *Studies in Political Economy*, 91 (1), 59–83.

Oberndorfer, L. (2015), 'From new constitutionalism to authoritarian constitutionalism: New economic governance and the state of European democracy', in J. Jäger and E. Springler (eds), *Asymmetric crisis in Europe and possible futures*, London: Routledge, pp. 186–208.

Pettifor, A. (2015), 'The euro, like the gold standard, is doomed to fail', *Social Europe*, 31 May, accessed 24 May 2018 at www.socialeurope.eu/the-euro -like-the-gold-standard-is-doomed-to-fail.

Polanyi, K. (n.d. [a]), *The fascist virus*, Montréal: Karl Polanyi Institute for Political Economy [18/08].

Polanyi, K. (n.d. [b]), *Marx on corporativism*, Montréal: Karl Polanyi Institute of Political Economy [19/11].

Polanyi, K. (1933), 'The mechanism of the world economic crisis', trans. Kari Polanyi-Levitt ['Der Mechanismus der Weltwirtschaftskrise', *Der Österreichische Volkswirt*, 25, 3–11].

Polanyi, K. (1935), 'The essence of fascism', in J. Lewis, K. Polanyi and D.K. Kitchin (eds), *Christianity and the social revolution*, London: Victor Gollancz [Montréal: Karl Polanyi Institute of Political Economy, 13/06].

Polanyi, K. (1937–8), *Conflicting philosophies in modern society*, Montréal: Karl Polanyi Institute of Political Economy [15/02].

Polanyi, K. (1939), *Coercion and defence*, Montréal: Karl Polanyi Institute of Political Economy [20/16].

Polanyi, K. (2001), *The great transformation: The political and economic origins of our time*. Boston: Beacon Press.

Presidenza Della Republica (2018), 'Declaration by the President of the Republic Sergio Mattarella at the end of consultations with Professor Giuseppe Conte', 25 May, accessed 2 June 2018 at www.quirinale.it/elementi/1417.

Savona, P. (2018), *Come un incubo e come un sogno: Memorialia e moralia di mezzo secolo di storia*, Soveria Mannelli: Rubbettino.

Scharpf, F. (2016), *Forced structural convergence in the Eurozone: Or a differentiated European monetary community*, MPIfG Discussion Paper 16/15, Köln: Max Planck Institute for the Study of Societies.

Streeck, W. (2014), *Buying time: The delayed crisis of democratic capitalism*, London and New York: Verso.

Streeck, W. (2018), 'Europe under Merkel IV', *American Affairs*, 2 (2), 162–92.

The Holy See (1891), *Rerum novarum: Encyclical of Pope Leo XIII: On capital and labor*, accessed 12 July 2018 at http://w2.vatican.va/content/leo-xiii/en/encyclicals/documents/hf_l-xiii_enc_15051891_rerum-novarum.html.

The Holy See (1931), *Quadragesimo anno: Encyclical of Pope Pius XI: On reconstruction of the social order*, accessed 12 July 2018 at http://w2.vatican.va/content/pius-xi/en/encyclicals/documents/hf_p-xi_enc_19310515_quadragesimo-anno.html.

The White House (2017), 'Remarks by President Trump and Prime Minister Tsipras of Greece in joint press conference', 17 October, accessed 1 March 2018 at www.whitehouse.gov/briefings-statements/remarks-president-trump-prime-minister-tsipras-greece-joint-press-conference/.

Traynor, I. and J. Rankin (2016), 'Greek failure to make IMF payment deals historic blow to Eurozone', *The Guardian*, 20 June, accessed 14 January 2018 at www.theguardian.com/world/2015/jun/30/eurozone-emergency-greece-without-financial-lifeline.

Wishart, I. (2018), 'EU smacks down German official over "lecture" to Italian voters', *Bloomberg*, 30 May, accessed 3 July 2018 at www.bloomberg.com/news/articles/2018-05-29/eu-smacks-down-german-official-over-lecture-to-italian-voters.

Zielonka, J. (2018), 'Harakiri, Italian style', *Social Europe*, 30 May, accessed 24 June 2018 at www.socialeurope.eu/harakiri-italian-style.

9. Political Islam as reactionary countermovement

Ayşe Buğra

Karl Polanyi's analysis of the basic incompatibility of the market economy with human society resonates well with our contemporary concerns about the social and human consequences of market expansion through the late twentieth-century economic globalization. Current discussions on rising inequality within and between nations, constant threat of unemployment and the increasing significance of precarious employment, and the alarming reality of environmental degradation are not difficult to frame in terms of a Polanyian approach. Yet, there is a second and less explored aspect of Polanyi's contemporary relevance, which is found in his approach to the political developments that have accompanied and followed the rise and fall of the "nineteenth-century civilization", whose "collapse" was announced in the opening sentence of *The Great Transformation*. His discussion of different political forms taken by the inevitable reaction of the society to the tensions inherent in the market economy offers important insights to the attempts to examine the political currents of our times.

This chapter draws on Polanyi's work in an investigation of the rise of political Islam in Turkey after the insertion of the country into the global market economy as a "reactionary countermovement" which presents a society-specific response to the social disruptions associated with market expansion. While the response was society-specific, it was also in line with the present context of global politics where the rise of reactionary political currents is now widely discussed with reference to the cases of "illiberal", "authoritarian" or "populist" political parties and politicians in many different countries including Western democracies (Krastev 2007; Mudde 2004; Müller 2016).

Reactionary approaches to politics and society have always been part of modernity and they are discussed in different ways in the literature (Hirschman

1991; Lilla 2016; Robin 2011).[1] In this chapter, the term reactionary is used to designate a particular imagination of history where the harmony of social existence is said to have been disrupted by a political intervention of a revolutionary or reformist character, and a conceptualization of justice which excludes the universalist ideals of Enlightenment thought.

The chapter draws attention to two developments which have been important in shaping the present context of global politics where political currents exhibiting the characteristics of such a reactionary outlook could appear as viable channels in which the feelings of insecurity caused by market-led socio-economic transformations could be expressed. First, the disappointing performance of both "actually existing socialism" and "national developmentalism" in late industrializing countries has left an important vacuum in the political arena. Second, the "cultural turn", which was situated in the same context with late twentieth-century globalization, has created an intellectual atmosphere where the claims of justice formulated in a language of individual liberties, political rights and socio-economic equality have been dominated by affirmations of cultural difference and the appeal of identity politics. This chapter argues that the recent trajectory of political Islam in Turkey was shaped by these characteristics of the global context as well as by domestic factors.

1.   POLANYI'S IDEA OF THE COUNTERMOVEMENT REVISITED

In *The Great Transformation*, we find an analysis of the market economy as a self-regulating order functioning on the basis of its own "natural laws". This economic order *disembedded* from society was, according to Polanyi, "a historical aberration", "a stark utopia" which had a devastating impact on the social and natural environment and presented a deadly danger to the society. An important aspect of the *disembeddedness* of the economy was the treatment of labour, land (or more broadly nature) and money as commodities, which, as Polanyi discussed in one of the most striking passages of *The Great Transformation*, presented a deadly danger to the human and natural substance of the society as well as its productive organization (Polanyi 1957, p. 73). No society could remain indifferent to such a threat, and the emergence of a defensive movement for the self-protection of society was inevitable. There was, therefore, an interaction between market expansion and the rise of protectionist demands translated into definite types of political intervention; hence, a "double movement" was set in motion in all market societies of the nineteenth

---

[1]   In these discussions, the names of Burke, Tocqueville and Hayek are often mentioned as prominent examples of reactionary thinkers.

century. As Polanyi put it: "For a century, the dynamics of modern society was governed by a double movement: the market expanded continuously but this movement was met by a countermovement checking the expansion in definite directions" (Polanyi 1957, p. 130).

Turkey entered the global market economy after the military intervention of 1980, in an environment where the left was severely repressed and the whole political arena was redesigned. At the same time, an unregulated market economy was established with economic policy changes consisting in the deregulation of major macroeconomic indicators such as the foreign exchange rate and the rate of interest, liberalization of trade and foreign direct investment and, at the end of the decade, financial liberalization. These were important steps towards the commodification of labour, land and money, a process which proceeded with further measures eliminating agricultural support mechanisms and deregulating labour markets.

At the end of the 1980s, there were some changes in the tightly controlled political environment where the redistributive dynamics of market expansion could continue without being challenged. These changes were followed by country-wide labour activism; while the labour movement could achieve initial success in blocking and even reversing the downward trend in wages, it was powerless to prevent the emergence of flexible employment relations. Practices such as subcontracting, outsourcing and home-based employment of especially women have emerged as part of an environment where labour was controlled even more effectively than by a repressive political regime. Formal employment in manufacturing shrank in size, labour market informality significantly increased while the dissolution of peasant agriculture continued.

While the ideological environment was clearly hostile to state intervention, the policy environment was not characterized by fiscal restraint and budgetary discipline. Government spending, internal borrowing and the budget deficit kept increasing. Both the inflationary pressures and the political tendency to interfere in the money market to keep the interest rates low in order to sustain economic growth could not be controlled. A major financial crisis which hit the country in 1994 clearly revealed the hazards of politically manipulating interest rates in the inflationary environment of a financially liberalized economy highly vulnerable to capital outflow.

It was in this environment that political Islam appeared as a promising alternative to the existing market-dominated economic order, as, in other words, the political form taken by the countermovement in Turkey. This was a development which could well be explained in Polanyian terms. As Polanyi wrote, the countermovement was neither shaped by narrowly defined economic interests of particular social classes nor by ideological positions. "At innumerable disconnected points it set in without any traceable links between the interests directly affected or any ideological conformity between them" (Polanyi 1957,

p. 149); the challenge of market expansion was to society as a whole, and the response came from society as a whole. Like the expansion of market relations, the societal reaction it triggered was global. Yet, the widespread call for the protection of the social and natural fabric of society had different political channels and was translated into different forms of intervention which were society-specific. In some countries the supporting political forces could be violently reactionary and anti-socialist while in others they could be liberal or social democrat (Polanyi 1957, p. 147).

An analysis of the forms these political forces take in the contemporary market economy would require an examination of the characteristics of the current context of global politics along with society-specific factors. One could begin such an examination by remembering an observation Polanyi made in the 1950s: "The great experience of the past thirty years is that fascism is possible and socialism can go wrong" (Rotstein 1956).

In the context of the return of the market economy with the late twentieth-century economic globalization, it was clear that socialism can go wrong, and the collapse of "actually existing" socialism has been significant in making the claim to universality of the market economy difficult to refute. At the same time, the transition to a market economy was presented also as a transition from authoritarianism to democracy, from state repression to individual freedom. This type of optimism, which was accompanied by the readiness to accept the basic tenets of the market economy, was especially strong in post-communist countries. In Turkey, the failure of the developmentalist state to achieve the objectives of stable economic progress and political democracy had led to a widespread critical reappraisal of the republican past in its economic as well as cultural dimensions. Much less attention was paid to the impact of the ongoing socio-economic transformations on the life and livelihood of Turkey. As political intervention was associated with the authoritarian state, economic regulation and planning ceased to be attractive subjects of discussion among economists.

Many Turkish intellectuals would in fact share Vaclav Havel's position in a "conversation" with Adam Michnik in 1991 (Matynia 2014). As Havel put it, "The fact that everything should be privately owned and that there is a law of supply and demand is for me obvious. But I don't treat it as ideology, as the meaning of life, or as a utopia, but rather as something that has been tested for several centuries, resonates with human nature, and functions in a natural way" (Matynia 2014, p. 72).

While Michnik felt the need to ask "Is the era of ideology really ending?", Havel found good reason to believe that "the era of ideology" was over and expressed his confidence in the disposition of human nature to pluralist thinking which would prevent ideological conflict in the new epoch (Matynia 2014, pp. 52–3). This was an interesting combination of the belief in a single "natural" economic order and in the "natural" inclination of people towards multiple ways of thinking about the world.

This perspective on the emerging world order resonated quite well with celebrations of "diversity" of cultures in the anti-universalist trends which accompanied the late twentieth-century economic globalization. In the atmosphere of the cultural turn, often justifiable attempts at highlighting the disadvantages related to ethnic identity went together with multiculturalist approaches (Gutmann 1994), which insisted on the legitimacy of culturally informed social relations, and the ideas of "alternative modernity"[2], where different social and political institutions said to be rooted in the society's culture were presented as part of the irrefutable reality of modern global order[3].

The call for the recognition of and respect for cultural difference often came from left liberal circles and reflected justified concerns with the cultural disadvantages which affected different minority groups' terms of integration in society. However, as writers such as Anne Phillips – who were clearly aware of the injustices stemming from such disadvantages – remarked, the emphasis of cultural difference at times overshadowed the problems of redistributive justice and deep-set economic inequalities stemming from the operation of market forces (Phillips 1999). The affirmations of cultural diversity were situated in a context where the standardization of economic institutions according to the logic of the market economy could proceed unchallenged given the demise of both the Keynesian welfare state and national developmentalism, and it was indeed remarkable that "the 'cultural turn' came in the midst of a headlong flight globally from a century long search for distributive and political justice" as Arif Dirlik observed (Dirlik 2013, p. 17).

Yet, as Bauman wrote, it was perhaps not surprising that the quest for cultural community constituted a channel for the expression of the need for security and belonging which the nation state, under pressure from the dynamics of economic globalization, could no longer provide (Bauman 1996). In this setting, it was also observed that the right was actually better placed than the left to appropriate and politically use the appeal to culture (Berman 2018; Hobsbawm 1996). The imagination of cultural specificity could thus appear as a salient element in a conservative discourse incorporating the promise of a life in harmony which hardly extended to the questioning of the market-generated disruptions in the livelihood of people.

---

[2]   See for example the issue on 'Multiple Modernities' of *Daedalus* 2000; for a critical evaluation of the idea, see Dirlik 2013.

[3]   For a discussion of these developments in relation to Polanyi's work, see Buğra 2018.

The global environment of the cultural turn was, therefore, also an environment conducive to the empowerment of reactionary political currents with a potential to fill the vacuum left by the demise of the socialist alternative to the market economy. It was in this context that a typically reactionary framing of justice, where the ideals of equality and individual freedom are replaced by the emphasis of social cohesion and harmony, where the claims for social rights are dominated by references to need and need satisfaction through private or public charity as a moral obligation, has become salient in the realm of politics and policy.[4] In a parallel vein, deviations from liberal democracy that are now globally observed have begun to present a challenge to equal political rights to question and to contest the political choices made by elected governments. Authoritarian interpretations of representational justice have become increasingly salient (Krastev 2007; Müller 2016).

Such attitudes towards social and political rights have been clearly present in the post-1980 trajectory of political Islam in Turkey.

2.   THREE LIVES OF POLITICAL ISLAM IN TURKEY

Islamic references had always been a crucial element in right-wing political discourse in Turkey and even the most ardent defenders of secularism would carefully avoid contesting the place of religion in the country's cultural universe. The explicitly Islamist "National Outlook Movement" made its appearance in the political scene at the beginning of the 1970s and was represented by a series of political parties, including the MSP (*Milli Selamet Partisi* – National Salvation Party) in the 1970s, the RP (*Refah Partisi* – Welfare Party) in the 1990s, and the AKP (*Adalet ve Kalkınma Partisi* – Justice and Development Party) since the 2000s; these parties all had their leaders and cadres formed in the National Outlook Movement. However, the continuity was accompanied by important changes both in the significance of the place of political Islam in the national political arena and in the discourse and strategy of the parties representing it.

---

[4]   The idea that private charity is the right way of dealing with indigence is a significant feature of reactionary thought. See, in particular: de Tocqueville [1835] 1997; Burke [1795] 2010. Writing against the Keynesian Welfare State in the 1950s, Hayek's rejection of public assistance was not as categorical as those of Burke and Tocqueville, but he shared the same reactionary spirit in his arguments around the inevitability of inequality and the socially dangerous nature of egalitarian social policy (Hayek 1960, pp. 85–102). For the salience of the approaches that insist on the role of philanthropy in contemporary social policy approaches in general and in Turkey in particular, see Buğra 2016.

In the 1970s, the MSP was part of three short-lived coalition governments. In one of these governments, the MSP was the junior partner of the centre-left CHP (*Cumhuriyet Halk Partisi* – Republican People's Party) and this was not met with a strong negative reaction from the very secularist constituency of the latter. Both parties appealed to the masses with their populist discourse and both made the big business community rather uncomfortable. In fact, the MSP's approach was very much in line with a national developmentalist orientation, where the protection of the national heavy industry and the policies supporting small and medium enterprises were emphasized. The party's discourse was strongly anti-Western which, in spite of the strong dose of anti-Semitism it incorporated, was not really out of line with the strategies of "de-linking with the imperialist world order" found in the dependency approach then very popular in development theory and policy.

After the military intervention of 1980, the MSP was closed along with all the other political parties. In the 1990s, in the chaotic environment of the market economy, political Islam, which was represented first by the RP and then the AKP, has enjoyed an increasing popular support and also begun to exhibit typically reactionary characteristics.

The RP, under the leadership of Erbakan who was also the leader of the closed MSP, was the winner of the municipal elections held in 1994. After these elections Erdoğan became the mayor of Istanbul; he would later appear as the founding leader of the AKP and become first the Prime Minister and then the President of the country with ever expanding powers.

In the general elections of 1995, the RP came out as the first party and formed a coalition government with a centre-right party. The RP was obviously not a marginal political actor like the MSP, which could at most get around 9 per cent of the popular vote by appealing to a largely uneducated and disadvantaged segment of the population, with more success in rural than in urban areas. The constituency of the RP included people from many different walks of life, which was not surprising since, in the absence of any viable left-wing opposition, the party appeared as the only political actor that could effectively respond to the widespread feelings of insecurity associated with the dynamics of market-oriented transformation.

The novel salience of Islamic politics, too, would not be surprising if one remembered how Polanyi insisted that the challenge of market expansion was to society as a whole and not only to its material existence but also to its cultural way of life[5]. However, in the Turkish case one feels compelled to ask what this cultural way of life threatened by the market society was. Turkey's cultural way of life challenged by market expansion had been shaped through

---

5   See, especially, Polanyi 1957, pp. 151–62.

more than half a century of republican secular modernization; social relations and institutions hardly conformed to Islamic norms. Turkey's insertion to the global market economy did not constitute, therefore, a challenge to a social order shaped around Muslim culture. It was, in fact, the secular republican order whose institutional fabric was being torn apart. Nevertheless, political Islam, which owed its electoral success to the frustrations caused by the new types of inequality and insecurity in the market economy, defined itself as a force of reaction to the secular republican order.

Those elements of a left-wing, third-worldist language of national developmentalism, which were salient in the MSP's discourse, were now replaced by a new type of emphasis on culture. While the MSP appealed to Islam as the centre-piece of the country's value universe rather than the basis of the institutional order of the economy and society, the RP's Islamism seemed to be more in line with Kymlicka's multiculturalist notion of a "civilizational culture", which does not only incorporate "shared memories and values, but common institutions and practices" (Kymlicka 1996, p. 76). A thorough institutional restructuring informed by Islamic norms was now on the agenda. The establishment of a "just order" was central to the RP's political programme and, at the level of discourse the project seemed to be aiming at a re-embedding of the economy in a Muslim society (Akgül 1991; Refah Partisi 1992).

The substantive content, on the other hand, did not really match the promise. The response to the commodification of labour largely consisted in statements about the mutual trust that would prevail between the employer, who is affectionate and just to his employees, and the worker, who is respectful and hard working. These statements were supported with reference to Koranic verses or the words attributed to the Prophet to set the cultural context. The question of credit was approached in a somewhat more systematic manner by insisting on the Islamic prohibition of charging interest on credit. An alternative Islamic model was presented to replace interest-based credit by what is called *selem* credit, extended against the promise of future delivery of goods at the time of their production. Nevertheless, even business actors and business-oriented intellectuals within the party were sceptical of such ideas, which some of them dismissed as "mere fantasies"[6].

Religion was more significant as an element in the revanchist attitude against the republican order which marked the radical Islamist project of starting off with a clean slate to establish a "just order" where social cohesion and economic efficiency would prevail together. As Mark Lilla wrote in *The Shipwrecked Mind*, "(Reactionaries) are, in their way, as radical as revolutionaries and just as firmly in the grip of historical imaginings." According to Lilla,

---

[6]   For several contributions around these arguments, see *İktisat Dergisi* 1993.

particularly significant to the making of the reactionary mind is a "narrative of history which begins with a happy state where people who know their place live in harmony, and continues with the alien cultural and intellectual developments which attacked the very roots of this well-ordered state, weakened and finally destroyed it" (Lilla 2016, pp. xii–xiii).The intense hostility of Islamist politics against the secular republican order could well be seen in this particular light.

3.   JUSTICE, EQUALITY AND DEMOCRATIC REPRESENTATION

The conceptualization of justice in the RP's – as later the AKP's – discourse was closely related to a reinterpretation of the "unjust" republican order and the imagination of a "just" society to be built by appealing to Islamic norms. In the political Islamist discourse, but not only there, the domination of the conservative Muslim majority by a secularist elite controlling the state was the underlying theme of justice-related debates. With supporting views also expressed by some respected secular intellectuals, the theme in question has become an established element in political debate, difficult to contest without being labelled as an authoritarian Kemalist or outmoded secularist (Seyhan 2017).[7] As far as the model of a just Islamist society was concerned, it was possible to see a rift between fundamentalist intellectuals who had a prominent position within the constituency of the RP and more pragmatic political and economic actors of the Islamist movement. The Islamist intellectuals were explicit in their rejection of the secularist and individualistic tenets of Western humanism, in which "Man was brutally torn apart from heavenly references", and they could declare, without much difficulty, that democracy and individual freedom are irrelevant to the organizing logic of a Muslim society (Bulaç 1993; Dilipak 1993).

The problem of democracy, which the fundamentalist Islamist intellectualist could afford to discuss with rather shallow criticisms of modern Western societies, constituted an important problem which the RP, as a democratically elected party, had to address in its discourse on justice. In its radical political orientation, the RP presented itself as the legitimate representative of the 98 per cent of the population constituted by Muslims and hence in a position to disregard minority views. A polarizing discourse, which divided the society

---

[7]   Although Seyhan's article does not provide a nuanced analysis of the different authors' views on Turkish politics and society in the republican era, it is useful to give an idea about the elements of the new critical historiography of the period which has unintentionally contributed to the reactionary orientation of political Islam.

into the supporters of the party as "the real people" and the opponents as the alien "others", was used to dismiss the concerns of the secularist opposition. This polarizing language would again surface as a salient characteristic of the political regime in the context of the alarming deviation from the norms of democracy in the later years of AKP rule.

The political right of the opposition to contest the vision and the practices of an elected government as a crucial feature of representative democracy was thus being disregarded with the emergence of a socio-political imaginary where social cohesion was based on the cultural values of the majority. The problem that emerged in the Turkish context was that this social imaginary was not shared by a very large segment of the population. Hence, the RP's electoral victories created an increasingly tense political environment and the tension was exacerbated by certain statements of the party leadership which implied that the means to realize the desired transformation they had in mind did not exclude violence. Particularly significant among these statements was one made after the municipal elections of 1994 when Erbakan, the leader of the party, said "The RP will bring the Just Order, this is clear. Whether the transition period will be smooth or hard, sweet or bloody, 60 million people will decide that".[8] This often quoted statement played an important role in the developments which have led to the collapse of the coalition government led by the RP and the subsequent closing of the party. Another coalition government then formed by centre-right and centre-left parties was unable to maintain the stability of an already very fragile economy and prevent the worst capitalist crisis of modern Turkey in 2001.

After this crisis, a series of market reforms endorsed by international financial institutions were introduced, with the prevention of discretionary political intervention in the economy as their major objective. This institutional restructuring and the accompanying stabilization policies were effective in controlling the crisis, but the population that was made to pay the price for economic stability was quite naturally inclined to accept any alternative to the political actors that were in power during the period of crisis and crisis management. It was, therefore, not difficult to understand the victory in the national elections of 2002 of the very recently formed AKP that had no responsibility in the crisis and the policies subsequently implemented; the outcome of the elections did not really require any explanation based on cultural disadvantage.

With the lessons learned from the predicament of the RP, the AKP was careful not to use a radical Islamist language. Nevertheless, religious refer-

---

[8]   For a "chronicle" of the events that have led to the collapse of the RP-led coalition government through the indirect intervention of the military, see Aljazeera Turk 2013.

ences have continued to be important in the strategy the party followed to maintain and expand its constituency. The developments in the realm of social policy constitute one area where this could be observed.

In this area, labour market reforms and the transformation of the pension and health systems have led to the dismantling of the country's former social security system and the loss of the acquired rights of people covered by this system such as civil servants and formally employed workers. At the same time, however, the newly introduced social assistance measures and family support policies have played a non-negligible role to contain the consequences of the commodification of labour in a market society. Poverty was recognized as a social problem and was dealt with by increasingly significant policies of means-tested social assistance. References to Islamic charity were particularly important in the approaches to this problem, and a large number of religiously motivated philanthropic associations began to be active in the field of social assistance along with public institutions (Göçmen 2014). In fact, the logic of charity has now extended to public social assistance and introduced an element of discretion to the allocation of benefits which has led to concerns about the use of social assistance for political purposes in the elections. Such concerns were not unjustified since the observed increase in social assistance spending prior to elections seemed to indicate that political authorities, too, were aware of the potential of social benefits to affect voting behaviour and shape the use of political rights (Buğra 2016).

There was a considerable increase in public assistance to the family in an approach characterized by a particular form of "supported familialism" designed to ensure that gender relations within the family conformed to the culturally given traditional norms. While the policy discourse also included references to "work–family reconciliation" to encourage female employment, motherhood was clearly what defined the position of women in society and policy framing was not of a nature to aim at their equal participation in working life (Alnıaçık et al. 2017). Today, the female employment rate in Turkey (around 32 per cent) is one of the lowest in the world. Moreover, over 40 per cent of women in employment are in the informal sector (TURKSTAT 2017).

Not only gender inequality but also the inequalities of class kept increasing under AKP rule. This was clearly reflected in the declining share of labour. Between 1995 and 2012, the share of labour has in fact declined in most G20 countries, but the trend was nowhere as strong as it was in Turkey (ILO/OECD 2015). Beyond income inequality, working conditions are extremely hard. Striking statistics on work accidents for example, are indicative of the nature of class relations in Turkey (İşçi Sağlığı ve İş Güvenliği Meclisi 2019).

The increasing inequalities of class were not unrelated to unemployment, which remained high even at times of high growth. The main beneficiaries of economic growth were the politically privileged big business actors, but also the small and medium enterprises that had outsourcing and subcontracting relations with them. They were the winners in an economic orientation where the investments in the construction sector and big infrastructure were the main engines of growth. To bring together the business actors with good relations with the AKP government, religion was used as a "network resource" by some business associations, which were formed and became important through the rise of political Islam since the 1990s. These associations have appealed to the religious identity of conservative Muslim business people and contributed to the development of collaborations in input supply, contract sharing or access to markets in a successful strategy of network formation. The emergence of a "Muslim bourgeoisie" was the result of this strategy, rather than a factor explaining the political success of the AKP as argued by some writers (see, for example, Demiralp 2009; Yavuz 2006). Associations that claimed to represent this Muslim bourgeoisie were prioritized while the others were marginalized by the government. The world of business has thus come to be characterized by the divide between business people and associations that were within the constituency of the AKP and the outsiders (Buğra and Savaşkan 2014).

The polarization of the associational environment was not limited to the realm of business. In social policy related areas, too, one could observe a proliferation of philanthropic associations and women's organizations with an Islamic outlook, as well as a few labour unions whose membership has significantly increased thanks to their good relations first with the RP and then the AKP. In this environment, labour unions and women's organizations with an egalitarian outlook have found themselves in a position to compete with politically privileged unions or NGOs that endorse the terms of a radical trans-formation project where class and gender equality hardly appears as a social objective.

Political Islam, which owed its success to the effect on society of the disruptions caused by the market economy, has thus ended up dividing the society into rival camps, while the country has remained inserted in the global economy. The political environment has been increasingly marked by the dynamics of this polarization. The affirmation of the legitimate right of an elected government to act as the representative of the will of the nation has eventually come to be a salient element in the AKP's political discourse and led to the presentation of the political opposition as a threat to the nation during the general elections. The demonization of the opposition parties has become a permanent feature of the political environment especially after the aborted coup attempt of July 2016, when tens of thousands of people were arrested and over a hundred thousand public employees have lost their jobs along with the possibility of civil employment (Kuran and Rodrik 2018).

The unprecedented dimension of the violations of the rule of law and democracy significantly contributed to the mounting economic problems associated with the way Turkey's market economy functioned. Economic growth in a heavily import dependent economy which relied on the continuous expansion of the construction sector and massive infrastructure investments went together with the uncontrolled increase of public and private debt. Hence, foreign capital inflow acquired a vital significance and the question of maintaining investor confidence constituted a crucial issue. At the same time, continued growth of the economy was necessary to satisfy the inner circle of AKP supporters and to control the rise of poverty. Credit expansion had to continue and the market rules which prevented the government from manipulating money supply and the rate of interest have become politically intolerable. In this environment, Erdoğan, now a president with immense powers over all economic and non-economic institutions began to make statements about keeping interest low, which contributed to a major currency crisis and showed how vulnerable a debt-ridden country was to a sudden halt in foreign lending. The crisis was exacerbated by the increasingly tense relations of Turkey with the USA and Europe. These tensions were largely related to the political situation in Turkey, which no longer seemed compatible with the stable functioning of a market economy.

As this chapter was being written, the anticipations about the possible collapse of the banking system created a chaotic economic environment, to which the political response came in the form of an increasingly nationalist discourse against the foreign and domestic enemies of the nation (Karnitschnig 2018; on the Turkish currency crisis see also Krugman 2018).

4.   IN LIEU OF CONCLUSION

In this chapter, Polanyi's analysis of the countermovement was revisited in a discussion of the political developments of the last two decades in Turkey. Notwithstanding the society-specific nature of these developments, the discussion in this chapter also presented some insights into the recent trends in global politics which now form the subject of intense debates on the rise of "illiberal", "authoritarian" or "populist" political parties and politicians in many different countries.

In Turkey, the crisis of democracy, which was caused by the reactionary political form of the countermovement, has played an important role in reaching the point where repairing the impaired self-regulation does not seem easy. At this point, one sadly remembers Polanyi's statement that "fascism, like socialism was rooted in a market economy that refused to function" (Polanyi 1957, p. 239). In the Turkish case, the emergence of a socialist alternative is a remote possibility, and it remains uncertain whether the country's "habitation" could be restored (Polanyi 1957, p. 249) in a genuine representative democracy.

REFERENCES

Akgül, A. (1991), *İslam davası ve adil düzen* [*The Islamic mission and the just order*], Istanbul: Risale Yayınları.

Aljazeera Turk (2013), *Kronoloji: 28 Şubat'a giden yo*, 27 May, accessed at www.aljazeera.com.tr/kronoloji/kronoloji-28-subata-giden-yol.

Alnıaçık, A., Ö. Altan-Olcay, C. Deniz and F. Gökşen (2017), 'Gender policy architecture in Turkey: Localizing transnational discourses of women's employment', *Social Politics*, 24 (3), 298–323.

Bauman, Z. (1996), 'On communitarians and equal freedom or how to square the circle', *Theory, Culture & Society*, 13 (2), 79–90.

Berman, S. (2018), 'Why identity politics benefits the right more than the left', *The Guardian*, 14 July, accessed at www.theguardian.com/commentisfree/2018/jul/14/identity-politics-right-left-trump-racism.

Buğra, A. (2016), 'Philanthropy and the politics of social policy', in B. Morvaridi (ed.), *New philanthropy and social justice*, Bristol: Policy Press, pp. 117–36.

Buğra, A. (2018), 'Revisiting "freedom in a complex society"', in M. Brie and C. Thomasberger (eds), *Karl Polanyi's vision of socialist transformation*, Montréal: Black Rose, pp. 77–90.

Buğra, A. and O. Savaşkan (2014), *New capitalism in Turkey: The relationship between politics, religion and business*, Cheltenham, UK and Northampton, MA, USA: Edward Elgar Publishing.

Bulaç, A. (1993), *İslam ve demokrasi* [*Islam and democracy*], Istanbul: Beyan Yayınları.

Burke, E. ([1795] 2010), *Thoughts and details on scarcity*, Whitefish, MT: Kessinger Publishing.

Daedalus (2000), special issue on 'Multiple modernities' (2000), *Daedalus*, 129 (1).

De Tocqueville, A. ([1835] 1997), *Memoir on pauperism*, Chicago: Ivan R. Dee.

Demiralp, S. (2009), 'The rise of Islamic capital and the decline of Islamic radicalism in Turkey', *Comparative Politics*, 41 (3), 315–35.

Dilipak, A. (1993), *Sorunlar, sorular ve cevaplar* [*Problems, questions and answers*], Istanbul: Beyan Yayınları.

Dirlik, A. (2013), 'Thinking modernity historically: Is "alternative modernity" the answer?', *Asian Review of World Histories*, 1 (1), 5–44.

Göçmen, İ. (2014), 'Religion, politics and social assistance in Turkey: The rise of religiously motivated associations', *Journal of European Social Policy*, 24 (2), 92–103.

Gutmann, A. (ed.) (1994), *Multiculturalism: Examining the politics of recognition*, Princeton, NJ: Princeton University Press.

Hayek, F. (1960), *The constitution of liberty*, London: Routledge & Kegan Paul.

Hirschman, A.O. (1991), *The rhetoric of reaction*, Cambridge, MA: Harvard University Press.

Hobsbawm, E. (1996), 'Identity politics and the left', *New Left Review*, 217, 38–47.

İktisat Dergisi (1993), 29 (343, November).

ILO/OECD (2015), *The labor share in G20 countries*, report prepared for the G20 Employment Working Group, Antalya, Turkey, 26–27 February, accessed at www.oecd.org/g20/topics/employment-and-social-policy/The -Labour-Share-in-G20-Economies.pdf.

İşçi Sağlığı ve İş Güvenliği Meclisi (2019), *2018 İş Cinayetleri Raporu [2018 Report on Work Murders]*, accessed 9 July 2019 at http://www .guvenlicalisma.org/site_icerik/2019/3mart/isig2018kapak.pdf

Karnitschnig, M. (2018), 'Europe watches as Turkey burns', *Politico*, August, accessed at www.politico.eu/article/recep-tayyip-erdogan-europe-watches -as-turkey-lira-currency-burns/.

Krastev, I. (2007), 'The populist moment', *Eurozine*, 18 September, accessed at www.eurozine.com/the-populist-moment/.

Krugman, P. (2018), 'Partying like it's 1998', *The New York Times*, 11 August.

Kuran, T. and D. Rodrik (2018), 'Economic costs of Erdoğan', *Project Syndicate*, August, accessed at www.project-syndicate.org/commentary/ how-erdogan-caused-turkey-collapse-by-timur-kuran-and-dani-rodrik -2018-08.

Kymlicka, W. (1996), *Multicultural citizenship*, Oxford and New York: Oxford University Press.

Lilla, M. (2016), *The shipwrecked mind: On political reaction*, New York: New York Review of Books.

Matynia, E. (2014), 'The uncanny era of post-communism', in E. Matynia (ed.), *An uncanny era: Conversations between Vaclav Havel and Adam Michnik*, New Haven: Yale University Press.

Mudde, C. (2004), 'The populist zeitgeist', *Government and Opposition*, 39 (4), pp. 541–563.

Müller, W.W. (2016), *What is populism?*, Philadelphia: University of Pennsylvania Press.

Phillips, A. (1999), *Which equalities matter?*, Cambridge: Polity Press.

Polanyi, K. ([1944] 1957), *The great transformation: The political and economic origins of our time*, Boston: Beacon Press.

Refah Partisi, R. (1992), *Adil düzen: 21 soru 21 cevap* [*The just order: 21 questions 21 answers*], Ankara: Refah Partisi.

Robin, C. (2011), *The reactionary mind: Conservatism from Edmund Burke to Donald Trump*, Oxford: Oxford University Press.

Rotstein, A. (1956), *Weekend notes*, Montréal: Karl Polanyi Institute of Political Economy [45/04].

Seyhan, A. (2017), 'Erdoğan and the intellectuals', *Telos*, 181, 205–17.

TURKSTAT (2017), 'Labour force statistics', accessed at www.turkstat.gov .tr/PreHaberBultenleri.do?id=24626.

Yavuz, H. (2006), 'Introduction: The role of the new bourgeoisie in the transformation of the Turkish Islamic movement', in H. Yavuz (ed.), *The emergence of a new Turkey: Democracy and the AK Parti*, Salt Lake City, UT: University of Utah Press, pp. 1–20.

10. "Freedom's utter frustration…": considerations on neoliberal social-policy reforms and the shift to the far-right through Polanyi's theory of fascism

Roland Atzmüller and Fabienne Décieux

1.   INTRODUCTION

In recent years the relevance of Karl Polanyi's approach (Block and Somers 2014; Buğra 2007; Polanyi 2001) for the analysis of the development of capitalist societies since the 1970s was vindicated by the financial and economic crisis of 2008 (Altvater 2010); the subsequent sovereign debt crisis and the imposition of so-called "austerity states" also in the Global North (Jessop 2015, 2017); and the social conflicts and struggles following from these developments. These tendencies were accompanied by the global upsurge of far-right and right-wing populist[1] movements and parties and their entry into governments in many countries (Campani and Sauer 2017; Heinisch 2016), which led to shifts towards illiberal democracies and authoritarianism in some (Becker 2018; Fabry 2019). From a Polanyian perspective, these developments raised the question whether the crises of marketization and financialization (Lapavitsas 2013) since 2008 together with the emergence of far-right and right-wing populist countermovements represent the collapse of financialized capitalism and mark the onset of another "great transformation" of capitalism or whether we are experiencing a radicalization of market expansion on a global scale further deepened by the austerity dominated strategies of crisis

---

[1]   Given the vast array of definitions of right-wing populism parties (Kaltwasser et al. 2017) we decided to use these two terms. Notwithstanding its ideological foundations, we use right-wing populist to depict the ability of certain movements and parties for mass appeal. We also use the term far-right to make clear that many of these movements are part of a longer history of political organizations of the radical right.

management. Against the background of Polanyi's substantivist approach to economics (Jessop 2008; Peck 2013) it would be problematic to debate these problems only on an abstract and formal level or to solely focus on the level of politics and political mobilization in a narrow sense. Therefore, we will try to analyse how the outlined dynamics affect (the re/production of) one of the so-called fictitious commodities (labour, land, money) – namely labour (power) – which constituted the most important of the factors of production for Karl Polanyi (2001, p. 130).

The emergence of a new "movement" of marketization and financialization to overcome the crisis of Fordism since the 1970s (Altvater 2010; Burawoy 2015) was closely related to and even pushed forward by neoliberal strategies to re-commodify labour power through the reorganization and reconfiguration of welfare regimes and social policies (Aulenbacher et al. 2018b; Peck 2001; Scherschel et al. 2012). In this context and given neoliberal aspirations to roll back the state two things are remarkable: first, the success of retrenchment strategies concerning the scope of welfare regimes appears rather limited as welfare expenditures show a remarkable degree of stability in most countries of the Global North so far (Hemerijck 2013; Obinger 2012; Pierson 2011). Thus, notwithstanding its contradictory dynamics the new "movement" of market expansion remains tied to certain social institutions, which regulate and organize the fictitious commodity status of labour (power) and its repro-duction. Second, right-wing populism is not a recent phenomenon that would only be geared against globalization. At least some of the neoliberal reform projects (in particular in the UK) were pushed forward and legitimized through "authoritarian populist" strategies (Hall 1980) of (welfare) state reform from the very start (Bruff 2013; Davidson and Saull 2017).

These developments raise three questions about the continuing relevance of Karl Polanyi's approach for the analysis of contemporary developments of capitalist societies. These questions concern the conceptualization of markets and their dynamics as well as relations – termed "social-embedding" (Gemici 2007) in a Polanyi inspired analysis – to other social spheres such as the state (Jessop 2016); the conceptualization of capitalist development between "movements" of marketization and so-called "countermovements" of society; and the conceptualization of far-right and right-wing populist "countermove-ments" and the political programmes and strategies they try to implement to tackle the crisis of capitalist market societies in particular. Given the inten-sifying attempts of right-wing populist and far-right parties and movements to develop and implement coherent policy programmes (Becker 2018; Fabry 2019; Heinisch 2016) it becomes necessary to understand how they grasp emerging tensions and contradictions in concrete social fields such as the reproduction of labour (power) as a fictitious commodity to assess their role in the recurring crises of capitalist societies. To offer some insights into these questions we will go back to Polanyi's conceptualization of fascism (Polanyi 2001, 2018a, 2018b, 2018c) as it offers a range of interesting conceptual tools to understand the role and function of far-right policies to tackle the crisis of capitalist societies.

In the field of labour market policies authoritarian and right-wing populist policies are defined by a merger of ever more punitive and disciplinarian activation and workfare oriented policies, which combine neoliberal strategies with an ethnicized ("immigration into the social system"), class-based and gendered understanding of unemployment, poverty and social exclusion. Furthermore, the benefit and entitlement regime is reorganized in order to segment beneficiaries according to ethnic but also age related, class-based and gendered lines thereby increasing inequalities among benefit recipients and delegitimizing entitlements of certain groups. This increasingly ties (reduced) benefit levels and access to labour market support services, such as training, to an autochthonous national background and combine them with enforced activities (in particular public work or participation in training or social values oriented education) expected from the poor or unemployed. The required efforts are not simply derived from alleged demands of labour markets but are increasingly framed in cultural and national terms (language and cultural trainings). Even access to basic social security is increasingly tied to age, years of work and tax contributions as an indicator for someone's willingness to work as well as continued presence in a certain state. Furthermore, and linked to this, tax and benefit regimes are reorganized in a way not simply to raise incentives for generative behaviour of the middle classes but to explicitly disadvantage families with a higher number of children, which is geared towards migrant families in particular.

In section 2, we will discuss the dialectics of "movements" and "countermovements" taking into account different possibilities for societies to protect themselves against market expansion. Section 3 will be focused on the relations between markets and states and the role and function the latter develops in and through social struggles – e.g. in the form of social policies – to secure the expanded reproduction of accumulation. In section 4, we will try to apply Polanyi's analysis of fascism for a deepened critique of current right-wing populist and far-right social policies to re-commodify labour (power).

2. THE DIALECTICS OF "MOVEMENTS" AND "COUNTERMOVEMENTS"

It has been highlighted in recent debates that a simplified reading of Polanyi's work – in particular *The Great Transformation* (2001) – runs into the danger of interpreting the development of capitalism as a kind of pendulum (for a detailed debate see Clarke 2014; Dale 2013; Harvey 2014). Thus, capitalism is understood to swing between phases in which market dynamics are more or less free from any social regulation and constraints and evolve in a "pure sense", and phases which are defined by the social embedding of capitalist markets emerging from the protective reactions of societies and states which can take different political and ideological forms (Kiely 2010; Streeck 2016). Such an interpretation could lead to a rather mechanistic conceptualization of history and an underestimation of its openness and non-synchronicity and deny the significance of social struggles and change which has been pointed out in recent critical debates about phases of capitalism and the problems of periodization (Jessop 2007).

One strength of Polanyi's concept of the "double movement" lies in its ability to highlight a fundamental dialectic of capitalist societies (Polanyi 2001, pp. 136 ff.). It remains unclear, however, whether the dialectics between the expansion of capitalist markets and the reactions of societies against it, can be reduced to a binary understanding of "movements" of marketization and protective "countermovements" which aim to socially embed the latter. *First*, protective reactions of societies and in particular social embedding tend to be reduced to state activities, which are understood to be geared against unfettered economic dynamics underestimating the significance of other social spheres (communities, families, etc.). Furthermore, focusing on the state's protective potentials also tends to underestimate the role and function of the state for the dynamics of capitalist markets. *Second*, "protective" reactions of society do not solely rely on the development of (political) institutions, which put constraints on market processes. Rather societies also try to protect themselves against the effects of market expansion through other mechanisms such as the externalization of its destructive dynamics – generally rolled forward by state activities – towards for example subordinated societies in the Global South order or towards certain strata within societies (migrants, ethnic minorities, the poor, women, etc.). For a long time critical analyses of the relations between the Global North and the Global South have pointed out that after 1945, the expansion of capitalism in the North came at the expense of the societies in the South. Recent analyses about the imperial mode of living (Brand and Wissen 2017) have argued that at least certain aspects of the social embedding of capitalism in post-Second World War modes of development rested on the externalization of its destructive effects (Lessenich 2016) on the environment and the Global South.

3.   MARKETS AGAINST WELFARE STATES?

A contemporary application of Polanyi's approach has to avoid to simply counterpose allegedly "pure" markets and their dynamics to socially embedded market dynamics and economics. Such an understanding is highly problematic as it does not transcend the assumption that "pure" market relations – devoid of all social ties and regulations – do and can really "exist" (even though their ability to reproduce might be viewed as limited) (critical: Aglietta [1979] 2000; for the relevance of Polanyi for regulation theory: Boyer and Saillard 2002). For such a perspective, the relations between markets and states might appear as a kind of zero-sum situation. This understanding does not transcend the neoliberal juxtaposing of markets and competition to state intervention and social regulations of the economy and narrows the possibilities to think of alternative modes to organize economy, state and society.

The Great Transformation (2001) is not completely devoid of the latter interpretation. In his later research Polanyi highlighted the fundamentally "instituted" character of the economy in general and markets in particular, even though the latter might reduce economic activities to the dominance of self-interest (Harvey 2014; Polanyi 1957, 1977). The debates about always embedded liberalism (Cahill 2015) also propose an interpretation of the Polanyian approach that aims to take into account the role of the state and politics in an adequate way. These analyses, which are well in line with recent critical debates about the state or the shift from a Fordist mode of development based on certain forms of regulation to the financialization of accumulation (Jessop 2016; Sum and Jessop 2015), make clear why the concept of pure markets constitutes an "economistic fallacy" (Polanyi 1977).

Taken together the outlined considerations were and are of crucial significance for a Polanyian inspired analysis of welfare regimes and social policies, which focus on the (re-)production of labour (power) as a fictitious commodity through its partial de-commodification (Esping-Andersen 1990; Offe 1993). The latter creates a range of tensions and contradictions within different welfare regimes, which are also affected by the actual structure of the economy (e.g. shift from industrial production to service or knowledge-based economies) but also gender divisions of labour or migration movements etc.

Thus, it was a crucial starting point of critical debates about welfare capitalism and welfare states since the 1970s (Esping-Andersen 1990; Offe 1993) to argue – based on a timely combination of Karl Polanyi and Karl Marx – that the (partial) de-commodification of labour (power) and its reproduction in and through welfare services, did not simply shield workers of the centres of capitalism against the risks of capitalist market expansion. Even though it emerged from the social struggles since the first half of the twentieth century it brought about the sustained dynamics of post-Second World War capitalism at the same time. The development of social institutions that protected labour (power) from its total and unlimited availability for capital – i.e. which limited its status as a fictitious commodity – allowed for the dynamics of the Fordist mode of development based on intensive accumulation (Aglietta [1979] 2000).

When Fordism entered into crisis in the 1970s the emerging struggles and conflicts pushed the varied institutional forms to (at least partially) de-commodify labour (power) and its reproduction through social policies centre stage. Neoliberal interpretations portrayed the de-commodifying limitations put on the usage of labour as one of the main reasons for the evolving crisis of the post-war growth models (Cahill et al. 2017). The emerging and triumphant neoliberal reform projects since the end of the 1970s began to restructure institutional settings of welfare regimes in order to enforce an encompassing re-commodification of labour (power) and to push back regulations that limited its availability for capital. On the one hand, so-called activation and workfare-oriented policies were rolled forward. They aim at focusing social policies towards activities to integrate the unemployed, as well as other economically inactive people who have no legitimate reason (e.g. motherhood) for non-participation, into the labour market as quickly as possible. Instead of changing markets to reach these goals these policies are focused on adapting people to the demands of increasingly flexible and precarious markets (Dörre and Haubner 2012; Lessenich 2012; Starke et al. 2016). On the other hand so-called social investment strategies (Hemerijck 2013, 2017; Morel et al. 2012), which aim at re-legitimizing the role of the state for the economy, have gained in importance in recent years. These strategies mainly focus on the permanent adaption and recomposition of the skills and competencies – i.e. their human capital – of individuals but also demand an expansion of childcare facilities to mobilize women for the labour market (Aulenbacher et al. 2018a).

The developments pushed forward by neoliberal reform projects pose a range of challenges for an adequate understanding of the tensions and ambivalences surrounding the evolution and crises of capitalist societies since the 1970s. The imposition of neoliberal reform projects to unleash a new "movement" of market expansion was often accompanied by and enforced through "authoritarian populist" mobilization and reform strategies, were geared against the Fordist mode of development and its crisis. This was in particular true for welfare reforms under Margaret Thatcher (UK) or Ronald Reagan (USA) (Davidson and Saull 2017; Kiely 2017) since the early 1980s but also for the developments in countries of the South such as Chile, which became the first laboratory of neoliberal economic and welfare reform after the coup d'état in 1973 and the installation of a dictatorship under Pinochet (Fischer 2009).

Notwithstanding its far-reaching triumph the polarizing and fragmenting dynamics of welfare reform under neoliberal dominance led to a range of aporias and contradictions. These emerge from the fact that neoliberal reform projects had to position themselves against the potential, albeit always contested universalism of the Keynesian welfare regimes which promised an improvement of living conditions for everyone. The latter constituted a field of social conflict and dynamics in which subjects could fight for greater individual autonomy (Vobruba 2003) from their social origin, gender, ethnic background, religious affiliation, etc. Against expanding state regulations of the struggles for autonomy, neoliberal welfare reforms reinstated the "self-regulating market" as a kind of universalist utopia – very much in the sense of how Polanyi had analysed it for the nineteenth century (2001). Re-commodification constituted a promise to give every able-bodied adult the opportunity of self-fulfilment through participation in gainful employment. Integration into the labour market at any cost became the fundamental tenet of neoliberal social policies assuming that this would help every hard working individual to climb the social ladder.

The gendered, ethnicized and class-based, but also ageist, structuration of capitalist labour markets, which bring about higher rates of unemployment, precarity and poverty for certain social groups, have been deepened by neoliberal reforms. In the recurrent crises of market expansion and financialization they are increasingly clashing with the universalist aspirations of neoliberal reform projects to secure enforced labour market participation for every able-bodied adult. However, instead of developing strategies to overcome the hierarchical structuration of capitalist societies that result from its divisions of labour, individualist conceptualizations of labour market dynamics as brought forward by neoliberalism are increasingly giving way to ethnicized and culturalist, class-based and gendered interpretations of labour market problems. Right-wing populist and far-right movements propose to interpret labour market problems and poverty as being the result of certain behavioural traits and normative orientations of certain social groups (immigrants, refugees, Muslims, underclass, etc.) and their attitude towards work. Unequal outcomes of capitalist labour markets are seen less as the result of individual effort but rather as the result of cultural, ethnic and other group-based deficits. It is here where Polanyi's account of fascism provides some insights to understand the connections between the aporias and contradictions of neoliberal welfare reform and the emergence of right-wing populist and far-right social policies, which capitalize on these.

4.   A FAR-RIGHT SOLUTION TO THE CRISIS? ABANDONING FREEDOM AND DEMOCRACY

Polanyi's conceptualization of fascism and its role for – what he called – the rescue of capitalism offers a range of interesting insights (Dale 2016; Harootunian 2006; Polanyi 2001, 2018a, 2018b, 2018c; Reynolds 2015) to understand the ambivalent character of far-right and right-wing populist "countermovements" and the policies they develop to impose a specific solution to the crisis of capitalist societies. This is important, as there are intensive debates whether the right-wing populist and far-right movements represent somehow mainly protective but exclusive reactions of societies against mar-ketization and the dominance of finance capital, which step into the vacuum emerging after democratic left parties and movements have accepted the relevance of market dynamics and the necessity to cut back on welfare. From such a perspective the authoritarianism and anti-democratic leanings as well as racism and anti-feminism of right-wing populist and far-right parties tend to be presented as secondary to the reactions against unfettered transnational market expansion.

So far, however, Polanyi's considerations on fascism in *The Great Transformation* (2001) but also in a number of other less well known papers such as 'The Essence of Fascism' from 1935 (2018b), have neither been analysed in a systematic way and articulated with his wider conceptualization of capitalist development (Reynolds 2015) nor have they been assessed in relation to other theories and analyses of fascism.[2] Nevertheless, his critique of fascist philosophy (in particular the work of the Austrian philosopher Othmar Spann) and its repudiation of a universalist concept of freedom and the individual at the expense of an understanding of race and nation that is based on struggle and survival (Polanyi 2018b, p. 103) could allow to articulate his approach with other critical theorizations of fascism.

Polanyi's perspective on fascism offers some interesting insights into how far a common ground between neoliberal strategies to economize and reorgan-ize (welfare) state activities, and social policies and far-right authoritarianism and right-wing populism, which ethnicize and culturalize social crises, is emerging. This becomes obvious in a speech Polanyi gave in 1933 (2005). He offered a discussion of the way fascism changes the relation between the economy and the state. This discussion has remarkable similarities to critical analysis of neoliberal strategies to retrench and to economize the state and politics:

> [. . .] fascism wants to abolish politics, and to absolutize the economy, to grab the state from its position, and to disincorporate the state from the economy. [. . .] Together with the sphere of politics fascism abolishes the idea of freedom. (Polanyi 2005, p. 219, own translation)

---

[2]   Any attempt to apply Polanyi's discussion of fascism to current developments must not overlook its limitations and blind spots. For example, in contrast to contem-poraries such as Wilhelm Reich or Erich Fromm and the Frankfurt Institute of Social Research (Wiggershaus 1993), Polanyi does not try to analyse the mass appeal of fascism nor does he provide an adequate analysis of the role of racism and in particular anti-Semitism even though he shows some awareness of the significance of the former for fascist movements (Dale 2016).

For Polanyi (2001, p. 247) fascism represents a move(ment) which aims at rescuing capitalism through first, an attack on and the destruction of democracy, and second, the replacement of individual freedom within society (Polanyi 2018b). From this perspective, fascism does not simply constitute an answer to the crisis and finally the collapse of societies dominated by market expansion. Rather, Polanyi depicts it as a reaction to a situation in which the stalemate between the unfettered international expansion of markets on the one hand and the limited and fragmented implementation of protective policies as well as the trend towards democratization after the First World War on the other hand could not be solved in a peaceful way (see the papers in Polanyi et al. 2018).

Against the background of the crisis of capitalist societies and the reactions to it, Polanyi tries to understand why fascism comes to view liberalism, Marxism/Bolshevism and democracy only as different facets of modern social and economic developments and their destructive effects on the people, the state and the economy (Polanyi 2018b). For him, fascism emerges as a social reaction to the deep and prolonged crisis of society, which could not be overcome through the existing form of democracy or state organized social protection. Rather, it frames the latter as reason for the economic and social crisis, and presents itself as the rescue of capitalism. For this, according to Polanyi, a revolutionary reorganization[3] of the whole state and social fabric was set in place, which amounted to a full scale attack on and abolition of all democratic institutions and processes, rights and organizations (Polanyi 2005, p. 219).

> The fascist solution of the impasse reached by liberal capitalism can be described as a reform of market economy achieved at the price of the extirpation of all democratic institutions, both in the industrial and in the political realm. The economic system which was in peril of disruption would thus be revitalized, while the people themselves were subjected to a re-education designed to denaturalize the individual and make him unable to function as the responsible unit of the body politic. This re-education, comprising the tenets of a political religion that denied the idea of the brotherhood of man in all its forms, was achieved through an act of mass conversion enforced against recalcitrants by scientific methods of torture. (Polanyi 2001, p. 245)

To be clear, Polanyi does not position the anti-democratic impetus of fascism against liberal understandings of democracy. Rather, he mobilizes a wider concept of democracy that has its roots in the socialist debates of the first half of the twentieth century (Brie and Thomasberger 2018). For him democracy is not confined to the political sphere in a narrow sense. Rather the expansion of democracy to other social spheres and in particular to the economy represents a crucial dimension of the emergence of protective "countermovements"

---

[3]   In the original version he talks about "Umgestaltung" and not transformation.

against the "liberal creed" and the expansion of market forces since the nineteenth century (Polanyi 2001). He expects that these developments will finally enable a transition to a socialist economy based on democratic planning and regulation, which would overcome the crisis and destruction brought upon society by an economy solely based on self-interest and uphold and expand freedom for all. For him, fascism and the transition to democratic socialism constituted two alternative solutions to the collapse and crisis of the "market society". For him, the fact that liberals denied this lies at the heart of the triumph of fascism.

> The extension of the democratic principle to the economy implies the abolition of the private property of the means of production, and hence the disappearance of a separate autonomous sphere: the democratic political sphere becomes the whole of society. This essentially is socialism. (Polanyi 2018b, pp. 105 f.)

However, Polanyi's account of fascism provides another aspect that helps to understand the role and function of far-right "countermovements". Contrary to the claim that Marxism and socialism are based on a fundamental enmity to the idea of personality/individuality, Polanyi points out that socialism is the heir of individualism as it is based on a universalistic concept of the individual. He does so, by highlighting the similarities and continuities between a Christian and a Marxist understanding of the dialectical relations and interdependencies between the individual and society. Thus, democracy and its expansion are the institutional connection between socialism and the individual, which is based on their fundamental equality. Universalist equality transcends not only economic differences but also "racial" or national ones (Polanyi 2018b). Fascism on the other side is anti-individualistic at its core and rejects universalist assumptions about the equality of individuals within society (Polanyi 2018b, p. 96). Taking these conceptualizations into account, it becomes obvious that Polanyi's analysis of fascism occupies an ambiguous position. Fascism constitutes a "countermovement" not only to market expansion but also to the emergence of tendencies to expand democratic processes and to enlarge the freedom of the individual based on a universalist concept of equality at the same time.

This ambiguity allows asking whether Polanyi's account of fascism can be used to deepen the understanding of whether and how current right-wing populist and far-right movements and parties can draw on the aporias and contradictions of neoliberal policies in different policy fields such as the (re-)production of labour (power) as a fictitious commodity. With his approach it is possible to identify (at least) three crucial fields in which fascism tries to reorganize and restructure the state and the social fabric as a whole for the rescue of capitalism. These fields encompass strategies to block the expansion of democratic participation beyond the political sphere in a narrow sense; the rejection of the equality of all individuals; and the attack on freedom in non-economic social spheres while expanding the freedom or market processes.

Against this background, three dimensions of the outlined reorganization and reconfigurations of welfare regimes under neoliberal dominance have to be pointed out. *First*, the neoliberal and "authoritarian populist" onslaught on de-commodifying welfare policies turned around tendencies to control and steer the capitalist economy and to expand democratic participation under the so-called Keynesian welfare national regimes (Jessop 2016) and the social struggles that were accompanying it. While these attacks on democracy could go as far as its outright abolition in countries such as Chile, in countries of the Global North rather a range of strategies of curtailing democratic institutions and processes were implemented (Kiely 2017). These include the confinement of trade union activities and collective bargaining but also their influence on policy making and welfare institutions under corporatist social partnership in many countries; the abolition or crippling of institutions of workers' representation on the shop floor and other forms of co-determination; the privatization and contracting out of social and public services (Frangakis et al. 2009) and the implementation of managerialism, which reduced public control and accountability. Recent debates about the hollowing out of democratic processes and the emergence of post-democracy (Crouch 2008) as well as authoritarian constitutionalism (Oberndorfer 2016) or the shift towards so-called illiberal democracies and their effect on voter disenchantment show that the dominance of neoliberal crisis management since the 1970s/1980s constituted some kind of a slippery slope towards a crisis of democracy that has recently been termed "authoritarian neoliberalism" (Bruff 2013).

Second, the emerging set of polarized social policies concerning the reproduction of labour power as a (fictitious) commodity between activation/ workfare and social investment are strongly focused on the subjectivities of individual workers and their abilities (defined as human capital) as well as willingness to take up employment and to act as commodified labour in a capitalist labour market (Atzmüller 2015). The enforced re-commodification of labour power includes and demands the permanent adaption of their "capacity for labour" (Arbeitsvermögen) (Marx 1972) through learning and other forms of self-improvement. The constant learning of new skills and competencies as well as the ability to cope with the demands of flexible and precarious employment come to define the position of individuals between economic demands and an increasingly economized social policy regime (Lessenich 2012). This narrows the scope of individual development to market conformism, which is beginning at the early development of children (Aulenbacher et al. 2018a). These changes of welfare regimes and social policies reverse the gains in individual autonomy (Vobruba 2003) that could be enforced through social policies and the social struggles that accompanied them.

Third, these activities are not simply based on cuts of welfare benefits. Rather, they tie benefit entitlements to certain expected behaviours and increase institutional control over individuals through the expansion of disciplinary and punitive measures (e.g. growth of sanction regimes of Public Employment Services) on the one hand and the growing demands to permanently adapt someone's self and capacity to work in order to sustain the valorization of one's own human capital. These developments have led to far-reaching tendencies of polarization and fragmentation in many societies bringing about high levels of unemployment and precarious employment, inequality and poverty (Scherschel et al. 2012).

5.   CONCLUSIONS

In this chapter we have shown that the neoliberal reconfiguration and reorganization of welfare states and social policies serve to actively re-commodify labour. The re-commodification of labour (power) cannot be conceptualized as process of disembedding through the retrenchment of social policies and regulations but rather as a contradictory reorganization and reconfiguration of welfare regimes that cannot be covered by the juxtaposition of marketization movements and protecting countermovements. Rather the state-induced re-commodification of labour (power) through activation/workfare and social investment constitutes an important mechanism to enforce structural change and to tackle (at least certain aspects) of the sustained crisis of capitalism in order to re-stabilize the movement of marketization. The recent upsurge of right-wing populist and far-right movements and parties reveal the aporias and contradictions of this enforced movement of market expansion, which led to a fragmentation and polarization of welfare systems and social policies. In the recurring crises of neoliberal market expansion the former constitute themselves as an alternative to tackle not only the crisis of market expansion but also to overcome the (emancipatory) continuities of a welfarist embedding of the economy that expanded individual autonomy and to enforce the hierarchical and exclusionist social order through its nationalist and ethnic closure.

Up to now, the overcome institutional features of welfare systems still block the externalization of the destructive effects of market expansion to certain strata of society defined through e.g. nationalist terms to a certain extent. However, the emergence of an ethnicized and culturalized view on social policies serves increasingly to de-legitimize the latter. Polanyi's conceptualization of fascism is helpful to depict the ambiguities of right-wing populist and far-right movements and policies (e.g. concerning the reproduction of labour power as a fictitious commodity). It offers insights as to why and how the latter are able to tie the crisis of marketization to an attack on welfare institutions and social policies which protect people from the former into an increasingly coherent social alternative.

REFERENCES

Aglietta, M. ([1979] 2000), *A theory of capitalist regulation: The US experience*, London and New York: Verso.

Altvater, E. (2010), *Der große Krach oder die Jahrhundertkrise von Wirtschaft und Finanzen, von Politik und Natur*, Münster: Westfälisches Dampfboot.

Atzmüller, R. (2015), 'Transformation der "zeitgemäßen Arbeitskraft" und Krisenbearbeitung', in R. Atzmüller, S. Hürtgen and M. Krenn (eds), *Die zeitgemäße Arbeitskraft: Qualifiziert, aktiviert, polarisiert*, Weinheim and Basel: Beltz Juventa, pp. 195–310.

Aulenbacher, B., F. Décieux and B. Riegraf (2018a), 'Capitalism goes care', *Equality, Diversity and Inclusion: An International Journal*, 37 (4), 347–60.

Aulenbacher, B., F. Décieux and B. Riegraf (2018b), 'The economic shift and beyond: Care as a contested terrain in contemporary capitalism', *Current Sociology*, 66 (4), 517–30.

Becker, J. (2018), *Neo-Nationalismus in der EU: sozio-ökonomische Programmatik und Praxis*, Wien: Kammer für Arbeiter und Angestellte für Wien.

Block, F.L. and M.R. Somers (2014), *The power of market fundamentalism: Karl Polanyi's critique*, Cambridge, MA: Harvard University Press.

Boyer, R. and Y. Saillard (2002), 'A summary of regulation theory', in R. Boyer and Y. Saillard (eds), *Régulation theory: The state of the art*, London and New York: Routledge.

Brand, U. and M. Wissen (2017), *Imperiale Lebensweise: Zur Ausbeutung von Mensch und Natur im globalen Kapitalismus*, München: Oekom.

Brie, M. and C. Thomasberger (eds) (2018), *Karl Polanyi's vision of a socialist transformation*, Montréal: Black Rose.

Bruff, I. (2013), 'The rise of authoritarian neoliberalism', *Rethinking Marxism*, 26 (1), 113–29.

Buğra, A. (ed.) (2007), *Reading Karl Polanyi for the twenty-first century: Market economy as a political project*, New York: Palgrave Macmillan.

Burawoy, M. (2015), *Public Sociology: Öffentliche Soziologie gegen Marktfundamentalismus und globale Ungleichheit*, Weinheim: Beltz Juventa.

Cahill, D. (2015), *The end of laissez-faire: On the durability of embedded neoliberalism*, Cheltenham, UK and Northampton, MA, USA: Edward Elgar Publishing.

Cahill, D., M. Konings and M. Cooper (eds) (2017), *The SAGE handbook of neoliberalism*, London: Sage Publications.

Campani, G. and B. Sauer (2017), 'The neo-fascist and neo-Nazi constellations', in G. Lazaridis and G. Campani (eds), *Understanding the populist shift: Othering in a Europe in crisis*, London and New York: Routledge, pp. 31–49.

Clarke, T.D. (2014), 'Reclaiming Karl Polanyi, socialist intellectual', *Studies in Political Economy*, 94 (1), 61–84.

Crouch, C. (2008), *Postdemokratie*, Frankfurt: Suhrkamp.

Dale, G. (2013), *Karl Polanyi: The limits of the market*, Oxford: Wiley.

Dale, G. (2016), *Karl Polanyi: A life on the left*, New York: Columbia University Press.

Davidson, N. and R. Saull (2017), 'Neoliberalism and the far-right: A contradictory embrace', *Critical Sociology*, 43 (4–5), 707–24.

Dörre, K. and T. Haubner (2012), 'Landnahme durch Bewährungsproben – Ein Konzept für die Arbeitssoziologie', in K. Dörre, D. Sauer and V. Wittke (eds), *Kapitalismustheorie und Arbeit: Neue Ansätze soziologischer Kritik*, Frankfurt/Main and New York: Campus, pp. 63–106.

Esping-Andersen, G. (1990), *Three worlds of welfare capitalism*, Cambridge: Polity Press.

Fabry, A. (2019), 'Neoliberalism, crisis and authoritarian-ethnicist reaction: The ascendancy of the Orbán regime', *Competition & Change*, 23 (2), 165–91.

Fischer, K. (2009), 'The influence of neoliberals in Chile before, during, and after Pinochet', in D. Plehwe and P. Mirowski (eds), *The road from Mont Pèlerin: The making of the neoliberal thought collective*, Cambridge, MA: Harvard University Press, pp. 305–46.

Frangakis, M., C. Hermann, K. Loran and J. Huffschmid (2009), *Privatisation against the European social model: A critique of European policies and proposals for alternatives*, Basingstoke: Palgrave Macmillan.

Gemici, K. (2007), 'Karl Polanyi and the antinomies of embeddedness', *Socio-Economic Review*, 6 (1), 5–33.

Hall, S. (1980), 'Popular-democratic vs. authoritarian populism: Two ways of "taking democracy seriously"', in A. Hunt (ed.), *Marxism and democracy*, London: Lawrence & Wishart, pp. 157–85.

Harootunian, H. (2006), 'The future of fascism', *Radical Philosophy*, 136, 23–33.

Harvey, M. (ed.) (2014), *Karl Polanyi: New perspectives on the place of the economy in society*, Manchester: Manchester University Press.

Heinisch, R. (2016), *Understanding populist party organisation: The radical right in Western Europe*, London: Palgrave Macmillan.

Hemerijck, A. (2013), *Changing welfare states*, Oxford: Oxford University Press.

Hemerijck, A. (2017), *The uses of social investment*, Oxford and New York: Oxford University Press.

Jessop, B. (2007), 'Was folgt dem Fordismus? Zur Periodisierung von Kapitalismus und seiner Regulation', in B. Jessop (ed.), *Kapitalismus Regulation Staa: Ausgewählte Schriften*, Hamburg: Das Argument, pp. 255–74.

Jessop, B. (2008), 'Polanyian, regulationist, and autopoieticist reflections on states and markets and their implications for the knowledge-based economy', in A. Ebner (ed.), *The institutions of the market: Organizations, social systems, and governance*, Oxford: Oxford University Press, pp. 328–47.

Jessop, B. (2015), 'Crisis construal in the North Atlantic financial crisis and the Eurozone crisis', *Competition & Change*, 19 (2), 95–112.

Jessop, B. (2016), *The state: Past, present, future*, Cambridge: Polity Press.

Jessop, B. (2017), 'Neoliberalism and workfare: Schumpeterian or Ricardian', in D. Cahill, M. Konings and M. Cooper (eds), *The SAGE handbook of neoliberalism*, London: Sage Publications, pp. 347–58.

Kaltwasser, C.R., P. Taggart, P.O. Espejo and P. Ostiguy (2017), 'Populism: An overview of the concept and the state of the art', in C.R. Kaltwasser, P. Taggart, P.O. Espejo and P. Ostiguy (eds), *The Oxford handbook of populism*, Oxford and New York: Oxford University Press, pp. 1–26.

Kiely, R. (2010), *The clash of globalisations: Neo-liberalism, the third way, and anti-globalisation*, Leiden and Boston: Brill.

Kiely, R. (2017), 'From authoritarian liberalism to economic technocracy: Neoliberalism, politics and "de-democratization"', *Critical Sociology*, 43 (4–5), 725–45.

Lapavitsas, C. (2013), *Profiting without producing: How finance exploits us all*, London: Verso.

Lessenich, S. (2012), 'Constructing the socialized self: Mobilization and control in the "active society"', in U. Bröckling, S. Krasmann and T. Lemke (eds), *Governmentality: Current issues and future challenges*, New York and London: Routledge, pp. 304–19.

Lessenich, S. (2016), *Neben uns die Sintflut: Die Externalisierungsgesellschaft und ihr Preis*, München: Hanser.

Marx, K. (1972), *Das Kapital: Marx-Engels-Werke: Band 23*, Berlin: Dietz.

Morel, N., B. Palier and J. Palme (eds) (2012), *Towards a social investment state: Ideas, policies and challenges*, Bristol: Policy Press.

Oberndorfer, L. (2016), 'Der neue Konstitutionalismus in der Europäischen Union und seine autoritäre Re-Konfiguration: WWU 2.0, New Economic Governance und Pakt(e) für Wettbewerbsfähigkeit', in H.-J. Bieling and

M. Große Hüttmann (eds), *Europäische Staatlichkeit: Zwischen Krise und Integration*, Wiesbaden: Springer VS, pp. 177–200.

Obinger, H. (2012), 'Die Finanzkrise und die Zukunft des Wohlfahrtsstaates', *Leviathan*, 40 (3), 441–61.

Offe, C. (1993), *Contradictions of the welfare state*, ed. J. Keane, London: MIT Press.

Peck, J. (2001), *Workfare states*, New York and London: Guilford Press.

Peck, J. (2013), 'Disembedding Polanyi: Exploring Polanyian economic geographies', *Environment and Planning A*, 45 (7), 1536–44.

Pierson, P. (2011), *The welfare state over the very long run*, ZeS-Arbeitspapier 2, Bremen: Zentrum für Sozialpolitik.

Polanyi, K. (1957), 'The economy as instituted process', in K. Polanyi, C.M. Arensberg and H.W. Pearson (eds), *Trade and market in the early empires: Economies in history and theory*, Glencoe, IL: Free Press, pp. 243–70.

Polanyi, K. (1977), *The livelihood of man*, New York: Academic Press.

Polanyi, K. (2001), *The great transformation: The political and economic origins of our time*, Boston: Beacon Press.

Polanyi, K. (2005), 'Die geistigen Voraussetzungen des Faschismus', in K. Polanyi, M. Cangiani, K. Polanyi-Levitt and C. Thomasberger (eds), *Chronik der großen Transformation: Artikel und Aufsätze (1920–1947): Menschliche Freiheit, politische Demokratie und die Auseinandersetzung zwischen Sozialismus und Faschismus*, Marburg: Metropolis.

Polanyi, K. (2018a), 'Fascism and Marxism', in K. Polanyi, M. Cangiani and C. Thomasberger (eds), *Economy and society: Selected writings*, Cambridge: Polity Press, pp. 125–35.

Polanyi, K. (2018b), 'The essence of fascism', in K. Polanyi, M. Cangiani and C. Thomasberger (eds), *Economy and society: Selected writings*, Cambridge: Polity Press, pp. 81–107.

Polanyi, K. (2018c), 'The fascist virus', in K. Polanyi, M. Cangiani and C. Thomasberger (eds), *Economy and society: Selected writings*, Cambridge: Polity Press, pp. 108–22.

Polanyi, K., M. Cangiani and C. Thomasberger (eds) (2018), *Economy and society: Selected writings*, Cambridge: Polity Press.

Reynolds, N. (2015), 'The crisis of market society and the fascist solution in the writings of Karl Polanyi: A preliminary investigation', accessed 16 January 2019 at www.academia.edu/24907916/The_Crisis_of_Market _Society_and_the_Fascist_Solution_in_the_Writings_of_Karl_Polanyi_A _Preliminary_Investigation.

Scherschel, K., P. Streckeisen and M. Krenn (eds) (2012), *Neue Prekarität: Die Folgen aktivierender Arbeitsmarktpolitik – europäische Länder im Vergleich*, Frankfurt/Main and New York: Campus.

Starke, P., M. Wulfgramm and H. Obinger (2016), 'Welfare state transformation across OECD countries: Supply side orientation, individualized outcome risks and dualization', in M. Wulfgramm, T. Bieber and S. Leibfried (eds), *Welfare state transformations and inequality in OECD countries*, London: Palgrave Macmillan, pp. 19–40.

Streeck, W. (2016), *How will capitalism end? Essays on a failing system*, London and New York: Verso.

Sum, N.-L. and B. Jessop (2015), *Towards a cultural political economy: Putting culture in its place in political economy*, Cheltenham, UK and Northampton, MA, USA: Edward Elgar Publishing.

Vobruba, G. (2003), 'Freiheit: Autonomiegewinne der Leute im Wohlfahrtsstaat', in S. Lessenich (ed.), *Wohlfahrtsstaatliche Grundbegriffe: Historische und aktuelle Diskurse*, Frankfurt/Main: Campus, pp. 137–55.

Wiggershaus, R. (1993), *Die Frankfurter Schule: Geschichte – Theoretische Entwicklung – Politische Bedeutung*, München: DTV.

11. *Völkisch* populism: a Polanyian-type movement?

Karina Becker and Klaus Dörre

1. STARTING SITUATION AND HYPOTHESES

Many countries are now finding themselves confronted with the rise of right-wing populist parties and movements that often constitute a critical juncture for the political system. Although populist parties generally recruit their voters from across all social classes and strata, they quite clearly enjoy particularly high levels of support from the working classes. US President Donald Trump owes his election victory not only to voters from the "middle class" and the petit bourgeois electorate but also to the production workers and their families living in the de-industrialized "Rust Belt" cities. The Brexit campaign spearheaded by the right-wing populist UKIP movement, for instance, also received a particularly positive response from the working classes. In the 2016 Austrian presidential election, 85 per cent of blue collar workers voted for the Freedom Party of Austria (FPÖ) candidate, Norbert Hofer (who won 46.2 per cent of the total vote), while his victorious rival, Alexander van der Bellen, only managed to secure a scant 15 per cent of the working-class vote. Since the 1990s, France's *Rassemblement National* (formerly *Front National*) has been winning landslide election victories in the former French Communist Party (PCF) strongholds. The election successes of the right-wing Alternative for Germany (AfD) party also fall into this pattern. Besides the Free Democratic Party (FPD), the AfD was the real victor in the 2017 German parliamentary election. Indeed, the results achieved in the eastern German states were, by and large, on par with what we would tend to expect of a major political party. In Saxony, with 27 per cent of the vote, the AfD even won more electoral votes than any other party. According to analyses conducted by Infratest dimap, during the 2017 election an above-average share of the blue collar, working-class, and unemployed electorate voted for the AfD (21 per cent in each case), but the party was also able to secure votes in the double-digit range from other occupational groups and from voters educated to intermediate secondary school level (Infratest dimap 2017). Among trade union members overall, the AfD attracted slightly above-average support with 15 per cent of the vote, while support among trade union members in Germany's east was as high as 22 per cent, putting it on par with the *Linkspartei* (The Left Party). The AfD made particularly high gains in the age cohorts dominated by the labour force, especially among men in the 25–59 age group. Among this group living in eastern Germany, the AfD recorded 26 per cent of the vote – an incredible 13 percentage points higher than for men living in western Germany – making it the strongest party for this group (Die Welt 2017).

This chapter takes this phenomenon as its point of departure and, based on the German case, asks what it is that makes right-wing populists so attractive to blue collar workers and trade unionists. In posing this question, the chapter seeks to contribute to the current intense and controversial debate in the social sciences and among the general public on the reasons behind the successes of the right-wing populist movement and on how we should respond to the situation (Becker et al. 2018). Some see the rise of right-wing populists as being primarily fuelled by the privileged middle classes' sense of entitlement that manifests itself in the form of racism. Others, however, refer to the "new workers' parties" (Gertz 2017; Nachtwey and Jörke 2017, p. 174), drawing on Didier Eribon (2014) or Arlie Hochschild (2016). Closely linked with the question of whether the phenomenon is thus a form of welfare chauvinism or whether it is more of a "right-wing workers' movement", i.e. the appropriation of the social question by right-wing forces, is the controversy surrounding the reasons for the spread of right-wing populist movements and parties, which, in this debate, is typically characterized by the dichotomy between socio-economic and cultural causes.

However, we are not convinced that there is a clear-cut "either/or" explanation for this phenomenon. Instead, in a bid to unravel the reasons for the rise of right-wing populism, we examine Karl Polanyi's "double movement" and countermovement concepts. Polanyi describes the "double movement" as a dynamic and contested development, the struggle between market and society which he observed from the end of the nineteenth/beginning of the twentieth century until the outbreak of the Second World War. In Polanyi's historical context, this movement was "the principle of economic liberalism, aiming at the establishment of a self-regulating market, relying on the support of the trading classes, and using largely laissez-faire and free trade as its methods" (Polanyi [1944] 2001, p. 138). The countermovement, on the other hand, is "the principle of social protection aiming at the conservation of man and nature as well as productive organization, relying on the varying support of those most immediately affected by the deleterious action of the market – primarily, but not exclusively, the working and the landed classes – and using protective legislation, restrictive associations, and other instruments of intervention as its methods" (ibid., pp. 138–9). After the historic experience of fascism, Polanyi did not think another phase of "market fundamentalism" (Burawoy 2015) possible. He perceived the attempts at the time to create a new socialist or fascist social order, and also the New Deal, as a social response to the destructive dynamics of an economy organized according to the principles of the "self-regulating market" (Polanyi [1944] 2001; Dale 2014).

In this chapter we discuss whether the *völkisch*[1] right-wing populism we are seeing today is a Polanyian-type countermovement. With this in mind, we present three hypotheses:

1. The countermovement is a conformist revolt seeking protection from market-driven competition. Perceived distributive injustice is redefined as competition between "insiders" and "outsiders".
2. Right-wing populist forces in Germany take up experiences of injustice, a sense of political disempowerment, and social criticism and turn them into ethnic issues.
3. During a time of diminishing solidarity, such forces thus provide the narrative of an exclusive national community.

The questions and hypotheses put forward here are explored using our own empirical studies. These studies are briefly outlined in the section below (section 2), which is followed by a more detailed examination of Polanyi's "double movement" concept (section 3). Lastly, we provide an in-depth description and interpretation of the subjective perspectives of the works council members who took part in our study. The hypotheses outlined at the outset will be evaluated for plausibility on the basis of these interviews (section 4). In the conclusion (section 5), the results will be summarized.

2.   EMPIRICAL BASIS AND METHODOLOGY

Practices of exclusive solidarity among wage-earners in Germany, which bring discrimination in their wake, have been observed for some time now (Dörre et al. 2013). During the course of labour market deregulation, these practices have focused primarily on employment status. They affect companies from various sectors and concern a number of different dimensions, for example different occupational safety standards for permanent and temporary staff as well as different levels of health protection (Becker and Engel 2015). This also leads to the collective devaluation of certain social groups by other, generally

---

[1]   The German adjective *völkisch* refers to something originating from the people and articulates notions of the "popular" with ethnic and racial homogeneity. With the rise of ethnic German nationalism in the nineteenth century, it was commonly used to refer to "Germanness" and was later a standard Nazi term.

more powerful groups (Becker 2015). Moreover, it is well known that there is significant potential in society for ostracizing and, in many cases, for hostile right-wing populist or extreme right-wing tendencies to develop (Heitmeyer 2018). Even the predisposition of unionized workers towards such political orientations is nothing new, nor is it a trend that has only recently become the subject of research. At the turn of the millennium, numerous studies had already highlighted the right-wing populist or right-wing extremist positions of trade union members (for a summary, see Bibouche et al. 2009). Ever since, it has been assumed that radical right-wing positions among trade union activists would be rejected outright and effectively combated through democratic participation (Zeuner et al. 2007). However, according to the findings of a research project entitled *Das Gesellschaftsbild des Prekariats* ("The Social Image of Precarity"), which comprised thematic interviews (n=66) conducted in 2017/2018 with employed and unemployed respondents from industrial and service enterprises based in eastern and western Germany, we can no longer rely on right-wing positions to be tackled with such a firm hand. The aforementioned survey also included a more in-depth sociological investigation of one region of Saxony (n=16) where different groups were questioned: works council members who positioned themselves as being either for or against the AfD and Pegida[2] (coded as Pro and Ant), full-time trade union staff (Sek), and youth and trainee representatives (JAV). The analysis focused in particular on works council members who publicly identified with the AfD, Pegida, or any other right-wing organization.

The aim of the interviews was to document respondents' subjective views on their own life situations, their employers, trade union activities, and their attitudes towards Pegida and the AfD. During the interviews, which were 60–90 minutes long, our interlocutors reported how they perceived and rated society and their own positions in that society; they spoke about their expectations of the future, outlined their thoughts on the notion of justice, and shared their views on the subject of migration (for a detailed description of the study, see Dörre et al. 2018).[3]

---

[2]   Pegida stands for "Patriotic Europeans Against the Islamization of the Occident" and is a German nationalist, anti-Islam, far-right, populist movement, which has been organizing public demonstrations and rallies since 2014.

[3]   The research project funded by the German Federal Ministry of Education and Research (BMBF), *das Gesellschaftsbild des Prekariats* ("The Social Image of Precarity") (duration: November 2015–September 2018), is part of the eLabour research consortium (headed by SOFI Göttingen). Those working on the project include Project Leader Klaus Dörre and also Sophie Bose, Jakob Köster, and John Lütten. Sophie Bose conducted an in-depth analysis of some of the interviews as part of her Master's thesis.

3.   POLANYI ON COUNTERMOVEMENTS

According to Polanyi, the development of capitalism can be described as a double movement. Accelerated by market fundamentalist ideologies, institutions and organizations that limit the scope of the market are weakened, markets become socially disembedded, and market-dependent individuals or groups are exposed to competition which only ever produces winners and losers. According to various contemporary interpretations (see, for example, Burawoy 2015, p. 161), this disembedding of markets, which results in the fictitious commodities of labour, land, and money being treated the same as any other market commodity, triggers primarily bottom-up global countermovements. Polanyi sees such countermovements ([1944] 2001) as different forms of counter-reaction from a society seeking protection from market encroachment. These include initiatives and measures such as state, political, and legal regulations that are implemented as a result of pressure from the labour movement. "For a century the dynamics of modern society were governed by a double movement: the market expanded continuously but this movement was met by a countermovement checking the expansion in definite directions" (ibid., p. 136).

This new countermovement is accompanied by a social science criticism of capitalism which does not focus on class-specific inequalities and exploitation, such as Karl Marx envisaged, but rather concentrates on the socially destructive consequences of disembedded markets. According to Marx, the relationship between capital and labour is structured by a causal mechanism which is based on the notion that the wealth of one person is conditional on the relative poverty and social insecurity of another. What emerges is a concept of class that rests on a particular type of relationship of power relations. According to this understanding, social mobilization against class rule aims to surmount and ultimately abolish this very domination.

Polanyi argues against what he sees as the Marxist, economically determinist understanding of classes. He believes that "class interests offer only a limited explanation of long-run movements in society" (Polanyi [1944] 2001, p. 159), because one-sided class-specific interests should ultimately always refer to "the situation of a society as a whole" (ibid., p. 159). Moreover, "the interests of a class most directly refer to standing and rank, to status and security, that is, they are primarily not economic but social" (ibid., p. 160). According to Polanyi, "an all too narrow conception of interest must in effect lead to a warped vision of social and political history" (ibid., p. 162), because it disregards the fact that purely economic matters are far less relevant to class behaviour than "questions of social recognition" (ibid., p. 160).

As we will now show, in view of the imagined revolts – ultimately compli-ant with the ruling class – of *völkisch* right-wing populism, Polanyi's argu-ments make sense. At the same time, we feel it would be useful to re-examine the link between Polanyi and Marx. With this in mind, we would like to outline a number of commonalities between the two thinkers, which are particularly evident in the class conception developed in the *Eighteenth Brumaire of Louis Bonaparte* (Marx [1852] 1963). One area of overlap between the two class concepts is the notion that classes are not homogeneous collective subjects which, moreover, do not act. On the contrary, they are organizations and representations of classes that most certainly *do* act. Class-specific inequalities can be central to a society's conflict dynamic, although this is not necessarily always the case. Over history, we have seen repeated non-class specific move-ments directed against the "satanic mill" of the market (Polanyi [1944] 2001, p. 35). Gender or race centred axes of inequality cannot be reduced to class differences. However, they do frequently have a class-specific dimension. Class awareness is more likely to be seen among the ruling classes. In the subaltern class factions, in contrast, competition, fragmentation, isolation, and cleavages are the norm. This normality is surmountable provided the requisite forms of social interaction and modes of communication allow the mobiliza-tion of class members. Decisive factors here are experience and educational processes which allow individuals to consciously transcend habitual practices geared towards rivalry. In essence, action by social classes serves to improve individual and/or collective positions in social space. Moreover, classes are defined by what they do or do not do. They are influenced by political and ideological cycles. Accordingly, phases of class dissolution and regeneration are very likely to repeatedly replace one another over the course of time (Marx and Engels [1848] 2012).

Polanyi's approach, focused on a criticism of capitalism, is also reflected in the classification of social movements. If we follow Beverly Silver's argument (2008), Polanyian-type movements are directed at a diffuse economic market power. But this market power seems vague and abstract, it can rarely be clearly defined, and criticism of it can be politicized by the left or the right. Like the earlier socialist labour movements, anti-market movements can pursue objectives which transcend the system. However, they can also simply call for protection against market-mediated competition. It is possible that these movements take on a reactive nationalist, even terrorist-like, quality, as is the case with fascist mobilization. In contrast to the implications of Marx's concept of a universal class, which posited that the "exploitation of the world market" would "give a cosmopolitan character to production and consumption in every country" (Marx and Engels [1848] 2012, p. 39), according to Polanyi, we have to anticipate the reverse happening. The levelling power of the market can encourage an "endemic tendency for workers to draw non-class borders and boundaries as a basis for claims for protection from the maelstrom [of the market]" (Silver 2008, p. 22).

4.   EMPIRICAL FINDINGS: INEQUALITY, EXPERIENCES OF INJUSTICE, APPROPRIATION OF DEMOCRACY, AND ETHNICIZED SOCIAL CRITICISM

4.1   Growing Inequality and Distributional Injustices

Nowadays, even liberal economists describe Germany as one of "the most unequal countries of the industrialized world" (Fratzscher 2016, pp. 9, 43 ff.). According to recently updated European Central Bank data, the assets of the 45 wealthiest households in Germany are roughly equivalent to those of the poorest half of the population. A total of 0.1 per cent own a 17.4 per cent share of the country's total assets (estimated at 9.5 trillion Euros). In contrast, 50 per cent of the population account for a mere 2.3 per cent share (Bach et al. 2018). Despite the German employment miracle and shortages of skilled labour, rising income polarization has been observed since reunification. As in any developed country, in Germany, too, the wage share (share of GDP accounted for by wages) has been on a steady downward slope since the 1980s, and only in the very recent past has this figure seen any improvement (International Monetary Fund 2017). In contrast to the above-average wage decreases seen among women employed in the service sector in particular, qualified and organized permanent staff in the export industry have been able to maintain their real wage level or have even experienced an increase (Hauptmann and Schmerer 2012, p. 3). In 2015, around half of all wage-earners made less in real terms than they had fifteen years earlier (Fratzscher 2016, p. 64).

This development of class-specific inequalities was certainly noted by our interview partners. Employees in the organization areas of the industrial trade unions were also not exempt from this. Only permanent skilled staff working for larger and medium-sized enterprises have benefited from wage increases of more than 50 per cent since the turn of the millennium. For those working in the supplier industries, IG Metall[4] negotiated staggered wage agreements across the former East Germany with the promise that "in ten years' time you will have the same wage agreement as in West Germany, a 35-hour week, and the same pay scale as West Germany" (Sek2). However, for the vast majority of companies, this promise has not been kept. Thus, not only does inequality

---

[4]   The industrial union IG Metall is the largest single trade union in Germany and the largest trade union in the world.

have an impact on the distribution ratio between labour and capital, it also causes fragmentation within the wage-earning classes. In eastern Germany this has led to resentment, particularly among the younger workers. For decades they or their parents have been forced to waive pay increases because otherwise – according to the "there is no alternative" mantra – they would no longer be able to count on having employment in their place of residence, and the survival of east German companies would be jeopardized. In order to be competitive with other companies, businesses subjected themselves to numerous rationalization and marketization processes, which led to an enormous increase in the workload of employees. In housing, health, and education, public goods and services were also commodified according to the constraints of the market.

Now, bailouts of ailing banks and southern European countries and, most recently, the admission of refugees have, in their eyes, turned the inevitability of commodification, marketization, and austerity politics on its head. This leads to resentment and frustration, evidence of which can be seen in the interviews conducted. In some cases, these feelings have resulted in protests against this inequality and lack of security accompanied by a market and alienation criticism that tie in with *völkisch* nationalist worldviews. This reinforces practices of exclusive solidarity, which, for the labour force, are now not only directed against those "at the bottom", i.e. those with precarious employment status (temporary workers or contractors), but also against ethnic "others", people who are perceived as rivals in a distributional conflict.

4.2 In the "Middle" of Society and Yet Still Abnormal

Also at the societal level, our interviews reveal status problems which culminate in the feeling of having been given a raw deal. For our respondents, living in a prosperous society does not, by any means, automatically give them hope of a better life or social advancement (Dörre et al. 2013). Indeed, a blue collar worker might perceive their having a steady income and a half-way secure job as having achieved everything they are going to achieve. Similarly, being a "worker" is not a source of pride, because those who have the opportunity either "go to university or get a desk job". With permanent full-time jobs, the workers interviewed see themselves as being in the "middle of society"; however, they do not believe that they are in a position to significantly improve their situation. A 20-year-old female worker elaborates on this during her interview: "Both my parents are workers. I don't have *Abitur* [German school-leaving qualification for university entrance] and didn't go on to study at university. I got my *Realschulabschluss* [vocational school leaving certificate] and then did an apprenticeship, and now I go out to work. And I'm pretty sure things will stay like that. I would certainly count myself as being in the middle range of the middle class but that's all it's ever going to be. This gap between the middle class [. . .] and the upper middle class, it's just massive. And I'll never be able to bridge that gap [. . .], it doesn't matter what I do. And that's simply the way it is for many, many people" (JAV1). For this respondent, the prospect of advancement is non-existent, while the possibility of slipping further down is very much present.

How perceived social devaluation processes tie in with nationalist world-views is illustrated by the example of a working-class family from a small town in eastern Germany. Both partners are in full-time employment, working 40 hours a week for a gross monthly wage of 1600 and 1700 Euros, respectively. Once all the fixed costs have been deducted, this family with two children have a net total of just 1000 Euros left each month, money which has to cover clothing, food, etc. On a budget like this, every single larger purchase, every car repair, for example, presents a problem. All the things that, subjectively speaking, make life good or are perceived by society as normal, whether a vacation or a meal in a restaurant on the weekend, are the very things this family, despite both partners working hard, simply cannot afford. This is the type of situation that results in people feeling abnormal through no fault of their own: "Every German citizen has an average basic income of 3300 Euros. So now I have to ask myself: what am I then? Am I not German?" (Pro3). Thus, "being German" becomes a cipher for being entitled to a "normal" life and equal opportunities, and being on level footing with other Germans. Since this entitlement is not fulfilled for our respondents, they believe it is exclusive and thus also not applicable to non-Germans. The example described reveals the subjective nature of how discrimination is processed – a process that involves the construction of a nationalist causal mechanism consisting of self-affirmation through the devaluation of others. Believing any attempt to resolve these distributional struggles – which they consider unjust – to be futile, the workers and works council members we interviewed tended to rein-terpret this conflict between "top and bottom" as a conflict between "insiders and outsiders", between indigenous Germans who are willing to work and foreigners who are not.

Right-wing populist forces take these tendencies towards exclusive soli-darity, which have been observed among wage-earners for many years now, and radicalize them. Originally founded as a market liberal party, the AfD has increasingly moved in a similar direction to older right-wing populist parties in Europe, such as the French *Rassemblement National*, i.e. towards becoming a *völkisch* populist social formation (Bieling 2017), despite this development being disputed within the party. In any case, the AfD has increasingly managed to capitalize on the widespread feelings of injustice, the criticism of social ine-quality as well as the problems of wealth distribution, turning these concerns into an ethnic issue. Parts of the AfD pose as attorneys for the "little people" whom they equate with German citizens, as the following statement by Björn Höckes, the most prominent representative of the *völkisch* nationalist wing of the AfD and the parliamentary party leader for the AfD in Thüringen, illustrates: "Today's social question" is not primarily the "redistribution of national wealth from the top to the bottom", but rather the "new German social question of the 21st century" is "the redistribution of national wealth from inside to outside" (quoted in Paulus 2017).

4.3   Problems beyond Poverty and Precarity

This view by no means only refers to material aspects, and it is not only shared by people with low income levels. Skilled workers with above-average incomes have also been known to refer to foreigners' incapacity to integrate into German culture. They cite other problems which, for many years, were not the focus of public debate and which, to some extent, still are not. These include increasing employee productivity to the detriment of their health (Detje and Sauer 2018, p. 202; Sauer et al. 2018, pp. 111–18; Becker 2016), disappointment over the pension ruling, and anger about crumbling infrastructure due to a lack of government investment as a result of commodification and austerity policies. These examples make it clear that it is not only the poor, long-term unemployed or those in precarious employment who are affected by the problems of injustice. For many social scientists, the disappearance of discussions of class relations as well as of dominance and exploitation from public debate leads to the analytical fallacy that anyone to whom the aforementioned financial and labour conditions do not apply is assigned to the middle class, where problems of injustice are not legitimate (Institut der Deutschen Wirtschaft Köln 2017; Lengfeld 2017). The "myth of the middle class" (Kadritzke 2017) thus distorts our view of the fact that even well-paid skilled workers are also wage-earners. Ignoring class in public discourse does not change the fact that everyone "who is objectively affected by the reality behind these terms feels collectively abandoned" (Eribon 2014, p. 122). This also applies to trade unionists and works council members, who are particularly sensitive to the growing income and wealth inequality in Germany. Subjectively speaking, it is also not a contradiction for them to be "happy with their own income" but at the same time to find that "those who people listen to are the ones with the power or the money", and that these people can "simply impose their [decisions] on others" (Pro2).

4.4   Appropriation of Democracy

The everyday consciousness of our interviewees is thus shaped by a multifarious source of social problems, which, according to the general tone of the interviews, established organizations and associations as well as the earlier traditional parties have all failed to put high enough on their agendas or to address successfully. The result in many cases has been frustration over political decisions such as the bank bailouts during the financial crisis and the humanitarian decision of the Merkel government to let refugees into the country by temporarily suspending the relevant entry requirements. The people we interviewed felt that all this was decided over their heads despite the impact these decisions would have on their standard of living. Movements such as Pegida, on the other hand, are seen as a driver of democratization. Even the left-leaning trade union secretaries have no doubt that the primary aim of the vast majority of Pegida demonstrators is to become subjects of political decision-making:

> "One of them expressed it as follows: I want my piece of the pie now, too. I've never had a piece, my parents never had their piece, and neither did my grandparents. The region where I live was deindustrialized, the trade unions only have a limited amount of power [. . .]. It's my turn now. And then there is this movement that is getting bigger every week and of course that's something you feel drawn to and say to yourself, wow, they can really make a difference. At first you don't really care about the *what*, but this feeling that there is something happening at last, that we can finally show the powers that be what we're made of. It's not necessarily about the content but is more about the emotions. It's all about wanting to be seen and heard" (Sek2).

The fact that extreme right-wing representatives are also taking part in Pegida demonstrations clearly does not seem to bother other participants or is simply seen as a matter of course.

The criticism directed at the prevailing democratic processes and representatives, however, by no means signifies the rejection of democracy. On the contrary, right-wing workers are now calling for more direct democracy: "Well, for me, well-functioning democracy would first mean calling a referendum. This is where you'd have to start. And, in my view, the second thing would be decent criminal law. Referendums that clearly show the mood among the country's population as opposed to some politician taking it upon himself to make a decision for everyone else, or that kind of thing" (Pro1). Democracy is thus reduced to the majority principle where the people must rule directly and the will of the people must be directly enforced. Here, "the people" are commensurate with good common sense. If the popular principle of reason can truly manifest itself, it is a foregone conclusion that the "right" opinions will prevail. At least this is the kind of logic that is almost identical to an identity-based understanding of democracy. The democratic subject is *éthnos*, a homogeneous nation of racially pure "indigenous" Germans or *Biodeutsche*, who autonomously determine their own destinies. According to this interpretation of democracy, human rights and people's rights are dispensable.

The appropriation of democracy represents a key difference between the "new right" and traditional right-wing extremism, which saw itself as unequivocally anti-democratic and aimed to establish a dictatorship.

4.5 Yearning for a National Community

Many of our interviewees say that in comparison to "earlier" times (meaning the German Democratic Republic (GDR), which the younger of them only know from their parents' stories) communality has eroded, and this is related to commodification, marketization, and economization processes. From their point of view, it would be good if egotism was limited. If this succeeds, then the will of the people can develop ideally. For radical right-wing workers, the people are a culturally based community. To some extent the desired national community existed in the old GDR. Of course, nobody wants a return to this GDR. At the top of their wish list is instead a national community that has not yet been destroyed by egotism, the struggle for perks, and a dog-eat-dog mentality: "I do not personally know the GDR itself. But if someone hears their parents talking about it, [. . .] there was more cohesion. It was more about the personal, about the human, and not about: how can I get even more money or whatever, so that [. . .] I can afford this or that" (Pro2).

The close link between market and alienation criticism, distribution disputes, and migration is what brings the trade unionists we interviewed into contact with right-wing populism. For our interviewees, it made sense to vote for the AfD because, in their view, it was the "only party" which "scrutinized the refugee question critically" (Pro2). This confirms something which can be read in many interpretations of the outcome of the last parliamentary elections: the AfD's above-average gains are the result of protest voting behaviour and because the refugee issue is the ideal topic as it can be linked with other problem areas, such as distributional injustice and social justice. At the same time, the "refugee crisis" also illustrates the new fragility of once clear boundaries. In today's globalized society, the former separation of foreign, domestic, and nation-state policy is increasingly disappearing. Right-wing populism, in contrast, promises to restore the past as part of its agenda for a future based on an imagined old order where the "us" (defined as an ethnically homogeneous "we") seemed to be doing well. The AfD's campaign slogan "Reclaim your country!" is in a similar vein. This notion provides a channel for the expression of all the fears of loss. Refugees are – as described by Zygmunt Bauman (2016) – bringers of misfortune. First, they remind people of their own social vulnerability, which they need to ward off. Second, they represent a decaying world order that allowed many people in the Global North to lead a hegemonic way of life, which cannot be generalized to the rest of the world. This old order, the social price of which had to be borne by others, is now at risk of slipping away. Right-wing populism is, therefore, a radical expression of and the radicalizing factor in a body politic that does not want to be affected by the world's suffering.

5.   CONCLUSIONS

The claim of state protection from inequality, the awareness of injustices in the world of work, the criticism of a loss of community, the feeling of being politically unrepresented and not having one's own interests present in the public sphere, and the lack of material and social recognition as workers are bound with racial resentment and are channelled in a nationalist, *völkisch* movement, all of which allow us to speak of a Polanyian countermovement. This movement is not directed against an exploitative class, capitalism, or the like but rather against a diffuse "system" and apparent cultural outsiders. Consequently, the boundaries between "us" and "them" do not follow class lines but instead are drawn according to achievement and "culture". The objective of this movement is not to question the actual social and economic roots of competition and to surmount that competition. Rather, it persistently opposes and rebels against the (alleged) social competition with migrants, the primary objective being to maintain its supporters' own statuses, their social security, and a continued "good life" into the future.

Unlike solidary class action, the right-wing populist revolt does not need a joint action by the subalterns. Following Marx, it can be described as "Bonapartist" (Beck and Stützle 2018). Where Marx deals with real class formation processes, he goes analytically far beyond the field of socio-economic class determinations. In *The Eighteenth Brumaire of Louis Bonaparte* (Marx [1852] 1963, pp. 111–207), he analyses the relations of forces and alliances between classes and class factions which characterized French society at the time. Using the example of the French parcel farmers, he explains why a class cannot be organized as a mobilized class due to its monadic mode of production, lack of means of communication, and low organization. Unable to constitute themselves as self-confident classes, they delegate their interests to authoritarian leaders who can only lead because they at least partially respect the interests of the subalterns (ibid., pp. 111–207). Structurally existing classes, therefore, do not deliberately produce agitating class movements on their own. On the contrary, demobilized classes without representative actors have little choice but to delegate their – always contradictory and therefore interpretable – interests to political actors who are capable of acting. Under completely different conditions, the demobilization of – this time wage-dependent – classes is also noticeable at present.

For many of the people we interviewed, their specific experiences in East Germany played a particularly decisive role. As a result of what was referred to as the *Wende*, the process of socio-political change which led to reunification in 1989/90, many East Germans experienced the sudden and rapid invalidation of almost everything that had been valid before. They were not only at an economic disadvantage compared to West Germans, but, from a cultural perspective, they also felt infantilized, devalued, and as though the realities of their lives were not acknowledged by West German policymakers, by employers, and by others. Feelings like this equate to tangible disadvantages and a lack of recognition, and East Germans are, even today, still underrepresented in high-level positions across all sectors and in the media. Wages and the quality of employment in today's eastern Germany remain lower than in western Germany. Since the far-reaching labour market, socio-economic, and demographic upheavals that were part of the *Wende* period, many East Germans have only recently regained some degree of normality and stability, and this is something they now perceive as being at risk once again as a result of the influx of refugees.

The negative categorization of East Germans reveals a mode of class formation which can impact various different groups. As long as the everyday consciousness of the subordinate classes lacks the direction that can lead to the development of mobilized collectives, class relations will continue to operate in the mode of competition. This is a result of the permanent division into winners and losers, and it works on the basis of collective devaluation and revaluation. Devaluation results in the formation of social strata which discriminate against everyone who has to deal with such a system.

With a view to the future, we believe that research which seeks to reduce the right-wing populist tendencies observed among wage-earners to just one or one key motive, thus pitting socio-economic against cultural causes, is not particularly helpful or expedient. Social classes develop in a multidimensional space (Bourdieu 1984), which will always encompass political and cultural dimensions alongside socio-economic strata. None of these multidimensional strata automatically generate binding courses of action or political orientations. Classes, including competitive classes, do not act. People, organizations, and class representations act. In this respect, we need to clarify why some of our interviewees interpreted their experiences of devaluation as being "to the political right" and others, in contrast, "to the political left". Comparative research which carves out the differences and commonalities between Polanyian-type market-critical, authoritarian, and democratic movements would not only be of analytical value but would also have the potential to provide a scientific basis for democratic adversarial policies.

REFERENCES

Bach, S., A. Thiemann and A. Zucco (2018), 'Looking for the missing rich: Tracing the top tail of the wealth distribution', DIW Discussion Papers 1717, Berlin: Deutsches Institut für Wirtschaftsforschung.

Bauman, Z. (2016), *Strangers at our door*, Cambridge: Polity Press.

Beck, M. and I. Stützle (eds) (2018), *Die neuen Bonapartisten: Mit Marx den Aufstieg von Trump & Co. verstehen*, Berlin: Dietz.

Becker, K. (2015), 'Macht und Gesundheit: Der informelle Handel um die Vernutzung von Arbeitskraft', *Berliner Journal für Soziologie*, 25 (1–2), 161–85.

Becker, K. (2016), 'Entgrenzte Organisationen – begrenzte Beschäftigtengesundheit? Arbeitspolitische Aushandlungen um Grenzverschiebungen im Arbeits- und Gesundheitsschutz', *Industrielle Beziehungen*, 23 (2), 142–62.

Becker, K., K. Dörre and P. Reif-Spirek (eds) (2018), *Arbeiterbewegung von rechts? Ungleichheit – Verteilungskämpfe – populistische Revolte*, Frankfurt/Main and New York: Campus.

Becker, K. and T. Engel (2015), 'Reduziertes Schutzniveau jenseits der Normalarbeit', *WSI-Mitteilungen*, 68 (3), 178–86.

Bibouche, S., J. Held and G. Merkle (2009), *Rechtspopulismus in der Arbeitswelt: Eine Analyse neuerer Studien*, Düsseldorf: Hans-Böckler-Stiftung.

Bieling, H.-J. (2017), 'Aufstieg des Rechtspopulismus im heutigen Europa: Umrisse einer gesellschaftstheoretischen Erklärung', *WSI Mitteilungen*, 8, 557–65.

Bourdieu, P. (1984), *Distinction: A social critique of the judgement of taste*, London: Routledge.

Burawoy, M. (2015), *Public Sociology: Öffentliche Soziologie gegen Marktfundamentalismus und globale Ungleichheit*, ed. B. Aulenbacher and K. Dörre, Weinheim: Beltz Juventa.

Dale, G. (2014), 'Karl Polanyi in Vienna: Guild socialism, Austro-Marxism and Duczynska's alternative', *Historical Materialism*, 22 (1), 34–66.

Detje, R. and D. Sauer (2018), 'Betriebliche Zustände – ein Nährboden des Rechtspopulismus? Eine arbeitsweltliche Spurensuche', in K. Becker, K. Dörre and P. Reif-Spirek (eds), *Arbeiterbewegung von rechts? Ungleichheit – Verteilungskämpfe – populistische Revolte*, Frankfurt/Main and New York: Campus, pp. 197–209.

Dörre, K., S. Bose, J. Lütten and J. Köster (2018), 'Arbeiterbewegung von rechts? Motive und Grenzen einer imaginären Revolte', *Berliner Journal für Soziologie*, 28 (1–2), Frankfurt: Springer VS.

Dörre, K., A. Happ and I. Matuschek (eds) (2013), *Das Gesellschaftsbild der LohnarbeiterInnen: Soziologische Untersuchungen in ost- und westdeutschen Industriegebieten*, Hamburg: VSA.

Eribon, D. (2014), *Returning to Reims*, Los Angeles: Semiotext(e).

Fratzscher, M. (2016), *Verteilungskampf: Warum Deutschland immer ungleicher wird*, München: Hanser.

Gertz, H. (2017), 'Superstar', *Süddeutsche Zeitung*, 30/31 December.

Hauptmann, A. and H.-J. Schmerer (2012), 'Lohnentwicklung im Verarbeitenden Gewerbe: Wer profitiert vom deutschen Exportboom?' *IAB-Kurzbericht*, 20, accessed 29 January 2019 at http://doku.iab.de/kurzber/2012/kb2012.pdf.

Heitmeyer, W. (2018), 'Autoritärer Nationalradikalismus: Ein neuer politischer Erfolgstypus zwischen konservativem Rechtspopulismus und gewaltförmigem Rechtsextremismus', in K. Becker, K. Dörre and P. Reif-Spirek (eds), *Arbeiterbewegung von rechts? Ungleichheit – Verteilungskämpfe – populistische Revolte*, Frankfurt/Main and New York: Campus, pp. 117–37.

Hochschild, A. (2016), *Strangers in their own land: Anger and mourning on the American right*, New York and London: The New Press.

Infratest dimap (2017), 'Bundestagswahl 24. September 2017: Ergebnisse und Schnellanalysen auf Basis der Kurzfassung des infratest-dimap-Berichts für die SPD', *Nachdenkseiten*, accessed 24 January 2019 at www.nachdenkseiten.de/upload/pdf/171009-Infratest-dimap-schnellanalyse-BTW-2017-SPD.pdf.

Institut der Deutschen Wirtschaft Köln (2017), 'Die AfD: eine unterschätzte Partei: Soziale Erwünschtheit als Erklärung für fehlerhafte Prognosen', accessed 29 January 2019 at www.iwkoeln.de/fileadmin/publikationen/2017/332686/IW-Report_7_2017_Die_AfD_Eine_unterschaetzte_Partei.pdf.

International Monetary Fund (2017), *World economic outlook April 2017: Gaining momentum?*, accessed 29 January 2019 at www.imf.org/en/Publications/WEO/Issues/2017/04/04/world-economic-outlook-april-2017.

Kadritzke, U. (2017), *Mythos 'Mitte': Oder: Die Entsorgung der Klassenfrage*, Berlin: Bertz und Fischer.

Lengfeld, H. (2017), 'Die "Alternative für Deutschland": Eine Partei für Modernisierungsgewinner', *Kölner Zeitschrift für Soziologie und Sozialpsychologie*, 69 (2), 209–32.

Marx, K. ([1852] 1963), *The eighteenth Brumaire of Louis Bonaparte*, New York: International Publishers.

Marx, K. and F. Engels ([1848] 2012), *The communist manifesto: A modern version*, London and New York: Verso.

Nachtwey, O. and D. Jörke (2017), 'Die rechtspopulistische Hydraulik der Sozialdemokratie', in O. Nachtwey and D. Jörke (eds), *Das Volk gegen die liberale Demokratie*, Leviathan Special Volume 32, Baden-Baden: Nomos, pp. 163–86.

Paulus, S. (2017), 'Eine Geschichte der Gegenwart: Zur Sozialen Frage im 21. Jahrhundert', *Theoriekritik*, accessed 29 January 2019 at www.theoriekritik .ch/?p=2920.

Polanyi, K. ([1944] 2001), *The great transformation: The political and economic origins of our time*, Boston: Beacon Press.

Sauer, D., U. Stöger, J. Bischoff, R. Detje and B. Müller (2018), *Rechtspopulismus und Gewerkschaften: Eine arbeitsweltliche Spurensuche*, Hamburg: VSA.

Silver, B. J. (2008), *Forces of labor: Workers' movements and globalization since 1870*, Cambridge: Cambridge University Press.

Die Welt (2017), 'Die Sorgen der Männer im Osten – "Integriert doch erst mal uns"', *Die Welt*, 26 September, accessed 24 January 2019 at www.welt.de/ politik/deutschland/article169032071/Die-Sorgen-der-Maenner-im-Osten -Integriert-doch-erst-mal-uns.html?wtrid=onsite.onsitesearch.

Zeuner, B., J. Gester, M. Fichter and R. Stöss (2007), *Gewerkschaften und Rechtsextremismus*, Münster: Westfälisches Dampfboot.

12. Cultural war 2.0? The relevance of gender in the radical populist-nationalist right

Birgit Sauer

Over the last ten years a consensus developed that the success of radical right-wing populist parties creates a huge challenge to democracies in Europe. In Hungary and Poland nationalist right-wing parties in government started to transform their countries into so-called "illiberal democracies". Despite the loss in the presidential elections the *Front National* (now *Rassemblement National*) has developed into a major actor in France's politics as have the *Dansk Folkeparti* (Danish Peoples' Party), the United Kingdom Independence Party (UKIP) and the Austrian Freedom Party FPÖ (*Freiheitliche Partei Österreich*). In Sweden only in the last twelve years a right-wing populist party, the Sweden Democrats, entered as a latecomer to the political stage. Similarly, Germany for a long time seemed to be immune to political strategies based primarily on right-wing anti-immigration resentments, but the recent electoral successes of the Alternative for Germany (AfD, *Alternative für Deutschland*) proved that this is no longer the case. Moreover, right-wing social movements like the German Pegida (Patriotic Europeans against the Islamization of the Occident) and the Identitarian movements across Europe challenge the values of European liberal democracies.

While right-wing groups and parties were re-established in several European countries after the Second World War, the emergence and growth of the "new" right is a relatively recent phenomenon of the last two decades (Birsl 2011, p. 11; Müller 2016b, p. 18). The transformation of the "old" right-wing parties into "new" *populist* parties is part of their success. At the same time, right-wing parties became more nationalist, nativist and authoritarian – and they aim at a new hegemonic anti-democratic compromise.[1]

---

[1]   Hans-Jürgen Bieling (2017, p. 557) identifies three waves of right-wing parties and movements' growth since the 1970s. I use the notion of right-wing *populist* parties for the third wave of "modernized" radical right parties, which explicitly discuss issues of national-social identity in an antagonistic mode.

While definitions of populism are contested, I will draw on Cas Mudde's notions in the following. Mudde (2004, p. 543) characterizes populism as a "thin-centred ideology", as a communicative strategy of appealing to and creating *first* a "we", "the" people, versus "them", the elite or the establishment (e.g. the EU, the old parties or mainstream media). Politics should be an expression of the *volonté général* of the people (Mudde 2004, p. 543). However, other ideologies can be attached to the populist thin ideology – such as nationalism, nativism and racism on the right or socialist and egalitarian ideologies on the left. What unites *right-wing* populist parties and movements despite their different national and historic backgrounds is a *second* antagonism, the opposition of the "we" to the "Others" (immigrants, asylum seekers, Muslims, LGBTIQ people,[2] feminists), who are supposedly posing a threat to the assumed autochthonous people. The "we" emerging in these right-wing antagonisms is an imagined "heartland", as Taggart writes (Taggart 2000), a homogeneous, morally pure, and nativist people. Mudde mentions a *third* feature of right-wing populism, namely an authoritarian element. Right-wing populist parties perceive politics as characterized by hierarchy and leadership. Hence, Stuart Hall (1985) coined the term "authoritarian populism" for the Thatcher government in Great Britain, which also fits for recent radical right populist strategies across Europe.

In the following I will first present Polanyian explanations of the emergence of the radical populist right in Europe. Second, I will discuss existing literature on right-wing populism as a gendered, male phenomenon in order to argue for the importance of a gendered perspective on the emergence and growth of the radical right. Third, I suggest explaining the success of right-wing populism with reference to gender relations. Finally, I will reflect on the right-wing gendered project of a new anti-democratic political hegemony.

1.   EXPLAINING THE GROWTH OF THE RADICAL POPULIST RIGHT: A POLANYIAN COUNTERMOVEMENT?

Similarly disputed as the concept of populism are the causes behind the rise of the political radical right. In political science, for instance, the growth of the radical right is explained by the transformation and failures of the party systems in Europe starting as early as in the 1960s, namely the oligarchization and cartelization of the catch-all parties and the emergence of a "political class" which is more interested in its own power positions than in the interests of the electorate (von Beyme 1996; Müller 2016a, p. 24). According to Mudde

---

2   LGBTIQ means lesbian, gay, bisexual, transgender, intersexual and queer.

(2004) a "populist Zeitgeist" emerged in the 1980s and since then has characterized more or less all parties in Western liberal democracies. This created an ongoing representational crisis of liberal democracies, the decline of the representational potential of the catch-all parties, the loss of trust in political elites leading to post-democratic (Crouch 2004) or – as Chantal Mouffe (2000) claims – to post-political conditions. The move to the centre of the catch-all parties and the search for consensus, Mouffe (2000, pp. 20 ff.) writes, opened the window of opportunity for the radical populist right, which politicizes the new antagonisms of "we", the people against the elite and the "Others".

While these post-democratic and post-political constellations constitute the background for the rise of right-wing populism, the dramatic transformations of liberal democratic hegemony must also be understood – and thus conceptualized – against the background of fundamental changes of capitalism over the last thirty years; changes which have been labelled as "neoliberal" – i.e. the dominance of the market over state and politics, which unleashes the globalization of capitalist economies as well as the transformation of states and state bureaucracies. Also, the crisis of neoliberalism since the 2008 financial crisis has been leading to major global turmoil, including processes of migration and flight. These conditions fuelled the rise of the populist radical right.

Here, Polanyi's conceptualization of the transformation of liberalism is helpful to understand these changes: The "great transformation" of capitalism and liberalism, i.e. the profound commodification of labour, facilitated the emergence of fascism and National Socialism at the beginning of the twentieth century (Polanyi 2001, pp. 24 ff., 31). According to Polanyi, political transformations cannot be simply deduced from capitalist structures but need to be embedded in social processes and activities in the production of meanings and identities (Bieling 2017, p. 559). Social and political tensions develop through the collision between the commodification of labour and the necessity to secure life and society, for instance through establishing a private, non-marketized sphere or through welfare state institutions. Political and social transformations of capitalist societies thus are characterized by a "double movement": "The one was the principle of economic liberalism, aiming at the establishment of a self-regulating market, relying on the support of the trading classes, and using largely laissez-faire and free trade as its methods; the other was the principle of social protection aiming at the conservation of man and nature as well as productive organization, relying on the varying support of those most immediately affected by the deleterious action of the market – primarily, but not exclusively, the working and the landed classes – and using protective legislation, restrictive associations, and other instruments of intervention as its methods" (Polanyi 2001, pp. 138f). Or to put it differently: "The extension of the market organization in respect to genuine commodities was accompanied by its restriction in respect to fictitious ones" (2001, p. 79). Polanyi labels the move towards restricting fictitious commodities as the countermovement of self-protection of society, i.e. of protecting the fictitious commodities of labour, land and money (2001, p. 79). Countermovements against capitalist commodification aim at re-establishing other interests than "money values" such as "professional status, safety and security, the form of a man's life, the breadth of his existence, the stability of his environment" (2001, p. 161). "The 'challenge' is to society as a whole; the 'response' comes through groups, sections, and classes" (2001, p. 160). Thus, as Bieling (2017, p. 558) points out, a Polanyian perspective of the double movement highlights not only economic issues but also the everyday life, interpretations, meanings and identities of different societal groups. However, movements against capitalist commodification, "'collectivist' countermovements", might take the shape of "socialism or nationalism" (Polanyi 2001, p. 151).

Following Polanyi, social scientists locate the growth and success of recent right-wing populist extremism since the 1990s in fundamental economic and social transformations, which are widely labelled as neoliberal restructuring and the financialization of capitalism. These transformations strengthened the interests of capital at the expense of the working class and parts of the middle class (Jessop 2016, p. 134). The deregulation of labour, austerity policies, the dismantling of public provisions, and cuts in social welfare resulted in rising unemployment, precarization, social insecurity and uncertainty, and an unequal distribution of wealth, i.e. growing poverty and the emergence of some super-rich (Piketty 2014). At the same time neoliberal subjectivation fostered individualization, responsibilization and competitiveness, and the decline of solidarity and care for others as a social value.

These transformations eroded the liberal democratic compromise – the consensus of welfare, equality and regulated political participation of the 1970s. In this context, right-wing populist parties and organizations, following Polanyi, can be seen as "movements against the impositions and compulsion of the capitalist market", movements against the disappointment over cuts in welfare and fears of losing wealth, as Klaus Dörre (2016, p. 2) writes.

Thus, the emergence of the radical populist right is a class-specific reaction, a movement against the deprivations of neoliberal economic globalization, job losses and cuts in social welfare. However, the success of right-wing populist extremism is not only a result of precarization and economic insecurity, i.e. it is not only a class issue, not least due to the fact that also parts of the middle class are afraid of loss of wealth and misrecognition. Moreover, right-wing populism has to be perceived as a gender issue, a "response" of "groups and sections" of the society in Polanyi's (2001, p. 160) words, in our case men. This chapter argues that recent right-wing populist mobilization is a gendered movement or male identity politics at the intersection of class, religion, ethnicity and sexuality. The importance of gender relations as explanatory factor is indicated by the right-wing populists' obsession with gender, the mobilization of gender bias over the last five years, their gendered organizational structures across Europe and their construction of an endangered masculinity and a "crisis of masculinity".

To give only two examples: in a talk in Berlin in September 2016 the French writer Michel Houellebecq called upon his audience to recognize that "The first enemy which our western societies want to eradicate is the age of masculinity, is masculinity itself" (quoted in *Die Zeit*, 29 September 2016, p. 45, translation B.S.). In a similar vein Björn Höcke from the AfD proclaimed at the party convention in 2015: "We have to rediscover our masculinity. Only if we rediscover our masculinity we will be manful. And only if we are manful will we be fortified; and we have to become fortified, dear friends!"[3]

Antagonistic gendered strategies, I want to argue, create the phenomenon of what is called the "new" right compared to the "old" right. Hence, the recent transformations of liberal democracies and the emergence and growth of the radical nationalist-populist right have to be located in simultaneous transformations of capitalist market societies and especially of the so-called male breadwinner systems. Moreover, the analysis of these transformations has to take into account a variety of social relations and ongoing social struggles over class, gender, ethnicity and race as these structures of difference and inequality have shaped national welfare states, i.e. protective movements against the commodification of labour, since their emergence in the nineteenth century.

2. RIGHT-WING POPULIST PARTIES AS "MÄNNERPARTEIEN": DESCRIPTION OF THE GENDERED PHENOMENON

Notwithstanding national differences across Europe, gender and sexuality have for a long time been important pillars of radical right-wing ideologies – like a gender binary which is perceived as natural and is combined with a traditional gendered division of labour in the heterosexual model of the male breadwinner and the woman as mother (Sauer et al. 2016, p. 113; Mayer et al. 2016). Moreover, hegemonic masculinity[4] in the right-wing narrative and imaginary is constructed as heroic masculinity, able to protect the weak and vulnerable woman, who is regarded as important for the heterosexual family, for the nation and the state (Rommelspacher 2011, p. 54). Thus, the extreme

---

[3] Speech at the party convention of the AfD, November 2015 at Erfurt (translation B.S.), accessed 30 November 2015 at www.youtube.com/watch?v=yBvy0MR3KBE.

[4] Hegemonic men or masculinities refer to the concepts of Raewyn Connell and James Messerschmidt (2005). They distinguish between hegemonic, subordinate and marginalized masculinities.

right's ideology has always been based on sexist assumptions. In this vein, Anders Breivik's so-called manifesto draws for instance on the fear of a "feminisation of European culture" (Breivik 2011, p. 36).

While the role of gender and sexuality in the new populist right has only recently received some scholarly attention (Spierings and Zaslove 2015; special volume of *West European Politics*, 40 (4), 2017) the most common gendered assumption is that right-wing populist and right-wing parties are "men's parties", *Männerparteien*, as Cas Mudde called them, referring to the German expression (Mudde 2007, ch. 4; Müller 2016b, p. 35; see also Rashkova and Zankina 2017).

The label *Männerpartei* includes five, though contested, changing and paradoxical dimensions. *First*, right-wing parties are "drawing especially from the support of male voters" (Erzeel and Rashkova 2017, p. 813). Nevertheless, this radical right gender gap in voting varies in different national contexts (Spierings and Zaslove 2017, p. 839; Harteveld et al. 2015). Nonna Mayer's (2013) research shows that Marine Le Pen appeals much more to women than her father Jean Marie Le Pen did and hence, that the gender gap in voting narrowed in the latest French elections. I suggest that the gender gap in voting is not fully explained by gender alone, but that dimensions of class, education, or race and ethnicity need also to be taken into account. In most European countries, the intersection of education, social status or class and gender explains the growth of the radical right in terms of mainly young, poorly educated or jobless men voting for the populist right (Mayer 2013, p. 162). In the last US presidential elections 52 per cent of white women casted their vote for Trump, while he only received 4 per cent of the vote from African-American women (Bump 2018). Hence, in the USA, race and gender are explanatory intersecting structures.

Second, gender differences in political opinions and motivations make right-wing parties "*Männerparteien*" and lead to the radical right gender gap in voting. Men, for instance, "have stronger populist [i.e. antagonistic, B.S.] attitudes than women" (Spierings and Zaslove 2017, p. 840); this means that the framing of a "we" against "Others" regarding the issue of migration appeals more to men than to women. Also, men seem to be more attracted by a masculinist-heroic leadership than women are (Birsl 2011, p. 12; Schellenberg 2012, p. 2).

The *third* characteristic of maleness refers to parliamentary representatives of right-wing parties. Traditionally, these parties attract a male constituency and this translates into a large proportion of male representatives in parliament, not least due to the rejection of quota regulations. However, this male picture in parliament gets blurred in different contexts. In the recent European

Parliament, for instance, the "Europe of Nations and Freedom" (ENF) group[5] has 34 per cent women representatives, while overall the EP has 36 per cent women representatives (Erzeel and Rashkova 2017, p. 814).

Fourth, while right-wing parties traditionally had "male charismatic leaders" (Erzeel and Rashkova 2017, p. 813) – e.g. Jörg Haider in Austria or Pim Fortuyn in the Netherlands – today women take over leadership positions in these parties. These women do not fit the right-wing image of motherhood – such as Marine Le Pen, Pia Kjærsgaard from the Danish People's Party, Siv Jensen from Norway's Progress Party or Alice Weidel, an openly lesbian mother, from the AfD. This "feminization" strategy or strategy of "de-demonization" (Mayer 2013, p. 161) allows right-wing parties to counter or relativize the image of being men's parties and to attract female voters. Nevertheless, these female leaders struggle with a masculinist party structure and thus have to perform their own form of political masculinity (for discussion of political masculinity see Bitzan 2000; Blee and Deutsch 2012; Meret 2015; Meret et al. 2016; Starck and Sauer 2014).

Fifth, substantive representation of women, i.e. acting for women and fighting for women's policies in parliament, is lower in right-wing parties than in others. Especially, right-wingers in parliament do not represent women's issues such as abortion, reproductive rights or quota regulations. Nevertheless, right-wing parties modernized their male-oriented programmes and their conservative gender ideology in order to "remain electorally successful" (Erzeel and Rashkova 2017, p. 816). Amesberger and Halbmayr (2002, p. 308) found for instance "modernized traditional gender images" within the Austrian FPÖ.

The genderedness of the radical populist right moreover shows in the recent development of a new "gender ideology" (Mudde 2007, p. 92) to enrich their "thin-centred ideology". In recent years right-wing populist antagonism includes an explicit reference to the scientific and political concept of gender in order to fight what they call "gender ideology" or "genderism", i.e. the fight against gender studies, gender mainstreaming, gender equality policies and the recognition of sexual diversity (Hark and Villa 2015; Kuhar and Paternotte 2017; for Austria see Mayer and Sauer 2017). Across Europe this anti-gender discourse modulates for instance resentment against the EU by presenting gender mainstreaming as imposed "from above", from Brussels. The anti-gender discourse also frames gender equality and gender studies as projects of a cosmopolitan feminist establishment or a feminist "metropolitan elite" (Cain 2016), which only pursues its own interests while neglecting the

---

[5]   Members of the ENF are inter alia the Austrian FPÖ, the Belgian *Vlaams Belang*, the French FN, the Italian *Lega Nord* and the Dutch *Partij voor de Vrijheid* (www .enfgroup-ep.eu).

interests of the "woman in the street". Finally, the recognition of sexual diversity is framed as a threat for children, especially for boys who are presented as in danger of being harassed by homosexual teachers (Mayer and Sauer 2017).

This "anti-genderist" move, however, draws an ambivalent picture when "it comes to the rights of Muslim women" (de Lange and Mügge 2015, p. 65): right-wing populist parties blame the backwardness, the pre-modern, patriarchal and misogynist barbarism and the violence of migrant and especially of Muslim men. The aim is to stigmatize Muslim "Others" in order to exclude them as not fitting to gender-equal Western societies. This "femonationalist" argument, as Sarah Farris (2017) calls it, or ethnosexist struggles (Dietze 2016) have been activated after the sexual assaults in Cologne on New Year's Eve 2015.

Hence, radical right-wing parties "couch their anti-immigrant proposals in gendered terms" (Morgan 2017, p. 888). But it would be too one-sided if we perceive gender only as being instrumentalized by the radical right for their anti-immigrant policies. Right-wingers' focus on gender points to both: that the growth of the radical right is based on transformations of gender relations and that it is part of ongoing gender struggles.

3. GENDERED EXPLANATION OF THE RISE OF THE RADICAL POPULIST RIGHT

In this section I want to expand the class perspective on the transformation of capitalist societies and politics and hence the emergence of nationalist movements against the commodification of labour. This argument expands Polanyian explanations by re-reading and re-conceptualizing Polanyi's argument of a double movement with an explicit gender dimension. For Polanyi one movement to protect society and the life of people is the creation of a private sphere, the family. While Polanyi did not discuss this protection as a movement at the expense of women's autonomy, he nevertheless realized that the capitalist market logic resulted in "the destruction of family life, the devastation of neighbourhoods" (Polanyi 2001, p. 139), i.e. one could add in the fundamental transformation of relations between men and women in the private sphere.

The gender perspective on the rise of the radical populist right therefore can draw on Polanyi's argument of movements which aim at social protection against the capitalist interests of the market. Monetary interests, Polanyi writes, "affect individuals in innumerable ways as neighbours, professional persons, consumers, pedestrians, commuters, sportsmen, hikers, gardeners, patients, mothers, or lovers" (2001, p. 161). Thus he concludes: "It appears reasonable to group our account of the protective movement not around class interests, but around the social interests imperilled by the market" (2001, p. 169) – to which we might add gender interests or struggles over gender at the intersection of class, sexuality, religion, ethnicity and race.

This opens the perspective towards gendered transformative contexts and countermovements. The emergence and growth of a new right-wing populist extremism over the last two decades is rooted in fundamental neoliberal transformations of the gender regimes in especially Western breadwinner oriented societies. Until the late 1970s the welfare consensus and gender regimes in most European countries rested on *in*equality between men and women, on the division between (male) paid labour and (female) unpaid care work which entailed women remaining dependent on a male breadwinner. The inclusion of women into higher education, the expansion of the so-called Keynesian welfare state and the struggle of women's movements since the late 1960s have been leading to more gender equality in European societies by slowly integrating women into the labour market. Neoliberal restructuring since the late 1980s resulted – with different pace in different European countries – in an acceleration of the inclusion of women into labour markets, in the intensified commodification of female labour, thus in an ambivalent "neoliberal gender equality" (Wichterich 2007). Hence, neoliberal arrangements allowed for a further ambivalent emancipation of women – especially of well-educated women, who became the target of affirmative action policies.

At the same time, male labour became more precarious and the "family wage" declined. Overall, the systematic erosion of the wealth of a low qualified working- and middle-class population through labour deregulation and cuts in welfare since the 1990s was accompanied by the erosion of hierarchical gender regimes and of male dominance in the private sphere of the family as well as in the public sphere of wage labour, politics and the state. These developments created a huge challenge to masculine hegemony and fostered the discourse about "failed patriarchs", i.e. men who are supposed to take over dominant or breadwinner positions but at the same time are confronted with their declining role on the labour market (Radhakrishnan and Solari 2015).

Against this background the radical right claims to compensate these losses and frames the marginalization of working- and middle-class men as caused by female labour market integration, gender equality and, of course, migration policies. They redefine the deprived class-status of "subordinated men" (Connell and Messerschmidt 2005) as hatred against well-educated women and migrants. The right-wing anti-gender discourse and the evocation of a "crisis of masculinity" is, hence, another facet of the re-signification process of growing social inequality while strategically confounding causes and consequences by mobilizing "angry white men" (Kimmel 2013).

In its discourse of boundary drawing, exclusion and "othering", right-wing populism moreover contributes to the self-affirmation of masculinity by offering points of reference for the re-establishment of traditional gender constellations and thus for the abolishment of gender equality policies. The right-wing interpellation of the "little man in the street" is hence part of a masculinist identity politics, which includes the promise that a charismatic male leader might increase the self-confidence of subordinated masculinities. Expanding Polanyi's notion of a double movement with an explicit focus on gender relations therefore helps to understand that right-wing populist mobilization of (a traditional) masculine identity is part of a discourse against commodification and of securing the everyday.

In the following I want to reflect on why gender is so important for right-wing populist mobilization and what the gender perspective tells us about the struggle over hegemony and the new political project of the radical populist right in a Polanyian perspective.

4.   GENDERED STRUGGLES FOR HEGEMONY: ELEMENTS OF A "DOUBLE MOVEMENT"?

Today, right-wing populist parties across Europe seem to have a single issue – they mobilize against immigration. However, a gender perspective reveals another project beneath the surface – the fundamental transformation of liberal democracies and welfare states. Right-wing anti-genderist mobilization must be seen as a "cultural war", which turns the critique of neoliberal global restructuring against the emancipatory movements of the 1960s and 1970s and against the Keynesian welfare state with its aims of limited social equality and democratization. In these cultural and political struggles, gender works as an "empty signifier" (Laclau 1996), which is able to connect new populist right-wing visions of society and the state, as for instance natural inequality, exclusion and authoritarianism, in order to modulate new hegemonic constellations and to forge new alliances with conservatives, with the Catholic Church as well as with liberals. Hence, the empty signifier "gender" becomes a catalyst in the movement of "self-protection of society" (Polanyi 2001, p. 79), at the expense, however, of gender equality in the private sphere of the family as well as in the sphere of wage labour.

As a binary concept, gender builds the paradigm for dividing societies into two distinct and hierarchical groups. Using gender legitimizes the fundamental inequality of people and thus of social hierarchies (Birsl 2011, p. 17; Lewandowsky et al. 2016, pp. 252 ff.). Eventually, referring to gender constructs a specific notion of "the people" in two discursive modes: *first*, gender symbolizes the natural, homogeneous and pure people (Diehl 2016, p. 17) and thus signifies the ethnopluralist idea of the people and the aversion towards a mix of supposedly different ethnicities. This nationalist-populist politics rejects plurality and legitimizes securitization, the walling off of the nation and the walling out of migrants and refugees (Brown 2010). *Second,* in the gender frame "the people" is constructed as weak and passive, without agency – a deceived victim of elites. "The people" needs to be saved from the seduction of corrupt political and intellectual elites – such as gender politicians or the media. The saviour is of course a right-wing populist leader. Hence, the interpellation of the people in right-wing populist political communication is part of the quest for more political leadership and thus for more authoritarianism. The paternalistic and patriarchal image of the people results in an anti-democratic move. Also, in this discourse democracy as sovereignty of the people seems impossible due to the inequality of people and their need of protection, hierarchy and leadership.

Overall, gender works as an empty signifier in the populist right's struggle, which fundamentally challenges social equality, non-discrimination and sovereignty through evoking the natural inequality of human beings and the nativist people in need of leadership. Referring to the Polanyian model of a double movement, the populist radical right tries to capture the fears of insecurity in the relations between men and women in order to safeguard against commodification of labour and life through restoring inequalities of gender relations. Against this background I suggest the need to further engage in studying (right-wing) politics as an intersectional struggle over social relations – class, gender, sexuality, religion and ethnicity, which have been embedded in Western liberal democracies and welfare states. Such an intersectional approach demands new coalitions in the struggle for democracy and democratization and against the radical populist right; it demands cooperation between social justice movements, such as the women's movements, leftist parties and trade unions.

REFERENCES

Amesberger, H. and B. Halbmayr (eds) (2002), *Rechtsextreme Parteien – eine mögliche Heimat für Frauen?* Opladen: Leske und Budrich.

Beyme, K. von (1996), 'The concept of political class: A new dimension of research on elites?', *Western European Politics*, 19 (1), 68–87.

Bieling, H.-J. (2017), 'Aufstieg des Rechtspopulismus im heutigen Europa – Umrisse einer gesellschaftstheoretischen Erklärung', *WSI Mitteilungen*, 8, 557–65.

Birsl, U. (2011), 'Rechtsextremismus und Gender', in U. Birsl (ed.), *Rechtsextremismus und Gender*, Opladen: Barbara Budrich, pp. 11–26.

Bitzan, R. (2000), *Selbstbilder rechter Frauen: Zwischen Antisexismus und völkischem Denken*, Tübingen: Edition Diskord.

Blee, K. and S.M. Deutsch (eds) (2012), *Women of the right: Comparisons and interplay across borders*, University Park, PA: Pennsylvania State University Press.

Breivik, A. (2011), *2083: A European declaration of independence*, London.

Brown, W. (2010), *Walled states, waning sovereignty*, New York: Zone Books.

Bump, P. (2018), 'Trump celebrates winning 52 percent of women in 2016 – which is only how he did among whites', *Washington Post*, accessed 10 March 2018 at www.washingtonpost.com/news/politics/wp/2018/03/10/trump-celebrates-winning-52-percent-of-women-in-2016-which-is-only-how-he-did-among-whites/?noredirect=on&utm_term=.f5c71ebe1b48.

Cain, R. (2016), 'Post-truth and the "metropolitan elite": Feminist lessons from Brexit', *feminist@law*, 6 (1), accessed 10 March 2018 at http://journals.kent.ac.uk/index.php/feministsatlaw/article/view/259.

Connell, R. and J.W. Messerschmidt (2005), 'Hegemonic masculinity: Rethinking the concept', *Gender & Society*, 6, 829–59.

Crouch, C. (2004), *Post-democracy*, Cambridge: Polity Press.

Diehl, P. (2016), 'Demokratische Repräsentation und ihre Krise', *Aus Politik und Zeitgeschichte*, 40–42, 12–17.

Dietze, G. (2016), 'Ethnosexismus: Sex-Mob-Narrative um die Kölner Sylvesternacht', *movements*, 1, accessed 10 March 2018 at https://movements-journal.org/issues/03.rassismus/10.dietze--ethnosexismus.html.

Dörre, K. (2016), 'Die national-soziale Gefahr: Pegida, Neue Rechte und der Verteilungskonflikt – sechs Thesen', in K.-S. Rehberg, F. Kunz and T. Schlinzig (eds), *PEGIDA – Rechtspopulismus zwischen Fremdenangst und 'Wende'-Enttäuschung?*, Bielefeld: transcript.

Erzeel, S. and E.R. Rashkova (2017), 'Still men's parties? Gender and the radical right in comparative perspective', *West European Politics*, 40 (4), 812–20.

Farris, S. (2017), *In the name of women's rights: The rise of femonationalism*, Durham, NC: Duke University Press.

Hall, S. (1985), 'Authoritarian populism: A reply to Jessop et al.', *New Left Review*, 1 (151), 115–24.

Hark, S. and P.-I. Villa (eds) (2015), *Anti-Genderismus: Sexualität und Geschlecht als Schauplätze aktueller politischer Auseinandersetzungen*, Bielefeld: transcript.

Harteveld, E., W. van der Brug, S. Dahlberg and A. Kokkonen (2015), 'The gender gap in populist radical-right voting: Examining the demand side in Western and Eastern Europe', *Patterns of Prejudice*, 49 (1), 103–34.

Jessop, B. (2016), 'The organic crisis of the British state: Putting Brexit in its place', *Globalizations*, 14 (1), 133–41.

Kimmel, M. (2013), *Angry white men: American masculinity at the end of an era*. New York: Nation Books.

Kuhar, R. and D. Paternotte (eds) (2017), *Anti-gender campaigns in Europe: Mobilizing against equality*, Lanham, MD: Roman & Littlefield.

Laclau, E. (1996), *Emancipation(s)*, London and New York: Verso.

Lange, S. de and L.M. Mügge (2015), 'Gender and right-wing populism in the Low Countries: Ideological variations across parties and time', *Patterns of Prejudice*, 49 (1), 61–80.

Lewandowsky, M., H. Giebler and A. Wagner (2016), 'Rechtspopulismus in Deutschland: Eine empirische Einordnung der Parteien zur Bundestagswahl 2013 unter besonderer Berücksichtigung der AfD', *Politische Vierteljahresschrift*, 57 (2), 247–75.

Mayer, N. (2013), 'From Jean-Marie to Marine le Pen: Electoral change on the far right', *Parliamentary Affairs*, 66 (1), 160–178.

Mayer, S. and B. Sauer (2017), '"Gender Ideology" in Austria: Coalitions around an empty signifier', in R. Kuhar and D. Paternotte (eds), *Anti-gender campaigns in Europe: Mobilizing against equality*, Lanham, MD: Rowman & Littlefield, pp. 19–30.

Mayer, S., I. Sori and B. Sauer (2016), 'Gendering "the people": Heteronormativity and "ethno-masochism" in populist imaginary', in M. Ranieri (ed.), *Populism, media and education: Challenging discrimination in contemporary digital societies*, London and New York: Routledge, pp. 84–104.

Meret, S. (2015), 'Female charismatic leadership and gender: Pia Kjærsgaard and the Danish People's Party', *Patterns of Prejudice*, 49 (1), 81–102.

Meret, S., B. Siim and E. Pingaud (2016), 'Men's parties with women leaders: A comparative study of the right-wing populist leaders Pia Kjærsgaard, Siv Jensen and Marine Le Pen', in G. Lazaridis and G. Campani (eds), *Understanding the populist shift: Othering in a Europe in crisis*, London and New York: Routledge, pp. 122–49.

Morgan, K.J. (2017), 'Gender, right-wing populism, and immigrant integration policies in France, 1989–2012', *West European Politics*, 40 (4), 887–906.

Mouffe, C. (2000), *The democratic paradox*, London and New York: Verso.

Mudde, C. (2004), 'The populist Zeitgeist', *Government and Opposition*, 39 (4), 541–63.

Mudde, C. (2007), *Populist radical right parties in Europe*, Cambridge: Cambridge University Press.

Müller, J.-W. (2016a), 'Populismus: Symptom einer Krise der politischen Repräsentation?', *Aus Politik und Zeitgeschichte*, 40–42, 24–9.

Müller, J.-W. (2016b), *Was ist Populismus? Ein Essay*, Berlin: Suhrkamp.

Piketty, T. (2014), *Capital in the twenty-first century*, Cambridge, MA: Harvard University Press.

Polanyi, K. (2001), *The great transformation: The political and economic origins of our time*, Boston: Beacon Press.

Radhakrishnan, S. and C. Solari (2015), 'Empowered women, failed patriarchs: Neoliberalism and global gender anxieties', *Sociology Compass*, 9 (9), 784–802.

Rashkova, E.R. and E. Zankina (2017), 'Are (populist) radical right parties Männerparteien? Evidence from Bulgaria', *West European Politics*, 40 (4), 848–68.

Rommelspacher, B. (2011), 'Frauen und Männer im Rechtsextremismus – Motive, Konzepte und Rollenverständnisse', in U. Birsl (ed.), *Rechtsextremismus und Gender*, Opladen: Barbara Budrich, pp. 43–68.

Sauer, B., R. Kuhar, E. Ajanovic and A. Saarinen (2016), 'Exclusive intersections: Constructions of gender and sexuality', in G. Lazaridis and G. Campani (eds), *Understanding the populist shift: Othering in a Europe in crisis*, London and New York: Routledge, pp. 104–21.

Schellenberg, B. (2009), 'Aktuelle Entwicklungen im europäischen Rechtsextremismus', *Bundeszentrale für Politische Bildung*, accessed 4 June 2016 at www.bpb.de/politik/extremismus/rechtsextremismus/41221/analyse-rechtsradikale-in-europa?p=0.

Spierings, N. and A. Zaslove (2015), 'Gendering the vote for populist radical-right parties', *Patterns of Prejudice*, 49 (1), 135–62.

Spierings, N. and A. Zaslove (2017), 'Gender, populist attitudes, and voting: Explaining the gender gap in voting for populist radical right and populist radical left parties', *West European Politics*, 40 (4), 821–47.

Starck, K. and B. Sauer (2014), *A man's world? Political masculinities in literature and culture*, Newcastle: Cambridge Scholars.

Taggart, P. (2000), *Populism*, Buckingham: Open University Press.

Wichterich, C. (2007), 'Globalisierung und Geschlecht: Über neoliberale Strategien zur Gleichstellung', *Blätter für deutsche und internationale Politik*, 6, 686–95.

PART III

"Fictitious commodities" and the challenges of "our time"

13. Contested social-ecological transformation: shortcomings of current debates and Polanyian perspectives

Ulrich Brand, Christoph Görg and Markus Wissen

1. INTRODUCTION

In international debates on sustainability and social-ecological issues, the term "transformation" – sometimes with reference to Polanyi – has become significant within the last years. A prominent case in point is the report *World in Transition* published by the German Advisory Council on Global Change and using the term "Great Transformation" in the title of the original German version (WBGU 2011). More recently the Wuppertal Institute on Environment, Climate and Energy published a study which also uses the term in its title (Schneidewind 2018). Scientific debate on the subject is intense (overviews in O'Brian 2012; Brie 2014; Nalau and Handmer 2015; Brand and Wissen 2017; Görg et al. 2017; Blühdorn et al. 2018).

It seems that discussions about transformation have a similar function to those around sustainable development in the 1990s, putting the ecological crisis into a larger context and uniting different fields of thinking and action against business-as-usual strategies. However, compared to the beginning of the era of sustainability concerns, the context has changed dramatically. The deepening of the ecological crisis during the last twenty-five years, the complexity and far-reaching consequences of problems as well as the urgent need to act are broadly acknowledged.

In this chapter we aim to address and assess the transformation debate from a Polanyian perspective. We argue that Polanyi's understanding of the historical "great transformation" towards capitalism as the root cause of the collapse of nineteenth-century civilization in the 1930s focuses the complex and highly problematic structural dynamics that are often ignored in current debates about social-ecological transformation (SET in the following).

We proceed as follows: In section 2, we outline some crucial aspects of current debates on social-ecological transformation. In so doing, we prepare a threefold argument that is developed in the following sections: With Polanyi we can enrich the debate on SET at the theoretical level by his understanding of a great transformation and his insistence that capitalism treats nature as commodity and therefore undermines its reproduction. Against the background of regulation theory we distinguish three types of transformation (section 3). With these theoretical reflections we can better understand the current ecological crisis as crucial element of the more comprehensive crisis dynamics of capitalism (section 3) and stress the necessity of political strategies that focus, among other things, on a decommodification of nature and argue for a democratization of societal nature relations (section 4). We conclude with a short discussion of the limits of a Polanyian approach to social-ecological transformation (section 5).

2. SOCIAL-ECOLOGICAL TRANSFORMATION: A CONTESTED EPISTEMOLOGICAL AND POLITICAL TERRAIN

In recent years, a series of political and academic reports and strategies has addressed the multiple and aggravating crises of capitalist societies: climate change, biodiversity loss, the economic crisis, the increasing inequality within many societies, the crisis of democracy, the tensions in international policy (OECD 2011; UNEP 2011; WBGU 2011; see Brand and Wissen 2017 for an overview). Most of the respective publications agree in considering the socio-environmental unsustainability of current societies as key to the understanding of many crisis phenomena and in stressing the urgent need for SET. The very concept of transformation, however, that is prevailing in the academic and political debates about (un-)sustainability remains vague. In particular, there is no agreement about the concrete causes of the crisis: there is neither agreement about the interlinkages between different dimensions of the crisis, nor a shared understanding of what the "urgent action" that is considered necessary actually means. Thus, Wolfgang Sachs's verdict on the formula of sustainable development seems also to be applicable to SET: it is "designed to maximize consensus rather than clarity" (Sachs 1999, p. 28).

Despite its rather vague character, there are some core elements of most concepts of SET: First, the common denominator of most reports and strategy papers is that they consider economic growth desirable, necessary and able to reconcile with the environment. They express a belief, akin to that which prevailed at the beginning of the sustainable development discourse in the early

1990s, that comprehensive win-win situations can be created: "the greening of economies is not generally a drag on growth but rather a new engine of growth; [...] it is a net generator of decent jobs, and [...] it is also a vital strategy for the elimination of persistent poverty" (UNEP 2011, p. 3). An important message thus is that SET is possible without fundamentally changing the mechanisms according to which capitalist societies function, in particular competition and growth. Instead, these mechanisms are seen as possible drivers of change if only the political framework conditions are shaped in favour of green capital factions. Power- and interest-driven processes are not in the focus of most contributions around SET and they show little understanding of the expansive logics and the conflict-driven character of modern societies.

Second, there seems to be a firm trust in the existing political and economic institutions and elites, which they see as both able and willing to guide this process. For instance, large parts of the SET debate assume that the state and its policymakers are interested in handling collective problems, and hence in creating general welfare. Currently, however, the emissions scandal in Germany (and probably also in other European countries) is a case in point where the German government mostly protects the unsustainable and profit-driven interests of the German automotive industry.

Third, most SET strategies towards a green economy hardly question that neoliberal open-market policies and fierce competition have led to a further commodification of nature around the world.

And finally, the strategies do not problematize the universalization of the Western mode of production via neoliberal globalization. We have analysed this model as implying an "imperial mode of living" (Brand and Wissen 2018): The logic of globalized liberal markets is reflected in the everyday practices in which access to cheap and often unsustainably produced commodities and labour power are normalized. Currently, this logic is being universalized among the upper and middle classes of economically fast growing semi-peripheral countries.

Without any doubt and despite all differences, the debate about the environmentally (and socially) destructive character of globalization under the header of SET goes beyond business-as-usual strategies to stabilize "brown" capitalism. In the broad debate on SET it is acknowledged that in the last three decades the ecological crisis deepened and an urgent transformation is required (cf. recently IPCC 2018). However, within this field epistemic and political power relations exist. They exclude or ignore more radical approaches which question dominant institutions like the market and the state as well as dominant logics like capitalist growth. Consequently, the debate on SET does hardly take into account the necessity of over-accumulated capital to look for profitable investment opportunities through the commodification of nature. One could therefore argue that there is a dominant "new critical orthodoxy" emerging (Brand 2016). Its rationale consists of seeing far-reaching problems and a deep ecological crisis and at the same time having a lot of trust in dominant dynamics like economic growth (of course, it should be "greened") and the mentioned prevailing institutions as well as the related power relations.

3.   UNDERSTANDING SOCIAL-ECOLOGICAL TRANSFORMATION WITH POLANYI

We argue that a Polanyian understanding of capitalist dynamics and its shaping of societal nature relations helps us to sharpen the analytical understanding of the ecological crisis and the strategic challenges ahead to cope with it. In the following we show that a Polanyian approach goes far beyond the semantic reference of most contributions of the "new critical orthodoxy" of SET to a great transformation (on various interpretations of Polanyi, cf. Gareth Dale's instructive distinction between a "soft" and a "hard" Polanyi; Dale 2016, pp. 4–7). In order to unfold its full potential, it must however be amended by other concepts and combined with other theories.

Regulation theory seems to be particularly useful in this respect (Aglietta 1979; Lipietz 1988; Atzmüller et al. 2013). On the one hand, it (implicitly) draws on a fundamental insight by Polanyi, namely that the capital relation is constitutively incomplete, it cannot "achieve self-closure, i.e. [. . .] reproduce itself wholly through the value form" (Jessop 2000, p. 235, and Chapter 6 in this volume) and thus needs extra-economic institutions in order to contain its self-destructive tendencies. On the other hand, regulation theory is broader because it does not focus mainly on the commodification of fictitious commodities, processes of disembedding and struggles over certain forms of re-embedding against the "Utopian experiment of a self-regulating market" (Polanyi [1944] 2001, p. 258). Instead, it addresses the complex and temporary institutional stabilization of inherently contradictory social relations. Moreover, regulation theory distinguishes different modes of capitalist development in space and time and thus helps to correct "Polanyi's homogenizing history of capitalism as a singular wave of marketization giving way to a singular countermovement" (Burawoy 2013, p. 38). This is not only a theoretical issue but also important for an adequate understanding of different forms of transformation that might emerge out of the current crisis.

3.1   Transformation

When Polanyi wrote *The Great Transformation*, he was convinced that the civilizational crisis of capitalism, particularly fascism, is not likely to be solved within liberal capitalism (Polanyi [1944] 2001, pp. 245, 267; Dale 2016; Brie and Thomasberger 2018). In contrast to regulation theory, he could not analyse *ex post* how this crisis was processed after the Second World War with the emergence of Fordism, decolonization and some remarkable advances within societies of the Global South as well as a relatively stable international order of "embedded liberalism" (Ruggie 1982) under the leadership of the United States, the rule of the Soviet Union in its sphere and some independent countries like China.

Following regulation theory, we suggest to distinguish three types of transformation: *First, incremental transformations* in and after "small crises" that accommodate society and economy. Capitalist societies transform themselves constantly and from time to time through crises. Permanent transformation is the very mode of reproduction of capitalism. It is its business as usual that distinguishes it from its predecessors.

In contrast to a small crisis and the resulting incremental transformation, a "great crisis" (Aglietta 1979; Boyer 1990) leads to a more *profound restructuring of the capitalist mode of production*, the modes of living, the technologies, the forms of the state, the dominant understandings of a good or at least functioning society, etc. This is the *second* type of transformation to be considered here. Struggles over hegemony take place in its course and even anti- and post-capitalist proposals and forces might gain relevance, but capital and the political forces related to it are usually able to maintain the basic structures of capitalism, although under new institutional conditions and based on a transformed regime of accumulation.

One could read the current debate on SET as a strategic claim to overcome fossil fuel-based capitalism, to cope with the social-ecological contradictions as they have been intensified by neoliberalism and to transform the resource base of the economy, i.e. to initiate a transformation towards a "green" capitalist mode of development. This would not question the capitalist mode of production and living, industry and further industrialization. It could, however, work as a countermovement against the self-destructive tendencies of neoliberal capitalism and industrial capitalism in general, temporarily containing the ecological crisis (Satgar and Williams, Chapter 14 this volume, call these the "ecocidal tendencies" of capitalism). However, under conditions of the dominant capitalist mode of production this would occur in a spatially and socially selective manner and create new forms of ecological contradictions, e.g. regarding the extraction and possible scarcity of the metals that are needed to sustain the growth of a "green" economy.

The *third* type of transformation is the one that results in forms of societalization (*Vergesellschaftung*) and societal nature relations beyond the capitalist mode of production. Polanyi's important point was that liberal capitalism of the nineteenth century led to a crisis or even collapse of civilization in the 1930s. Here we can understand that capitalist globalization since the 1970s increasingly provides evidence for such a collapse, particularly in ecological but also in cultural and political terms. However, and this is the strategic implication of a critical and emancipatory understanding of SET, there might arise social practices and forces that point to post-capitalist modes of production beyond an authoritarian "brown" or a more or less regulated "green" capitalism. We elaborate on that point below.

It is important to note that the regulation theoretical typology of crises and transformations is not totally in line with Polanyi's approach. On the one hand, there is a coincidence of Polanyi's *Great Transformation* and the institutional, technological and economic restructuring that results from a *great crisis* of capitalism, i.e. the second type of transformation in regulation theoretical terms. Thus, both Polanyi and regulation theory would coincide in their assessment of the capitalist crisis starting in 1929. They would, however, differ regarding the crisis of Fordism in the 1970s. For regulation theory, the latter is another great crisis of capitalism that, like the one in the 1930s, gave way to major changes in the industrial paradigm, the regime of accumulation and the institutional forms through which social contradictions are processed. From a Polanyian perspective, however, one would stress the differences between the two crises. The crisis of the 1930s was driven by *countermovements* that politicized the socially destructive tendencies of the preceding wave of marketization (either progressively, like the labour movement in the USA, or in a reactionary way, like the Nazis in Germany). It resulted in a *re-embedding* of the economy into society. In contrast, the crisis of the 1970s was driven by the *movement* of neoliberal forces that increasingly gained influence in academia, in the media and in state apparatuses like central banks and managed to politicize the contradictions of an embedded capitalism. It resulted in a *dis-embedding* of the economy from society in particular at a global scale and a new wave of marketization since the second half of the 1970s (Altvater and Mahnkopf 1996; critique in Brand and Görg 2001).[1]

For Polanyi, a great transformation may therefore indeed emerge out of a great crisis in the sense of regulation theory, but only insofar as this crisis follows from the contradictions that have been intensified by a preceding wave of marketization. Furthermore, a great transformation in the understanding of Polanyi may either take the form of a major restructuring of the mode of regulation and the regime of accumulation, i.e. a transformation *of* capitalism (type two of regulation theory) or mark the beginning of a process that ends

---

[1]   It was also driven by social movements that criticized an authoritarian welfare state, a confining educational system, patriarchal gender relations and destructive societal relations with nature. However, as Boltanski and Chiapello (2003) have shown, the neoliberal critique managed to absorb central notions of the *critique artiste* of social movements and partially redirect it into a new wave of marketization.

in completely different forms of societalization, i.e. a transformation *beyond* capitalism (type three of regulation theory).

3.2   Land and Nature

A further theoretical insight of Polanyi that is largely neglected in the SET debate is his very understanding of modern societies and the limits of liberal ideologies, particularly that "the concept of a self-regulating market was Utopian" (Polanyi [1944] 2001, pp. 148, 157). For Polanyi, the utopian liberal ideologies led to severe crises and the emergence of the social forces of the "protective countermovement" that struggled for certain forms of re-embedding by restricting the overuse of fictitious commodities (Polanyi [1944] 2001, introduction, particularly chapters 11, 12; cf. the contributions of Sauer, Chapter 12, and Satgar and Williams, Chapter 14 in this volume).

Polanyi's understanding of the dynamic development of the "market society" and the "stark utopia of self-regulated markets" in the nineteenth century was intrinsically linked to the question of land. We should equate land today with a more comprehensive understanding of nature, soil and ecosystems. Concerning the biophysical foundations of social life and the tendency to its commodification, Polanyi stated: "What we call land is an element of nature inextricably interwoven with man's institutions. To isolate it and form a market for it was perhaps the weirdest of all the undertakings of our ancestors" (Polanyi [1944] 2001, p. 187). Land is, beside labour and money, for Polanyi one of the fictitious commodities – fictitious in the sense that it is not produced for sale: Biological evolution is an enormously complex and contingent process and biophysical processes, even if they are transformed by labour and technology, are based on laws of their own (Polanyi [1944] 2001, pp. 45–69). Thus, nature cannot be produced as a commodity. Throughout history, nature was appropriated by human labour and embedded in social rules and norms. However, in societies with a dominant capitalist mode of production it is *treated* as a commodity with an exchange value whose realization on the market contributes to capital accumulation.

Referring to the example of England, Polanyi distinguishes three "stages in the subjection of the surface of the planet to the needs of an industrial society" (Polanyi [1944] 2001, p. 188). First, land was isolated from its communal or feudal usage – as the direct producers were liberated from personal dependency but also from their direct means of (re-)production and they became wage labourers. Private property on land and the right to exchange it became a crucial element of individual freedom. Second, the basic provision of most people with their means of living became market dependent. Until the second half of the eighteenth century, the means of reproduction were largely produced for own use or for exchange on local markets. Then they were more and more transported and sold over increasingly large distances for the growing population in industrial cities whose population had no more to sell than its labour power. This dynamic was, third, repeated at the global scale. Particularly through free trade, "the industrial-agricultural division of labour was applied to the planet" (Polanyi [1944] 2001, p. 190). The industrial centres imported mineral and metal resources as well as agrarian products for individual and "productive" (i.e. industrial) consumption.

This commodification of land – or better said: of nature – is one of the core drivers of capitalist globalization as well as of the ever more severe ecological crisis. The central contradiction of this commodification lies in the fact that nature is appropriated for societies and, at the same time, put in danger or even destroyed. To treat nature as commodity implies getting the maximum economic revenue from it. This can go so far that the reproduction of nature or certain elements of it is threatened.

3.3 Recent Waves of Commodification as Attempts to Deal with Capitalist Crises

With Polanyi we consider the further commodification of nature as a danger-ous dynamic. We give some examples for the above mentioned three stages in order to clarify our argument. A case in point for the first stage of commod-ification is the prominent example of *land grabbing* (Peluso and Lund 2012; Brad et al. 2015). Land that is used as common, often in extensive manner and with non-codified rules, is first subsumed under formal rules and then privat-ized in order to cultivate cash crops for exports.

An example for the second stage, i.e. the conversion of the basic provi-sions of the means of reproduction of people through commodities, is the breath-taking pace of industrialization and urbanization in countries with "emerging economies" such as on the east coast in China (Huan 2008). This attracts or forces people from the countryside into commodity cycles who formerly lived on a semi-subsistent basis. As wage labourers they move to the industrial centres and become dependent on commodities in their personal reproduction – and require for that the maintenance of a wage-income.

And finally, the crisis of Fordist capitalism since the 1970s and more recently the crisis of 2007/2008 were tackled by dominant actors through an ever more intense commodification of labour and nature at a global scale. Agro-industrial and pharmaceutical companies of the Global North buy the intellectual property on biological diversity in countries of the Global South (Brand et al. 2008). In sum and from a Polanyian perspective, a far-reaching SET that really intends to cope with the driving forces of the crisis of societal nature relations needs to block the various commodification dynamics.

4. STRATEGIES OF A GREAT TRANSFORMATION: POST-CAPITALIST SOCIETAL NATURE RELATIONS

In the last chapter of *The Great Transformation* Polanyi states in the second paragraph: "After a century of blind 'improvement' man is restoring his 'habitation'. If industrialism is not to extinguish the race, it must be subordinated to the requirements of man's nature" (Polanyi [1944] 2001, p. 257). Polanyi argued for "the shifting of industrial civilization onto a new nonmarketing basis" (Polanyi [1944] 2001, p. 258) which can be read as an overcoming of the imperatives of the capitalist market, i.e. the third type of transformation we introduced above. At the same time, Polanyi was aware that dealing with the civilizational crisis is a highly contested process. The transformation process "may happen in a great variety of ways, democratic and aristocratic, constitutionalist and authoritarian" (Polanyi [1944] 2001, p. 259).

More concretely this means for perspectives of a SET that beside authoritarian tendencies and the prevailing predominance of "brown industries" there is also the danger that the corridor of both top-down *and* bottom-up alternatives tends to be systematically narrowed down to a form of capitalist ecological modernization.

Polanyi had serious doubts whether the social and ecological problems of his time could be solved under conditions of a "market society" (a synonym for liberal capitalism). In that sense, he was not just a theorist of the "double movement" and a social reformer but a socialist who experienced the Red Vienna of the 1920s and socialist experiments in Eastern Europe at that time (Brie and Thomasberger 2018, pp. 13–14; Bockman 2018; Novy, Bärnthaler, and Stadelmann, Chapter 16 in this volume).

Concerning the mentioned dynamics of the commodification of nature, Polanyi suggested particularly two things to counter it: the de-commodification of nature and – in our words – the democratization of societal nature relations. In his *Great Transformation* Polanyi does not use explicitly the term "de-commodification". But he clearly argues that the commodification of land (beside labour and money) is the key driver of the crisis of civilization (Polanyi [1944] 2001, chapter six, also pp. 137, 167). This suggests that for a Polanyian perspective on SET, probably the most important issue is the *de-commodification* of nature. This is more than its mere protection or conservation – like many environmental discourses suggest – but it means very different forms of the societal appropriation of nature to fulfil human and societal needs, i.e. different forms of organizing alimentation and clothing, housing and infrastructures, mobility and communication, etc.

This requires rules and norms not to overuse nature and to block its commodification (Ostrom 1990). Those rules and norms need to be achieved through social struggles. And indeed, throughout history, the commodification of nature and particularly its negative consequences have led to countermovements. Polanyi saw that they were often politically reactionary, for instance, when the large-scale land owners resisted the "mobilization of the land" (Polanyi [1944] 2001, p. 192) and fought for protectionism in the agrarian sector of a country. On the other hand, progressive countermovements struggled for land reforms in order to withdraw land from liberal market logics as well as from the reactionary rule of large-scale land owners. Those experiences of commoning or public control contribute to the de-commodification of nature and, therefore, anticipate environmentally sustainable social and economic forms beyond capitalism (on Polanyi and commoning cf. Mendell 2018).

Polanyi saw the need for economic planning and coordination. But he saw also the tendencies of bureaucratization. Therefore, an important principle is that planning does not take place at the expense of freedom and that the respective institutions are subject to democratic control.

This brings us to another dimension of a profound SET. With Polanyi we can also argue that the question of a *democratic shaping* of society and of societal nature relations is crucial. Of particular importance is the securing of individual freedom which is linked to questions of democracy. For instance, Polanyi argues that "the problem of industry would resolve itself through the planned intervention of the producers and consumers themselves. Such conscious and responsible action is, indeed, one of the embodiments of freedom in a complex society" (Polanyi 1947, p. 117).

The claims for a de-commodification of nature and a democratization of societal nature relations emerge out of crises and contradictions and the incapacity of existing institutions to deal with them (Pichler et al. 2018). The concrete politicization of crises and contradictions require social actors that claim and propose alternatives to a further commodification – be it as parts of "brown" or "green" capitalist strategies – as well as emerging everyday practices that contribute to such a de-commodification and democratization.

5.   LIMITS TO A POLANYIAN UNDERSTANDING OF SOCIAL-ECOLOGICAL TRANSFORMATION

To apply and further develop a Polanyian thinking on the ecological crisis, societal nature relations and far-reaching SET, we propose some aspects that should be considered in more detail.

First, in line with Polanyi the commodification of nature and the conversion of many elements of nature into (fictitious) commodities are major drivers of the dynamics of capitalism that result in ecological and social-economic crises. However, the causes of the ecological crisis are much broader including the very perception of nature and discourses about it, the subjectivities and every-day practices of people, the negative effects of fossil fuel-based capitalism as climate change, and the possible overuse of nature through non-commodified practices. Public policies, too, and their partial de-commodification have often adverse ecological effects. Therefore, the dominant mode of production and living is at stake when the ecological crisis should be dealt with. We propose to mark this broader understanding of the social-ecological crisis with the term "imperial mode of living" that is, in fact, an "imperial mode of production and living" (Brand and Wissen 2018). This concept helps us to better understand both the persistence and spread of unsustainable patterns of production and consumption that deepen the crisis *and* the increasingly contradictory charac-ter of these patterns that results from their very deepening and spread.

This brings us to a *second* core element concerning the ecological crisis. Polanyi understood the ecological crisis as mainly caused by the commod-ification of land with severe social and ecological implications. Today, the ecological crisis clearly has a global dimension. Of course, many destructive impacts such as mining, pollution or resource scarcity are local and regional but the drivers stem from the globalizing dynamics of the capitalist mode of production and living. At the same time, the scale of climate change and the overuse of resources are global. This makes its politicization and adequate policies, particularly at the level of the nation state, more difficult. Such an argument is no excuse for the non-willingness or incapacity of the state to deal more seriously with the ecological crisis. But it sheds light on the necessity of multi-scalar approaches from the everyday life of people and institutions to the international scale (Görg et al. 2017).

Third, Dale argues in his reconstruction of *The Great Transformation* that Polanyi "tends to overstate the 'protective' attributes of the state" (2016, p. 121). For today and despite many concrete successes of environmental policies, the state at all spatial scales largely secures dominant and destructive forms of the appropriation of nature. Therefore, the role of the state needs to be reflected more carefully in Polanyian approaches (Brand and Görg 2001). The state is not just an institution or social actor that delivers the rules of the game – for powerful actors and promoting commodification – but it is a social relation that is in its very structure linked to the capitalist economy, to related power relations and to everyday life (Poulantzas 1978).

Finally, many current conflicts about existing societal nature relations and entry points for SET take place in very concrete forms and often at local levels (for a typology see Dietz and Engels 2018). Therefore, we see a certain restric-tion in the metaphor of the "double movement" in the sense that in such "big concepts" the concrete conflicts tend to be subsumed under overarching logics.

However, those conflicts are diverse, contradictory and contingent and they need to be carefully analysed and in political struggles considered.

In that sense, Polanyi offers us many elements to think today about the deep ecological crisis as a crisis of capitalist societal nature relations (and not one of an abstract "humankind"), and to see some limits of many approaches to SET, particularly the blindness of commodification dynamics. However, we should also think beyond Polanyi to fully grasp crisis dynamics and existing as well as potential alternatives.

REFERENCES

Aglietta, M. (1979), *A theory of capitalist regulation: The US experience*, London: Verso.

Altvater E. and B. Mahnkopf (1996), *Grenzen der Globalisierung: Ökonomie, Ökologie und Politik in der Weltgesellschaft*, Münster: Westfälisches Dampfboot.

Atzmüller, R., J. Becker, U. Brand, L. Oberndorfer, V. Redak and T. Sablowski (eds) (2013), *Fit für die Krise? Perspektiven der Regulationstheorie*, Münster: Westfälisches Dampfboot.

Blühdorn, I., F. Butzlaff, M. Deflorian and D. Hausknost (2018), *Transformation research and academic responsibility: The social theory gap in narratives of radical change*, IGN-Interventions January 2018, accessed 10 November 2018 at www.wu.ac.at/ign/forschung/aktuelle-publikationen/.

Bockman, J. (2018), 'Not the new deal and not the welfare state: Karl Polanyi's vision of socialism', in M. Brie and C. Thomasberger (eds), *Karl Polanyi's vision of a socialist transformation*, Montréal: Black Rose, pp. 200–208.

Boltanski, L. and E. Chiapello (2003), *Der neue Geist des Kapitalismus*, Konstanz: UVK.

Boyer, R. (1990), *The regulation school: A critical introduction*, New York: Oxford University Press.

Brad, A., A. Schaffartzik, M. Pichler and C. Plank (2015), 'Contested territorialization and biophysical expansion of oil palm plantations in Indonesia', *Geoforum*, 64, 100–111.

Brand, U. (2016), '"Transformation" as new critical orthodoxy: The strategic use of the term "transformation" does not prevent multiple crisis', *GAIA – Ecological Perspectives for Science and Society*, 25 (1), 23–7.

Brand, U. and C. Görg (2001), 'The regulation of the market and the transformation of the societal relationships with nature', *Capitalism, Nature, Socialism*, 12 (3), 67–94.

Brand, U., C. Görg, J. Hirsch and M. Wissen (2008), *Conflicts in Environmental Regulation and the Internationalisation of the State: Contested Terrains*, London and New York: Routledge.

Brand, U. and M. Wissen (2017), 'Social-ecological transformation', in N. Castree, M. Goodchild, W. Liu, A. Kobayashi, R. Marston and D. Richardson (eds), *International encyclopedia of geography: People, the earth, environment, and technology*, Hoboken: Wiley-Blackwell/Association of American Geographers.

Brand, U. and M. Wissen (2018), *The limits to capitalist nature: Theorizing and overcoming the imperial mode of living*, London: Rowman & Littlefield.

Brie, M. (ed.) (2014), *Futuring: Transformation im Kapitalismus über ihn hinaus*, Münster: Westfälisches Dampfboot.

Brie, M. and C. Thomasberger (2018), 'Introduction', in M. Brie and C. Thomasberger (eds), *Karl Polanyi's vision of a socialist transformation*, Montréal: Black Rose, pp. 5–16.

Burawoy, M. (2013), 'Marxism after Polanyi', in M. Williams and V. Satgar (eds), *Marxism in the 21st century*, Johannesburg: Wits University Press, pp. 34–52.

Dale, G. (2016), *Reconstructing Karl Polanyi: Excavation and critique*, London: Verso.

Dietz, K. and B. Engels (2018), *Field of conflict: Ein relationaler Ansatz zur Analyse von Konflikten um Land*, Berlin: GLOCON.

Görg, C., U. Brand, H. Haberl, D. Hummel, T. Jahn and S. Liehr (2017), 'Challenges for social-ecological transformations: Contributions from social and political ecology', Sustainability, 9 (7), accessed 6 November 2018 at https://pdfs.semanticscholar.org/b92d/e2c3623be3f38 756ca8f443065d8c98b1d05.pdf.

Huan, Q. (2008), 'Growth economy and its ecological impacts upon China: A red-green perspective', *International Journal of Inclusive Democracy*, 4 (4), 7.

IPCC – Intergovernmental Panel on Climate Change (2018), *Global warming of 1.5 °C – an IPCC special report on the impacts of global warming of 1.5 °C above pre-industrial levels and related global greenhouse gas emission pathways, in the context of strengthening the global response to the threat of climate change, sustainable development, and efforts to eradicate poverty*, accessed 6 November 2018 at www.ipcc.ch/report/sr15/.

Jessop, B. (2000), 'The crisis of the national spatio-temporal fix and the tendential ecological dominance of globalizing capitalism', *International Journal of Urban and Regional Research*, 24 (2), 323–60.

Lipietz, A. (1988), 'Accumulation, crises, and ways out: Some methodological reflections on the concept of "regulation"', *International Journal of Political Economy*, 18 (2), 10–43.

Mendell, M. (2018), 'Commoning and the commons: Alternatives to a market society', in M. Brie and C. Thomasberger (eds), *Karl Polanyi's Vision of a Socialist Transformation*, Montréal: Black Rose, pp. 221–40.

Nalau, J. and J. Handmer (2015), 'When is transformation a viable policy alternative?', *Environmental Science & Policy*, 54, 349–56.

Ostrom, E. (1990), Governing the commons: The evolution of institutions for collective action, Cambridge: Cambridge University Press.

Peluso, N. L. and C. Lund (2012), 'New frontiers of land control: Introduction', *The Journal of Peasant Studies*, 39 (2), 667–81.

Pichler, M., U. Brand and C. Görg (2018), 'The double materiality of democracy in capitalist societies: Challenges for social-ecological transformations', *Environmental Politics*, doi: 10.1080/09644016.2018.1547260.

Polanyi, K. ([1944] 2001), *The great transformation: The political and economic origins of our time*, Boston: Beacon Press.

Polanyi, K. (1947), 'Our obsolete market mentality', *Commentary*, 3 (2), 109–17.

Poulantzas, N. (1978), *State, power, socialism*, London and New York: Verso.

Ruggie, J. G. (1982), 'International regimes, transactions, and change: Embedded liberalism in the postwar economic order', *International Organization*, 36 (2), 379–415.

Sachs, W. (1999), 'Sustainable development and the crisis of nature: On the political anatomy of an oxymoron', in F. Fischer and M. Hajer (eds), *Living with nature: Environmental politics as cultural discourse*, Oxford: Oxford University Press, pp. 23–41.

Schneidewind, U. (2018), *Die Große Transformation – Eine Einführung in die Kunst gesellschaftlichen Wandels*, Frankfurt/Main: Fischer.

UNEP – United Nations Environment Programme (2011), *Decoupling natural resource use and environmental impacts from economic growth. Report by the International Resource Panel*, accessed 6 November 2018 at http://resourcepanel.org/reports/decoupling-natural-resource-use-and -environmental-impacts-economic-growth.

WBGU – Wissenschaftlicher Beirat der Bundesregierung Globale Umweltveränderungen (2011), *World in transition: A social contract for sustainability, flagship report*, accessed 6 November 2018 at www.wbgu .de/fileadmin/user_upload/wbgu.de/templates/dateien/veroeffentlichungen/ hauptgutachten/jg2011/wbgu_jg2011_en.pdf.

14. Polanyi, nature and the international: the missing dimension of imperial ecocide

Vishwas Satgar and Michelle Williams

1.　INTRODUCTION

The ecological crises we face today are both temporally urgent and on a planetary spatial scale. This dual dimension means the effects of the crises are felt by orders of magnitude greater than anything previously experienced and are felt across the globe. For example, the climate crisis – which is one among many ecological crises – threatens to lead to the mass extermination of entire species, including human beings. But these ecological crises did not just materialize on their own. Rather they are inherent to the logic of capitalism itself.

In this chapter we argue the climate crisis is ecocidal and to understand it we engage Karl Polanyi's work. We focus on Polanyi's rich conceptual thinking about nature and the international in *The Great Transformation* (1944) to help us understand contemporary dimensions of ecological crises and the link between imperialism, ecology and historical capitalism. We argue that since its emergence in the European centre, and in its relations with peripheries, capitalism has been grounded in particular forms of imperial ecocide. Extending Polanyi's analysis in this way allows us to examine contemporary capitalism's domination of nature and ecological crises and the challenges for contemporary resistance.

2.　CAPITALISM'S SYSTEMIC CONTRADICTION: CLIMATE CRISIS ECOCIDE

Capitalist accumulation has come up against serious natural limits. The assumptions of endless growth, infinite resources and externalizing the costs of waste and pollution in a linear system of capitalist accumulation devastate eco-systems. Scientists warn us of the dangers of violating planetary boundaries in relation to carbon dioxide, nitrous oxide, ocean acidification, marine fish capture, tropical forest loss, and terrestrial biosphere degradation, amongst others. Overshooting these natural boundaries greatly accelerated in the 1950s (Steffen et al. 2015, p. 7) and as a result there are multiple simultaneous ecological crises in the making, the most dangerous of which is the climate crisis. A heating earth with planetary temperature increases of three, four or five degrees would make human life impossible. We are thus living in an age of "climate crisis ecocide" as we hurtle down a path that promises to undermine the conditions that sustain human and most of non-human life.

According to the science on climate change the world is heating at an unprecedented rate. While the United Nations (UN) multilateral process produced the 2015 "Paris Climate Agreement", setting a 2 °C increase as the upper threshold in planetary temperature and 1.5 °C as an immediate goal, the scientific evidence shows these limits are being ignored (IPCC 2018). This is an epic failure of global ruling elites and classes to take the climate crisis seriously. While the Paris Climate Agreement was cobbled together through a series of compromises, after twenty wasted years of US recalcitrance, it has failed to deal with the main causes of climate change such as the extraction of carbon, the global transport industry, and the globalization of carbon-centric value chains. Rather it has merely anchored the global political economy in a weak pledge and review mechanism to lower nationally determined emissions. Current commitments under the Paris Climate Agreement are inadequate and an overshoot of 3.3 °C is expected by the end of the twenty-first century (Milman 2018)[1].

On 29 August 2017, the International Geological Society formalized the Anthropocene as a planetary geological epoch in which humans are shaping planetary conditions subject to the confirmation of certain geological markers. With current heating trends recording the hottest years on record, the planetary temperature increase – measured since before the industrial revolution – now stands at 1 °C. The effects of this increase are vividly seen with Arctic ice melting at an unprecedented rate, releasing dangerous levels of methane (a more deadly greenhouse gas than carbon), taking the planet closer to uncontrollable global warming (Carson and Peterson 2016). Climate shocks – extreme weather events – register annually with devastating consequences for human and non-human nature. For example, over the 2018 summer in the Global North, California experienced fourteen severe wild fires and ten countries in Europe experienced wild fires in the midst of an extreme heatwave, while across Korea a heatwave killed 4.5 million farm animals. At the same time, the southern state of Kerala, India experienced its worst monsoon flood

---

[1]   Climate projections are continuously being revisited as climate change accelerates. The data in this chapter was the most up to date at the time of publication.

in a century, displacing a million people. In 2019 Mozambique experienced two massive cyclones within five weeks of each other (cyclones rarely if ever hit this region), killing thousands of people and displacing over three million. As climate shocks register, the costs are disproportionately borne by poorer countries with financial challenges and poorer peoples within countries having fewer security nets to help recover from such devastation. As the climate crisis worsens, the economic costs are certain to spiral, while climate shocks will further complexify the challenges faced as food, water, energy and social infrastructure necessary for human survival are threatened. The ecocidal logic of contemporary global capitalism treats these realities as unintended consequences that can be externalized from capitalism. It is thus the peoples of the world – and all life forms – that suffer the consequences both of the events themselves and their aftermath.

It is in this context that we engage Polanyi's perspectives on nature and the international in understanding contemporary climate ecocide. While Polanyi was writing in a different historical context against market liberalism, there are marked similarities to the past three decades of financialized neoliberalization, which intensified the restructuring of states, economies and societies to promote the primacy of the globalized market.

3.   NATURE IN POLANYI

Polanyi was not the first social scientist to engage ecological issues, yet nature commanded a significant place in his macro-historical and political economy understanding of the perilous role of a self-regulated market society. In *The Great Transformation*, nature features in his analysis through different lines of enquiry.

First, Polanyi is critical of the way in which liberal philosophy draws on natural sciences to think about social change. He problematizes the embrace of biological evolution, as a model for society, and the way in which liberal thought naturalized the self-regulated market within economic history of Western civilization (Polanyi [1944] 2001, pp. 59–70). His critique of "spontaneous" and natural progress targets the liberal misreading of history which critically obscures the role for the government, even in the context of managing the pace and rate of change of enclosures in England and the role of state regulation in engendering internal trade in Europe. Moreover, the naturalization of the market economy also invokes a conception of the "Economic Man", which, Polanyi tells us (1944 [2001], p. 47), was based on a Eurocentric understanding of ten thousand years of civilizational history. Crucial in this liberal revisionism was a fallacious equation of the division of labour with bartering and exchange. In his reading of anthropology and history, Polanyi demonstrates that a market economy is anything but natural. He concludes:

> The outstanding discovery of recent historical and anthropological research is that man's economy, as a rule, is submerged in his social relationships. [. . .] every step in that process is geared to a number of social interests which eventually ensure that the required step is taken. These interests will be very different in a small hunting or fishing community from those in a vast despotic society, but in either case the economic system will be run on non-economic motives. (Polanyi [1944] 2001, p. 48)

Polanyi convincingly argues that liberal economic history elides this rich historical past of embedded market–society relations based on varied degrees and combinations of reciprocity, redistribution and householding, and instead asserts a self-regulated market economy. The myth of a self-regulating market was not only unprecedented, but was married to a conception of naturalized social change which obscures the deleterious impacts of market engineering on human and social life. This paradox of habitation versus improvement comes through Polanyi's description of how the lives of common people are exposed to great harms in the context of the industrial revolution but yet rationalized as progress of the market economy. Polanyi ([1944] 2001, p. 41) writes:

> The laboring people had been crowded together in new places of desolation, the so-called industrial towns of England; the country folk had been dehumanized into slum dwellers; the family was on the road to perdition; and large parts of the country were rapidly disappearing under the slack and scrap heaps vomited forth from the "satanic mills."

Polanyi, like Karl Marx and Friedrich Engels, had an acute appreciation of violence, alienation and human degradation as central to industrialization. However, Polanyi develops as part of his critique of market economy and liberalism a conception of fictitious commodities that reveals the deep alienation between humans and nature. This is the second conception of nature at work in Polanyi. Polanyi's understanding of human alienation from nature is very similar to Marx's conception of the metabolic rift (Foster 1999). Polanyi, recognizing the self-regulating market economy as anachronistic, identifies a crucial commodifying mechanism consistent with the logic of market economy through using prices and maximum monetary gain. He argues the assumption of market self-regulation suggests that all production is for sale and, thus, generates incomes. This idea assumes a historical shift in the nineteenth century from state regulation to self-regulated markets in which society separates into economic and political spheres. This bifurcation is a necessary precondition and together with the creation of a market society enables commodification of what is required for a market economy.

However, for Polanyi two consequences arise in the context of creating labour, land and money as fictitious commodities. First, there is a deepening rift between labour and land – as part of nature – and the market (Polanyi [1944] 2001, p. 75). Subsuming labour and land essentially means nature is dominated by the rationality and laws of the market. For Polanyi market domination of nature (labour and land) is an instrument to meet the needs of market economy. Nature becomes a means to meet the limitless appetites of markets. Polanyi ([1944] 2001, p. 188) cogently summarizes this process:

> The first stage was the commercialization of the soil [. . .] The second was the forcing up of the production of food and organic raw materials to serve the needs of a rapidly growing industrial population on a national scale. The third was the extension of such a system of surplus production to overseas and colonial territories. With this last step land and its produce were finally fitted into the scheme of a self-regulating world market.

The second consequence of the market creating fictitious commodities is the reproduction of a paradox. While markets and industry need labour, land and money, none of them are commodities due to inherent features that render them incapable of being commodities. Therefore to be commodities they have to be commodified by the market as fictions. Polanyi ([1944] 2001, p. 75) argues:

> But labor, land and money are obviously not commodities; the postulate that anything that is bought and sold must have been produced for sale is emphatically untrue in regard to them. In other words, according to the empirical definition of a commodity they are not commodities. Labor is only another name for a human activity which goes with life itself, which in its turn is not produced for sale but for entirely different reasons, nor can that activity be detached from the rest of life, be stored or mobilized; land is only another name for nature, which is not produced by man; actually money, finally, is merely a token of purchasing power which, as a rule, is not produced at all, but comes into being through the mechanism of banking or state finance. None of them is produced for sale. The commodity description of labor, land and money is entirely fictitious.

For Polanyi ([1944] 2001, p. 187), labour (central to life) and land (nature) are relational parts of a unitary whole. This leads to a third conception of nature at work in Polanyi: nature as an object of market destruction. Throughout *The Great Transformation* Polanyi shows how utopian market self-regulation results in the annihilation of society and nature. The market's destruction of society was simultaneously the destruction of nature and vice versa. The corollary to this reveals a fourth conception of nature at work in Polanyi's ([1944] 2001, p. 138) understanding of market liberalism: the notion of the double movement. The double movement refers to the battle between economic liberalism and social protection. Economic liberalism organizes self-regulating markets based on laissez-faire and free trade methods. Social protection, by contrast, aims at protecting society and nature, through regulation, restrictive associations and other methods to limit the destructiveness of markets. Polanyi demonstrates the myriad historical examples of society pushing back to protect itself such as the Speenhamland squires' attempt to organize against the advent of the labour market, the Owenites' commitment to cooperatives and intentional utopian societies, and the Chartists' demand for universal suffrage. History is littered with struggles rallying particular class and social forces to protect society against increased marketization. However, it is not just humans and the social world that the double movement protects. For Polanyi the protection of nature is an integral part of the struggle to protect society.

4.   THE INTERNATIONAL IN POLANYI

Polanyi invoked an international perspective to explain the recurring crisis of market regulated society in the late nineteenth century and the interwar years. Like Marx, he transcended contemporary disciplinary boundaries of international relations, economics and historical sociology, and remained true to his project of a political economy analysis of civilizational crises and the role of the international.

There are four aspects to Polanyi's conception of the international and its role in market-centred crisis. First, Polanyi has a relational understanding of the international in which states are situated in relation to social location and international developments (in stark contrast to many theorists of international relations such as Realism and Neo-Realism who work with reified units of states). For example, in understanding the nineteenth century, he holds a relational view on the role of feudal elites – interrelations among aristocracies, kings and the church – the role of high finance, great states, the centrality of the British Empire, and the colonial outside. This expansive understanding of the international is reflected in his conceptions of agency, international relations and geo-politics. States were actors but were always embedded in wider social relations that shaped and were in turn shaped by states. For instance to secure peace in Europe:

> The Holy Alliance contrived to achieve this with the help of instruments peculiar to it. The kings and aristocracies of Europe formed an international of kinship; and the Roman Church provided them with a voluntary civil service [. . .] The hierarchies of blood and grace were fused into an instrument of locally effective rule [. . .] supplemented by force to ensure Continental peace. (Polanyi [1944] 2001, p. 9)

Second, Polanyi's conception of the international is strikingly historical. The making of international orders in Europe – from the mid-nineteenth century through the interwar years – brought together agential forces that buttressed different conjunctures distributing power. For instance, the conjunctures of the Holy Alliance in Europe, the Concert of Europe, and the interwar years each had its own logic and distribution of power. Polanyi shows that the continuity in international market arrangements over these conjunctures and institutions led to a collapse of the economic order. His explanation of the First World War – the end of 100 years of relative peace – and what comes after, including the Second World War, highlights the continuities in these arrangements. Two points about Polanyi's historicization and method are worth highlighting. First, his explanation for the First World War differs from other prominent thinkers of that era. Lenin used monopoly capital – banking and industrial – to explain inter-imperial rivalries in the First World War. By contrast, Polanyi argues that recurring market arrangements brought the collapse of the system and the descent into the First World War. Second, his historical method shows ruling class inability to learn lessons from history and appreciate the limits of market-centred international arrangements.

The third aspect of Polanyi's conception of the international is the importance of institutions and the difference between war and peace. Four institutions are central to his analysis: the system of balance of powers, which patterns variegated relationships in different conjunctures, the international gold standard, the self-regulating market, and the liberal state. Polanyi maintains that the gold standard brought down the system as it failed to ensure currency values, adjustments in national contexts, and trade relations. As the gold standard's failings registered in national contexts, protectionism rose. Yet after the First World War the ruling elite fail to learn historical lessons and the same institutional arrangements are repeated with disastrous consequences. Both national and international arrangements are locked into the market-centred institutions that undermine the possibility of other international institutions that could avert crisis and collapse. Thus, whether war or peace prevails in Polanyi's analysis hinges on whether market-centred institutions organize international relations and the world economy. His conclusion is prescient for today: a world economy organized through market institutions leads to collapse and war. It has already happened twice in Europe according to Polanyi.

Fourth, Polanyi locates the double movement to protect society within the international. While organized in the national space and grounded in political-economic relations, the double movement has international implications in making the world order and international conflict. After the First World War, Polanyi ([1944] 2001, p. 24) observes:

> In the early thirties, change set in with abruptness. [. . .] While at the end of the Great War nineteenth century ideals were paramount, and their influence dominated the following decade, by 1940 every vestige of the international system has disappeared

and, apart from a few enclaves, the nations were living in an entirely new international setting.

5.   IMPERIALISM, ECOLOGY AND HISTORICAL CAPITALISM

Reading Polanyi's *Great Transformation* in the contemporary capitalist context is instructive in understanding the dangers of climate ecocide. Polanyi appreciates (a) how market capitalism naturalizes itself against nature through its own rationality, (b) how markets commodify and create fictitious commodities of land, labour and money, and (c) how markets treat nature as objects of destruction. In our neoliberal times, the world has now seen over three decades of marketization through the neoliberal class project. Markets have been dis-embedded to prevail over state, society and nature with disastrous impacts including for eco-systems and the natural limits confronting global capitalist accumulation. According to Burawoy (2013) Polanyi provides us the tools to extend the periodization of marketization to a third wave from 1973 through the present with nature being the primary fictitious commodity. The marketization of nature essentially extends property relations to every type of natural commons. As Burawoy demonstrates, Polanyi's understanding of marketization and nature explains the contemporary destruction of nature, including the advance of climate ecocide.

Polanyi's analysis assists in situating social forces – state and non-state – that shape the international including hegemonic states. He provides a framework for thinking about and historicizing conjunctures of international ordering, the importance of institutions in shaping the international, and the role of national double movement practices in shaping international politics. While Polanyi enriches social theory and political economy to engage the ecocidal logic of contemporary capitalism there are a number of issues that need further developing in order to think with Polanyi in the present. We focus on the idea of imperial ecocide,[2] missing in Polanyi's work, which requires unpacking three conceptual challenges.

The first challenge relates to the historical roots of imperial ecocide. The three moments of marketization of Western civilization (late nineteenth-century, interwar years, and 1970s onwards to neoliberalization) do not date back far enough in history as imperial ecocide is moored in the originary moments of capitalism (that is, primitive accumulation) and the metabolic rift found in Marx's thought (Satgar 2018b). Taking different historical forms in different periods, imperial ecocide is integral to the expansionist imperial logic of capi-

---

[2]   Climate ecocide is part of imperial ecocide.

talism. Imperial expansions of the northern centres of capitalism have not only sought political, economic, military and geopolitical domination, but have sought to conquer nature through controlling natural resources, eco-systems and human and non-human life. The ecocidal logic of military mercantilism – from the Columbian moment of 1492 – led to genocidal violence against indigenous peoples, dehumanization through slavery, the mass destruction of species, the eradication of eco-systems and destructive transformation of landscapes. This long history of imperial ecocide continues today with the United States – as today's dominant imperial force – further deepening the logic of imperial ecocide in its international relations and the industrial scale violence it unleashes on the metabolic conditions of all life forms. Recognizing the centrality and historical specificity of US imperial relations in exacerbating climate ecocide deepens a Polanyian understanding of the present. This is developed further below.

The second challenge relates to analytically locating the agentic forces reproducing imperial ecocide and contemporary capitalism. Anthropocene theory – which has become part of United Nations and climate discourses – provides for a generic (class blind) explanation of the ecological challenges facing planet Earth (Satgar 2018b). It suggests that all humans are equally responsible for causing the climate crisis as humans have become a geological force affecting conditions on Earth. The problem with this rendition of causation is that it elides the real source of climate change. On the one hand, US-led imperial ecocide has conjoined to the expansion and growth of carbon capital and finance since the Second World War. Carbon states, ruling classes and the global carbon fraction of transnational capital has embraced complex hydrocarbons including fracking, deep sea drilling and tar sands to keep the global oil spigot flowing, despite the bleak warnings from climate science (Klare 2012). Similarly, these vested interests actively block the transition to socially owned and democratic renewable energy systems. Given the power of these interests to pursue an ecocidal path, it is fallacious to blame all of humanity for the climate crisis. Rather, the political economy of the Anthropocene reveals that globalizing capital is the geological force shaping planetary conditions particularly the climate crisis (Satgar 2018b). On the other hand, the ruling classes – both within nation states and at the helm of the interstate system – are to blame for not mustering the collective will and democratic mandates from citizens to lead just transitions in their societies. Instead, weak global agreements such as the Paris Climate Agreement divert attention from the real issues of ecocidal capitalism, which spells disaster for humanity and non-human life forms (Guerrero 2018). In this moment of deep crisis, the world needs deeply democratic climate emergency governance in national states and the multi-lateral system. But what we have seen instead for over three decades of neoliberalization is the remaking of nation states into market democracies that are impervious to citizens' voices and have undermined social contracts with labour. Market democracies privilege the needs of markets, while deepening precarity, inequality and disciplining of labour.

The third conceptual issue is imperial ecocide's inherent racism and gender oppression. US-led imperial ecocide has been functional to racist interests, despite the rhetoric and liberal foreign policy of the US state. For instance, the USA has not resolved the white supremacist oppression of its African minority, despite its civil war and the civil rights movement. Today, #BlackLivesMatter has placed the spotlight on the continued racial violence against African Americans through policing, incarceration and ghettoization. With Hurricane Katrina and its disproportionate impact on black residents in New Orleans, the neglect of the US state was visible for the world to see. Despite the historic Obama presidency, the race war continues in the USA and has intensified with Trump's white nationalism and neo-fascist disposition. The majority of climate-change deniers in the USA are white males with secure incomes, and who are over-confident about their views (Klein 2014, p. 46). The racist and gendered dimensions of US imperial ecocide are felt far beyond its borders. For example, in Africa and across the Global South, women small-scale farmers and peasants are hit hardest by climate shocks and women face the deleterious brunt of extractivism by corporate giants. At the same time, women are at the forefront of resisting further land dispossession, carbon extraction and pollution of their communities and societies in many parts of the African continent (Terreblanche 2018, pp. 174–6).

Contemporary US-led imperial ecocide is at the centre of the climate crisis by enabling carbon capital to continue extracting, exchanging and burning the planet. It has continued the racial and gendered practices imbricated in historical capitalist social relations. Imperial ecocide is, thus, central to the making of climate ecocide and the destruction of life conditions for human and non-human nature. The historical logic of imperial ecocide that took root in the foundational phase of capitalism (that is, military mercantilism), manifested in different historical forms, continues into the present. Adding imperial ecocide to Polanyi's analysis of conjunctures of international ordering suggests that our global institutions and national states are leading humanity to a perilous place. Using these Polanyian-inspired insights, we now look at contemporary US-led imperial ecocide.

6.   CONTEMPORARY IMPERIAL ECOCIDE

As the global climate crisis worsens, the logic of ecocide is further entrenched. Donald Trump's administration has elevated climate change denial to state policy and increased carbon extraction. His policy interventions undermine the global consensus to address the climate crisis. Under Trump's leadership, the USA is set to become the largest oil producer in the world surpassing Saudi Arabia and Russia (News Corp Australia Network 2018), which inadvertently encourages more carbon extraction in other parts of the world. In a perverse cycle of extraction, the more the USA extracts the more others look to extraction.

The irrationality of this trajectory comes into sharp relief when we look at Oxford University's data from tracking global carbon emissions, which tells us that we are over 600 million tons of cumulative carbon emissions.[3] We are perilously close to a 2 °C increase, which, under the current emissions trajectory, is likely to happen over the next twenty years. At close to 2 °C, studies on tipping points – such as the Arctic becoming ice free or major retreats in Himalayan glaciers – show that eighteen out of thirty-seven abrupt changes will occur (Drijfhout 2015).

In response, plutocratic class fractions, ruling classes, and social forces lording over the planet propose a renovated climate capitalism (also known as green neoliberalism) (Bond 2012). The institutions, regulatory frameworks and ideological structures built over the past three decades – despite the worst economic crisis on record – are the anchor for this new climate capitalism. This climate capitalism does not attempt to solve the climate crisis, but rather promotes solutions that continue the (ir)rationality of market-centred economics such as carbon trading, carbon offsets, utilizing forests as sinks, nuclear power and geo-engineering solutions. While nature was commodified in the third wave of marketization, we now see commodification of the ecocidal destructive tendencies of capitalism – that is, the climate crisis – through the marketization of climate. The climate is now a commodity bought and sold on the market (such as carbon trading) in a spectacular site of market conquest. Polanyi's historical sequence of self-regulated market madness is repeating itself.

The US-led bloc and its global power structure have not heeded historical let alone recent lessons. While the earlier disasters led to world wars and millions of lost lives, the consequences of today's crisis are ecocidal and could lead to species extinction, including humanity's extinction. Polanyi warned against the terminus for the human species in his critique of market liberalism. Little could he realize how prescient his warning would be.

7.   CONCLUSION

While Polanyi's analysis of what went wrong in the early twentieth century has much to teach us, he also invites us to think about the double movement

---

[3]   http://trillionthtonne.org.

against market-centred ecocide. In this regard, the variegated social forces that emerged in the mid-twentieth century – New Deal, Social Democracy, Soviet Socialism and Fascism – are instructive for how we think about the present. Expanding carbon capitalism, together with globalizing financialized markets – including climate markets – have brought to the fore various forms of resistance, including religious fundamentalism (for example Taliban, India's BJP, US Christian fundamentalists), ethno-nationalism (for example Europe's far right), petro-nationalism (for example Andean carbon capitalism in Bolivia), and global justice movements (for example World Social Forum, La Via Campesina, food sovereignty movements and social justice movements in myriad countries). The global justice movements represent attempts to advance a climate justice politics to engender deep, just transitions to sustain life (Satgar 2018a). Systemic alternatives – such as climate jobs, socially owned renewable energy, rights of nature, solidarity economy, food sovereignty, democratic planning, integrated clean energy public transport, the basic income grant, zero waste – are being championed in many local and national spaces. At the same time, history is uncertain and the tectonic shifts taking place in global politics could produce a post-neoliberal world order that turns into a neo-fascist world and ecocidal destruction. Indeed, imperial ecocide is part of an eco-fascist outcome.

Thinking with Polanyi about contemporary capitalism, particularly the challenge of climate ecocide, enriches our understanding on many levels. His critique of liberal economics was deeply ecological and attentive to the international workings of a dis-embedded market economy. Indeed, Polanyi is more relevant today given the marketization of neoliberalism. Yet today's crisis catastrophically combines economic and climate crises. The dangers, limits and madness of neoliberalism suggest that Hayek's (1944) valorization of the self-regulating market – *The Road to Serfdom* published at the same time as Polanyi's *Great Transformation* – won out against the prudent warnings of Polanyi's careful analysis. Neoliberalism cannot be the end of history as imperial ecocide makes our choices stark: end ecocidal market capitalism or perish. The human impulse to survive is powerful and together with citizens organizing into climate justice movements, there is still hope that through a double movement we will (re)find a world beyond the tide of a rising eco-fascism. In this context, Polanyi might still triumph.

REFERENCES

Bond, P. (2012), *Politics of climate change: Paralysis above, movement below*, Pietermaritzburg: University of KwaZulu-Natal Press.

Burawoy, M. (2013), 'Marxism after Polanyi', in M. Williams and V. Satgar (eds), *Marxisms in the 21st century*, Johannesburg: Wits University Press, pp. 34–52.

Carson, M. and G. Peterson (2016), *Arctic resilience report*, Arctic Council, Stockholm Environmental Institute and Stockholm Resilience Centre, accessed 9 September 2018 at www.arctic.council.org/arr.

Drijfhout, S. (2015), 'What climate "tipping points" are – and how they could suddenly change our planet', *The Conversation*, 9 December, accessed 17 August 2017 at https://theconversation.com/what-climate-tipping-points -are-and-how-they-could-suddenly-change-our-planet-49405.

Foster, J.B. (1999), 'Marx's theory of metabolic rift: Classical foundations for environmental sociology', *American Journal of Sociology*, 105 (2), 366–405.

Guerrero, D. (2018), 'The limits of capitalist solutions to the climate crisis', in V. Satgar (ed.), *The climate crisis: South African and global democratic eco-socialist alternatives*, Johannesburg: Wits University Press, pp. 30–46.

Hayek, F. (1944), *The road to serfdom*, Chicago: University of Chicago Press.

IPCC – Intergovernmental Panel on Climate Change (2018), *Global warming of 1.5 °C – an IPCC special report on the impacts of global warming of 1.5 °C above pre-industrial levels and related global greenhouse gas emission pathways, in the context of strengthening the global response to the threat of climate change, sustainable development, and efforts to eradicate poverty*, accessed 9 September 2018 at www.ipcc.ch/sr15/.

Klare, M. (2012), *The race for what's left: The global scramble for the world's last resources*, New York: Metropolitan Books.

Klein, N. (2014), *This changes everything*, London: Penguin Books.

Milman, O. (2018), 'Climate change: Local efforts won't be enough to undo Trump's inaction, study says', *The Guardian*, 30 August, accessed 9 September 2018 at www.theguardian.com/environment/2018/aug/29/local -climate-efforts-wont-undo-trump-inaction.

News Corp Australia Network (2018), 'The United States is set to surpass Saudi Arabia as top producer of crude oil', accessed 9 September 2018 at www.news.com.au/world/north-america/the-united-states-is-set-to-surpass -saudi-arabia-as-top-producer-of-crude-oil/news-story/dcd7677d9377bc68 d9f952352541970c.

Polanyi, K. ([1944] 2001), *The great transformation: The political and economic origins of our time*, Boston: Beacon Press.

Satgar, V. (2018a), 'The climate crisis and systemic alternatives', in V. Satgar (ed.), *The climate crisis: South African and global democratic eco-socialist alternatives*, Johannesburg: Wits University Press, pp. 1–28.

Satgar, V. (2018b), 'The Anthropocene and imperial ecocide: Prospects for just transitions', in V. Satgar (ed.), *The climate crisis: South African and global democratic eco-socialist alternatives*, Johannesburg: Wits University Press, pp. 47–68.

Steffen, W., W. Broadgate, L. Deutsch, O. Gaffney and C. Ludwig (2015), 'The trajectory of the Anthropocene: The great acceleration', *The Anthropocene Review*, 2 (1), 1–18.

Terreblanche, C. (2018), 'Ubuntu and the struggle for an African eco-socialist alternative', in V. Satgar (ed.), *The climate crisis: South African and global democratic eco-socialist alternatives*, Johannesburg: Wits University Press, pp. 168–89.

15. Soy expansion and countermovements in the Global South: a Polanyian perspective

Karin Fischer and Ernst Langthaler

1. INTRODUCTION: INVESTIGATING DOUBLE MOVEMENTS

Capitalism in the age of neoliberalism has expanded the logic of capital to spheres that were previously not considered for sale on the market. New forms of marketization depend to a great extent on the control over and the access to land. While export-oriented monocultures and industrial food production have been a consistent feature of corporate agriculture in the Global South for decades, the growing demand for cash crops like soy, used for animal feed and agro-fuels in the Global North, has further accelerated the "global land grab" (McMichael 2013).

Based on a Polanyian perspective, we focus on movements and countermovements around the marketization of land and its agricultural products. To form a market for land and make it a tradable commodity was, in the eyes of Polanyi, "perhaps the weirdest of all the undertakings of our ancestors" (Polanyi [1944] 2001, p. 187). Accordingly, the marketization of land motivated countermovements which sought to increase state intervention, protective institutions and alternative forms of socio-economic organization. Polanyi considers countermovements as socio-cultural and politico-economic dynamics based on definite social forces. They organize themselves within different contexts and represent local articulations of a broader structural movement. Their struggles can be seen as attempts to (re-)gain social and political control of land in the face of increased commodification, here defined as a process of deepening commodity relations within the cycle of reproduction (Friedmann 1980, p. 158).

In our chapter, we take the expanding soy production in South America as an example (see Figure 15.1) and analyse the scope and limits for protective countermovements. Among soy-producing countries, we have chosen three

Table 15.1   *Socio-economic features of countries under study*

	Argentina	Bolivia	Brazil
GDP per capita (USD) in 2016	18 585	6708	14 077
Average dietary energy supply (kcal/cap/day) in 2016	3250	2355	3184
Employment in agriculture (%) in 2016	0.6	27	10
Agricultural share of GDP (%) in 2016	6	11	4
Soybeans on arable land (%) in 2016	50	30	41
Urban population (% of total) in 2018	92	69	86
Indigenous population (% of total) in 2010	2	62	0.5

Source: ECLAC 2014; FAO 2018; United Nations Population Division 2018.

cases with similar political regimes and diverse socio-economic features (Gerring and Cojocaru 2016). What the countries have in common is that from 2003/2006 onwards left-wing governments promoted social protection and a diverse economy. Here we pursue Polanyi's argument that a countermovement involves the state and protective legislation designed to check the action of the market (Polanyi [1944] 2001, pp. 79–80). Additionally, the societies differ in their socio-economic conditions. Our cases include, on the one hand, Argentina as a relatively rich and urbanized society which is highly specialized in soy production and, on the other hand, Bolivia as a relatively poor and rural society – with a high proportion of indigenous populations – which shows a more diversified land use. Brazil ranges somewhere in between these poles (see Table 15.1), while it stands out for its strong rural social movement.

From a historical and comparative perspective, we outline the drivers and effects of soy expansion, the mobilization of social movements as well as the role of agribusiness and government in each country. A countermovement involves policies and regulations. We thus analyse the state policies in respect to land and agriculture and ask what role the state plays in conflicts around the marketization of land. Our focus here is on the progressive governments in the three countries under study: the governments of Lula and Rousseff in the case of Brazil (2003–16), Argentina under the Kirchners (2003–15) and Morales in Bolivia (since 2006). To capture state–society–capital relations, we follow Polanyi's concept of the double movement (marketization vs. countermovement) in combination with critical state theory, more precisely with a strategic relational approach focusing on (semi-)peripheral contexts (Becker 2008; Jessop 2008).

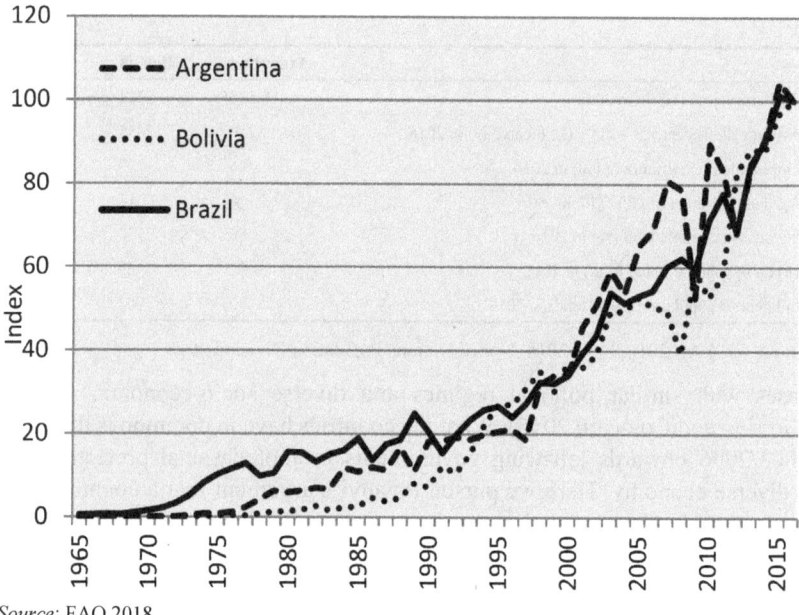

Source: FAO 2018.

Figure 15.1   *Soy production in Argentina, Bolivia, and Brazil, 1965–2016*
               (in physical terms, index 2016 = 100)

2.   SOY EXPANSION AND THE DISARTICULATED COUNTERMOVEMENT IN BRAZIL

The production of soybeans began to grow from the mid-1960s onwards, as the military regime invested in state-led agroindustrial development. In the 1970s, soybeans were converted from a green fertilizer and oilseed of secondary importance into one of the most important globally traded commodities, first and foremost as a protein-rich animal feed for the livestock industry in the Global North. Due to attempts to reduce dependency on US supply, Western Europe and Japan transferred capital and technology to Brazil for fuelling soy expansion. Brazil's hyperinflation in the 1980s, accompanied by the resignation of the military regime, permitted multinationals such as Archer Daniels Midland, Bunge, and Cargill to buy large parts of the state-sponsored soy complex. The government supported the agroindustrial powerhouses through trade liberalization in the framework of GATT/WTO and Mercosur agreements (Patel 2008, pp. 181–7; Oliveira 2015, pp. 350–7; Turzi 2017, pp. 83–5).

A veritable soy boom took off in the mid-1990s, when neoliberal deregulation in combination with growing European and Chinese demand fuelled Brazilian exports. Between 1990 and 2016, harvested area multiplied by 2.9, from 11.5 to 33.2 million hectares, and production volume multiplied by 4.8, from 19.9 to 96.3 million tonnes (FAO 2018). As the soy frontier moved northward to the savannah region (*cerrados*) and the Amazonian rainforest, the state of Mato Grosso in the midwest of the country emerged as the major producer. Since herbicide-resistant varieties of genetically modified (GM) soy were legalized in Brazil only in 2005, seeds were illegally imported from Argentina, where they had already been approved in 1996, and other neighbouring countries. Alongside the multinationals, capitalist farmers of mostly European or North American descent, driven by profit-maximizing "frontier mentality", soon adopted the technological package for simplified cultivation (large-scale machinery, GM seeds, agrochemicals, etc.). By 2014, 93 per cent of the soybeans planted in Brazil were herbicide-tolerant (Oliveira 2015, pp. 357–66).

Brazil's soy expansion was not only a burden on the environment, with regard to deforestation, greenhouse gas emission, reduced biodiversity, soil health, and water purity; it disorganized rural society as well. Since the 1980s, concentration of farm size in soy production and, thus, income inequality has proceeded faster than in the rest of agriculture. The market-driven and state-supported expansion of large-scale commercial farms threatened the livelihoods of indigenous and peasant communities. Cases of direct violence are documented in large numbers. In conflicts between peasants and ranchers and soy planters, for instance, 390 Indians were killed in Mato Grosso do Sul between 2003 and 2014. Moreover, peasant families were displaced by the collateral damages of agroindustrial farming. Most disastrous were agrochemical drifts from large soy fields, harming neighbouring people as well as their livestock and crops. The more peasant farms became enclosed by big soy *cultivares* as well as cut off from the social networks of their communities, the more they tended to abandon their land. Displaced people partly resorted to rural–urban migration to make a living; others stayed in the countryside, often lacking a roof over their heads, to serve as underpaid wage labourers; and many of them flocked to rural social movements (Patel 2008; Lapegna 2016, pp. 84–114; Turzi 2017, pp. 95–6).

Besides the environmental issue of deforestation in the Amazon basin, the social issue of access to land has been in the centre of the public debate on the soy boom. Though the distribution of land in Brazil has been concentrated since colonial times, recent land policies have failed to retard the cycle of concentration. Despite the 1988 constitution, which enabled the state to redistribute land lacking a "social function", the national governments of the 1990s either ignored the land issue or limited agrarian settlements to a low level. Simultaneously, a series of land conflicts led to the formation of the

Landless Rural Workers' Movement (MST), the largest social movement in Latin America. Through land occupation, the MST resettled landless peasants on active or fallow *latifundias*, gaining public visibility and pushing land reform onto the political agenda. The MST advocates cooperative forms of work and decision-making to improve the sustainability of peasant communities and their environment. In the wake of the MST's rise, the Cardoso administration refocused the land issue. It authorized the MST to do a social, non-state, bottom-up, direct land reform, which was politically less risky than a government-led agrarian reform against the interests of powerful landowners (Robles and Veltmeyer 2015, pp. 189–95; Turzi 2017, pp. 95–6).

The MST was an integral part of the social movements' coalition that brought Lula, the candidate of the Workers' Party (PT), to presidency in 2003. Thus, the MST's land reform was expected to proceed by both its supporters and opponents. However, under the PT governments, the land issue received the *coup de grâce* by the fracturing of the landless movement. Despite initial promises, Lula refused expropriation for the purpose of land reform; accordingly, his plan to settle one million families was cut in half. The number of actually settled families declined year by year, hitting the bottom under the Rousseff's presidency (Turzi 2017, pp. 95–6). In 2012, the founder and coordinator of the MST wearily stated that the PT government "had abandoned agrarian reform" as it "could not even solve the social problem of 150,000 families encamped, some for more than five years, along Brazilian roads" (Turzi 2017, p. 96). How can the downturn of land reform, thought to be a protective institution, be explained?

In addition to divisions within the MST due to conflicts over community work and life, the state–movement relations were anything but favourable to check the action of the market and respond to the lived experience of marketization. First, the PT's "pro-poor" social programmes eroded the MST's social base, since they distracted the working class from the struggle for agrarian reform. Increased social expenditures reduced support for land occupations. Co-optation of labour leaders isolated the MST from its urban ties, thereby fracturing the movement's representation spectrum and hindering their mobilizing capacity. All in all, the MST's dependence on the PT did not serve it well (Robles and Veltmeyer 2015, pp. 191–3; Turzi 2017, p. 95).

Second, the federal government authority for settlement, the National Institute for Colonization and Agrarian Reform (INCRA), only reluctantly settled peasants and failed to adequately provide post-settlement programmes. Therefore, the newly settled peasants suffered from lack of access to educational, financial, technological and marketing resources. Though the MST challenged the state to confront this precarious situation, the established programmes were incoherent, underfunded, and administered by urban-based development experts without involvement in rural communities. Moreover,

INCRA was accused of corruption with regard to land-grabbing issues. INCRA's doubtful role undermined not only the land reform, but also the MST's position (Robles and Veltmeyer 2015, pp. 190–1; Turzi 2017, pp. 96–7).

Third, the MST's orientation towards food sovereignty met harsh opposition by agribusiness. Though the landed elites did not enjoy hegemony in the public sphere, they relied on strong power alliances to defend their interests. Their congressional arm across different political parties, the *bancada ruralista*, enabled them to block or vote through legislative initiatives. Outside the parliament, large landowners, in alliance with provincial and municipal authorities, successfully used the courts to challenge land expropriations. Most importantly, the PT government sided with export-oriented agribusiness as a revenue-increasing model of development, encouraging its growth with legal and financial incentives. In line with the compromise between political and economic power, Lula even appointed an agribusiness advocate as Minister of Agriculture. Contrary to what one might have expected, the "post-neoliberal" governments empowered the neoliberal agribusiness elite, including soy producers, processors and traders, over the MST's core clientele, the indigenous populations and landless peasants (Robles and Veltmeyer 2015, pp. 193–4; Turzi 2017, p. 96).

3.   SOY EXPANSION AND THE DEMOBILIZED COUNTERMOVEMENT IN ARGENTINA

Soy production took off in Argentina in the mid-1970s, as Brazil and other South American countries began to challenge the USA as the world's leading supplier since the Second World War. From the 1990s onwards, neoliberal reforms by the Argentinean government as well as rising demand for animal feed on the world market fuelled a veritable soy boom, centring in the Pampa provinces of Córdoba, Santa Fe and Buenos Aires. Between 1990 and 2016, harvested area multiplied by 3.9, from 5.0 to 19.5 million hectares, and production volume multiplied by 5.5, from 10.7 to 58.8 million tonnes (FAO 2018).

In 1996, Argentina was the first country in South America to approve GM soy. Encouraged by the pro-business climate, transnational agribusiness companies promoted the biotechnological package, soon adopted by large-scale Argentinean farmers. By 2006, GM seeds already occupied 99 per cent of the total acreage of soybeans planted in the country. Despite the changes of Argentinean governments, the soy boom and with it the prosperity of agribusiness continued (Rodríguez and Seain 2007; Rodríguez 2010; Lapegna 2015, pp. 71–2; Torrado 2016, pp. 696–8).

Though the soy boom has been less contested among social classes in Argentina than in neighbouring territories (Turzi 2017, p. 117), the adverse effects on rural communities and their environments became obvious from the mid-1990s onwards. First, the growing demand for soybeans increased pressures for supplies of arable land in the Argentine countryside, especially in the low-price northern provinces, with large farms increasingly encroaching on the small properties of peasant families and indigenous communities. The forced marketization of land resulted in violent conflicts, including murders of activists, while leaders and members of peasant and indigenous movements were permanently harassed. Second, the expansion of soy production resulted in large-scale deforestation, amounting to about 700,000 hectares of native forest between 1998 and 2008. Since forests are commonly used by peasant families for grazing livestock, deforestation severely harmed rural livelihoods as well. Third, the widespread application of GM seeds in combination with herbicides has resulted in agrochemical runoff into water supplies and drifts contaminating the air, thereby harming the health of rural and suburban populations as well as livestock and non-GM crops (Cáceres 2014; Leguizamón 2014; Lapegna 2015, pp. 75–6; Torrado 2016, pp. 595–6; Lapegna 2017, pp. 316–18).

The neoliberal restructuring of the 1990s, including the social and environmental disruptions by the soy boom, resulted in a cycle of protest and led to the creation of new peasant and indigenous social movements in northern provinces and the Patagonia region. For instance, the Peasant Movement of Santiago del Estero (MOCASE) was founded in 1990 as an umbrella organization of local movements at the province level, combating the eviction of peasant families due to precarious landed property rights (Wald et al. 2012, pp. 171–9). MOCASE was instrumental in creating the National Peasant and Indigenous Movement (MNCI) in 2005. Though MOCASE with 9,000 members is the largest peasant movement in Argentina, it is quite small compared to the organizations with an industrial and urban focus. Despite their ideological and organizational differences, the variegated *piquetero* movement of mostly unemployed people from urban areas became a key political actor of the countermovement in the late 1990s and early 2000s. The series of roadblocks (*piquetes*) put the disruptive consequences of neoliberalization on the public agenda. The government responded to these challenges by repressing social movements, dismissing their protests, or providing piecemeal resources to quell contention (Villalon 2007; Lapegna 2015, pp. 71–2; Lapegna 2017, p. 320).

Against this backdrop, the leaders and members of the countermovement drew hope from the accession of the new government in 2003, since Kirchner's "post-neoliberal" rhetoric resonated with popular social movements. However, instead of further strengthening through cooperation with the government, the popular social movements of the 1990s lost their ability to mobilize people. The demobilization of the lower-class countermovement is indicated by the participation rate of *piqueteros* in roadblocks, which declined from over 60 per cent in 2003 to 10 per cent in 2006. Conversely, the share of middle-class activists (*vecinos*) in the same period rose from 10 to 50 per cent. Thus, the scenery of social movements fundamentally changed in the 2000s: simultaneously with the decline of the old (counter-)movement, a new movement emerged, based upon middle-class activists in support of agribusiness and adopting similar forms of anti-government protest (Lapegna 2015). How can we explain that?

Soon after inauguration in 2003, the Kirchner administration tried to build alliances with popular social movements. Kirchner's approach contrasted with that of his predecessors: he tolerated roadblocks, met with *piquetero* leaders, and established a relationship of mutual support. The affinities between the administration and popular social movements translated into institutional collaboration, including access to bureaucratic functions and federal funds. This strategy buttressed specific government policies and provided political support at critical moments. For instance, the MNCI was offered the control of the Social Agricultural Programme, which enabled them to address not only material but also power inequalities, guided by the model of the Brazilian MST. Activists, empowered through legal authority and job security, gained autonomy vis-à-vis the provincial government and agribusiness leaders. However, the political and economic benefits also made them more and more dependent on the functions and funds of the public administration. Thus, the co-optation of the popular social movements by the government went hand in hand with their demobilization (Ronconi and Franceschelli 2007; Wolff 2007; Lapegna 2015, pp. 72–6; Lapegna 2016, pp. 115–35; Lapegna 2017, p. 321).

The Kirchner administration faced severe opposition by the neoliberal movement of agribusiness interests. In 2002, the interim government reinstated the taxes on agricultural exports which had been eliminated in the 1990s. The Kirchner administrations considerably raised these taxes to 35 and finally to 44 per cent in order to gain revenues for financing the ambitious social programmes, thereby instituting "export-oriented populism" (Richardson 2009). The tax increase of 2008 met harsh opposition by medium and large landowners, farmers' associations and agribusiness companies under the label "the countryside" (*el campo*), strongly supported by the mass media. This broad coalition of agricultural producers, processors and traders organized a series of roadblocks in order to put the consumers and, thus, the national government under pressure. As a reaction, popular social movements mobilized in Buenos Aires in support of the Kirchner administration. Strikingly, middle- and upper-class protest adopted the form of action – the roadblock – that had been frequently used by lower-class social movements. As *piquetero* leaders moved from the roads to the offices, the agribusiness coalition moved from the farms to the roads (Cáceres 2014; Lapegna 2015, pp. 76–9; Lapegna 2017, pp. 322–5; Turzi 2017, pp. 117–25).

The government's immediate attempt to mitigate the 2008 agribusiness protest failed: a bill which modified export taxes by adjusting them to the fluctuations of international prices was defeated in Congress. In the long run, however, the Kirchner administration responded to the challenge more effectively: first, it created new institutional spaces to newer social movements from the 2000s, thereby marginalizing its long-time *piquetero* constituencies. Second, it expressed support for global agribusiness corporations (e.g. approval of new GM seeds), thereby creating ambiguities that puzzled many of the peasant movements (Lapegna 2015, pp. 79–82). The government regarded the export-oriented soy complex as a "cash cow" which had to be fed in order to yield. Accordingly, collateral damages such as the social and environmental disruptions of the soy boom were to be taken into account, even though harming the livelihoods of its rural supporters. Paradoxically, Argentina's "post-neoliberal" turn in the 2000s reproduced the neoliberal food regime through an active developmental state, combining global marketing of GM soy and national redistribution of its returns (Torrado 2016).

4.   SOY EXPANSION AND THE FRACTURED COUNTERMOVEMENT IN BOLIVIA

Soy production in the Eastern Lowlands, Bolivia's most productive agricultural zone, began to expand in the mid-1980s, with the transition to neoliberal, free-market policies. The state promoted the sector both by implementing infrastructure and facilitating access to credit for agro-exporters. Money from the state and the World Bank drove the process forward, together with the introduction of new technologies and the influx of foreign investors. Being a relative latecomer, soy production in Bolivia has since made a big jump upwards. Between 1990 and 2016, production multiplied by 13.8, from 232,743 tonnes to 3.2 million tonnes per year. Cultivated land for soybeans increased by 9.3, from 143,372 hectares in 1990 to 1.3 million hectares in 2016. A handful of multinationals – ADM-SAO, Cargill, FINO and Gravetal – control about two-thirds of the Bolivian output and exports. Chinese investors and *translatino* capital from Brazil, Argentina, Venezuela, Peru and Columbia alongside Bolivian firms do the rest (McKay and Colque 2016; Castañón Ballivián 2017; FAO 2018). Beside deforestation, biodiversity loss and pollution, social groups and civil organizations raised the problem of GM seeds. Due to legal and technical weaknesses and sharp opposition, even among government officials, the formal approval of GM seeds came rather late in 2005. At present soy is the only legally authorized GMO crop in Bolivia, and the government restricts the use of GMOs to just one variety of soybean resistant to glyphosate (Catacora-Vargas 2007, pp. 236–9).

In 2006, Morales was elected president. The ruling party *Movement for Socialism* evolved out of the combined movements of coca growers, indigenous communities, and peasant workers, the so-called "Unity Pact". The first years of the self-proclaimed "government of the social movements" were characterized by open confrontations with the right-wing, secessionist agro-industrial elite of the Eastern Lowlands. The battle over the future of (agrarian) social relations in Bolivia was not only fought in the Constituent Assembly which was established to write a new constitution for the country. Violent attacks on movement activists and local representatives of the government happened frequently and culminated in an unsuccessful coup in 2008, led by agribusiness landlord Marinkovic (Soruco 2008; Webber 2017).

In a first phase, the government's agrarian reform made land distribution easier and extended the communitarian land of indigenous communities – in Polanyian terms, a decommodification of land. This was an important recognition of territorial rights which potentially offers some kind of refuge from market forces. The scope of these measures, however, remained limited since the vast majority of transfers were from state-owned land located in the highlands. By contrast, in the fertile lowlands the already slow process of registration and land titling soon came to a halt (Colque et al. 2016, pp. 155–84; Vergara-Camus and Kay 2017, p. 419).

After a referendum a new constitution was set in force in 2009. It set a maximum land-size ceiling of 5,000 hectares. Nevertheless, the government started negotiations with agro-industrial groups and incorporated an additional provision allowing that limit to be multiplied by the number of associates participating in an agribusiness, essentially rendering the land ceiling obsolete. Moreover, the ceiling is not binding on pre-existing large properties. The ongoing commodification of land in the "agrarian extension zone" did not result in protective countermovements – despite the fact that the peasant and indigenous movement in Bolivia was among the strongest in Latin America, challenging neoliberalism in the 1990s and bringing Morales to power. How can we explain that?

First, a state–agribusiness alliance evolved while at the same time state–social movement relations became burdened by conflicts. After the failed coup and the strong support base for the government, the landed elite of Santa Cruz decided to seek an alliance with the government rather then continued conflict. For the government, however, the revenues from the commodity boom represented an important resource to finance pro-poor expenditures and maintain legitimacy among its constituencies. The novel agro–capital–state alliance culminated in the joint announcement of a "productive pact" with the aim to boost the area of land under cultivation and transform Bolivia into one of the leading soy producers in Latin America (Colque et al. 2016, pp. 10–11, 179–80, 183–4; Webber 2017).

Second, the success of agribusiness under favourable economic conditions enhanced the market integration of rural households. Following the Brazil model, the state-owned *Company to Support the Production of Foodstuffs* (EMAPA) provides family farmers with inputs (fertilizer, seeds and fuels) and credit (EMAPA 2018). Nonetheless, the highly mechanized and capital-intensive character of the soy complex makes it extremely difficult for small producers to enter the industry. As a result, small farmers without sufficient land and savings are increasingly excluded from working their land (McKay and Colque 2016). More generally, the type of exclusionary and inclusionary dynamics of the export-oriented agriculture led to a social differentiation among the rural population. This constitutes a further obstacle to the formation of a countermovement.

Small landholders and peasants with a plot size of around 50 hectares or fewer lease rent out their land to agro-industrial firms who control the soy value chain or to capitalist farmers who have the necessary equipment to be integrated in the chain. Those "middle peasants" receive 25 per cent of the net sales of the final harvest which is usually enough to cover the basic expenditures of the family. Members of the extended family combine this income from land rent with rural and off-farm work, e.g. as part-time wage workers, informal workers or small-scale informal entrepreneurs (Urioste 2017). They profit from the marketization of their land which gives them a relatively stable and risk-free income from rent and their economic interests and expectations become aligned with the agro-capitalist class as better harvests result in higher rent payments. A small group of capitalist farmers, among them Mennonite communities, integrate themselves successfully – although subordinated to the agribusiness and dependent on international markets – in the soy chain. They hire poorer or landless peasants as wage workers or subordinate them under other forms (Castañón Ballivián 2015, pp. 44, 80; McKay and Colque 2016, pp. 584–6, 596, 605).

The forms of interlocking between agribusiness and different social groups placed a wedge between the richer, poorer and landless peasantry and rural workers. If the crisis and neoliberal restructuring of the 1990s created fertile ground for class unity among them, the economic boom of the mid-2000s blurred things. Peasants with sufficient land and some saving, as well as unionized rural workers, saw the importance of a thriving agribusiness sector. Land struggle or agrarian reform, not to mention a radical transformation of the export-driven agricultural model, was no longer a priority for them (Vergara-Camus and Kay 2017, p. 426).

Finally, the emerging state–capital alliance and selective co-cooptation split the popular movement. The planned "Tipnis highway" that cuts through an indigenous territory and National Park prompted the organizations of the lowland *indígenas* to leave the Unity Pact. Their organizations CONAMAQ and CIDOB withdrew their support for the Morales government and stayed outside the "productive pact" (McKay 2018).

5. CONCLUSION: DISARTICULATED, DEMOBILIZED AND FRACTURED SOCIAL MOVEMENTS

In all three countries under study the relations between state, civil society and capital were conflict-ridden and contested. While many aspects of social movements were incorporated into state policy, the left-wing governments sooner or later tended to lean towards agribusiness interests. This can be explained by a conception of the state as a social relation and a site of strategy that reflects and modifies the balance of class forces (Jessop 2008). Organized political forces with different power compete for political influence in the state and within civil society. In (semi-)peripheral contexts we have to consider a strong dependency on exports of primary goods and foreign capital. The fiscal and material basis of the state and, thus, room for political manoeuvre depend on (foreign exchange) revenues from exports and royalties (Becker 2008). Even if progressive governments intend to change world market integration, not least to broaden the space for policymaking and increase the government's political legitimacy before its constituencies, this is not an easy task, quite the contrary. Domestic and transnational capital interests have privileged access to and/or control over state capacities and, thus, are able to lead state agency in directions that conserve established power structures. Even where a reform of the state itself was enacted as was the case in Bolivia with a new constitution, it is apparently difficult to alter the "strategic selectivity" inscribed into the state: the state apparatus in Brazil, Argentina and Bolivia was more accessible to the interests and strategies of the movement than to those of the countermovement.

We further observe a social differentiation among popular classes, deepened by processes of (ex- and re-)commodification of land and labour. Landless and land-poor peasants are threatened by the involuntary exclusion from the (labour) market. Being outside the market means marginalization not autonomy (in the sense of defending a self-governed resource base). Protective regimes such as communal land titles exist in some places in Brazil, Bolivia and Argentina; the Brazilian government encouraged cooperatives of landless and family farmers. But their capacity for self-governed, alternative forms of socio-economic organization which Polanyi envisioned as protective answers to marketization cannot be assumed. "Middle" peasants and organized rural workers are integrated into the circuits of agribusiness, though in a precarious and subordinated way, and became aligned with the agro-capitalist class. For many family farmers, farming for export still comprises the hope and the promise of social advancement. Strategies pursued by rural people are indeed realizations of the kinds of "social disintegration" Polanyi predicted (Polanyi [1944] 2001, pp. 159, 164, 257).

Small landholders became (part-time) wage labourers, informal and migrant workers and entrepreneurs. But they perceive themselves neither as petty bourgeois nor as proletarians or peasants (for Bolivia see Urioste 2017, pp. 69–71). Semi-proletarianization and multi-locality of the peasantry is by no means a new phenomenon and consequences on rural households are always an empirical question. From our case studies we assume that pluri-activity and multi-locality make it difficult to acquire a clear class consciousness, in other words to acquire a body of ideas and understandings which reflect the common interests, the historical path and the future of a class.

With regard to movement and countermovement dynamics, social movements were strong in challenging neoliberalism in the 1990s. When they became involved in state policies they lost mobilization capacity. In all three cases, social movements experienced fractures, culminating in the separation of the Unity Pact in Bolivia, and were disarticulated by selective cooptation. Moreover, agrarian movements based on the countryside remained largely isolated from their urban counterparts. This is especially true for Argentina. The *piquetero* movement was mainly fuelled by unemployment and marginalization in urban areas and centred on urban cooperativism. The murder of land rights activists in 2011/12 drew more public attention to (indigenous) peasant organizations and their demands but the export-oriented agricultural model and the soy complex are not in the centre of mobilizations. We also observe that in Argentina and Brazil a transformation of the social base of social protest took place, from popular classes towards middle-class sectors. The protest of new and traditional middle classes, disappointed about minimal opportunities for upward social mobility or deprived of their old privileges respectively, often turned to the right and distanced themselves from popular demands. The political alliance between middle-class fractions and popular/ peasant-indigenous movements which brought the progressive governments to power turned out to be short-lived and fragile.

We thus conclude that the development strategy to promote exports in extractive industries and use the "extractive rents" for social spending and to diversify the economic structure has failed. In all the countries under study, the state has prioritized the needs for capital accumulation over maintaining its legitimacy among its constituencies. The state – in Polanyi's view a central actor that establishes protective institutions and regulations – diluted popular demands. Thereby, countermovements of soy expansion and other facets of neoliberalism became disarticulated (Brazil), demobilized (Argentina) and fractured (Bolivia). Beyond totally pessimistic or optimistic accounts about the agency of progressive countermovements, our results call for a more realistic assessment, thereby taking into account both the room for manoeuvre and its limits.

REFERENCES

Becker, J. (2008), 'Der kapitalistische Staat in der Peripherie: politökonomische Perspektiven', *Journal für Entwicklungspolitik*, 14 (2), 10–32.

Cáceres, D.M. (2014), 'Accumulation by dispossession and socio-environmental conflicts caused by the expansion of agribusiness in Argentina', *Journal of Agrarian Change*, 15 (1), 116–47.

Castañón Ballivián, E. (2015), 'Discurso empresarial vs. realidad campesina: la ecología política de la producción de soya en Santa Cruz, Bolivia', *Cuestión Agraria*, 2, 65–86.

Castañón Ballivián, E. (2017), *Empresas transnacionales en el agronegocio soyero: Una aproximación a sus estrategias y relaciones con los pequeños productores campesinos*, La Paz: Fundación TIERRA.

Catacora-Vargas, G. (2007), 'Soya in Bolivia: Dependency and the production of oleaginous crops', in J. Rulli (ed.), *United soy republics: Realities about soya production in South America*, Asuncion: GRR, pp. 235–51.

Colque, G., E. Tinta and E. Sanjinés (2016), *Segunda reforma agraria: Una historia que incomoda*, La Paz: Fundación TIERRA.

ECLAC (2014), 'Indigenous peoples in Latin America', accessed 25 January 2019 at www.cepal.org/en/infografias/los-pueblos-indigenas-en-america -latina.

EMAPA/Empresa de Apoyo a la Producción de Alimentos (2018), *Rendición de cuentas final, gestión 2017*, La Paz: EMAPA/Ministerio de Desarrollo Productiva.

FAO (2018), Faostat database, accessed 25 July 2018 at www.fao.org/faostat.

Friedmann, H. (1980), 'Household production and the national economy: Concepts for the analysis of agrarian formations', *Journal of Peasant Studies*, 7 (2), 158–84.

Gerring, J. and L. Cojocaru (2016), 'Selecting cases for intensive analysis: A diversity of goals and methods', *Sociological Methods & Research*, 45 (3), 392–426.

Jessop, B. (2008), *State power: A strategic-relational approach*, Cambridge: Polity Press.

Lapegna, P. (2015), 'Popular demobilization, agribusiness mobilization, and the agrarian boom in post-neoliberal Argentina', *Journal of World-Systems Research*, 21 (1), 69–87.

Lapegna, P. (2016), *Soybeans and power: Genetically modified crops, environmental politics, and social movements in Argentina*, Oxford: Oxford University Press.

Lapegna, P. (2017), 'The political economy of the agro-export boom under the Kirchners: Hegemony and passive revolution in Argentina', *Journal of Agrarian Change*, 17, 313–29.

Leguizamón, A. (2014), 'Modifying Argentina: GM soy and socio-environmental change', *Geoforum*, 53, 149–60.

McKay, B. (2018), 'The politics of agrarian change in Bolivia's soy complex', *Journal of Agrarian Change*, 18 (2), 406–24.

McKay, B. and G. Colque (2016), 'Bolivia's soy complex: The development of "productive exclusion"', *The Journal of Peasant Studies*, 43 (2), 583–610.

McMichael, P. (2013), *Food regimes and agrarian questions*, Halifax and Winnipeg: Fernwood Publishing.

Oliveira, G. de L.T. (2015), 'The geopolitics of Brazilian soybeans', *The Journal of Peasant Studies*, 43 (2), 348–72.

Patel, R. (2008), *Stuffed and starved: Markets, power and the hidden battle for the world food system*, London: Portobello Books.

Polanyi, K. ([1944] 2001), *The great transformation: The political and economic origins of our time*, Boston: Beacon Press.

Richardson, N. (2009), 'Export-oriented populism: Commodities and coalitions in Argentina', *Studies in Comparative International Development*, 44 (3), 228–55.

Robles, W. and H. Veltmeyer (2015), *The politics of agrarian reform in Brazil: The landless rural workers movement*, New York: Palgrave Macmillan.

Rodríguez, J. and C. Seain (2007), 'El sector agropecuario Argentino, 1990–2005', in K. Forcinito and V. Basauldo (eds), *Transformaciones recientes en la economía Argentina*, Buenos Aires: Prometeo Libros, pp. 57–78.

Rodríguez, J.L. (2010), 'Consecuencias económicas de la difusión de la soja genéticamente modificada en Argentina, 1996–2006', in A.N. Bravo, H.F. Centurión, D.I. Domínguez, P. Sabatino, C.M. Poth and J.L. Rodríguez (coord.), *Los señores de la soja: la agricultura trangénica en América Latina*, Buenos Aires: CLASCO, pp. 155–259.

Ronconi, L. and I. Franceschelli (2007), 'Clientelism, Public workfare and the emergence of the piqueteros in Argentina', in N. Dinello and V. Popov (eds), *Political institutions and development: Failed expectations and renewed hopes*, Cheltenham, UK and Northampton, MA, USA: Edward Elgar Publishing, pp. 228–52.

Soruco, X. (2008), 'De la goma a la soya: El proyecto histórico de la élite cruceña', in X. Soruco (coord.), W. Plata and G. Medeiros, *Los barones del Oriente: El poder en Santa Cruz ayer y hoy*, Santa Cruz: Fundación TIERRA, pp. 1–100.

Torrado, M. (2016), 'Food regime analysis in a post-neoliberal era: Argentina and the expansion of transgenic soybeans', *Journal of Agrarian Change*, 16 (4), 693–701.

Turzi, M. (2017), *The political economy of agricultural booms: Managing soybean production in Argentina, Brazil, and Paraguay*, Cham: Palgrave Macmillan.

United Nations Population Division (2018), 'World urbanization prospects 2018', Urban/Rural Population database, accessed 25 January 2019 at https://population.un.org/wup/DataQuery/.

Urioste, M. (2017), *Pluriactividad campesina en tierras altas: "Con un solo trabajo no hay caso de vivir"*, La Paz: Foro Andino Amazónico de Desarrollo Rural.

Vergara-Camus, L. and C. Kay (2017), 'The agrarian political economy of left-wing governments in Latin America: Agribusiness, peasants, and the limits of neo-developmentalism', *Journal of Agrarian Change*, 17 (2), 415–37.

Villalon, R. (2007), 'Neoliberalism, corruption, and legacies of contention: Argentina's social movements, 1993–2006', *Latin American Perspectives*, 34 (2), 139–56.

Wald, N., C. Rosin and D. Hill (2012), '"Soyization" and food security in South America', in C. Rosin, H. Campbell and P. Stock (eds), *Food systems failure: The global food crisis and the future of agriculture*, New York: Earthscan, pp. 166–81.

Webber, J.R. (2017), 'Evo Morales, *transformismo*, and the consolidation of agrarian capitalism in Bolivia', *Journal of Agrarian Change*, 17 (2), 330–347.

Wolff, J. (2007), '(De-)mobilising the marginalised: A comparison of the Argentine piqueteros and Ecuador's indigenous movement', *Journal of Latin American Studies*, 39 (1), 1–29.

16. Navigating between improvement and habitation: countermovements in housing and urban infrastructure in Vienna

Andreas Novy, Richard Bärnthaler and Basil Stadelmann

In the "socialist municipality" that was later called Red Vienna (1919–34), Karl Polanyi felt at home (Dale 2010, p. 379). He was impressed by its cultural achievements to offer "freedom for all" and "experienced an epiphany akin to that which George Orwell described ten years later in Barcelona: suddenly, workers 'looked you in the face and treated you as an equal'" (Dale 2016a, p. 100). Polanyi's daughter, Kari Polanyi-Levitt (1990, p. 123), is convinced "that the shock of the passage from Red Vienna to the slums of Britain [. . .] burnt into his consciousness – as it did in mine" which explains "the passion in the pages of *The Great Transformation* that accuse the owning classes of sacrificing 'Habitation for Improvement'".

In this chapter, we will investigate the history of Vienna by dwelling more systematically on the dialectics between improvement and habitation. Polanyi describes the drama of the industrial revolution as a profoundly disruptive transformation, a metamorphosis, differing from continuous growth (Polanyi [1944] 2001, p. 44). On the one hand, the nineteenth-century industrial revolution brought progress as the "linear unfolding of the universal potential of human improvement" (Cowen and Shenton 1996, p. 14): material benefit, increasing productivity, efficiency, and profitability. On the other, it represented a catastrophe to important strata of society, undermining habitation (defined as routinized and secured livelihood) as well as status and well-being leading to forced migration, misery, and uprooting. The pace at which improvement strategies – "a crude utilitarianism combined with an uncritical reliance on the alleged self-healing virtues of unconscious growth" (Polanyi [1944] 2001, p. 35) – are implemented was essential for Polanyi. In this context, he stresses the oblivion and discrediting of "elementary truths of political science and statecraft": "it should need no elaboration that a process of undirected change, the pace of which is deemed too fast, should be slowed down, if possible, so as to safeguard the welfare of the community" (Polanyi [1944] 2001, p. 35). The mere focus on improvement during the industrial revolution, however, "appears to take for granted the essence of purely economic progress, which is to achieve improvement at the price of social dislocation" (Polanyi [1944] 2001, p. 36).

Polanyi did not oppose improvement *in principle*. He was no anti-modernist in this respect. Holmes (2018, p. 29) observes that "the social value of habitation and improvement are, in Polanyi's account, simply incommensurable" and decisions are, thus, unavoidable. Such an understanding of Polanyi's writing is essential to prevent misinterpretations: Polanyi did not axiomatically prefer habitation over improvement. Fraser (2014, p. 544), for example, insinuates that *The Great Transformation* (TGT) "demonizes marketization" and "idealizes social protection". We will use the Viennese case to problematize this reading. In our understanding, the whole attempt of TGT was to understand how fascism could have become a successful countermovement (Polanyi [1944] 2001, p. 32). Improvement and habitation comprise the dialectics of modern industrial civilization (Berman 1988; Cowen and Shenton 1996), of ongoing change and restless growth on the one hand and a sense of belonging and routinized and secure livelihoods on the other. This also poses a pressing problem from a contemporary perspective as far-right and right-wing populist movements and parties are on the rise. While dismantling welfarist social security, Trump, Orbán, and the Austrian right-wing FPÖ appeal directly to habitation as an imagined community protected against immigration. Their specific framing of habitation, thus, fosters versions of authoritarian capitalism.

This chapter narrates historical struggles in housing and infrastructure in Vienna to identify contemporary potentials and limits for enabling improvement and securing habitation. These struggles can roughly be divided into five phases comprising an anti-liberal phase before 1918 (first), the creation of a social-democratic countermovement between 1918 and 1933 (second) which was replaced by a phase of fascist (Austro-fascism and Nazism) countermovements (third). The developments after the Second World War can roughly be divided into two phases. The period of an institutionalization of the social-democratic countermovement between 1945 and 1989 (fourth) is followed by a still unfolding phase of its erosion (fifth) (see Table 16.1). This analysis requires scrutinizing the ambivalences of anti-market countermovements to overcome a flawed understanding of movements for social protection as *always* promoting social security, social cohesion and emancipation. In this regard, we will show that habitation and improvement have been framed and implemented very differently in different historical contexts and by different historical actors, thus, having different societal consequences. In short, improvement is not always destructive and habitation not always unifying. Their outcomes depend on their specific form of implementation and framing.

1.   AN ANTI-LIBERAL COUNTERMOVEMENT (VIENNA BEFORE 1918)

The stock market collapse of 1873 opened a period of economic insecurity and damaged faith in the "liberal creed" of self-organizing markets. Those who denounced liberalism as the "anarchism of the bourgeoisie" (Hobsbawm 2003, p. 40) were empowered. Capitalist modernization and demographic growth, however, continued. From 1869 to 1910, Vienna's population surged from 890 000 to more than 2.08 million (Resch and Eigner 2001), often offering horrible living conditions to newcomers. Dealing with this dark side of modernization (Berman 1988) two countermovements, both anti-liberal, emerged all over Europe: the working-class parties and movements as well as "demagogic anti-liberal and anti-socialist parties" (Hobsbawm 2003, p. 358). In Vienna, the latter was politically organized in the populist Christian-Social Party, the "blacks".[1] The ideological base of Karl Lueger, the first elected Christian-Social mayor (1897–1910), was the anti-liberal and anti-Semitic leanings of the Catholic Church. Lueger framed Vienna as a familial, pre-industrial, middle-class *Vaterstadt* based on paternalism, authority and patrimony (Maderthaner and Musner 2002). He allied with landlords, local business, and the lower middle class – the majority of the voting population who were threatened by industrialization and unsettled by cultural moderni-zation. What was even called "municipal socialism" promised protection that small proprietors and shopkeepers needed from monopolists (Johnston 1983, p. 64; Killion 2015, p. 7), but was fiercely opposed to social policies (Förster 2002, p. 2). Therefore, Lueger confronted liberal elites who even allied with the Emperor to avoid him taking office in 1895 (Schorske 1982, p. 132). Given the huge importance of Jewish professionals, artists and entrepreneurs, Lueger's anti-elitism was framed as anti-Semitism. In light of the huge migra-tion from the Habsburg hinterland, his populism was xenophobic, based on German assimilationist policies. Lueger was responsible for a new "political culture that incited the masses against the (old) elites and the 'integrated' against the 'outsiders'" (Maderthaner and Musner 2002, p. 867).

However, Lueger did not only offer protection and habitation symbolically by using exclusionary frames but effectively administered a rapidly growing city. While propagating an anti-socialist narrative, he expanded Vienna's urban infrastructure and took over from heretofore private foreign-owned enterprises

---

[1]   Due to its alliance with the Catholic clergy, vested in black.

Table 16.1   *Five historical countermovements in housing and urban infrastructure in Vienna*

Time Period	Countermovements	Improvement	Habitation (material & cultural dimension)
Anti-liberalism (until 1918)	Anti-liberal countermovement **against liberal elite and secularized Marxism**	Improvements as urban modernization for and against the market: **municipalization of urban infrastructure** (pragmatic and problem-oriented: "planning was not planned")	**Conservative, exclusionary and religious** framing of habitation; systematic exclusion of working classes (from democracy and welfare)
Red Vienna (1919–34)	**Social-democratic countermovement** with transformative aspirations focused on housing; inclusion of formerly excluded workers and propertyless classes	Slow economic recovery after military defeat; **fiscal straitjacket** limits economic growth	**Rent control and municipal housing**, decommodified housing and sustained socio-economic habitation; cultural habitation based on dignity of formerly excluded segments of the population (e.g. emancipation of women)
Austro-fascism and National Socialism (1934–45)	Fascist countermovement against failure of liberal elite and socialist threat	Economic crisis and war impede improvement; socio-economic improvement strategies were based on distributing the wealth of expropriated Jews and exploiting the conquered countries	Cultural habitation based on **Catholicism / German people**; socio-economic habitation is lacking (Austro-fascism) or based on **Aryanization** (Nazi-fascism)

Time Period	Countermovements	Improvement	Habitation (material & cultural dimension)
Welfare capitalism (1945–89)	**Institutionalization of the social-democratic countermovement**; loss of transformative character	Reconstruction, **high economic growth rates; spread of consumer society and marketization**	Inclusionary **security-based form of habitation "for all"** within national power container; guest workers with precarious citizenship from the 1960s onwards
Contested neoliberalization (from 1989 onwards)	**Erosion of the socio-democratic countermovement**; market-centred improvements, as well as reactionary countermovements, gain in importance	Competitiveness as prerequisite for sustaining the welfare state; embedding of improvement in market logic; deepening of possessive individualism	**Defending municipal ownership of urban infrastructure and housing** and experiments with socio-economic infrastructure (e.g. mobility and public spaces); increasing importance of insider–outsider dynamics in offering "habitation" (e.g. access to housing)

a wide range of essential services like gas, electricity, water, sanitation, and tramway (Johnston 1983; Weihsmann 1985, pp. 8 f.). This paved the way for a decommodified form of collective consumption, but also political patronage. Investments were financed by regressive taxes on consumption and housing rents. Lueger even founded a municipal savings bank in 1907 (Weihsmann 1985, p. 14). Individually, these initiatives tackled urgent problems ad hoc. "While laissez-faire economy was the product of deliberate state action, subsequent restrictions on laissez-faire started in a spontaneous way. Laissez-faire was planned; planning was not" (Polanyi [1944] 2001, p. 147). In its totality, however, these measures triggered a paradigm shift in the perception of the municipal government "as having an obligation and responsibility" (Killion 2015, p. 16) for the health and well-being of its population.

Strikingly, there was one main policy field that was exempt from decommodification efforts. Due to Lueger's alliance with landlords, residential construction remained almost entirely in private hands and "rents could be increased at any time" (Förster 2002, pp. 2 f.). Most apartments were lacking a toilet, a water conduit, gas supply or electric light, yet rent made for up to 25 per cent of a worker's (and employee's) monthly wage (Weihsmann 1985, pp. 16 f.).

To sum up, Lueger's anti-liberal countermovement (1897–1918) revolted against the liberal elite as well as secularized Marxism. Improvement strategies were implemented as urban modernization for and against the market. *For*, because it provided the necessary infrastructure for capitalist accumulation.

Against, because it municipalized foreign-owned companies or concessions and used municipal companies to finance urban infrastructure. At the same time, Lueger constructed clear visions that appealed to the needs for habitation. By forming a bloc of "assimilated insiders" in a time of dislocation and confusion, Lueger created an imagined community of "we" *against* "them" (Sennett 1998, p. 138). His legacy includes a reactionary, conservative, exclusionary, and religious framing of habitation based on a culturalized "insider–outsider" distinction.

2.   A SOCIAL-DEMOCRATIC COUNTERMOVEMENT (RED VIENNA, 1919–34)

The dissolution of the Habsburg Empire paved the way for the proclamation of a democratic republic based on strong welfare pillars. On a national level, between 1918 and 1920, a coalition government of social democracy and the Christian Social Party implemented various progressive policies, laws and constitutional reforms significantly empowering citizens, especially women, and enhancing the conditions of workers (for example unemployment protection, the eight-hour working day, and paid vacation) (Tálos et al. 1995). From 1920 onwards, the Christian Social Party, governing with right-wing parties, allied with the League of Nations to implement a flawed and unaccomplishable strategy of habitation *via* improvement. It insisted on severe austerity programmes to fight inflation, arguing that livelihood could only be sustained through access to financial markets (Holmes 2018). This resulted in severe fiscal constraints on local governments.

In Vienna, however, two other changes facilitated political agency. In 1917, rigorous rent regulations were implemented to protect tenants from the soaring costs of living. These regulations did not end with the war but have been sustained until today. This has dramatically reduced rents in the pre-war buildings (Förster 2002, p. 3), protecting tenants since then from the imponderables of the housing market. It devalued housing as a commodity. Confronted with high inflation and without the option to raise their rents, apartments lost their "commodity form" (Weihsmann 1985, p. 36). Many landlords opted to sell their estates, and land prices dropped. The second change was the constitutional separation of Vienna from Lower Austria, creating an independent Federal State in 1922. Thereby, the capital city gained financial sovereignty (Weihsmann 1985, p. 22), allowing for a radical redistributive change in fiscal policy (Becker and Novy 1999, p. 134).

When social democracy took over the municipality in 1919, unemployment was high and dwelling space scarce and precarious (Weihsmann 1985, p. 15). It was a rewarding strategic decision to make housing policy, the neglected policy field of Lueger's modernization project, the centre of a social-democratic political project. To finance these investments, the city-state implemented a set of progressively staggered consumption taxes on luxury goods such as cars, riding-horses, hotel rooms as well as private servants. Besides, a housing construction tax (*Wohnbausteuer*) was introduced, taxing small apartments with only 2 per cent of the pre-war rent while villas and luxury apartments were taxed with up to 36 per cent. Notably, the most expensive 0.5 per cent of taxed objects accumulated to roughly 45 per cent of the revenue (Weihsmann 1985, pp. 32 f).

Already in 1918, settlers occupied free spaces on the outskirts of the city to cultivate and grow vegetables and to raise livestock (Förster 2002, pp. 3 ff.). Driven out of the city by the insufferable urban conditions, they promoted self-construction. Social-democratic leadership accepted the settlers' movement but was sceptical of its autonomy and petty-bourgeois leanings. Nevertheless, mayor Reumann "promised the purchase and development of land, the supply of building materials and professional assistance" (Förster 2002, p. 4). Although a municipal settlement office coordinated the building of cooperative housing, the dominant solution to the housing crisis were comparably spacious and bright apartments in centrally-coordinated council housing (Weihsmann 1985, pp. 41 ff.). Social amenities such as laundries, libraries, kindergartens, shops, youth centres and medical care were common (Lewis 1983, p. 336). Neither rent nor any of the attached services covered more than the operating costs, drastically reducing the financial burden of housing. Colossal apartment complexes such as the *Karl-Marx-Hof* or leisure facilities such as a public natatorium (*Amalienbad*), were lighthouse projects signalling strength, solidarity but also livelihood in the city. Nevertheless, the 64 000 new council apartments, housing one-tenth of Vienna's inhabitants, remained enclaves of an unaltered imperial and bourgeois urban setting.

Social democracy explicitly fostered urban citizenship of those born in the city, independent from their nationality. Reformist measures ranged from social assistance, health care, child care, and women's empowerment to cultural and educational reforms. Red Vienna's transformative narrative was in line with the "hard" Polanyi who "advocated a socialist mixed economy dominated by redistributive mechanisms" (Dale 2010, p. 370). Nonetheless, Austro-Marxism lacked a "consistent economic strategy" (Becker and Novy 1999, p. 134), distributing a cake which was still being baked by means of capitalist accumulation (Weihsmann 1985, p. 39). Red Vienna, with all its merits, never went beyond progressive social policies and infrastructure provisioning. Its most effective economic policy was public investment, predominantly in the ambitious housing programme (Weber 1995, p. 539). The municipal sector of decommodified collective consumption was in large part resumed from Lueger.

Progressive taxation as well as high-quality public services, however, were perceived as a threat by those accustomed to the privileges of the liberal order (Hayek [1944] 1994, p. vi). Red Vienna was denounced as "city hall dictatorship" and "tax and finance terrorism" (Wassermann 2014, p. 2). At the same time, it was not only redistribution but also cultural modernization and new gender roles that appalled traditional segments of the population. The Christian Social Party led broad formal as well as informal alliances of conservative and reactionary groups to combat the City of Vienna. In an apparent Red Vienna, media and universities remained strongholds of "Black Vienna" (Wassermann 2014). The national government started to strangle the municipality fiscally by reducing federal funds. This became increasingly effective from 1929 onwards due to the Great Depression.

To sum up, Red Vienna's (1919–34) social-democratic countermovement had transformative aspirations focusing on housing and social policies. It included the formerly propertyless classes. In terms of improvement, a slow economic recovery after the war, as well as a fiscal straitjacket, limited economic growth. Habitation was constructed predominantly via social policies, rent controls and council housing. An essentially decommodified housing sector sustained socio-economic habitation, which was framed culturally based on the dignity of the formerly excluded segments of the population such as women.

3.   FASCIST COUNTERMOVEMENTS (1934–45)

In 1934, a short civil war ended democracy, and the conservatives installed an Austro-fascist government which lasted until Austria's annexation to Germany in 1938 (Becker and Novy 1999, p. 134). The two fascist periods differed dramatically in violence but shared anti-democratic, anti-liberal, and anti-socialist convictions. Both were countermovements against the failure of economic liberalism and the socialist threat. The cultural backlash for gender roles, social innovations, and creativity must not be underestimated. Very few intellectuals returned to Vienna after the war – and were in no way encouraged to do so (Becker and Novy 1999). During Nazi-fascism the politically "dangerous" and "multi-culturally oriented" city was downgraded. Vienna became the experimental field of Aryanization (Aly and Heim 1993): 200 000 Viennese citizens were either deported to concentration camps and killed or had to flee the country. The Jewish population that exceeded 200 000 in the 1920s was reduced to a few thousand in 1945 (Steidl 2015, pp. 426 f.).

Socio-economic improvement strategies were based on distributing the wealth of expropriated Jews and exploiting the conquered countries. Cultural habitation was initially based on Catholicism and an Austrian identity, then on the community of the German people – radical versions of the insider–outsider divide.

4.   INSTITUTIONALIZATION OF A SOCIAL-DEMOCRATIC COUNTERMOVEMENT (1945–89)

After the Second World War, welfare capitalism led to high economic growth rates, spreading consumer society and marketization. In line with a "soft" Polanyi, the "market should remain the dominant coordinating mechanism but should be complemented by redistributive institutions" (Dale 2010, p. 370). All over Western Europe, access to mass consumption was opened to the working classes. In Austria, housing became a key pillar in the post-war corporatist welfare consensus (Matznetter 2002). These welfare states of "embedded liberalism" (Ruggie 1982) never attracted Karl Polanyi's interest, not only due to their timid attempts to put the economy under democratic control (Dale 2010, p. 375; Dale 2016b, pp. 4 ff.), but especially because social democracy abandoned the interwar strategy of radical reformism of constructing habitation based on a solidaristic culture beyond greed and materialism.

A specific anti-fascist consensus was at the core of post-war Austria. While it avoided any systematic coming to terms with its past, it constituted a class compromise and consensus-oriented politics based on social rights and full employment. Red Vienna's cultural project of offering social infrastructure to foster a non-capitalist mode of living gave way to technocratic provisioning of housing, which started to increasingly suggest that improvement via marketization automatically leads to secured livelihoods. This cannot only be ascribed to ideological changes. A shift of fiscal competencies to the federal scale – already initiated before the Second World War – further diminished the room for manoeuvre of place-based urban planning (Becker and Novy, 1999, p. 134). "The progressive cultural and intellectual cosmos did not recover" (Becker and Novy 1999, p. 137), as only few of the surviving intellectuals, researchers, or artists returned. Not only revolutionary ideas, but also innovation and creativity were eyeballed sceptically.

Post-war reconstruction took place in a shrinking city next to the Iron Curtain. The provision with basic private living spaces had priority, while investment in communal and educational infrastructure like libraries and playgrounds within the housing complexes was restrained. Housing policy was led by (cost-)efficiency, which was facilitated by more peripheral sites for public housing, creating a "*city of long distances*". Apartments' average size increased, and generous green spaces around the housing complexes were provided. "The aspiration to support and 'shape' people's life-, education-, or cultural behaviour through housing was [however] abandoned" (Ruhsmann and Wippel 2018, own translation). From the 1970s onwards, the housing shortage in the still shrinking city was overcome. Policy concern shifted to soft urban renewal of pre-war buildings with the clear aspiration of incumbent upgrading – improvements with limited displacement of renters.

To sum up, post-war policies focused on socio-economic habitation, facilitated by high growth rates, as fascism has discredited radical cultural habitation strategies. The social-democratic countermovement institutionalized decommodified infrastructures and an inclusionary security-based form of habitation "for all" within a national power container. But it abandoned transformative aspirations.

5.   EROSION OF A SOCIAL-DEMOCRATIC COUNTERMOVEMENT (1989 ONWARDS)

In the 1980s it became apparent that social-democratic civil society was severely weakened. The consumer cooperative *Konsum* and the party journal *Arbeiterzeitung* were extinct; the municipal savings bank was privatized. New elite networks, selectively integrating civil society and experts, emerged (Novy et al. 2001). Viennese social democracy shifted from a cultural avant-garde, building an alternative social infrastructure "for all", to a right-wing social democracy focusing on enabling access to mass consumption for formerly excluded segments of the population. During the 1990s, the right-wing party FPÖ got over 20 per cent of the votes in the municipal elections and even surpassed 30 per cent in areas with a high density of tenants in council housing.

Vienna, which has always been governed by social democracy (alone or in coalition governments) under democratic regimes, has been a latecomer to neoliberal urban reforms (Becker and Novy 1999). The anti-liberal heritage of Lueger has survived too. Nevertheless, neoliberal policies gained momentum after the fall of the Iron Curtain which reoriented Vienna towards Eastern Europe. Due to the focus on austerity of European economic governance, the municipality has found itself increasingly unable to finance necessary investment and, as a result, public–private partnerships were facilitated (IFIP and SRZ 2007, p. 14).

The "end of Red Vienna" (Novy et al. 2001) as radical reformism must not be conflated with the abandonment of a distinctively decommodified sector of housing and public infrastructure. Up to today, the municipality has avoided privatization and re-commodification. Vienna has maintained 100 per cent municipal ownership over large parts of its infrastructure, especially public housing, although municipal companies, from public utilities to the management of public housing, were transformed into private legal form. Favourable multi-level alliances facilitated this persistence. At the national level, coalition governments led by social democracy allowed for local deviance (Becker and

Novy 1999). At the European level, the city of Vienna was able to orchestrate a city alliance against the forced privatization of services of public interest (Reinprecht 2014).

Of Vienna's over 1.8 million inhabitants, 43 per cent live in socially rented housing encompassing council housing and limited-profit housing associations, 33 per cent in private-rented dwellings, in part protected by rent controls, and 19 per cent live in owner-occupied residencies (Tockner 2017, p. 10).[2] Rent controls are still valid for apartments built before 1945. Tenants with old rental contracts are protected from soaring rents, as are inhabitants of council housing where rents are on average 1.3 euros per m^2 below average. Furthermore, there are "generous possibilities for tenants to hand over rental contracts within the family" (Kadi 2015, p. 258). Together with tenants in council housing, these households represent the insiders of Vienna's decommodified housing sector. In 2004, the municipality of Vienna abandoned its council housing construction programme (Kunnert and Baumgartner 2012, p. 57) and delegated construction to limited-profit housing associations (Kadi 2015, p. 248).[3] Between 2011 and 2014, 17 000 new apartments were built by limited-profit housing associations alone (Mattern 2016, pp. 12 f.). Average land price for limited-profit housing rose from 575 to 961 euros per m^2 from 2000 to 2010. As a consequence, this has increased cooperative-share requirements by tenants to up to 25 000 euros, limiting access for less affluent households (Kadi 2015, p. 254).

The same is true for new forms of housing such as *Baugruppen* and co-housing which focus on the provision of shared and communal spaces in which residents can interact and live together in non-commodified ways (for example through moneyless trading markets, learning spaces, and atelier rooms). These projects are, except for the newly designed city quarter *Seestadt*, rather small-scale and participating requires "a certain level of skills, knowledge, and financial resources" (Reiss 2017, p. 66). Hence, they have difficulties to overcome their middle-class bias, although they often make explicit attempts to build bridges to disadvantaged segments of the population (e.g. refugees, homeless).

The combination of comparatively low housing prices and a still-to-be commodified housing sector offers potential gains for financial agents (Aalbers

---

[2]	The remaining 5 per cent encompasses other legal forms (for example rent free, gratuitously used dwellings).

[3]	The so-called Austrian Federation of Limited-Profit Housing Associations (*Gemeinnützige Bauvereinigungen* – GBV) is composed of limited-profit organizations and cooperatives that are granted tax advantages and special access to housing subsidies and that, in return, are *inter alia* obliged to limit their profits and reinvest their surplus equity in social housing.

2017, pp. 117 ff.). As mobility rates in the decommodified sector have decreased, access to affordable housing is increasingly difficult. Regulations for renting new private apartments have eroded. Therefore, the burden of deteriorating housing markets has to be carried by those looking for apartments, be it young families, newcomers from the interior of Austria, migrants, or poor households. While overall rents increased by 37 per cent from 2001 to 2010, they rose by 67 per cent for regulated private-rental units in pre-war buildings (Tockner 2012, p. 10). New rent contracts in the private sector rose by 43 per cent in the period from 2008 until 2016 (Tockner 2017, p. 12). In this market segment, the share of households that spend more than 25 per cent of their income on housing costs has risen from 39 per cent to 45 per cent between 2005 and 2011, as new contracts are significantly more expensive (Kadi 2015, p. 256).

In this increasingly insecure economic context, a right-wing national government has attacked the remaining Viennese public sector and also European regulations are hostile to a decommodified sector outside competition law (Gruis and Priemus 2008). Nevertheless, the current red–green city government (from 2010 onwards) has begun to timidly revive policies of Red Vienna (Vollmer and Kadi 2018, pp. 257 f.). First, it has started to build new council housing at a modest level. The first 4000 apartments are expected to be ready in 2020. Second, new construction regulations were introduced in 2018 to tackle soaring land prices by introducing a new zoning category "subsidized housing construction" (see section 6). This is expected to cap land prices at under 188 euros per m^2 and net rent at under five euros per m^2 (Vienna City Administration 2018). In providing affordable public transportation with an annual ticket at 365 euros as well as improving bicycle infrastructure and public spaces, the city also pursues timid decommodification strategies of public infrastructure with immediate impact on purchasing power.

To sum up, from 1989 onwards market-centred improvement as well as populist, xenophobic and racist countermovements have gained importance. Building on its position as Vienna's second largest party since 1991, the FPÖ has reached 30.8 per cent of votes in the 2015 municipal elections. Improvement strategies are increasingly embedded in a market logic, deepening tendencies of possessive individualism. The growing importance of city rankings is only one example of the key role attributed to competitiveness for sustaining welfare. Social housing has become stigmatized while supranational and national directives facilitate home ownership. Right-wing populism, invoking insider–outsider dynamics in offering habitation, has gained prominence, often in the form of ethnicizing conflicts that have severe socio-economic implications, such as the regulation of access to council housing. Liberalization in Vienna, however, has been modest, municipal ownership of urban infrastructure as well as housing has been secured, and experiments with innovative urban infrastructure have been started.

6.   CONCLUSION

There have been impressive improvements in living conditions over the last 150 years in Vienna. This, however, did not impede the proliferation of powerful countermovements to oppose the velocity and destructiveness of economic and socio-cultural change. Both anti-liberal countermovements against marketization – Lueger and Red Vienna – offered habitation, routinized and secured livelihood, and *Gemeinschaft*, characterized by apparent social unity (Dale 2010, p. 381), be it a traditional-Catholic community or a vivid social-democratic mode of living. Both defended livelihoods directly rather than indirectly through an abstract process of economic improvement (Holmes 2018, p. 143). Red Vienna inspired Polanyi's concrete utopia of a social order based not on liberal freedom for "assimilated insiders", but "freedom for all" (Polanyi [1944] 2001, pp. 257–68). Supported by strong pressure "from below", Red Vienna delivered social protection "from above"; subordinating the logic of gain and profit to delivering high-quality urban infrastructure. But the socio-cultural achievements of this emancipatory countermovement would have hardly been possible without the foundations laid by populist forces which municipalized infrastructure. Although incentives for democratic participation or civic involvement were controlled "from above", Red Vienna implemented innovative and profound reforms which turned workers into citizens by offering "livelihood for all".

Fascism radicalized exclusion and oppression but also paved the way for consensual policy-making after the war. Social democracy increasingly pursued a strategy of habitation via mass consumerism, and transformative aspirations of habitation strategies were largely lost. Over the last decades, neoliberalism had its imprint on the city. Entitlements and services were increasingly differentiated between groups of urban inhabitants. The share of households considered at risk of poverty grew from 12.7 per cent in 2005 to 19.2 per cent in 2011 (Kadi 2015, p. 253). The part of the eligible population that cannot vote due to lack of Austrian citizenship reached 27 per cent, questioning the legitimacy of the existing form of democratic citizenship (City of Vienna 2017, p. 8).

But different from most other European cities, the strong public sector is still structuring politics and life in Vienna. Paradoxically, the partial decommodification of housing created a secure private sphere and facilitated the spread of mass consumption, possessive individualism, and a culture of commercialization – exactly this liberal culture which is currently most dismissive of public and political agency. As a consequence, rising, often elder segments of "the insiders" in the housing market have become conservative, sometimes even reactionary in distinguishing themselves from "the outsiders". Council housing has become a stronghold of the right-wing FPÖ, reaching up to 40 per cent of votes in the 2015 municipal elections. Thus, when talking about habitation and protection, the FPÖ has for now abandoned pleas for privatization of public housing, focusing instead on restricting access to housing and labour markets and radicalizing anti-Islam discourses. In many respects, these protective and clientelist discourses have similarities with Lueger's habitation strategy as they also ethnicize socio-economic conflicts.

To sum up, countermovements are ambivalent. Improvement is not always destructive and habitation not always unifying. Their outcomes depend on their specific form of implementation and framing. Housing and urban infrastructure are not just about the technical provision of material well-being, but have cultural implications as well. They bear positive, but also negative potentials to foster holistic forms of social cohesion, a peaceful communal life, and emancipation. What will be actualized depends on how habitation is conceived and framed and how improvement is carried out. A promising attempt to actualize positive potentials is the new building law amendment that intends to enjoin investors to devote two-thirds of future housing projects to a new zoning category "subsidized housing construction", in which rents must not exceed five euros net per m^2. It will discourage investments in the high-priced housing sector, and thereby – in line with Vienna's reformist history – devalue housing and land as a commodity.

To erode the attractiveness of the divisive outsider–insider discourse, an emancipatory cultural hegemony has to be built on a common agenda for insiders *and* outsiders. Such alliances have to mobilize insiders and outsiders for a project "for all". As many of the outsiders are not entitled to vote (yet), democratic electoral alliances have to be broad. They have to improve access to housing for outsiders via council housing or cheaper social housing, but also defend the rights of the insiders in the decommodified housing sector. Furthermore, access to decommodified urban infrastructure "for all" in a broad sense – mobility, education, health, care, and leisure – is crucial for alliance building, as it improves the quality of life for outsiders as well as insiders in the housing market. Both are empowered by spaces of encounter for all inhabitants. Such a public infrastructure could be the foundation of an inclusive and solidaristic project that can challenge authoritarian, exclusionary neoliberalism and antagonistic imaginaries of habitation.

REFERENCES

Aalbers, M.B. (ed.) (2017), *The financialization of housing: A political economy approach*, London: Routledge.

Aly, G. and S. Heim (1993), *Vordenker der Vernichtung: Auschwitz und die deutschen Pläne für eine neue europäische Ordnung*, Frankfurt/Main: Fischer Taschenbuch.

Becker, J. and A. Novy (1999), 'Divergence and convergence of national and local regulation: The case of Austria and Vienna', *European Urban and Regional Studies*, 6 (2), 127–43.

Berman, M. (1988), *All that is solid melts into air*, New York: Penguin.

City of Vienna (2017), *Diversitäts- und Integrationsmonitor 2013–2016*. Wien: Stadt Wien/Magistratsabteilung 17.

Cowen, M.P. and B.W. Shenton (1996), *Doctrines of development*, London: Routledge.

Dale, G. (2010), 'Social democracy, embeddedness and decommodification: On the conceptual innovations and intellectual affiliations of Karl Polanyi', *New Political Economy*, 15 (3), 369–93.

Dale, G. (2016a), *Karl Polanyi: A life on the left*, New York: Columbia University Press.

Dale, G. (2016b), *Reconstructing Karl Polanyi: Excavation and critique*, London: Pluto.

Förster, W. (2002), '80 years of social housing in Vienna', accessed 22 June 2018 at www.wien.gv.at/english/housing/promotion/pdf/socialhous.pdf.

Fraser, N. (2014), 'Can society be commodities all the way down? Post-Polanyian reflections on capitalist crisis', *Economy and Society*, 43 (4), 541–58.

Gruis, V. and H. Priemus (2008), 'European competition policy and national housing policies: International implications of the Dutch case', *Housing Studies*, 23 (3), 485–505.

Hayek, F. ([1944] 1994), *The road to serfdom*, Chicago: University of Chicago Press.

Hobsbawm, E. (2003), *The age of empire: 1875–1914*, London: Abacus.

Holmes, C. (2018), *Polanyi in times of populism: Vision and contradiction in the history of economic ideas*, London: Routledge.

IFIP and SRZ (2007), 'Eigentümerstruktur im Wiener Privaten Althausbestand: Analyse der Veränderungen und deren Auswirkungen auf den Wohnungsmarkt in Wien', accessed 12 July 2018 at https://media.arbeiterkammer.at/wien/PDF/studien/Studie_Eigentuemerstruktur_Althausbestand.pdf.

Johnston, W.M. (1983), *The Austrian mind: An intellectual and social history, 1848–1938*, Oakland: University of California Press.

Kadi, J. (2015), 'Recommodifying housing in formerly "red" Vienna?', *Housing, Theory and Society*, 32 (3), 247–65.

Killion, J.A. (2015), 'Changing cities, changing roles: Municipal developments and the urban social contract in nineteenth century Vienna', paper presented at the Graduate Student Conference – Chronopolis: Time & Urban Space, Western Michigan University, 31 October.

Kunnert, A. and J. Baumgartner (2012), 'Instrumente und Wirkungen der österreichischen Wohnungspolitik', accessed 12 July 2018 at https://media .arbeiterkammer.at/wien/PDF/studien/Wohnungspolitik_2012.pdf.

Lewis, J. (1983), 'Red Vienna: Socialism in one city, 1918–27', *European History Quarterly*, 13, 335–55.

Maderthaner, W. and L. Musner (2002), 'Textures of the modern: Viennese contributions to cultural history and urban studies', *Cultural Studies*, 16 (6), 863–76.

Mattern, P. (2016), 'Wohnungsversorgung in Berlin und Wien: Bedarfs- und Angebotsentwicklung seit der Jahrtausendwende', accessed 12 July 2018 at https://media.arbeiterkammer.at/wien/PDF/studien/Mattern_Wohnungsver sorgung_in_Berlin_und_Wien_2016.pdf.

Matznetter, W. (2002), 'Social housing policy in a conservative welfare state: Austria as an example', *Urban Studies*, 39 (2), 265–82.

Novy, A., V. Redak, J. Jäger and A. Hamedinger (2001), 'The end of red Vienna: Recent ruptures and continuities in urban governance', *European Urban and Regional Studies*, 8 (2), 131–44.

Polanyi, K. ([1944] 2001), *The great transformation: The political and economic origins of our times*, Boston: Beacon Press.

Polanyi-Levitt, K. (1990), 'The origins and significance of *The Great Transformation*', in K. Polanyi-Levitt (ed.), *The life and work of Karl Polanyi*, Montréal: Black Rose, pp. 111–24.

Reinprecht, C. (2014), 'Social housing in Austria', in K. Scanlon, C. Whitehead and M. Fernández Arrigoitia (eds), *Social housing in Europe*, Chichester: Wiley, pp. 61–73.

Reiss, V.R.S. (2017), 'Viennese planning culture: Understanding change and continuity through the Hauptbahnhof', Master's thesis, Vancouver: University of British Columbia.

Resch, A. and P. Eigner (2001), 'Stadtwirtschaft Wien – langfristige Entwicklungen, Vienna', accessed 28 July 2018 at www.demokratiezentrum .org/fileadmin/media/pdf/eigner_resch_entwicklungen.pdf.

Ruggie, J.G. (1982), 'International regimes, transactions, and change: Embedded liberalism in the postwar economic order', *International Organization*, 36 (2), 379–415.

Ruhsmann, B. and J. Wippel (2018), 'Wiener Gemeindebau – Blick in die Vergangenheit mit Zukunft', accessed 19 August 2018 at http://forumw ohnbaupolitik.at/barbara-ruhsmann-und-joerg-wippel-wiener-gemeinde bau-blick-in-die-vergangenheit-mit-zukunft/http://forumwohnbaupolitik .at/barbara-ruhsmann-und-joerg-wippel-wiener-gemeindebau-blick-in-die -vergangenheit-mit-zukunft/.

Schorske, C.E. (1982), *Wien: Geist und Gesellschaft im Fin de Siècle*. Frankfurt/Main: Fischer.

Sennett, R. (1998), *The corrosion of character: The personal consequences of work in the new capitalism*, London: Norton.

Steidl, A. (2015), 'Ein attraktiver Anziehungspunkt für Zuwanderer aus ganz Europa: Wanderungsmuster nach Wien, 1740–2010', in A. Weigl, P. Eigner and E.G. Eder (eds), *Sozialgeschichte Wiens 1740–2010*, Innsbruck: Studienverlag, pp. 375–434.

Tálos, E., H. Dachs, E. Hanisch and A. Staudinger (eds) (1995), *Handbuch des Politischen Systems Österreichs: Erste Republik 1918–1938*, Wien: Manz.

Tockner, L. (2012), 'Mietensteigerung in Österreich und Wien: Auswertungen aus dem Mikrozensus', accessed 11 July 2018 at http://media.arbeiterkammer .at/wien/PDF/mietensteigerungen_studie.pdf.

Tockner, L. (2017), 'Mieten in Österreich und Wien 2008 bis 2016', accessed 11 July 2018 at https://media.arbeiterkammer.at/wien/PDF/studien/Mieten _in_Oesterreich_und_Wien_2008_bis_2016.pdf.

Vienna City Administration (2018), *Verbesserungen im Wiener Baurecht*, accessed 12 August 2018 at www.wien.gv.at/bauen-wohnen/ bauordnungsnovelle.html#widmungskategorie.

Vollmer, L. and J. Kadi (2018), 'Wohnungspolitik in der Krise des Neoliberalismus in Berlin und Wien', *PROKLA Zeitschrift für kritische Sozialwissenschaft*, 191 (2), 247–64.

Wassermann, J. (2014), *Black Vienna: The radical right in the red city, 1918–1938*, Ithaca, NY: Cornell University Press.

Weber, F. (1995), 'Staatliche Wirtschaftspolitik in der Zwischenkriegszeit', in E. Tálos, E. Dachs, E. Hanisch and A. Staudinger (eds), *Handbuch des politischen Systems Österreichs: Erste Republik 1918–1933*, Wien: Manz, pp. 531–51.

Weihsmann, H. (1985), *Das Rote Wien: Sozialdemokratische Architektur und Kommunalpolitik 1919–1934*, Wien: Promedia.

17. The "fictitious commodity" care and the reciprocity of caring: a Polanyian and neo-institutionalist perspective on the brokering of 24-hour care

Brigitte Aulenbacher and Michael Leiblfinger

Post-1989, with the new phase of globalisation, the international sociology of care diagnoses a deep going transformation of care regimes. Scholars emphasise three interrelated tendencies: the transnationalisation of labour, work and policies; the forced commodification of care and care work; and new governance and the reorganisation of the welfare state. How these tendencies are interconnected differs from country to country depending on the welfare, employment, gender and migration regimes. Nevertheless, common patterns emerge (Anderson and Shutes 2014; Klenk and Pavolini 2015; Kofman and Raghuram 2015). One such pattern is the emergence of new care markets, which are embedded in and partially regulated by the (welfare) state. We will focus on the case of 24-hour care in Austria and on home care agencies as brokers recruiting care workers predominantly from Eastern Europe and selling care. The reason for selecting this case is that Austria is a forerunner state of the marketisation of 24-hour care. It combines the conservative ideal of the home care society with neoliberal cash-for-care policies, which reduce the responsibility of the welfare state at the expense of the private household in the framework of strong legalisation of formerly informal work (Shire 2015), allowing brokers to flourish. The chapter discusses the Austrian case of 24-hour care brokered by home care agencies from a Polanyian and neo-institutionalist perspective.[1] The first part addresses how far caring is characterised by

[1] This research is part of the D-A-CH-project "Decent Care Work? Transnational Home Care Arrangements", a cooperation of Aranka Benazha, Helma Lutz, Iga Obrocka and Ewa Palenga-Möllenbeck from Goethe University Frankfurt/Germany, Brigitte Aulenbacher, Michael Leiblfinger and Veronika Prieler from Johannes Kepler University Linz/Austria and Karin Schwiter, Jennifer Steiner and Anahi Villalba from the University of Zurich/Switzerland. It is funded by the German Research Foundation DFG project no. LU 630/14-1, by the Austrian Science Fund FWF project no. I 3145

unequal reciprocity and care has become a "fictitious commodity", (Polanyi 2001) how it is put at risk and how we can investigate home care agencies. The second part analyses how 24-hour care is embedded in the Austrian care regime and what this means for brokering care workers and selling care. The third part draws on empirical findings to show which problems and solutions home care agencies as care providers and mediators between care receivers, their relatives and care givers describe and how they concern care and care work. The conclusion will come back to the topic of care as a "fictitious commodity" (Polanyi 2001) and the reciprocity of caring.

1.   APPROACHING THE UNEQUAL RECIPROCITY OF CARING AND CARE AS A "FICTITIOUS COMMODITY"

The established understanding of care focuses on the relations between human beings and includes the relationship between human and non-human nature, as Berenice Fisher and Joan Tronto (1990, p. 40, without authors' emphasis) state: "On the most general level, we suggest that caring be viewed as a species activity that includes everything that we do to maintain, continue, and repair our 'world' so that we can live in it as well as possible. That world includes our bodies, ourselves, and our environment, all of which we seek to interweave in a complex, life-sustaining web." Care includes self-care as well as care for others. In such an ontological perspective human beings are considered to be "homines curans" (Tronto 2017), who are facing the contingency of life as dependent and vulnerable, not only in case of childhood health issues and elderly care, but also in everyday life and over the whole lifespan (Klinger 2013). "Relationships can be seen as the backbone of care, of its realm, its context and its functioning" (Weicht 2015, p. 37) and care can be understood as "work on, with, and against the contingency of life" (Klinger 2013, p. 84, own translation). The relations of care are asymmetrical in regard to reciprocity, which often is not or not fully given between care receivers and givers and also, concerning the interdependencies between them, with regard to relations of power. Under these auspices, decent care – in an emphatic sense including respect of the care givers and receivers for each other as autonomous individuals and responsibility for needs for reasons of humanity – is not given but has to be built up in the relations and practices of caring as a continuing process

G-29, and by the Swiss National Science Foundation SNSF project no. 170353. This chapter refers to a survey of all websites of Viennese home care agencies and the in-depth analysis of 20 of them, 11 expert interviews with their representatives and the investigation of one care arrangement including episodic interviews with all participants, among them care receivers and givers, all done by the Austrian team.

(Tronto 2017, pp. 31 ff.). To deal with (unequal) reciprocity between those who are needy and those who feel responsible for meeting these needs, this is not only part of individual interaction but also depends on the context. As Eleonore Kofman and Parvati Raghuram (2015, pp. 52 f.) emphasise in regard to the societal organisation of care and social reproduction, there is "a set of values and norms guiding human action and the interdependent relationships established with others". This is, in Western Europe, connected, interwoven, and/or in conflict with other principles in the societal organisation of care and care work in the private sector, the (welfare) state, the third sector, the private household, and social networks, their normative and institutional orders. In other words and focusing our topic: the ever given asymmetrical, power-prone and rarely reciprocal relations between care givers and receivers refer to norms and ideals of, in the broadest sense and whatever this means in each sector, decent care and meet, under the auspices of a capitalist economy, ideas of competition, rationalisation, rentability and profit. In this context scholars rediscover Karl Polanyi's (2001, pp. 45 ff.) work. His concept of "fictitious commodities" (Polanyi 2001, pp. 71 ff.) and his distinction between four organizational principles of economy – "reciprocity", "redistribution", "house-holding" and (market) "exchange" – have been of interest in the recent debate.

The concept of "fictitious commodities" (Polanyi 2001, pp. 71 ff.) is useful to understand the societal organisation of care under the auspices of its forced commodification (Aulenbacher et al. 2018a; Fraser 2013; Lutz 2017; Tronto 2017). With 24-hour care in mind, three Polanyian arguments are of interest for us: first, "fictitious commodities" in the Polanyian sense are "essential elements of industry; they also must be organized in markets; in fact, these markets form an absolutely vital part of the economic system", but these "elements" never have been produced for sale (Polanyi 2001, p. 75). Similar to his characterisation of labour as "a human activity which goes along with life itself" (Polanyi 2001, p. 75) we can state that the primary aim and purpose of care is to sustain livelihood (Tronto 2017), which is the precondition of society including its economy, and not to be sold. Second, for Karl Polanyi (2001, p. 76) the "commodity fiction [. . .] supplies a vital organizing principle in regard to the whole society affecting almost all its institutions in the most varied way". In the case of care, "commodification", "marketization" and "corporatization" of care (Farris and Marchetti 2017) are oriented on other values than its primary orientation towards the needs of human beings and the relationships it depends upon by subordinating them to the mechanisms of supply and demand; principles of a profit-oriented, competitive economy and rationalisation strategies have to be mentioned (Aulenbacher and Dammayr 2014, pp. 125 ff.). Third, for Karl Polanyi (2001, pp. 71 ff.) the liberal idea of the "self-regulating market" goes along with destructive tendencies. "To allow the market mechanism to be sole director of the fate of human beings and their natural environment indeed, even of the amount and use of purchasing power, would result in the demolition of society" (Polanyi 2001, p. 76). The transnational commodification and marketisation of care is an instructive example. It goes hand in hand with care gaps between the wealthy countries, which can afford to recruit migrant care workers, and the poor(er) countries with their already insufficient care provisions, from which the migrant carers come, and unequal relationships and arrangements, which are established in this constellation (Kofman and Raghuram 2015; Lutz 2017, 2018). Investigation on the question how far care has become a "fictitious commodity" (Polanyi 2001) is focused on its forced commodification and the relation between care givers and receivers and, in case of domestic care, their relatives (Aulenbacher et al. 2018a; Fraser 2013; Lutz 2017; Tronto 2017). The paradigmatic case of reciprocity, as Polanyi understands it, is the gift exchange, which does not need to be balanced, because the relationship is the primary aim. Anna Safuta and Florence Degavre (2013, p. 426) take up this Polanyian perspective to show how "reciprocity", partially combined with "redistribution", has become the informal, but nevertheless important practice between care workers enabling each other to care for their selves. However, investigation of the relations between care givers and receivers and their relatives in terms of "reciprocity" *and* of care as a "fictitious commodity" (Polanyi 2001) is a blank space. The forced "commodification", "marketization" and "corporatization" of care and care work (Farris and Marchetti 2017) lead to asking how they and reciprocity come or collapse together. Furthermore, we ask how this happens under given conditions of unequal division of labour, particularly interrelated with the established relations of gender, race, class, and subsequent inequalities which are – to a greater or lesser extent – legitimated in the meritocratic order of the modern capitalist society, contested or scandalised (Aulenbacher et al. 2017).

Investigating the transnational brokering of care workers and sale of care services, this chapter focuses on a facet of care arrangements built up in the context of marketisation and corporatisation of care. It seems useful to add a neo-institutionalist perspective to come closer to the home care agencies as organisations with increasing influence on care provision (Aulenbacher et al. 2019; Österle et al. 2013). Referring to Royston Greenwood et al. (2011), home care agencies can be investigated as organisations operating in the care market depending on their own constitutions and the relations, not least the competition, in the field, but also shaping it by their own agenda setting. Embedded in wider society, organisations face "institutional complexity" (Greenwood et al. 2011) with "prescriptions" and "proscriptions" (Greenwood et al. 2014, pp. 1213 ff.). These are established, in the terms used by Patricia Thornton et al. (2012, pp. 3, 73 ff., 104 ff.), in different historically emerged "institutional orders", such as family, community, religion, state, market, profession, corporation, with their respective "institutional logics", beliefs, norms and values. They influence how individuals and organisations organise their everyday practice, create their identities and legitimate what they are doing (Thornton et al. 2012, pp. 3, 73 ff., 104 ff.). "Logics [. . .] provide guidelines on how to interpret and function in social situations. [. . .] Typically, organizations face multiple logics, that may – or may not – be mutually incompatible [. . .]. To the extent that the prescriptions and proscriptions of different logics are incompatible, or at least appear to be so, they inevitably generate challenges and tensions for organizations exposed to them" (Greenwood et al. 2011, p. 318). From this perspective home care agencies do not orientate themselves solely to the logics of the market or the corporation. They also have to consider demands which are connected with, in our focus, the logics of the state, the family, and the profession when they deal with the "fictitious commodity" (Polanyi 2001) of care and face the "institutional complexity" (Greenwood et al. 2011) of the care regime in which the Austrian care market is embedded.

2. THE AUSTRIAN 24-HOUR CARE MARKET AND THE ROLE OF THE HOME CARE AGENCIES

Over the last decade, economic, socio-structural, and political developments led to changes in familial care. Austria developed a "modernized male breadwinner model" (Haas 2005, p. 496) without breaking with the ideal of a home care society, leaving the main responsibility of care to relatives and, within families, predominantly to women. Their increased participation in the (paid) labour market nonetheless led to less intergenerational care (Appelt and Fleischer 2014). The introduction of the Federal Long-Term Care Benefit Act (*Bundespflegegesetz*) in 1993 and Austria's proximity to countries of post-communist Eastern Europe led to the creation of an irregular market for live-in care. After years of turning a blind eye and a heated public debate during the general election in 2006, the Home Care Act (*Hausbetreuungsgesetz*) of 2007 legalised the previously irregular practice of employing live-in carers and created a new occupation: "personal care worker" (*PersonenbetreuerIn*) (Leiblfinger and Prieler 2018). Although the law allows for an employer–employee relationship, self-employment[2] of the predominantly female care givers from Eastern European countries has since become the predominant form.[3] Legalisation was the main reason for the Home Care Act, with affordability being another major concern. Besides a means-tested benefit to help

[2] In Austria, the self-employed are integrated in the general social insurance system with a comprehensive, but slightly less extensive coverage compared to employees.
[3] About 99.8 per cent of 'personal care workers' are self-employed (BMASGK 2018, p. 4).

cover social insurance costs, the self-employment model provides households with more flexibility and lessens the bureaucratic and financial burden as self-employed carers have no claim to minimum wage, paid vacation, regular working hours, or guaranteed breaks (Österle and Bauer 2016, pp. 196 f.; Leiblfinger and Prieler 2018). Like all self-employed individuals, "personal care workers" are responsible for the results of their work including all accompanying risks or mistakes (Aulenbacher et al. 2018b). The construction of self-employed care workers in the private household, combining the logics of the market, the state, the profession and the family, is the core element that makes Austria the forerunner for commodification and marketisation of 24-hour care by undermining all standards of workers' rights and the usual social protections connected to regular employment.

The 24-hour care arrangement builds on shuttle migration and the underlying economic and welfare gaps between East European countries and Austria, which, despite the given conditions, make care workers available. The most important sending countries are Romania and Slovakia.[4] Care workers are predominantly recruited and brokered by home care agencies on the rapidly growing care market, which allows them to define and shape many conditions of the care arrangement (Aulenbacher et al. 2018b).[5]

The legal structures of these agencies vary greatly: even though sole proprietors make up more than half of, for example, Viennese home care agencies, limited liability companies (*Gesellschaften mit beschränkter Haftung*) also play a big role while not-for-profit organisations (*Vereine*) and other commercial partnership forms (*KG, OG*) are less common (cf. Aulenbacher et al. 2018b, 2019), a shift from previous research where LLCs and NPOs were more common than sole proprietors (Österle et al. 2013, p. 166). Some of their representatives, mostly from the larger enterprises, are strongly connected with and able to influence economic or political stakeholders in the field.

Usually home care agencies broker two "personal care workers", who alternate in typically two-to-three-week periods as live-ins. On their websites, most home care agencies advertise that they visit regularly to ensure the quality of

---

[4]   Currently, more than 62 600 care workers are registered with the Chamber of Commerce (WKO 2018, p. 11): 95 per cent are female, more than 80 per cent come from Romania and Slovakia, and about two-thirds are between 41 and 60 years old (authors' correspondence with Sozialversicherungsanstalt der gewerblichen Wirtschaft in January 2018 regarding the number of socially insured "personal care workers" and selected demographic characteristics).

[5]   In 2007, a study found 37 home care agencies. A comprehensive internet search identified 133 brokers, with approximately a third located outside of Austria, in late 2011 (Österle et al. 2013, pp. 163, 165 f.). By the end of 2017, 738 home care agencies were registered with Austria's Chamber of Commerce alone (WKO 2018, p. 11; registration is mandatory).

care. Even though agencies offer services to both households and "personal care workers",[6] the majority primarily address (potential) care receivers, as clients, or their relatives, as customers, rather than care givers (Aulenbacher et al. 2019). Recruiting strategies vary, but are influenced by the logics of the market, the family and the profession. One of our interviewees, the head of an agency's home care activities, describes the process as follows (AG 08, pp. 1 f., ll. 5–46): after being contacted by (usually) relatives of the potential client via email or telephone, the first questions to be dealt with are pricing and affordability. After a visit directly with the care receiver, where not only the care needs but also the relevant medical history is taken, the family is consulted about their wishes for the carers, e.g. age, (non)smokers, pet friendliness, etc. This agency then uses a partner in Eastern Europe that tries to identify potential care workers according to the anamnesis, who in turn will be checked by the home care agency before they broker them into the household. On the first day, they accompany the carers and after going through all relevant contracts and forms, the family is asked to give it a try with the live-in. This process description was similar for other interviewees, though some home care agencies do not rely on external partners for recruitment.[7]

3.   COMPLEX, CONTRADICTORY AND CONFLICTING DEMANDS OF HOME CARE AND THE AGENCIES AS BROKERS AND MEDIATORS

Embedded in the care regime with its logics of the family, the state and the profession, the Austrian care market is a paradigmatic case for a politically shaped market (Polanyi 2001) as well as concerning the question how organisations face "institutional complexity" (Greenwood et al. 2011) and how they act. In this chapter, we focus on two aspects of the self-conception home care agencies describe: they consider themselves as brokers offering care services to private households (section 3.1) and as mediators in the event of conflicts (section 3.2). Both roles include broad common sense about the field, which is shared by all representatives of the home care agencies we have interviewed: from their perspective, Austrian 24-hour care only works as a low-cost model of self-employment instead of employment. The reason is that neither the

---

[6]   Most home care agencies at the very least offer help with the mandatory registration at the Chamber of Commerce, although this service is sometimes advertised as one for care receivers and their families.

[7]   Other home care agencies recruit directly, having their own, sometimes Eastern European language-speaking, recruitment personnel (e.g. AG 01) or using Facebook groups (e.g. AG 06) to find carers looking for work.

welfare state nor private households would be able or willing to pay for such an alternative. And this means that it only works combined with shuttle migration from poor(er) countries, where the economic situation (unemployment, low wages, insufficient pensions, etc.) pushes people to go. Both points make us aware of the "commodity fiction" (Polanyi 2001) which belongs to the commodification and marketisation of care and puts its relationships at risk in respect of reciprocity and subsequently self-care and care for others in the relation of care receivers, their relatives and care givers.

3.1   Home Care Agencies' Services and Offers for Care Receivers and Their Relatives

In addition to 24-hour care, most home care agencies offer short-term home care. Both forms typically rely on shuttle migration and are predominantly advertised as relief for care giving relatives, addressing the logics of family and (welfare) state in the home care society. Some agencies (additionally) offer hourly or nightly home care, still using self-employed "personal care workers" who moved to Austria (e.g. AG 05, 06). This form is seen by some as an advancement, especially when those carers change residence with children (e.g. ST 08). But whatever form home care agencies offer, they typically not only recruit and broker care workers into households but offer additional services, often also used as arguments for (monthly) fees that households typically have to pay the agency. Apart from the needs assessment with the (potential) care receiver, which home care agencies are legally required to do in person, they often advertise help with the forms for relevant benefits, on-site introduction of the "personal care workers" into the households on their first day, the mediation of any conflicts between households and carers, and regular visits to the households to ensure the quality of care (Aulenbacher et al. 2019). As some home care agencies found a niche for hourly care, others started to offer not just the replacement of what is advertised as affectionate familial lay-care but an alternative to nursing homes, which are repeatedly described with a negative connotation, with those brokers positioning their services in between medical and professional care[8] (e.g. AG 09):[9]

> I explain to [the nurses] in detail what is important for the patient. What are the issues to watch out for, what do you have to do about them. Then, everything is accurately documented and gets constantly reviewed. Even laypeople can do it,

---

[8]   Although not required to be trained nurses, "personal care workers" can – as laypeople and under certain conditions – perform medical and professional care tasks.

[9]   Other home care agencies specifically distance themselves from such practices, offering only non-medical care (e.g. AG 06).

ultimately. I have one patient or another and have to see, that for each patient the optimum of care and reactivating care is brought out. (AG 09, p. 11, ll. 353–65)[10]

Following the competitive logic of the increasingly crowded market, home care agencies therefore try to find their own niche to separate themselves and their services from others, either by offering additional services like hourly or nightly home care or differentiating themselves with professional or medical care services.

However, home care agencies do not only offer services, but also follow their own agenda with the logic of the profession playing a prominent role. Together, the three NPOs Caritas, Hilfswerk, and Volkshilfe, who are important players in Austria's long-term care in general, developed quality standards for 24-hour care which all three organisations adhere to. This quality seal, which is not open to other agencies, is used prominently in their advertising and, among other things, commits the three home care agencies to standards in the selection of "personal care workers", including their education. Such ambitious projects are connected with the logics of the market and the family insofar as high quality should be an argument for the clients and customers not to look solely at prices. Similarly, the Chamber of Commerce has long pushed for a quality seal of its own in an attempt to influence the market by having standards with which high-quality home care agencies can distinguish themselves from so called "black sheep" (cf. Steiner et al. 2019). Such strategies of the not-for-profit and for-profit organisations and the stakeholders in the field are part of the dealing with complex, contradictory and conflicting demands in the interplay of the logic of the market, state, profession and family. At the core we can identify the problem that – under given conditions of this form of care provision – decent care is requested without facilitating decent work. From a Polanyian perspective, demands and claims going along with the "commodity fiction" (Polanyi 2001) and expectations of reciprocity between care receivers, their relatives, and care givers are conflicting which will be visible in regard to the home care agencies' role as mediators.

3.2 Commodification and Marketisation of Care and the Question of Reciprocity

Although home care agencies as brokers primarily address care receivers and their relatives in their advertising (Aulenbacher et al. 2019), many of them see themselves as mediators between households and care givers. In the narratives

---

[10] This interviewee used the German term for nurses instead of carers or "personal care workers".

in which they give insight into this part of their self-conception, problems become visible which touch on the already difficult question of reciprocity in care and the relations of power. Although all representatives of the home care agencies committed themselves to the Austrian model of self-employment, this is accompanied by criticism regarding the practice and, especially, the competitive care market, other home care agencies, the care receivers and their relatives, the care workers, and the insufficient political regulation concerning social policies, costs and control of professional standards but rarely – if ever – their own business and activity. Nevertheless, as experts in the field, striving to deal successfully with the complex and conflicting demands in the interest of their organisations, they are keen-eyed observers of problems.

From the perspective of one of the bigger home care agencies which try to influence stakeholders in the field, the Austrian ideal of the home care society builds the fundament of 24-hour care and the economic gap between countries makes it possible, but in future this may change and should challenge the state and politics:

> It is true that this model survives because the economic differences are so big. We are seeing this in Slovakia, there are fewer and fewer care workers. There are so many job opportunities in Bratislava and the wages are already at the level of what carers can earn in 14 days. So we have hardly any carers from that area. Politics ought to create incentives to make the work really attractive for care givers and keep it that way in future. Conditions must be right and no exploitative practices should happen there. (AG 01, pp. 37 ff., ll. 1236–64)

The background of such ideas of stronger political regulation are experiences of competition in widely unregulated international care markets and the – from the perspective of the care agencies – insufficient support by the state which does not enable private households to buy care services at an appropriate price. This inability of appropriate pricing also means that carers are not given an appropriate honorarium for their work. Furthermore, although most of the home care agencies address the middle classes as clients and customers, this does not mean that they are willing to pay more than necessary:

> If you look at the market, the price structure alone shows huge differences. Also for the personal care workers, I see that some get maybe 30 Euros a day. Slavery in my opinion. That is such a problem area, where customers often call us and say: 'No, I have found this other agency that is cheaper.' Where we say: 'Fine, no problem, it's a free market.' And then, three days later, two weeks later, three months later, we get the call: 'We would like to give you a try after all, it has not worked quite as expected'. (AG 08, pp. 21 f., ll. 667–99)

On the care market the honorarium for 24 hours varies between €30, the rate offered by the so-called "black sheep" (cf. Steiner et al. 2019) brokering care by price dumping, and approximately €100, in rare cases of intense cure and care up to €150, just as different contracts set out with different working conditions for the care workers. Some home care agencies differentiate the honorarium with reference to the qualification and tasks of the care workers (AG 01, 08, 11), while others offer the same honorarium for all (AG 09). However, competition is not only generated by the prices; the controlled quality of care up to professional standards is seen as the most important factor for maintaining the agency's own position on the market (AG 01, 04, 08, 10) or for developing profitable new niches (AG 09), which may be at odds with the working conditions found in the households.

Care workers and, if they mediate, home care agencies are confronted with a lot of problems. On the one hand insufficient board and lodging, the expectation of 24-hour availability of the care worker including extra work in house and garden, and for relatives, jealousy and problems of living together in the established household order, and sexual harassment are persistent issues in the narratives (AG 01, 04, 08, 10). They mirror the care givers' status as a cheap, but highly available workforce and female migrant "denizens" (Standing 2011, pp. 159 ff.), the relations of power, which are unfolded in the barely controlled intimacy of the private household (Geissler 2018), and the lack of workers' rights going along with self-employment. On the other hand, as the flipside of the economic pressure to migrate and work under given conditions of 24-hour care, the narratives show how care workers try to narrow down the burden of the expected hard work (AG 08, 09). The owner of a highly specialised home care agency with professional agenda setting quotes the request of a care worker for "a vacancy with a bedridden patient living alone in a flat or house in or near Vienna", which was refused on the assumption that the expectations underlying it would not be compatible with intense cure and care in case of morbidity (AG 09, p. 10, ll. 315–23). The ever difficult question of reciprocity in the field of care and the expected availability of the workforce are conflicting.

The home care agencies describe different strategies to handle such constellations. If mediation between care giver and receiver – or their relatives – doesn't work, interviewees claim they "have to exchange" carers (AG 05, p. 20, l. 662; AG 08, p. 5, l. 140). Though fluctuation among care workers can be very high – "With new customers, it is usually the case that you have to exchange two to three times anyway" (AG 08, p. 5, ll. 139–40) – agencies admit they rarely drop customers. As one owner put it: "You cannot exchange customers. Not possible" (AG 05, p. 20, l. 662). Other home care agencies do so, but it is the exception after a long history of sexual harassment, assignment of overtaxing caring tasks, etc. (AG 08, 09). Under given conditions, the logic of the market providing the option to exchange care givers becomes the solution if not even a minimum of reciprocity in the care arrangement is given. That notwithstanding, through the logic of the state and especially the legalisation the Austrian model has been formalised (Kretschmann 2010), and relationships making the arrangement work will be organised formally and informally.

Formally, from the perspective of the home care agencies one of their main tasks is matching, which means finding those care givers whose profiles – in terms of qualification as well as personality, often emphasising the latter – are best aligned with the demands and expectations of the care receivers and their relatives. Successful matching is considered to be the core element of a well-functioning home care arrangement (AG 01, 09) and it is not only combined with professional logics, but also with informal aspects. What agencies call "good chemistry" (AG 01, 03, 04, 05, 07), care givers call a "good family" (A102, A107.2): "If the chemistry is right, almost everything goes. If the chemistry is not right, [. . .] it won't work. I have to exchange her, game over" (AG 07, p. 12, ll. 375–7). This owner of a small home care agency insisted that nursing and language qualifications or professionalism of carers are much less important than both care givers and receivers getting along. However, agencies and carers have entirely different opinions on how long it takes to settle in, which also means that they have different perspectives on the relationships of care. While agencies are thinking of days or a week (e.g. AG 07, p. 1, ll. 19–28), care givers are talking about weeks and months until both care giver and receiver got accustomed to another (e.g. A104, p. 18, ll. 568–74), which mirrors the expectation of successful commodification of care by adequate matching on the one hand and the expectation of a reciprocal process of building up a working home care arrangement on the other hand. While one of the carers we refer to stressed that both care giver and receiver have to find the middle ground, some home care agencies, despite the problems described above, blame care workers alone for not compromising and making it work (e.g. AG 03, p. 6, ll. 175–83).

From the perspective of the home care agencies, successful care arrangements (AG 01, 04, 08, 10) are not only stories of the successful matching, but also of the informal and personal organisation of reciprocity referring to the logic of the family (Aulenbacher et al. 2019). A home care agency, which is part of a transnational corporation and works with a lot of organised exchanges of care workers in case of conflict, describes a visit in a household which is not problematic: "It is really a family atmosphere where you sit together and the carer is really fully integrated into the family. We have customers with the same two carers for six years, when you reach that point, care is really good, everyone is happy, no matter who you are talking to individually" (AG 08, pp. 20 f., ll. 651–60). This is part of the "institutional complexity" (Greenwood et al. 2011), in which commodified and marketised, more or less professionalised care, on the one hand, substitutes the former tasks of relatives. On the other hand, the logic of the family, as everyday experience of those who are obliged to work as 24-hour live-ins, restricts the logics of the market in its demolishing power concerning the "fictitious commodities" (Polanyi 2001) labour and care. The inclusive family becomes the informal substitute for the lacking regulation of working conditions and goes along with conditions facilitating more or less reciprocal relations.

4. CONCLUSION: "COMMODITY FICTION" AND RECIPROCITY IN 24-HOUR CARE

Although the transnational commodification of care is nothing new at all, home care agencies are protagonists of the forced marketisation of care, going along with its formalisation, standardisation, and professionalisation on the one hand. On the other hand, market-driven competitive commodification and marketisation of care with price dumping, and substitution of work force instead of protected employment undermine the conditions for building up reciprocity between care receivers and givers and creating the relationships which enable human beings to react to the contingency of life.

The case of 24-hour care is a result of a Polanyian "commodity fiction" (2001, p. 76): the idea is to bridge intergenerational care gaps by commodification and marketisation of care, to organise care for the Austrian middle classes at the cost of the mostly female migrant "denizens" (Standing 2011), and to narrow down the costs for the Austrian welfare state by hazarding the consequences of growing care gaps in the poor(er) countries.

This is neither a plea for nostalgia, harking back to the male breadwinner model with its gender arrangement and intergenerational contract, nor a rejection of embedded markets as forms of institutionalised exchange. It is a criticism of marketisation, pushed so far and combined with the relations of gender, race and class in the Austrian care regime, that it destroys the relationships of care, with at the core, the ever difficult reciprocity, which would make it possible to deal with the contingency of life – from the perspective of the care receivers as well as the care givers, in regard to decent care as well as decent work.

REFERENCES

Anderson, B. and I. Shutes (eds) (2014), *Migration and care labour: Theory, policy and politics*, Basingstoke: Palgrave Macmillan.

Appelt, E. and E. Fleischer (2014), 'Familiale Sorgearbeit in Österreich: Modernisierung eines konservativen Care-Regimes?', *Soziale Welt*, Sonderband 20, 401–22.

Aulenbacher, B. and M. Dammayr (2014), 'Zwischen Anspruch und Wirklichkeit: Zur Ganzheitlichkeit und Rationalisierung des Sorgens und der Sorgearbeit', *Soziale Welt*, Sonderband 20, 125–40.

Aulenbacher, B., M. Dammayr and B. Riegraf (2017), 'Gesellschaftliche Widersprüche, institutionelle Logiken, alltägliche Anforderungen: Sorgearbeit, Leistung und Gerechtigkeit illustriert an der Altenpflege', in B. Aulenbacher, M. Dammayr, K. Dörre, W. Menz, B. Riegraf and H. Wolf (eds), *Leistung und Gerechtigkeit: Das umstrittene Versprechen des Kapitalismus*, Weinheim and Basel: Beltz Juventa, pp. 155–72.

Aulenbacher, B., F. Décieux and B. Riegraf (2018a), 'The economic shift and beyond: Care as a contested terrain in contemporary capitalism', *Current Sociology Monograph*, 66 (4), 517–30.

Aulenbacher, B., M. Leiblfinger and V. Prieler (2018b), 'Ein neuer Sorgemarkt im Wohlfahrtsstaat: 24-Stunden-Betreuung in Österreich und Dienstleistungsangebote von Wiener Vermittlungsagenturen', in U. Filipič and A. Schönauer (eds), *Zur Zukunft von Arbeit und Wohlfahrtsstaat: Perspektiven aus der Sozialwissenschaft*, Wien: ÖGB, pp. 47–56.

Aulenbacher, B., M. Leiblfinger and V. Prieler (2019), '"Jetzt kümmern sich zwei slowakische Frauen abwechselnd um meinen Vater . . .": Institutionelle Logiken und soziale Ungleichheiten in der agenturvermittelten 24h-Betreuung', in M. Seeliger and J. Gruhlich (eds), *Intersektionalität, Arbeit und Organisation*, Weinheim and Basel: Beltz Juventa, pp. 160–174.

BMASGK – Bundesministerium für Arbeit, Soziales, Gesundheit und Konsumentenschutz (2018), 'Anfragebeantwortung Nr. 1517/AB vom 19.10.2018 zur Anfrage 1550/J betreffend Pflegekräfte in Österreich', accessed 23 October 2018 at www.parlament.gv.at/PAKT/VHG/XXVI/AB/AB_01517/imfname_714869.pdf.

Farris, S.R. and S. Marchetti (2017), 'From the commodification to the corporatization of care: European perspectives and debates', *Social Politics* 24 (2), 109–31.

Fisher, B. and J.C. Tronto (1990), 'Toward a feminist theory of caring', in E.K. Abel and M.K. Nelson (eds), *Circles of care*, Albany, NY: SUNY Press, pp. 36–54.

Fraser, N. (2013), 'A triple movement? Parsing the politics of crisis after Polanyi', *New Left Review*, 81, 119–32.

Geissler, B. (2018), 'Haushaltsarbeit und Haushaltsdienstleistungen', in F. Böhle, G. Voß and G. Wachtler (eds), *Handbuch Arbeitssoziologie: Band 2: Akteure und Institutionen*, Wiesbaden: Springer VS, pp. 767–99.

Greenwood, R., C.R. Hinings and D. Whetten (2014), 'Rethinking institutions and organizations', *Journal of Management Studies*, 51 (7), 1206–20.

Greenwood, R., M. Raynard, F. Kodeih, E. Micellota and M. Lounsbury (2011), 'Institutional complexity and organizational responses', *Academy of Management Annals*, 5 (1), 317–71.

Haas, B. (2005), 'The work–care balance: Is it possible to identify typologies for cross-national comparisons?', *Current Sociology*, 53, 487–508.

Klenk, T. and E. Pavolini (eds) (2015), *Restructuring welfare govern-ance: Marketization, managerialism and welfare state professionalism*, Cheltenham, UK and Northampton, MA, USA: Edward Elgar Publishing.

Klinger, C. (2013), 'Krise war immer . . . Lebenssorge und geschlech-tliche Arbeitsteilung in sozialphilosophischer und kapitalismuskri-tischer Perspektive', in E. Appelt, B. Aulenbacher and A. Wetterer (eds), *Gesellschaft: Feministische Krisendiagnosen.* Münster: Westfälisches Dampfboot, pp. 82–104.

Kofman, E. and P. Raghuram (2015), *Gendered migrations and global social reproduction*, Basingstoke: Palgrave Macmillan.

Kretschmann, A. (2010), 'Mit Recht regieren? Zur Verrechtlichung transmi-grantischer 24-Stunden-Carearbeit in österreichischen Privathaushalten', in K. Scheiwe and J. Krawietz (eds), *Transnationale Sorgearbeit: Rechtliche Rahmenbedingungen und gesellschaftliche Praxis*, Wiesbaden: VS Verlag für Sozialwissenschaften, pp. 199–226.

Leiblfinger, M. and V. Prieler (2018), *Elf Jahre 24-Stunden-Betreuung in Österreich: Eine Policy- und Regime-Analyse* (Linzer Beiträge zu Wirtschaft – Ethik – Gesellschaft), Linz: Katholische Privat-Universität Linz.

Lutz, H. (2017), 'Care as a fictitious commodity: Reflections on the inter-sections of migration, gender and care regimes', *Migration Studies*, 5 (3), 356–68.

Lutz, H. (2018), *Die Hinterbühne der Care-Arbeit: Transnationale Perspektiven auf Care-Migration im geteilten Europa*, Weinheim and Basel: Beltz Juventa.

Österle, A. and G. Bauer (2016), 'The legalization of rotational 24-hour care work in Austria: Implications for migrant care workers', *Social Politics: International Studies in Gender, State & Society*, 23, 192–213.

Österle, A., A. Hasl and G. Bauer (2013), 'Vermittlungsagenturen in der 24-h-Betreuung', *WISO – Wirtschafts- und sozialpolitische Zeitschrift*, 36, 159–72.

Polanyi, K. (2001), *The great transformation: The political and economic origins of our time*, Boston: Beacon Press.

Safuta, A. and F. Degavre (2013), 'What has Polanyi got to do with it? Undocumented migrant domestic workers and the usages of reciprocity', in L. Oso and N. Ribas-Mateos (eds), *The international handbook on gender, migration and transnationalism: Global and development perspectives*,

Cheltenham, UK and Northampton, MA, USA: Edward Elgar Publishing, pp. 420–438.

Shire, K. (2015), 'Family supports and insecure work: The politics of household service employment in conservative welfare regimes', *Social Politics: International Studies in Gender, State & Society*, 22 (2), 193–219.

Standing, G. (2011), *The precariat: The new dangerous class*, London: Bloomsbury Academic.

Steiner, J., V. Prieler, M. Leiblfinger and A. Benazha (2019), 'Völlig legal!? Legalitätsnarrative in der 24h-Betreuung in Deutschland, Österreich und der Schweiz', *Österreichische Zeitschrift für Soziologie*, 44 (1), 1–19.

Thornton, P.H., W. Ocasio and M. Lounsbury (2012), *The institutional logics perspective: A new approach to culture, structure, and process*, Oxford: Oxford University Press.

Tronto, J.C. (2017), 'There is an alternative: Homines curans and the limits of neoliberalism', *International Journal of Care and Caring*, 1 (1), 27–43.

Weicht, B. (2015), *The meaning of care: The social construction of care for elderly people*, Basingstoke: Palgrave Macmillan.

WKO – Stabsabteilung Statistik (2018), 'Personenberatung und Personenbetreuung: Branchendaten', accessed 6 December 2018 at http://wko.at/statistik/BranchenFV/B_127.pdf.

18. The commodification of informal care: joining and resisting marketization processes

Bernhard Weicht

1. INTRODUCTION

Migrant domestic care has become a crucial feature of the Austrian arrangements of long-term care and has since received widespread attention in the social-scientific literature (Weicht and Österle 2016). Situated within the context of the traditional, gendered care regime of Austria (Österle and Bauer 2012), informal care gaps arising from increasing labour market participation of women and widespread resistance to institutional care settings have fostered a system in which live-in migrant care workers substitute the idealized family carer in people's households (Da Roit and Weicht 2013; Weicht 2010). Not least due to a lack of public services the phenomenon of migrant domestic care work features particularly in family-like care regimes and fulfils roles and functions previously held by women within families (Da Roit and Weicht 2013; Degiuli 2007; Escriva and Skinner 2008; Österle and Bauer 2016).

In Austria the formerly illegal arrangements of employing migrant workers to live in the household of and care for an older person for 24 hours, on the basis of usually fortnightly shifts, gained public interest in the run-up to national elections in 2006. After an initial amnesty and subsequent legalization process, a system was established that mainly fosters a model in which various agencies arrange the engagement of formally self-employed migrant care workers, financed to a large extent by a generous cash-for-care scheme and additional government subsidies (see Bachinger 2016; Weicht 2015a; Weicht and Österle 2016). As a consequence, an ever-increasing market has been established in which predominantly women from Eastern European countries seek and find awaited employment opportunities (Österle and Bauer 2016). This (here briefly sketched) market for domestic care work resembles many features of widespread international processes of marketization, transnationalization and new forms of governance in the field of care (Aulenbacher et al.

2018b). From a Polanyian perspective a process of marketization has taken shape in which a particular sector – traditionally not belonging to the market sphere – is increasingly commodified. On the surface this process could be understood as an inevitable expansion of capitalist production which "requires the continuous occupation of a previously not or not fully commodified other" (Becker et al. 2018, p. 362). In Polanyi's terms the organizing principle of the market, "aiming at the establishment of a self-regulating market, relying on the support of the trading classes, and using largely laissez-faire and free trade as its methods" is expanding its reach and taking over areas of life originally characterized by "the principle of social protection aiming at the conservation of man and nature as well as productive organization" (Polanyi [1944] 2001, pp. 138–9). One crucial feature of this type of analysis lies in the exposure of opposing movements and tendencies. However, while countermovements against the economic shift in the field of care can certainly be identified (Aulenbacher et al. 2018a; Radicioni and Weicht 2018) a strictly and exclusively dualistic logic of marketization and social protection veils important dynamics that characterize the field of care. Polanyi himself emphasized the essential embeddedness of markets and the parallel evolution of markets and regulation (Polanyi [1944] 2001, p. 71). However, analytically the double movement still remains based on a struggle between markets and social protection where the latter is thought of as an indispensable answer to the threat of a decline of societal cohesion.

Remarkably, however, in the Austrian case described above, the legalization of migrant care work and subsequent marketization processes were met by widespread public support. The current version of marketized care needs to be read as a particular mix of legislation, social policy, markets and family that requires a context-dependent analysis of markets within societal structures. In particular, I argue, the movements around or against marketization need to be understood not as general processes applied to the field of care but rather as expressions of the specific context and content of the organization of care in Austria. Drawing on Fraser's utilization of Polanyi's concept of the double (triple) movement, I seek to demonstrate that due to different national systemic conditions both increasing marketization (in the care workers' countries of origin) and resistance to market- and state logics in care (in Austria) meet in generating a unique transnational market of care. The particular empirical context of Austria in that sense supports a more precise and situated identification of those aspects which a more nuanced theory of marketization seeks to understand.

Three analytical angles should capture the specificities of the empirical context and allow a necessary extension of the analytical framework. First, care needs to be analysed in its character as reproductive work. This means that if care is becoming commodified, it not only functions as fictitious commodity

(Aulenbacher et al. 2018a) in Polanyi's ontological meaning but is threatened in its structural nature as enabling markets in the first place (Fraser 2013). Second, the current Austrian solution to long-term care needs fundamentally relies on cross-border markets and thus requires a transnational perspective in order to capture intersecting and interdependent movements in different nation states. Third, beyond its necessity for reproduction of society itself, care involves and embodies closeness and intimacy. This requires an investigation of possible marketization or rejection of commodification of affection and intimacy as well. These three analytical angles should convey a broader and, by drawing on the specific empirical context of the Austrian care system, more empirically specific and justified lens onto what could be called the commodification of informal care, which is both embraced and resisted and alternates depending on the geographical, political and family location or perspective.

Moral resistance to both an increasing marketization and an extension of state provisions, as well as moral longing for informal care, need to be seen as part of the process that has generated and boosted the development of a sector enabling the self-marketization of Eastern European care workers.

2. CARE AS COMMODITY?

The first analytical angle takes care's specific nature as gendered reproductive work as its starting point. In her critical appraisal of Polanyi's work Nancy Fraser argues that due to the duality of markets and social protection, the consequences of women's reproductive work and care in particular are missing in Polanyi's *The Great Transformation*:

> Focused single-mindedly on harms emanating from disembedded markets, the book overlooks harms originating elsewhere, in the surrounding "society". Occulting non-market-based forms of injustice, it also tends to whitewash forms of social protection that are at the same time vehicles of domination. Focused overwhelmingly on struggles against market-based depredations, the book neglects struggles against injustices rooted in "society" and coded in social protections. (Fraser 2013, p. 229)

Fraser pronounces Polanyi's account of disembedded markets as too dark and as uncritically romanticizing the realm of society (Fraser 2013, 2014) – a domain that has historically ensured women's subordination through society's material and moral constitution. In order to be able to integrate the layer of those society-induced injustices and marginalizations, which are often "encoded in social protections" (Fraser 2013, p. 229), Fraser extends the concept of the double movement and introduces a third possible dynamic – emancipation, which aims to overcome forms of subjection rooted in society (Fraser 2013). Emancipation, she argues, can not only be reached with the help of public provisions and protection but has often been secured through alignment with marketization processes. More specifically, women's emancipation from subordination requires other arrangements of care, which then can be realized through public or market-based means (with, obviously, different consequences). Before situating this discussion in the empirical context of Austria, another one of Fraser's considerations on care seems imperative. The care crisis, Fraser argues, is an inherent component of capitalism and takes specific forms of social-reproductive contradictions in the latest period of financialized capitalism (Fraser 2016). Every capitalist society, as she calls it, "free rides on [. . .] activities of provisioning, care giving and interaction that produce and maintain social bonds, although it accords them no monetized value and treats them as if they were free" (Fraser 2016, p. 101). Increasing commodification and marketization require increasing recruitment of labour and thus also continuously new ways of social reproduction (Becker et al. 2018).

In the Austrian case these processes can be observed in two steps. First, it needs to be recognized that (elder) care in Austria is fundamentally based on the family with social protection predominantly aimed at social support for family carers (Appelt et al. 2014). This means care has traditionally been embedded in both family structures and state institutions securing and enabling those structures. The analysis of the marketization process therefore needs to start from the point of emancipation for Austrian (middle-class) women precisely from those limiting structural embeddings through their own participation in (labour) markets. This first movement of marketization (of labour) has thus coincided with (at least potential) defamilialization of care. However, since needs ought to be addressed, other forms of securing care had to be realized. In a (analytical) second step, resisting movements can be identified which reject defamilialization of care as requiring increasing bureaucratization or institutionalization. This (morally charged) movement thus negotiates different versions of embeddedness between state- and family structures. As has been argued, the Austrian system of migrant domestic care work needs to be understood as realization of family care beyond the family, of a commodified version of informal, family-based care. The emancipation through marketization movement of Austria's potential informal carers has thus been achieved while at the same time public provision of care through institutionalization has been rejected. This has been made possible through a utilization of social inequalities that allowed an inclusion of family-based care within the realm of markets. The result of these processes within modern capitalist society, Fraser (2016, p. 104) demonstrates, "is a new, dualized organization of social reproduction, commodified for those who can pay for it and privatized for those who cannot, as some in the second category provide carework in return for (low) wages for those in the first".

3. TRANSNATIONAL MOVEMENTS

This dualized organization of care is furthermore instigated by significant international social and economic relations of inequality which enable and foster labour migration. A transnational perspective of the marketization movement and possible countermovements is required for two reasons. First, it needs to be recognized that all movements can stimulate and accelerate divergent consequences in different (national) contexts. Fraser diagnoses that "the idea that state-territoriality can serve as a proxy for social effectivity is no longer plausible. Under current conditions, one's chances to live a good life do not depend wholly on the internal political constitution of the territorial state in which one resides" (Fraser 2008b, p. 24). This means that due to economic, political and social interrelations, movements towards marketization, social protection and emancipation can trigger reactions in other territorial areas. In the field of care, different concepts, such as Global Care Chains or Care Circulation, that seek to capture the inter- and transnational relations and their consequences due to national care arrangements, have been introduced (Aulenbacher et al. 2018b; Lutz 2018). Joan Tronto (2013) thus poignantly argues for an extension of (citizenship) rights along the lines of transnational care relations since decisions on the arrangement of care in one country strongly affect people and their care relations in another (Andersson and Kvist 2014; Lutz 2018; Tronto 2013; Tronto and Weicht 2014). Related to these observations is the second imperative for a transnational perspective – the problem of misframing (Fraser 2008a). With this concept Fraser emphasizes that political claims of movements can only be formulated within particular national frames: "Because the frame limits the scope of justice to intra-state institutions that organize relations among fellow citizens, it systematically obscures transborder forms and sources of gender injustice" (Fraser 2008a, p. 112). Countermovements to marketization or emancipation movements are therefore often limited to address a polity that might only be partially affected by the very processes at hand. Transnational levels of policy making require the formulation of other claims and frames.

In the Austrian example of migrant care work, EU regulations and policies, such as the free mobility principle, create the location for transnational marketization (Österle and Bauer 2016). Against this backdrop several other processes of marketization take place. The search for higher income, problematic labour market situations in the home countries and the seeking of a better future for oneself and one's children are identified as main drivers of care migration (Bahna 2016; Österle and Bauer 2016; Safuta et al. 2016). For many women pursuing attractive wages, flexible shift arrangements, the possibility of combining work with family (due to the fortnightly arrangements), and the design of more individually shaped career plans (Österle and Bauer 2016) the so-called circular migration option allows for increasing participation in the labour market. Related shifts in gender structures and within women's families can thus eventually foster processes of emancipation through marketization. However, it remains indisputable that the working conditions are highly precarious (Österle and Bauer 2016) and that inequality is the main variable in enabling this particular kind of cross-border market. Bahna (2016) demonstrates that while previously care migration from Slovakia was based on middle-aged, highly qualified women seeking higher income, a gradual reduction in the wage differences between Austria and Slovakia has made the sector less attractive and recruitment has shifted to those having difficulty in finding employment at home. Currently, care-related labour migration is thus particularly an option for less educated women from poorer areas and backgrounds (see also Safuta et al. 2016).

But marketization is not limited to those seeking work. Especially after the legalization a considerable rise in the industry surrounding the scheme, such as agencies or transport organizations, could be observed (Bahna 2016; Österle et al. 2013). From the perspective of migrant care workers and the industry around it an incentive for the embracing of commodification of migrant work seems inevitable (see Samaluk 2016). For the Austrian situation the marketization and liberalization allows an extension of the "regular army of labour" (Farris 2015) so that an increased number of women are available for the labour market, both as domestic care workers and for the "regular" labour market as family members are freed from care obligations. The implicit consequences – highly flexible and available workers for low wages and reduced social security – emerge as a case in point for Polanyi's observation of the marketization of labour:

> This makes clear what the employers' demand for mobility of labour and flexibility of wages really means: precisely that which we circumscribed above as a market in which human labour is a commodity. (Polanyi [1944] 2001, p. 185)

In other words, one country's solution for both the marketization of women's labour and the subsequent crisis of care (through marketization) shows considerable consequences and effects for marketization and emancipation in other countries. Movements for and against marketization in different countries affect each other and produce intersections of marketization, social protection and emancipation delineated by citizenship rules and status. The clarification of those sets of definitions of citizenship, the so-called citizenship regime (Jenson and Sineau 2003; Luppi et al. 2015; Weicht 2015a), thus circumscribes the perspective of movement and countermovement and how these are situated in relation to each other (Holmwood 2016). While intersections of the economy, local politics and international regulations indeed define the possibilities and limits of both marketization and emancipation an explanation of the concrete Austrian variation of migrant care work requires one additional institutional angle: the nature of the imagination of care itself.

4.   RESISTING INDIVIDUALIZATION AND INSTITUTIONALIZATION

So far it has been argued that an analysis of marketization of migrant care work in Austria needs to recognize, first, the nature of reproductive work as traditional women's work and, second, the different national and transnational frames, as well as international relations and inequalities that define limits and consequences of both marketization and emancipation. An inquiry into the broad public and political support and the specific nature of the Austrian case, however, requires a third analytical angle: an understanding of care as affective labour. Personal feelings related to family associations form a constitutive part of (idealized) care provision (Ungerson 2005). Above, it has been argued that recognition of the embeddedness of care within the family structure is crucial for an understanding of marketization as possible emancipation. I now want to point to an additional effect, though: the moral constitution and construction of care can lead to commodification, based on a rejection of increased institutional social protection.

In discussing care as fictitious commodity, it can be argued that the necessity of addressing care needs makes care an inevitable factor of production. In Polanyi's understanding of commodification, care's flexible availability has to be ensured and its provision organized through individual contracts; what makes it a fictitious commodity, however, is that it is not primarily produced for the market and exchange (see Aulenbacher et al. 2018a; Fraser 2012, 2013). In relation to fictitious commodities, Polanyi ([1944] 2001, p. 171) discusses the artificial differentiation of labour from other aspects of human life and the former's commodification means "to annihilate all organic forms of existence and to replace them by a different type of organization, an atomistic and individualistic one". The unfeasibility and undesirability of isolating labour or, in the present context, care, from the human and relational circumstances restricts the potential commodification, so that "even professional, paid forms of care work always contain elements which awkwardly resist rationalization and commodification" (Becker et al. 2018, p. 364). Liberal values of choice, individual freedom and control only marginally apply to personal care relations (Shutes 2012). In her extension of the Polanyian framework Fraser recognizes these limits as well. Emancipation from family-based embedding, which can produce liberation from domination, can also challenge "the fabric of existing solidarities" and therefore further "clearing the way for marketization" (Fraser

2013, p. 236). In these accounts, the affective, the solidarity and the familial limit an all-embracing commodification of care. Care constructed as labour of love thus excludes a strict marketization almost by definition (Lynch 2007). In the specific Austrian case, however, this analysis is at least partly misleading. In fact, I would argue, the affective is an integral part of what is actually commodified.

The legalization of migrant care work in Austria needs to be understood as endorsement of a practice that prolongs informal family-based care with the help of the transnational market. In its regularization of existing patterns the state never challenged the deeply engraved primacy of family (Aulenbacher et al. 2018a; Österle and Hammer 2007) or provided alternative social provision of care services. Migrant care workers have continuously been constructed as angels or fictive kin who substitute family members in fulfilling people's wishes to stay in their own home (Weicht 2010). This specific construction of domestic care work inevitably challenges the position of migrant care workers as it has clouded the problematic home-based employment situation even more (Weicht 2015a). In fact the introduction and enablement of the market for migrant care work allowed for continuous existence of a morally charged longing for (informal) family care within a context of increasing marketization (Weicht 2016). In other words, marketization of care has happened on the basis of and with the aim of care profoundly being embedded within family structures and with the explicit rejection of increased social protection, manifested through the image of the cold institution (Weicht 2015b). Ideologically the present commodification of care is embedded in family values and can be seen itself as a countermovement to unwanted and feared institutionalization (Kontos 1998). A more nuanced understanding of the opposition of the double or triple movement is therefore necessary to capture the role of the affective in promoting and fostering increasing commodification, as Hochschild (2012) has demonstrated in various fields of social relations. Rejecting increasing state provision of care, markets have been firmly embedded within the family logic and context. By emphasizing the personal, the affective and the relational components of care, the migrant care work arrangements have been positioned as a market-based possibility of informal care.

5.   CONCLUSION

In the introduction to this contribution I raised the question whether the Austrian migrant care arrangements should be understood as continuing commodification of more and more areas of life, despite the lack of public protest. I suggested that a more detailed and context-dependent analysis is required in order to use the Austrian case to delineate the various movements and countermovements arising from transnational processes of marketization. For this endeavour I have presented three perspectives that should provide analytical extensions for the analysis of the concrete Austrian context. First, the role of care as reproductive labour and its relation to traditional women's work within families bears the potential of marketization as emancipation, in particular for women. Second, an analysis of the transnational processes identifies various emancipation movements, fostered by both marketization and protection in different countries. Third, recognizing care as affective labour emphasizes that the present system of marketization of domestic care work needs to be understood as a rejection of increasing social protection due to widespread moral resistance to institutionalization.

While marketization unquestionably promotes precarious, highly problematic employment situations it is crucial to recognize that, on the other hand, it enables several processes of emancipation: of middle-class women from family care duties and of a substantial number of poor, unemployed migrant women. Marketization at the same time allows a persistence of the rejection of social protection as institutionalization and the continuous embeddedness in family structures and logics. For this specific outcome, the interrelation of several structural factors needs to be emphasized: "[l]ogics of the state [. . .], the market [. . .], the family [. . .] and the profession [. . .] mesh with one another" (Aulenbacher et al. 2018a, p. 352).

However, starting from the specific nature and context of care allows a more distinct understanding of what exactly is commodified. While agencies can be described as clear agents of the market the process of marketization of care seems more complex. In the Austrian welfare system not care but *informal* care could be called the fictitious commodity since commodification takes the place of informality and familiarity, i.e. what makes it fictitious is commodified. The introduction of the system of migrant care work in Austria thus needs to be depicted as both joining and resisting marketization. Rather than being the aim of structural or political interventions, non- decisions and non-political engagements resulted in a process of marketization. However, despite its unintended nature (potentially) harmful consequences have arisen both for currently employed migrant care workers and the Austrian social system as a whole. The danger of an extension of markets into the private and affective sphere, which might coincide with the danger to "subordinate the substance of society itself to the laws of the market" (Polanyi [1944] 2001, p. 75) is only clouded by its embeddedness in family structures. In that sense it needs to be held that the "challenge is not merely to embed markets, but to embed them in such a way that they simultaneously reinforce the embedding of individuals in social and political communities" (López 2016, p. 245). This recognition, however, requires nuanced political consciousness that focuses on the complex interplay of the triple movement: first, to recognize the underlying, cross-national emancipatory struggles; second, to situate these struggles within an extension and democratization of social protections (Fraser 2013, p. 241); and, third, an attention to the meanings of the actual longings and concerns (Sayer 2011) regarding the embedding and rejection of institutional solutions. In particular the personal, the private and the affective define and constitute the possibilities and limits of the commodification of care. Potential countermovements thus need to relate to those claims directly.

REFERENCES

Andersson, K. and E. Kvist (2014), 'The neoliberal turn and the marketization of care: The transformation of eldercare in Sweden', *European Journal of Women's Studies*, 22 (3), 274–87.

Appelt, E., E. Fleischer and M. Preglau (eds) (2014), *Elder Care: Intersektionelle Analyse der informellen Betreuung und Pflege alter Menschen in Österreich*, Innsbruck: Studienverlag.

Aulenbacher, B., F. Décieux and B. Riegraf (2018a), 'Capitalism goes care: Elder and child care between market, state, profession, and family and questions of justice and inequality', *Equality, Diversity and Inclusion: An International Journal*, 37 (4), 347–60.

Aulenbacher, B., H. Lutz and B. Riegraf (2018b), 'Introduction: Towards a global sociology of care and care work', *Current Sociology Monograph*, 66 (4), 1–8.

Bachinger, A. (2016), 'Von der 24-Stunden-Betreuung zur Personenbetreuung: Arbeitsmarkt-, Migrations- und Care Regime und die Nutzung migrantischer Arbeitskraft', in B. Weicht and A. Österle (eds), *Im Ausland zu Hause pflegen: Die Beschäftigung von MigrantInnen in der 24-Stunden-Betreuung*, Wien: LIT Verlag, pp. 31–58.

Bahna, M. (2016), 'Slowakische 24-Stunden-BetreuerInnen in Österreich: Nur ein weiterer Migrationsstrom aus der Slowakei?', in B. Weicht and A. Österle (eds), *Im Ausland zu Hause pflegen: Die Beschäftigung von MigrantInnen in der 24-Stunden-Betreuung*, Wien: LIT Verlag, pp. 199–220.

Becker, K., K. Dörre and Y. Kutlu (2018), 'Counter-Landnahme? Labour disputes in the care-work field', *Equality, Diversity and Inclusion: An International Journal*, 37 (4), 361–75.

Da Roit, B. and B. Weicht (2013), 'Migrant care work and care, migration and employment regimes: A fuzzy-set analysis', *Journal of European Social Policy*, 23 (5), 469–86.

Degiuli, F. (2007), 'A job with no boundaries: Home eldercare work in Italy', *European Journal of Women's Studies*, 14 (3), 193–207.

Escriva, A. and E. Skinner (2008), 'Domestic work and transnational care chains in Spain', in H. Lutz (ed.), *Migration and domestic work: A European perspective on a global theme*, Aldershot: Ashgate, pp. 113–26.

Farris, S.R. (2015), 'Migrants' regular army of labour: Gender dimensions of the impact of the global economic crisis on migrant labor in Western Europe', *Sociological Review*, 63 (1), 121–43.

Fraser, N. (2008a), 'Mapping the feminist imagination: From redistribution to recognition to representation', in N. Fraser (ed.), *Scales of justice: Reimagining political space in a globalizing world*, Cambridge: Polity Press, pp. 100–115.

Fraser, N. (2008b), 'Reframing justice in a globalizing world', in N. Fraser (ed.), *Scales of justice: Reimagining political space in a globalizing world*, Cambridge: Polity Press, pp. 12–29.

Fraser, N. (2012), 'Can society be commodities all the way down?', Working Paper Series, accessed 22 July 2013 at https://halshs.archives-ouvertes.fr/halshs-00725060/document.

Fraser, N. (2013), 'Between marketization and social protection: Resolving the feminist ambivalence', in N. Fraser (ed.), *Fortunes of feminism: From state-managed capitalism to neoliberal crisis*, London: Verso, pp. 227–41.

Fraser, N. (2014), 'Can society be commodities all the way down? Post-Polanyian reflections on capitalist crisis', *Economy and Society*, 43 (4), 541–58.

Fraser, N. (2016), 'Contradictions of capital and care', *New Left Review*, 100 (July–August), 99–117.

Hochschild, A.R. (2012), *The outsourced self: Intimate life in market times*, New York: Metropolitan Books.

Holmwood, J. (2016), 'Moral economy versus political economy: Provincializing Polanyi', in C. Karner and B. Weicht (eds), *The commonalities of global crises: Markets, communities and nostalgia*, London: Palgrave Macmillan, pp. 143–66.

Jenson, J. and M. Sineau (2003), 'The care dimension in welfare state redesign', in J. Jenson and M. Sineau (eds), *Who cares? Women's work, childcare, and welfare state redesign*, Toronto: University of Toronto Press, pp. 3–18.

Kontos, P.C. (1998), 'Resisting institutionalization: Constructing old age and negotiating home', *Journal of Aging Studies*, 12 (2), 167–84.

López, J.J. (2016), 'Disembedding the embedded/disembedded opposition', in C. Karner and B. Weicht (eds), *The commonalities of global crises: Markets, communities and nostalgia*, London: Palgrave Macmillan, pp. 223–47.

Luppi, M., R. Oomkens, T. Knijn and B. Weicht (2015), *Citizenship in the context of migrant care work: Regimes, rights & recognition*, Utrecht University.

Lutz, H. (2018), 'Care migration: The connectivity between care chains, care circulation and transnational social inequality', *Current Sociology*, 66 (4), 577–89.

Lynch, K. (2007), 'Love labour as a distinct and non-commodifiable form of care labour', *Sociological Review*, 55 (3), 550–570.

Österle, A. and G. Bauer (2012), 'Home care in Austria: The interplay of family orientation, cash-for-care and migrant care', *Health and Social Care in the Community*, 20, 265–73.

Österle, A. and G. Bauer (2016), 'The legalization of rotational 24-hours care work in Austria: Implications for migrant care workers', *Social Politics*, 23 (2), 192–213.

Österle, A. and E. Hammer (2007), 'Care allowances and the formalisation of care arrangements: The Austrian experience', in C. Ungerson and S. Yeandle (eds), *Cash for care in developed welfare states*, Basingstoke: Palgrave Macmillan, pp. 13–31.

Österle, A., A. Hasl and G. Bauer (2013), 'Vermittlungsagenturen in der 24-h-Betreuung', *WISO – Wirtschafts- und sozialpolitische Zeitschrift des ISW*, 35 (1), 159–72.

Polanyi, K. ([1944] 2001), *The great transformation: The political and economic origins of our time*, Boston: Beacon Press.

Radicioni, S. and B. Weicht (2018), 'A place to transform: Creating caring spaces by challenging normativity and identity', *Gender, Place & Culture*, 25 (3), 368–83.

Safuta, A., A. Kordasiewicz and S. Urbańska (2016), 'Verpasste Kreuzung: Polen als Herkunfts- und Zielland für migrantische Pflege- und Haushaltskräfte', in B. Weicht and A. Österle (eds), *Im Ausland zu Hause pflegen: Die Beschäftigung von MigrantInnen in der 24-Stunden-Betreuung*, Wien: LIT Verlag, pp. 221–44.

Samaluk, B. (2016), 'Neoliberal moral economy: Migrant workers' value struggles across temporal and spatial dimensions', in C. Karner and B. Weicht (eds), *The commonalities of global crises: Markets, communities and nostalgia*, London: Palgrave Macmillan, pp. 61–85.

Sayer, A. (2011), *Why things matter to people: Social science, values and ethical life*, Cambridge: Cambridge University Press.

Shutes, I. (2012), 'The employment of migrant workers in long-term care: Dynamics of choice and control', *Journal of Social Policy*, 41 (1), 43–59.

Tronto, J.C. (2013), *Caring democracy: Markets, equality, and justice*, New York: New York University Press.

Tronto, J.C. and B. Weicht (2014), '"As long as care is attached to gender, there is no justice": An interview with Joan C. Tronto', *Tijdschrift voor Genderstudies*, 17 (3), 362–81.

Ungerson, C. (2005), 'Care, work and feeling', *Sociological Review*, 53 (2), 188–203.

Weicht, B. (2010), 'Embodying the ideal carer: The Austrian discourse on migrant carers', *International Journal of Ageing and Later Life*, 5 (2), 17–52.

Weicht, B. (2015a), 'Employment without employers: The public discourse on care during the regularisation reform in Austria', in A. Triandafyllidou and S. Marchetti (eds), *Employers, agencies and immigration: Paying for care*, Farnham: Ashgate, pp. 113–30.

Weicht, B. (2015b), *The meaning of care: The social construction of care for elderly people*, Basingstoke: Palgrave Macmillan.

Weicht, B. (2016), 'State, market, or back to the family? Nostalgic struggles for proper elder care', in C. Karner and B. Weicht (eds), *The commonalities of global crises: Markets, communities and nostalgia*, London: Palgrave Macmillan, pp. 115–41.

Weicht, B. and A. Österle (eds) (2016), *Im Ausland zu Hause pflegen: Die Beschäftigung von MigrantInnen in der 24-Stunden-Betreuung*, Wien: LIT Verlag.

19. Polanyi's double movement and the making of the "knowledge economy"

Antonino Palumbo and Alan Scott

[W]e are the witnesses of a barely perceptible transformation in ordinary language: verbs which formerly expressed satisfying actions have been replaced by nouns which name packages designed for passive consumption only – "to learn" becomes "to accumulate credits". (Illich 1978, p. 8)

1.   INTRODUCTION

In this chapter, we want to re-evaluate the heuristic role of Polanyi's double movement by suggesting an alternative reading that could answer several criticisms that have been levelled against it. Moreover, we believe that this reading can give us greater insight into both the nature of the current crisis and its failure to unravel the neoliberal consensus.[1] According to our reading, since the Speenhamland measures introduced in 1795 in Britain, faulty welfarist solutions have had the ability to undermine the political force of countermovements calling for protective measures while helping pro-market coalitions to periodically regenerate themselves. For us, this means that the future resolution of the current crisis is likely to restart a new cycle in what looks uncannily like the "Groundhog Day" of modernity.[2] As a result, we should expect not

---

[1]   The crisis we are referring to is the one that started with the 2008 credit crunch – in reality, several intersecting crises have been affecting different domains and reinforcing each other ever since. The credit crunch affected financial markets worldwide and, by extension, the international economy. The crisis of the international economy required the intervention of political institutions to compensate for the failure of the self-regulating market system, but the way interventions occurred has revealed all the limitations of liberal democratic arrangements; hence the concerns about a political crisis. Both the economic and political crises are, in addition, contributing to the ecological and social crises that have come to dominate public debates in the new century.

[2]   The reference here is to the 1993 American movie of the same name, starring Bill Murray and Andie MacDowell.

only the deepening of previous drives to commodify land, labour and money, but also a full-blown attempt at commodifying novel fields of activity and social resources. Knowledge is, in the context of the information age, the most likely candidate to be turned into another (fourth) fictitious commodity. This, we shall argue, explains the tensions arising in those sectors engaged in the managerial and intellectual activities which in the last four decades have been the target of New Public Management (NPM).[3]

2. MARKET SOCIETY AS A DYNAMIC, MULTISTAGE PROCESS

The "double movement" thesis represents an enduring aspect of Polanyi's account of the rise and fall of earlier attempts to realize a self-regulating market economy. And, obviously, this is also the feature of his work that has attracted the critical attention of successive generations of social and political theorists who have shared his concerns. Polanyi's thesis concerning the double movement is introduced in the final paragraphs of chapter six of *The Great Transformation* (hereafter TGT) in a passage worth quoting at length, even if in abridged form:

> To allow the market mechanism to be sole director of the fate of human beings and their natural environment, indeed, even of the amount and use of purchasing power, would result in the demolition of society. [. . .] Robbed of the protective covering of cultural institutions, human beings would perish from the effects of social exposure; they would die as the victims of acute social dislocation through vice, perversion, crime, and starvation. Nature would be reduced to its elements, neighborhoods and landscapes defiled, rivers polluted, military safety jeopardized, the power to produce food and raw materials destroyed. [. . .] But no society could stand the effects of such a system of crude fictions even for the shortest stretch of time unless its human and natural substance as well as its business organization was protected against the ravages of this satanic mill. (2001, pp. 76–7)

From this he concludes that "human society would have been annihilated but for protective countermoves which blunted the action of this self-destructive mechanism" and that the social history in the nineteenth century was thus "the result of a double movement: the extension of the market organization in respect to genuine commodities was accompanied by its restriction in respect to fictitious ones" (2001, p. 79).

Concerning Polanyi's remarks, the first thing we want to suggest is that the countermovement he refers to in these passages should not be viewed as

---

[3]   Unveiling the structure, relevance and rationale of the NPM is the aim of our 2018 book, *Remaking Market Society*, upon which this chapter draws.

a single unitary phenomenon (see, for example, Polanyi-Levitt and Seccareccia 2016, figure 18.1), but as a process composed of many interlinked phases. These are characterized by their own distinctive double movement which, in turn, prepares the ground for the restarting of the market experiment on an even larger scale. Each of these phases is kick-started by specific events and has at its "core" distinct social actors and rationales.

The stages discussed by Polanyi upon which we shall focus are related to: (a) the social reaction against the attempt to turn land into a fictitious commodity that resulted in the Speenhamland system (1795–1834); (b) the full blown attempt to commodify labour after that system was dismantled, "until in the 1870s the recognition of the trade unions offered sufficient protection" (Polanyi 2001, p. 86); (c) the transformation of money into another fictitious commodity at the turn of the century, and the eventual collapse of the liberal economic order following the 1929 financial crash. Of these events, the most extended analysis carried out by Polanyi in TGT pertains to the commodification of labour, which is used as paradigmatic of the *modus operandi* of the market mechanism; the commodification of land and money are treated in a more cursory manner.[4] It is also worth noting that Polanyi's attempt to highlight the epistemic limitations of political economy is part of a more ambitious sociology of culture that he uses as a general framework, but to which we cannot do justice here. The next sections contain a quite detailed reconstruction of Polanyi's historical analysis and must necessarily cover some issues already familiar to Polanyian scholars, but we would ask the reader to bear with us as this level of detail is necessary to make our broader point: Polanyi identifies a recursive process that is still working itself out.

3.   THE ATTEMPT TO TURN LAND INTO A FICTITIOUS COMMODITY

Speenhamland, the historical case at the centre of TGT (chapters seven and eight), deals with the agricultural revolution that preceded industrialization. Here the countermovement emerges as a decentralized and bottom-up act of resistance against the commodification of land promoted by the enclosure of open fields and other types of commons.[5] Polanyi discusses a set of related state interventions to deal with the displacement of the rural population.

---

[4]   The enclosure movement receives only few scattered references; the financialization of the economy caused by the passing of the joint-stock company laws and the creation of national stock markets, and which occurred in the second half of the nineteenth century, is not even mentioned.

[5]   For a work in which various types of commons are identified and their relevance highlighted see Palumbo and Scott (2005).

Speenhamland refers to the allowance system established by local magistrates in Berkshire in 1795, but which, according to Polanyi, was copied by many other local authorities. Those protective measures will be followed by other pieces of legislation which will interact together, causing what he calls disruptive strains. These are: (a) the partial repeal of the 1662 Act of Settlement, (b) the abolition of the 1563 Statute of Artificers and (c) the passing of the Anti-Combination Laws of 1799–1800.

The countermovement involves two main social actors: first, the local landlords, who are interested in the removal of feudal norms regulating the tradability of estates and the appropriation of common land, but keen on retaining a steady workforce no longer tied to their villages; second, the commoners, who are deprived of the protection afforded them by both the cottage economy and the guilds system, but forbidden to establish concerted actions to boost their bargaining power. According to Polanyi, both actors hold ambivalent attitudes towards those changes:

> The allowance system will appear as a device contrived by squirearchy to meet a situation in which physical mobility could no longer be denied to labor, while the squire wished to avoid such unsettlement of local conditions, including higher wages, as was involved in the acceptance of a free national labor market. (2001, p. 93)

Thus Speenhamland reinforced the supremacy of the squirearchy while weakening the influence of the rural middle class.

For their part, the commoners are likewise concerned about the loss of protection assured by past arrangements, but keen to free themselves from the ties that bound them to their locality and lords. The Speenhamland system represents a political compromise reached by the magistrates who were called to address these contrasting pressures coming from above, in support of extant social hierarchies, and below, intending to undermine them.

At the same time, Polanyi develops a powerful analysis of the unintended consequences brought about by that compromise. First, as already noted, he considers the social role and attitude of the local aristocracy which is able to influence the norm-making process directly. Second, he explains that the allowance system imposed as the result of the squirearchy's wishes starts a vicious dynamics leading to the blurring of the distinction between the working poor and paupers that will undermine the work ethic of rural labourers: "Within a few years the productivity of labor began to sink to that of pauper labor, thus providing an added reason for employers not to raise wages above the scale" (2001, p. 83). Finally, Polanyi clarifies how the allowance system interacts with the other pieces of legislation mentioned above creating an unstable blend that will undermine the rural social coalition supporting those protective measures:

> In conjunction with the Anti-Combination Laws, which were not revoked for another quarter of a century, Speenhamland led to the ironical result that the financially implemented "right to live" eventually ruined the people to whom it was ostensibly design to succor. (2001, p. 85)

4.   THE ATTEMPT TO TURN LABOUR INTO A FICTITIOUS COMMODITY

In Polanyi's account, a proper market economy takes shape only in the 1830s, as a result of a full blown attempt to commodify both rural and urban labour. Once again, the changes that brought about the industrial revolution and will set the scene for establishing an urban-dominated social order are related to several legislative interventions: the abolition of the Poor Law in 1834, Peel's Bank Act of 1844 and the repeal of the Corn Laws of 1846. As a result of those reforms, rural workers are no longer receiving outdoor relief but are being forced to choose between employment in the manufacturing industries at increasingly competitive rates or the hellish regime of the workhouse. Competitive wages are, in turn, established by a developing system of international trade that provides cheap imports of corn from abroad, something made possible by the abolition of the pre-existing system of duties and of a newly emerging centralized monetary regime dedicated to fostering free trade. In reaction, we have the start of a new countermovement, which in Polanyi's account develops in two distinct steps reflecting the fragmentation undergone by the rural coalition in the meantime. The first step represents the last act of resistance of a traditional rural order against a rising new industrial urban order, while the second is due to the mobilization of the working classes under the banner of socialism.

Polanyi writes that "The protection of society, in the first instance, falls to the rulers, who can directly enforce their will" (2001, p. 173), and then goes on explaining that

> [. . .] when, in 1834, the Reform Parliament abolished Speenhamland, the landlords shifted their resistance to the factory laws. The church and the manor were now rousing the people against the mill-owner whose predominance would make the cry for cheap food irresistible, and thus, indirectly, threaten to sap rents and tithes. [. . .] the repeal of Speenhamland and the growth of the factories actually prepared the way for the success of the Anti-Corn Law agitation, in 1846. [. . .] The Ten Hours

Bill of 1847, which Karl Marx hailed as the first victory of socialism, was the work of enlightened reactionaries (2001, p. 174).[6]

Although the working classes up to the late 1840s have not yet acquired their own self-awareness as a distinctive social force, the events recalled by Polanyi are meant to show that they are in the process of emancipating themselves from past loyalties. Thus, in one instance they side with the urban middle classes and support the repeal of the Corn Laws, while in another they side with the rural elites and back the passing of the Ten Hours Bill.

The events that mark the onset of the working classes' emancipation from their rural masters are, according to Polanyi, traceable to the events that characterized British life in the first half of the 1830s:

> Politically, the British working class was defined by the Parliamentary Reform Act of 1832, which refused them the vote; economically, by the Poor Law Reform Act of 1834, which excluded them from relief and distinguished them from the pauper. (2001, p. 174)

The Owenite and Chartist movements epitomize the inception of the new era of autonomous working-class struggle based on a radical political programme seeking to protect them from dislocation without necessarily preserving the past social order. Socialism, on this view, is a forward-looking search for a novel form of habitation able to re-embed the market within a progressive social milieu. Polanyi, however, notes that, notwithstanding the success of the Ten Hours Bill, the implosion of the rural coalition allows the entrenchment of the market mechanism within British society. By the end of the 1840s, "the beginning of the Golden Age of capitalism obliterated the vision of the past" (2001, p. 175) and brought about the demise of the Chartist movement in the same year, 1848, that continental Europe was engulfed in the flames of a socialist revolution.

In the following decades, the diverging fragments of the anti-market coalition will manage to support a raft of legislative measures designed to ameliorate working conditions. A proper re-birth of the countermovement is going to happen only in the 1880s, after, that is, a decade-long crisis that will ravage the manufacturing industry and the countryside worldwide – what economic historians call the First Great Depression (Hobsbawm 1989, pp. 34–55). This

---

[6]   Weber made a similar point in his 1906 St Lewis Lecture (Weber 2005, pp. 334–5): in the "old *Kultur*" of Europe anti-capitalist coalitions consist of the Church (both Catholic and Lutheran), the aristocracy, the *"Bildungsaristokratie"* (educated professionals) – "enlightened reactionaries" – plus "the disciplined masses of working-men".

second step is pre-eminently led by the trade union movement that is developing across the industrialized world. This movement will use collective bargaining and political mobilization at the international level to engender both extensive forms of democratization and means of social insurance. It is also a historical phase in which conservative political forces succeed in supporting widespread protective measures that aim at accomplishing the market economy at national level, but that will obstruct international trade, creating a new set of tensions. Polanyi's account of such "disruptive strains" has striking contemporary resonances. World trade via self-regulating markets turns "nations and peoples" into "mere puppets in a show utterly beyond their control" (2001, p. 226). However, the protectionist measures introduced as a response serve to make manifest "a debility of the world market system": internationally, "the import tariffs of one country hampered the exports of another" (2001, p. 226), while domestically: "protectionism helped to transform competitive markets into monopolistic ones" (2001, p. 227). Two incompatible imperatives are at work here: the necessity of political intervention and upholding the "institutional separation of the political from the economic sphere" that is "constitutive to market society and had to be maintained whatever the tension involved" (2001, p. 227).

5.   FINANCIAL DRIVES TO COMMODIFY MONEY

This second phase overlaps with sustained attempts to commodify money and financialize the market economy. These changes prepare the ground for the emergence of a new type of financial capitalism that will cause the imperial drives responsible for the outbreak of the Great War, and the subsequent collapse of the liberal order in the 1930s. Polanyi's discussion here focuses on the reasons behind the development of free trade and the adoption of the gold standard. Particularly engaging are, in relation to those topics: (a) the distinction between "token" and "commodity" money; (b) the tensions between domestic and international policies; and (c) the effects produced by the emancipation of the economic sphere from the political one. We shall discuss these in turn.

To the commodification of money Polanyi dedicates only a short chapter (chapter sixteen), in which he discusses the reasons behind establishing a double currency regime: one required by the domestic economy, which relies on token money; another needed for international trade, which uses gold as commodity money. The two regimes are interconnected and operate through the intermediation of two distinct institutional actors whose goals are not always overlapping, generating periodic tensions. These are the national central banks and *haut finance*: the former is concerned to assure a steady supply of token money to prevent monetary deflation and stimulate economic growth, while the latter is preoccupied with exploiting the opportunities offered by free trade and imbalances in exchange rates. Chapter sixteen deals exclusively with the operation of central banks and their monetary policies; *haut finance* and its *modus operandi* receive a few observations in chapter one. Chapter sixteen opens with an explanation of the economic reasons pushing for the commodification of money:

> If profits depend upon prices, then the monetary arrangements upon which prices depend must be vital to the functioning of any system motivated by profits. [. . .] if the price level was falling for monetary reasons over a considerable time, business would be in danger of liquidation accompanied by the dissolution of productive organization and massive destruction of capital. Not low prices, but falling prices were the trouble. (2001, p. 201)

For Polanyi, the rationale for the evolution of token money and the institutions of central banking charged with its management is clear: due to the deflation consequent upon the expansion of trade combined with the scarcity of commodity money (usually gold or silver) industrial production and the market economy are not possible "without the medium of artificial money" (2001, p. 202). From this he concludes that "it was possible to avoid the wholesale dislocation of business and employment involved in deflation in such a way as to absorb the shock and spread its burden over the whole country" by centralizing the supply of credit at the national level. In this way central banks were able to cushion the "immediate effects of gold withdrawals on the circulation of notes as well as of the diminished circulation of notes on business" (2001, p. 203).

Economic reasoning and the relevance acquired by token money, as opposed to currencies based on precious metals like gold (specie), show, according to Polanyi, the dependence of the market mechanism on non-market elements that cannot be fully commodified and remain, therefore, fictitious commodities. Token money is a means of payment rather than a commodity in its own right; a form of purchasing power with no intrinsic utility. A society dependent upon such counters is "entirely different from market economy" (2001, p. 205).

Transactions *between* economic operators belonging to different countries could not be carried out by using the same type of currency, but required instead a proper commodity currency based on gold. Joining the gold standard thus became, for Polanyi, a necessary requirement to enjoy the benefits of free trade at the global level. This however entailed maintaining the separation between the domestic and international spheres, and adopting two operating logics that could easily enter into contradiction with each other.

Accomplishing a self-regulating market requires not only the building of national markets unhindered by internal obstacles, but also the removal of duties and tariffs that set limits to imports and exports. To have competitive rates in the manufacturing industries, he reminds us, meant repealing the system of Corn Laws' duties erected in the past to protect domestic farming. To have a flourishing industrial apparatus also requires foreign markets to which the manufactures thus produced could be freely exported, and from which the factors of production sourced. In short, the viability of a domestic market economy depends on its connection with international trade routes and a system of free trade that keeps those routes open across national borders. In an international order based on the nation states system, where each state claims an absolute and exclusive form of sovereignty, this could be achieved only through the nexus of the gold standard and the intermediation of a financial system independent of state power.

However, in Polanyi's view, this is revealed to be highly problematic: if, at a theoretical level, the international order seemed to rely on a voluntaristic mode of compliance, in practice this order rested on an unequal distribution of powers and resources among states through which compliance was forcefully imposed on each occasion. While "in liberal theory Great Britain was merely another atom in the universe of trade" (2001, p. 216) ranked alongside smaller nations, in reality the world was divided along a number of lines the consequences of which could not be ignored in practice: lending vs. borrowing nation; exporting vs. "practically self-sufficient" ones; varied vs. limited exports.

For Polanyi this means that the anomic sets of changes effected at the national level to engender the market mechanism in the domestic realm will have to be replicated at the international level as well; otherwise the whole economic edifice would collapse under its own weight. And once again, given the impossibility to effect those changes spontaneously, the international market-building enterprise would have to be delegated to the state, whose intervention would be dictated by the logic of power politics; a rather different utilitarian calculus from the one advocated by liberal political economists.

Finally, Polanyi tries to clarify the problems brought about by these two competing logics by discussing another prerequisite of the liberal creed, the separation between the economic sphere and the political sphere. In doing so, he draws a logical parallel between the domestic realm and the international setting:

> The strains emanating from the market were thus to shifting to and fro between the market and the other institutional zones, sometimes affecting the working field of government, sometimes that of the gold standard or that of the balance-of-power system. [. . .] It was the relative autonomy of the spheres that caused the strain to accumulate and to generate tensions which eventually exploded in more or less stereotyped forms. (2001, p. 220)

In TGT, Polanyi offers us a very dynamic account of social change at the core of which we have his notion of the double movement. The book is structured and reads like a film script, with each chapter representing an edited sequence illustrating parts of the general thesis. Some of the sequences are longer and more detailed than others, some are only sketched and some are missing – but they can be figured out quite easily. Rather than producing a stable and sustainable steady state, the regulation and re-embedding of the market create further "disruptive strains", which in turn herald a new phase and further initiatives to commodify novel areas of human activity.

Our aim in the remaining part of this chapter is to show that the recursive sequence Polanyi identified carries on well beyond the iteration at which his analysis stopped. To this end, we shall seek to apply the double movement argument, as we have read it here, to more contemporary developments.

6. POLANYI'S DOUBLE MOVEMENT AND CAPITALISM'S GROUNDHOG DAY

In Palumbo and Scott (2018) we suggested seeing the political and institutional changes introduced since the 1980s through New Public Management (NPM) as an attempt to expand the self-regulating market mechanism by enclosing the common of the mind and commodifying knowledge (Boyle 2008). In a Polanyian spirit, we contended that in this context too the remaking of market society is, above all, an exercise in statecraft having a twofold objective: (a) to undermine the system of tangible and intangible commons from which societal agents and sub-state units derive their autonomy and legitimacy; (b) to entice the corporate entities whose help is needed to achieve this goal. Here there is space only for a very quick reprise of this analysis.

The case studies offered in our book seek to link the body of literature on the information society with the one concerned with the development of NPM. In our view, the public sector is being used as a large-scale laboratory to test how far the (re)commodification of managerial and intellectual labour can reach. By using different combinations of privatization, liberalization and marketization, managerial and intellectual work is being parcelled into discrete sequences and routinized. *Ex ante* and *ex post* forms of assessments are then used to measure the degree of conformity of each individual located along the production line. In this digital version of Taylorism, conformity is rewarded by allowing a tiny minority to move up the ranks, whereas non-conformity is strongly discouraged by the ease with which any individual could be replaced along the digital conveyor belt by a growing number of part-time and temporary white-collar workers seeking more secure positions. As Brown et al. explain:

> Digital Taylorism is not only deskilling many white-collar workers, but it also incites a power struggle within the middle classes, as corporate reengineering reduces the autonomy and discretion of some but not all managers and professionals. It encourages the segmentation of talent in ways that reserve permission to think to a small proportion of elite employees responsible for driving the business forward, functioning cheek by jowl with equally well-qualified workers in more Taylorized jobs. (2011, p. 81)

Moreover, in order to differentiate Polanyi's account of change from the competing Marxist one, our focus on these intellectual fields of activities endeavours to integrate his analysis by developing two themes that he only touches upon briefly: the proactive role of the state and the supportive role of technology.

By attributing to the state the role of good employer and making public bodies such as the civil service and the universities largely self-regulating, the welfare state granted middle-level managers, technicians, and salaried professionals significant forms of autonomy that often set them apart from those operating in the private sector. This privileged position was taken by other white-collar workers as a benchmark for bettering the working conditions of the private sector as well; elements that in economic conditions of nearly full employment enormously reduced the bargaining power of corporate businesses. Such a position of strength was further reinforced by the fact that welfare policies generated new types of "commons" that white-collar employees could exploit to insulate themselves from competition and retain an independent power base. For us, this explains the converging interests of state actors and private corporations affected by widespread legitimation crises to join forces and reconstitute, once again, the pro-market coalition. It also explains why the restarting of the commodification process in the 1980s has been carried out in parallel with repeated top-down attempts at undermining the viability of the commons upon which those categories depended. Finally, it shows that technological innovations are not the main determinants of change, but play a secondary role; in an alternative scenario, ICTs *could* be used to move beyond such an obsolete Tayloristic managerial mentality, and engender post-capitalistic forms of social organizations. In line with our above reconstruction of Polanyi's historical analysis, Keynesianism and the welfare state induced further "disruptive strains", which precipitated a conservative backlash regenerating the old pro-market coalition. But let us look at this new sequence in slightly more detail.

Polanyi attributes to successful countermovements the ability to regenerate tangible and intangible commons that help check the commodification process.

Within industrial society, the most tangible commons assumed the form of pension funds and other types of social insurance systems managed by labour organizations either directly or indirectly (Van Leeuwen 2016), and mutualist and cooperative activities making up the moral economy (Booth 1994; Fassin 2009; Götz 2015). Less tangible commons are related to labour legislation, collective bargaining systems, practices of codetermination and other demo- cratic activities which give workers voice in managerial matters. This explains the relevance trade unionists and progressive thinkers like Polanyi attached to industrial democracy (Burkitt and Hutchinson 2006). Despite the limitations noted in our book, the post-war settlement ended up producing new types of commons, having a growingly intangible nature, related to the ability of civil servants and salaried professionals to determine the terms and conditions of their activities and influence the determination of their salary levels through collective bargaining (Mau 2003). Such "decommodification" created potential resources, which, from the perspective of market actors, appear underutilized and ripe for recommodification. Recommodification has, therefore, entailed not only undermining trade unions and repealing labour legislation offering legal protection to disruptive categories of white-collar employees; it has also meant enclosing the commons from which those societal actors derived their autonomy, and rolling back the neo-corporatist arrangements which gave them political leverage.

What we have – once again – seen with the introduction of neoliberal policies and instruments is thus a shift from state-sponsored commons to state-sponsored markets. From a Polanyian perspective – in contrast to a Marxist one – this shift is not the product of the logic of capitalism as such, but the result of state-led policies. It is – in our terms – a new form of state- craft in which state actors seek to transfer some of the responsibilities they acquired onto market actors while retaining indirect control, and in the process opening up new opportunities for recommodification. In this context, we have witnessed the flourishing of an expanding new set of intellectual property rights (IPRs) and associated regulatory regimes (Kapczynski 2015). Designed to protect individual authors and stimulate innovation, IPRs are inevitably hijacked by the corporate actors operating within a cultural industry committed to rewarding rent-seeking activities (Gillespie 2007).

The counter-reaction of all negatively affected interests is dealt with in the ways discussed by Polanyi. At a theoretical level, an increasing number of neoliberal think tanks, Astroturf groups, and political economists are enrolled by pro-market coalitions to supply justifications appealing to any deonto- logical and instrumental reason available interchangeably. In doing so, past arguments used to justify property rights and the enclosure of commons are freely recycled even when (a) rights are attributed to legal entities rather than physical persons and their enforcement requires the systematic violation of traditional civic liberties (Patry 2009); (b) enclosure pertains to intangible cultural objects and practices that digital technologies are making non-depletable and are, therefore, reproducible at close to zero cost (Rifkin 2014). The upshot is a humourless "comedy of the commons" (Rose 1986) that is replacing the melodramatic "tragedy of the commons" staged in the past (McManis and Yagi 2013).

At a more practical level, state authority is systematically deployed to criminalize entire communities involved in a flourishing gift economy producing cutting-edge innovation and interesting forms of democratic experimentation (Krikorian and Kapczynski 2010). Hence the commitment of central governments and inter-governmental organizations to "collibration" strategies the goal of which is to raise the costs of collective action faced by antagonistic movements, the establishing of collusive pro-market coalitions and reforming efforts at both national and transnational levels wishing to turn educational institutions at all levels into assembly factories for the training of useful idiots; that is, an atomized and depoliticized cybertariat (Huws 2014).

7. CONCLUSION: NEOLIBERAL CHANGE IN A POLANYIAN PERSPECTIVE

In this chapter we have carried out a twofold task. First, we have suggested an alternative reading of Polanyi's double movement. Second, we have tried to use this revised version of Polanyi's thesis to propose an interpretation of current efforts to engender a knowledge economy. The revised notion of double movement tells us that faulty solutions to the dislocations caused by the market economy could end up generating vicious, vortex-like cycles. The failure of the Speenhamland system to stop the commodification of land brought about both a continuing intensification of that process, and a full-blown and persistent effort to commodify labour. The failure of nineteenth-century socialist movements to reverse the commodification of labour set the ground for the financialization of the economy and the commodification of money, producing more vicious and large-scale dislocations. Finally, the failure of the welfare state to redress the problems generated by financial capitalism promoted a neoliberal form of globalization that is extending the market mechanism in all directions and entrenching it by pushing for the commodification of knowledge in its many aspects. If this Polanyian account is at all plausible (and we think it is), failure to properly address the current set of interlinking economic, political, social and ecological crises this time around would restart the vicious cycle anew.

REFERENCES

Booth, W.J. (1994), 'On the idea of the moral economy', *American Political Science Review*, 88 (3), 653–67.

Boyle, J. (2008), *The public domain: Enclosing the commons of the mind*, New Haven, CT: Yale University Press.

Brown, P., H. Lauder and D. Ashton (2011), *The global auction: The broken promises of education, jobs, and incomes*, Oxford: Oxford University Press.

Burkitt, B. and F. Hutchinson (2006), *The political economy of social credit and guild socialism*, London: Routledge.

Fassin, D. (2009), 'Les économies morales revisitées', *Annales: Histoire, Sciences Sociales*, 64 (6), 1237–66.

Gillespie, T. (2007), *Wired shut: Copyright and the shape of digital culture*, Cambridge, MA: MIT Press.

Götz, N. (2015), '"Moral economy": Its conceptual history and analytical prospects', *Journal of Global Ethics*, 11 (2), 147–62.

Hobsbawm, E. (1989), *The age of empire 1875–1914*, London: Vintage.

Huws, U. (2014), *Labor in the global digital economy: The cybertariat comes of age*, New York: New York University Press.

Illich, I. (1978), *The right to useful unemployment and its professional enemies*, London: Marion Boyars.

Kapczynski, A. (2015), 'Intellectual property's leviathan', *Law & Contemporary Problems*, 77, 131–45.

Krikorian, G. and A. Kapczynski (eds) (2010), *Access to knowledge in the age of intellectual property*, New York: Zone Books.

Mau, S. (2003), *The moral economy of welfare states: Britain and Germany compared*, London: Routledge.

McManis, C.R. and B. Yagi (2013), 'The Bayh-Dole Act and the anticommons hypothesis: Round three', *George Mason Law Review*, 21, 1049–91.

Palumbo, A. and A. Scott (2005), 'Bureaucracy, open access, and social pluralism: Returning the common to the goose', in P. du Gay (ed.), *The values of bureaucracy*, Oxford: Oxford University Press, pp. 267–93.

Palumbo, A. and A. Scott (2018), *Remaking market society: A critique of social theory and political economy in neo-liberal times*, London: Routledge.

Patry, W. (2009), *Moral panics and the copyright wars*, Oxford: Oxford University Press.

Polanyi, K. ([1944] 2001), *The great transformation: The political and economic origins of our time*, Boston: Beacon Press.

Polanyi-Levitt, K. and M. Seccareccia (2016), '"The political movement that dared not speak its own name": Thoughts on neoliberalism from a Polanyian perspective', accessed 2 August 2018 at www.ineteconomics.org/uploads/papers/Polanyi_Seccareccia_on_Mirowski.pdf.

Rifkin, J. (2014), *The zero marginal cost society: The internet of things, the collaborative commons, and the eclipse of capitalism*, Basingstoke: Palgrave Macmillan.

Rose, C.M. (1986), 'The comedy of the commons: Commerce, custom, and inherently public property', *The University of Chicago Law Review*, 53 (3), 711–81.

Van Leeuwen, M.H. (2016), *Mutual insurance 1550–2015: From guild welfare and friendly societies to contemporary micro-insurers*, Dordrecht: Springer.

Weber, M. ([1906] 2005), 'The relations of the rural community to other branches of social science', edited and annotated by P. Ghosh as 'Max Weber on The Rural Community: A critical edition of the English text', *History of European Ideas*, 31, 327–66.

20. Polanyi and the digital transformation of labour: on fictitious commodities and real conflicts

Hans-Jürgen Urban

1. INTRODUCTION

Karl Polanyi's *The Great Transformation* ([1944] 2001) can be read as a classic of economic history or of economic and institutional sociology. It centres on how divorcing the market from its social circumstances resulted in the emergence of liberal market societies, and how these toppled into fascist regimes. The argumentation amounts to the thesis "that the origins of the cataclysm lay in the Utopian endeavour of economic liberalism to set up a self-regulating market system" (Polanyi [1944] 2001, p. 31). Because "the idea of a self-adjusting market implied a stark Utopia" and because a market system left to its own devices could not survive over any prolonged period of time "without annihilating the human and natural substance of society", society saw itself forced into a countermovement in the form of measures for its own protection. These measures impaired the functioning of the market system, however, and led to a disorganization of industrial development. "It was this dilemma which forced the development of the market system into a definite groove and finally disrupted the social organization based upon it" (Polanyi [1944] 2001, pp. 3 f.).

Historically oriented, politico-economic and sociological research has diagnosed many analogies between Polanyi's analyses and the developments of contemporary capitalism. A similar disembedding of capitalist markets from state regulation is observed in the current transition from welfare state capitalism under the nation state to global financial market capitalism. And again, the destructive forces of unregulated markets create rifts in society; again, tendencies towards social instability and post-democratic authoritarianisms are evident (Crouch 2008; Deppe 2013; Streeck 2016).

The question to be asked in the following is what role the digitalization of work plays in this process (Schröder and Urban, 2016).[1] The thesis will be formulated that digitalization is driving a new surge of marketization and rationalization which promotes a double transformation: the transformation of labour in the sense of a restructuring of work processes and organization; and concurrently, the transformation of the institutional setting of social protection rights, on which the previously attained degree of decommodification of labour power in the welfare state depended. The Polanyi-type great transformation is followed by a digital transformation of its own kind.

Left to its own devices, i.e. as a market-driven process, the development ought to follow Polanyian paths. Already set in motion by neoliberal deregulation and privatization policy, a continuing liberation of work from regulation by employment and social law is foreseeable. To resist the ensuing weakening of labour and the consequential damage to society, a countermovement would be called for. This would have to counter the top-down digital rationalization with a bottom-up humanization of labour policy, and the dismantling of welfare state institutions with the reconstruction of intervention rights to strengthen labour power (Urban 2016). The following remarks first explain the thesis of a new digital transformation and draw attention to the considerable potential of the Polanyian approach as a stimulus for sociological analysis of digital revolutions (section 2). Next the digitalization of industrial added value ("*Industrie 4.0*") will be used as an example to illustrate that transformation conflicts in the sphere of interest politics are the locus of decision-making about the developmental path of digitalization, and that special significance attaches to the democratization of economic decisions as a prerequisite for labour and social policy successes (section 3). Finally the assumption is discussed that the marketization of data and knowledge resulting from these digitalizations could instigate a new double movement in the Polanyian sense (section 4).

2.   THE "GREAT" AND THE "DIGITAL" TRANSFORMATION

Polanyi localizes the cause of the collapse of Western European liberal-capitalist civilization in the social and technological upheaval that brought forth the "market society" in the nineteenth century. In the latter, the regulation of

---

[1]   In the following, a terminological distinction will be made between the *digitalization of work* and *digital work*. Whereas digitalization denotes the *process* whereby work is pervaded by digital technologies, digital work means the *new quality of work* that has evolved from the process (also Hoose 2018, pp. 3 f.).

goods production and distribution was completely left to the unregulated market mechanism. Labour, land and money also became objects of exchange that were traded in markets. But incorporating these into the "satanic mill of market" was not without its consequences. "To include them in the market mechanism means to subordinate the substance of society itself to the laws of the market" (Polanyi [1944] 2001, p. 75). Indeed, in Polanyi's view, their commodification is based on a fiction. Labour, land and money cannot be treated like any other commodities without sustaining damage to their substance and their social function. "Labour is only another name for a human activity which goes with life itself" (Polanyi [1944] 2001, p. 75). Labour power cannot exist without human beings. "For the alleged commodity 'labour power' cannot be shoved about, used indiscriminately, or even left unused, without affecting also the human individual who happens to be the bearer of this peculiar commodity" (Polanyi [1944] 2001, p. 76). Similarly destructive consequences, in the form of environmental destruction or inflation, accompany the commodification of land and money. In order to protect the fictitious commodities and hence the substance of society from devastating market forces, society intervened in the market mechanism by means of regulatory institutions. "While on the one hand markets spread all over the face of the globe and the amount of goods involved grew to unbelievable dimensions, on the other hand a network of measures and policies was integrated into powerful institutions designed to check the action of the market relative to labour, land, and money" (Polanyi [1944] 2001, p. 79).

2.1 Labour in the "Third Wave of Marketization" and in the Transition to Financial Market Capitalism

Polanyi interpreted the dynamic of market fundamentalism and countermovement as a unique, historically concluded process. Not so Michael Burawoy in his sociological reconstruction of the Polanyian analysis. He reconstructs the development of capitalism as both a sequence and an interplay of at least three waves of marketization, in which the commodification of labour, money and nature each plays its own special role and invokes corresponding countermovements to protect the fictitious commodities. In his heuristic model "each successive wave of marketization is characterized by a new combination of fictitious commodities. In the first wave the (de)commodification of labour takes the lead, in the second wave we see the intersection of the (de)commodification of labour and money with money taking the lead. The third wave is characterized by the articulation of the (de)commodification of labour, money and nature, in which the (de)commodification of nature will ultimately take the lead" (Burawoy 2010, p. 308).

Burawoy's "three waves" model provides an interpretative foil for the renewed transformation of capitalism, extending Polanyi's idea of the wave-like double movement. The starting point of the third wave of capitalist transformation, impelled by the neoliberal offensive since the beginning of the 1970s, is an economic-institutional constellation which had the intervening welfare state at its centre. The latter, a historic project of social democracy, was expanding until well into the 1970s. Through a combination of market-opening and market-correcting interventions along with systems of social protection, it realized profitable growth for businesses and material risk compensation for dependent labour for the eventualities of sickness, unemployment and old age. However, after crisis struck the regulated market economies and private profit production was too heavily regulated, deregulation and privatization strategies heralded in the transition from national state-organized welfare capitalism to global financial market capitalism. This third transformation plays out as a transnational dynamic and encompasses nature to an extraordinary degree. The emerging financial market capitalism is influenced not only, but substantially, by the key actors and rules of play of the global financial markets. Fundamental changes took place (and are still taking place to date) in business management and control, in the labour and social constitution and in social policy (Urban 2013, pp. 17 ff.). In businesses the dominance of the financial markets heightens external pressure for return on investment and promotes a reorientation of corporate structures, work organization and human resources strategies. Terms like "financialization" of business management and control, "marketization" of labour and social relations, and indirect forms of control of human resources describe the transformation.

The changes precipitate not only an "organizational revolution" in labour but also a general socio-economic upheaval "which – far beyond business and labour – is concerned with the transformation of the European and the specifically German production and social model" (Sauer 2013, p. 8, own trans.). These are flanked by the reconfiguration and dismantling of the welfare state, which go hand in hand with benefit cuts and more stringent conditions for claims, and a general precarization of work. It was this renewed disembedding of the market economy from the set of regulatory institutions which brought social insecurity back into the existence of waged labour via the recommodification of labour (Castel 2000), and which in turn culminated in a major crisis, the financial market crisis of 2008 and the following years.[2]

---

[2]   It was rightly noted that the Polanyian approach is particularly well-suited to drawing out the "structural similarity between the Great Depression of 1929 and the collapse of 2008" (Moucaurant and Plocinicziak 2013, p. 527).

2.2 Institutional Regulation, Contested Technology and Dominance Paths

As digitalization progresses, the thesis contends, this transforming dynamic of the capitalist conditions gathers pace. In politico-economic terms it can be expressed as a technology-based reorganization of capital structures, which encompasses the micro, meso and macro levels of the social reproduction process. Not only does digitalization pervade economic added value chains; it also forms the technological basis of a new "capitalist Landnahme" (Dörre 2015), which embraces the economy, the world of work and society in equal measure. Digitalization promotes a metamorphosis of constant (fixed) capital, whereby fixed capital acquires a new material form. It is accompanied by a surge of real subsumption of labour among the capital bound up in the "digital machinery" (Barthel and Rotenbach 2017, own trans.).

Digitalization thus sets in motion a metamorphosis of the material form of fixed capital, which unleashes new forms of subordination of labour power, new strategies of corporate dominance, new antagonisms in interest politics and new social conflicts. Thus the very institutional arrangements which regulate capital–labour relations in the corporate and societal worlds also come under pressure. Since the digitally informed labour and dominance processes do not shed their capitalist form, their antagonisms of interest continue to exist. These are played out in contested and power-based negotiation processes, which are ultimately decided by the conflict resources of the actors involved.

These conflict-based negotiations can be understood as transformation conflicts. They mould the institutions whose job is to regulate developments. Effectively they specify the milestones of the digitalization path. Whoever dominates the institutions dominates the rules of the digital game and makes the choice between path-change and continuity. The power-based transformation of institutions is thus of special importance for a politico-economic analysis of digitalization. With this in mind, it is principally the turning points of institutional developments ("critical junctures", Beyer 2005) that are addressed by Polanyi and representatives of New Institutional Economics (North 2005; Didry and Vincensini 2011; Maucourant and Plociniczak 2013). Both approaches emphasize the significance of institutions as factors structuring economic and social action, and both conceive of markets as such institutions. They immediately differ, however, in their assessments of the significance of social contexts and historical aspects for markets and institutions. While institutional economics largely interprets markets and market transactions as ahistorical, (as it were) primordial phenomena, Polanyi emphasizes their processual historicity and the significance of social contexts for market activity. "To conceive of economy and markets as institutionalized processes, as Polanyi does, contradicts the belief in the naturalness, the asocial universality and the ahistorical nature of the market" (Maucourant and Plociniczak 2013, p. 526).

It is self-evident that Polanyi's historically oriented approach to the analysis of current upheavals is more appropriate than an ahistorical modelling which weights elegant abstractions more highly than links to historical reality. Polanyi's institution-theoretical approach in particular calls for vigilance against a widespread "technological determinism" (Lutz 1987). As other advances in technology have done, here digital technologies provide the basis for possible development paths. Which of the possibilities becomes reality, however, depends on the power-based interplay of technology with organizational, personnel and institutional factors in "socio-technical systems" (Botthof and Hartmann 2015; Hirsch-Kreinsen et al. 2018). In the capitalist company, conceivable technological solutions are assessed for their "economic efficiency" and hard calculations are made of investment and opportunity costs as well as capital payback times. No less important are their conjectured impacts on the corporate dominance structure and the balance of power between capital and labour. In other words, profit analysis and power calculus act as innovation filters which either block or open up development paths.

From a perspective informed by capitalism theory and institutional theory, the path-dependent integration of digitalization into the present transformation is more probable than a change of path in the direction of the digitalization-based humanization. And as a factor in the capitalist restructuring process, the digital offensive might well aim principally at harnessing new efficiency potentials that come to light thanks to the new technologies – with concomitant risks for employment, remuneration and working conditions. Yet acknowledgement of the rationalization character of digitalization by no means requires denial of the logic of humanization which is likewise inherent in the new technologies. Undoubtedly they also hold latent potential to alleviate work stress and strains on health; reduced workloads and enriched work tasks are conceivable outcomes. An imaginable transformation based on humanization politics would be a counter-tendential project and would be premised on a powerful countermovement of politically effective actors. But the trade unions lack power and the neoliberal state has no such will.

3. *INDUSTRIE 4.0* – THE DIGITALIZATION OF INDUSTRIAL ADDED VALUE

A suitable field of practice for examining the rationalization thesis is the digitalization of industrial added value. This is referenced in the German debate with the buzzword *"Industrie 4.0"*.[3] Great uncertainty still prevails in empirical research regarding the consequences of digitalization for forms of work, working conditions, employment, social relations and competitiveness (Frey and Osborne 2013; Bauer et al. 2014; Brynjolfsson and McAfee 2014; Heng 2014; Brzeski and Burk 2015).[4] Relevant studies show, however, that to date *Industrie 4.0* (as yet?) remains a vision rather than a reality (on this, see WSI-Mitteilungen 2018). At this point a significant "differentiation and diversification of different patterns of work" are observed, which follow the paths of institutional settings (Hoose 2018, p. 34, own trans.; also Kirchner and Wolf 2015; Ahlers 2018). On the one hand digitalization promotes new models of business and work organization such as digital platforms, which are regarded as the nucleus of a new "Platform Capitalism" (Srnicek 2017) but have shown few signs of proliferating so far. Above all, the ultimate objective of *Industrie 4.0* is clearly geared towards complex production and added value networks in all parts of industrial production. These networks try "as far as possible to integrate all elements of production processes, the flanking services and the linking logistics processes digitally with one another; to merge the material with the digital" (Pfeiffer 2015, p. 7, own trans.). In the influential final report of the *Industrie 4.0* Working Group of the Industry-Science Research Alliance (*"Forschungsunion"*) and the German Academy of Science and Engineering (*"acatech"*), the following description is found:

> In the future, businesses will establish global networks that incorporate their machinery, warehousing systems and production facilities in the shape of *Cyber-Physical Systems (CPS)*. In the manufacturing environment, these Cyber-Physical Systems comprise smart machines, storage systems and production facilities capable of autonomously exchanging information, triggering actions and controlling each other independently. This facilitates fundamental improvements to the industrial

---

[3]   *Industrie 4.0* represents a technology-oriented view whereby the digitalization of industry marks a new and radical (fourth) revolution in industrial added value. "The 'fourth industrial revolution' refers to the sequence of major (disruptive) stages in the advancement of industrial production, which have manifested as great upheavals based on technical and technological innovations. *Mechanization* by means of water and steam power at the end of the eighteenth century (the first industrial revolution), *electrification* and the use of mass production at the beginning of the twentieth century (the second industrial revolution), the *computerization* and automation of production processes since the 1970s (the third industrial revolution), and now the fourth industrial revolution, the *digitalization and networking of production*" (Ittermann and Niehaus 2018, p. 36; own trans., emphasis in original). The term was coined in the technology-policy debate about the digitalization of German industry but has since passed into use in the discourses of other European countries (European Commission 2017).

[4]   A survey of the current research state of the art is provided by Hoose 2018.

processes involved in manufacturing, engineering, material usage and supply chain and life cycle management. The *smart factories* that are already beginning to appear employ a completely new approach to production. Smart products are uniquely identifiable, may be located at all times and know their own history, current status and alternative routes to achieving their target state. The embedded manufacturing systems are vertically networked with business processes within factories and enterprises and horizontally connected to disperse value networks that can be managed in real time – from the moment an order is placed right through to outbound logistics. (Kagermann et al. 2013, p. 5; emphasis in original).[5]

3.1   Power Shifts in the Company and Labour Policy Transformation Conflicts

That honouring the interests of labour in the digitalization process is a conflict-prone undertaking is confirmed by the experiences of works council and staff council members. They report of the condensation and intensification of work resulting from corporate digitalization processes (Ahlers 2018).[6] Studies investigating the shifts in interests and power also support the thesis whereby live work is being repositioned by digitalization within the corporate production and dominance structure. For instance, in their longitudinal analysis, Schwemmle and Wedde point out "that digitalization increasingly acts as a power factor in the relationship between labour and capital. To a growing extent it opens up potentials for unsecuring, decollectivizing and disempowering human labour power. If the technical-organizational upheavals seemingly happen by themselves but are de facto driven and influenced by calculations of entrepreneurial efficiency and control, digitalization alters the dynamic in favour of 'capital' and to the detriment of 'labour'." "In order to prevent this", they continue, "there is a need for labour policy interventions and labour law regulations" (Schwemmle and Wedde 2018, p. 5, own trans.). Whether such interventions and regulations will succeed, only the future will show. The German employers' associations are resisting them (BDA 2015). At this juncture, some axes of conflict can be identified, around which the institutional design of the digital industrial work might develop (Figure 20.1). They mark out labour policy transformation conflicts, and hence the terrains on which the

---

[5]   Note that the observed hype surrounding *Industrie 4.0* is "not the causal consequence of a real status of technical developments but, considered in terms of discourse analysis, a case of professional *agenda building*" (Pfeiffer 2015, p. 9; own trans., emphasis in original). It is backed by interest-led ambitions and hopes, keeping in mind that digitalization can be expected to generate substantial research projects, consultancy contracts and new markets.

[6]   Surveys of employees in digitalized companies point in the same direction; see Schmucker 2018.

contours of digital work will be fought out, with the trade unions as key actors of any Polanyian countermovement called upon to offer regulatory concepts of their own.

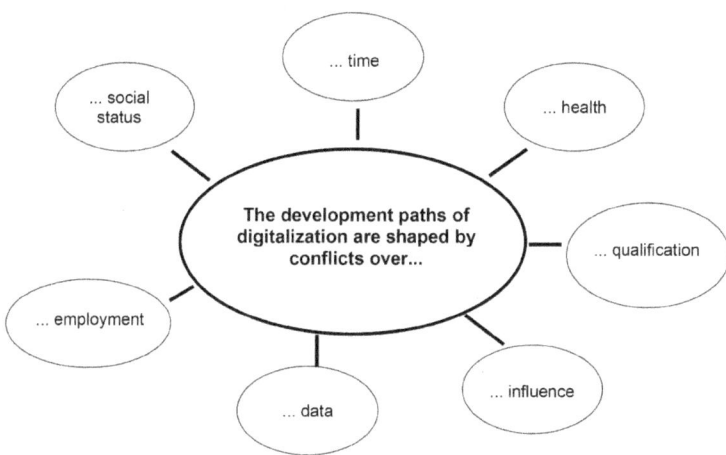

Source: own presentation.

Figure 20.1   Transformation conflicts of digitalization

3.1.1   The conflict over social status: precarious entrepreneurs or protected knowledge workers

The digitalization of work promotes the use of labour in new forms such as cloudworking or crowdsourcing. In these models, a not always clearly defined volume of workers take part in assignments that are advertised via digital platforms (Boes et al. 2015; Srnicek 2017). If tasks and activities are outsourced and/or employees transferred to self-employed status, a simultaneous displacement into a different legal space occurs (Däubler and Klebe 2015). In many cases a considerable worsening of income, working hours and employment security is the consequence.

The reform options are plain to see: either the dependent self-employed are reintegrated into the protection of the labour and social systems as quasi-employees, or the systems open up for forms of dependent work outside the parameters of employee status. This would require a redefinition of the group of socially insured individuals. At the same time it requires all those employed under contracts for work to be included in the codetermination and control rights of works councils and staff councils.

3.1.2   The conflict over time: flexibility or sovereignty

The digital communication technologies enlarge the scope for decoupling of the workplace and the performance of work. The "mobile work" away from the workplace thus facilitated ranges from classical homeworking (e.g. telework) and the service, maintenance and sales work carried out on the customer's premises to quickly dealing with tasks on the move (via smart phones or mobile devices) or working on business trips. It is obvious that in the context of mobile work, occupational safety regulations geared towards the workplace come under pressure, since constantly changing places of work make controls more difficult. At the same time, mobile work is frequently associated with a loss of boundaries around working hours and ever more pervasive access to employees' personal time in its entirety.

In the societal debate, a lack of childcare establishments, poor support with caring tasks or rigid school hours are often criticized as stressors for employees. The performance and working hours regimes in businesses, on the other hand, are left unquestioned. Yet real gains in sovereignty will only arise if the regulations in workplaces are changed, if the needs of private individuals become the fixed variable and the time demands of companies the adjustable one. This will not be achievable without robust regulation in collective bargaining agreements, works agreements and individual rights of autonomy. And fixed points are needed, such as maximum daily and weekly working hours, around which latitude for flexibility can be designed (Urban 2017).

3.1.3   The conflict over health: economization or prevention

It is also foreseeable that the growing prevalence of "intelligent robots" ("cyber-physical systems", CPS) will give rise to hybrid labour systems in which human–machine interaction gains new significance. A conceivable form of progress on the humanization side might be the avoidance of undue physical and mental demands. Workplaces characterized by forced postures, hazardous substances or heavy lifting and load-carrying can be automated.

But even digital work is by no means free of monotony and psychological distress. It normally entails condensation of performance and intensification of work. If strains on health are to be averted, the soonest possible interventions in the organization of work are needed by employees and representations of collective interests. It is a matter of exerting influence on the use of technology, working procedures and staff assessments. In this way the risks of autonomous human–machine collaboration can be minimized and performance standards regulated. Regulations to protect psychological health must also be brought in.

3.1.4 The conflict over qualification: competence or personality development

Even though concepts of "work organization conducive to learning" are being discussed in the labour studies debate (Botthof and Hartmann 2015), reliable findings on the changing task and competence profiles in the digital factory are scarce as yet (Ahrens and Spöttl 2015). One thing is clear: the transformation in the spectrum of tasks and activities also alters the demands placed upon employees in terms of knowledge, skills and competences. Steering, controlling, servicing and information-procuring tasks are taking on greater importance. Accordingly, the necessary technical, social and cognitive competences are becoming more highly valued (Hausner et al. 2015).

The field of qualification policy is yet another instance where corporate interests do not coincide with labour interests and negotiation conflicts are to be expected. The demands of constant continuing education can be welcomed as an opportunity for professional development but also perceived as a burdensome pressure. It generates an expectation within the company, which not everyone is equipped to meet. Fear that informal qualifications could be devalued and the sense of constant pressure to engage in continuing education could amplify status anxieties. At the same time, constant continuing education is linked to rising costs, and the conflict over distribution could well escalate. Trade union education policy must therefore increasingly discuss vocational education and training as a distribution issue. Ultimately it is incumbent on representations of interests to stand up to the danger of a technical-functionalist truncation of the concept of education and competence. The digitalized world of work generates not only professional but also complex social work demands. It requires personal competences and personality development as well as the willingness and capability to pursue individual and collective interests.

3.2 Digitalization, Humanization, Democracy

The collisions of interests associated with digitalization lend special significance to the conflict over influence on corporate decisions. New possibilities of digital communication are altering social relations. Not uncommonly, all-embracing access to employees' work capacity is combined with (mostly rather symbolic) offers of a voice and feedback, which are certainly well received in staff bodies. With "agile management" methods, new models of work organization and communication are used to accommodate employees' needs for involvement by making systematic offers of participation (Häusling and von Gloeden 2014).

Ambitions of this kind come together in the concept of the "democratic enterprise", which is a strategy design with hegemony potential. The message is that employees elect their managers themselves and perhaps vote them out again; have sovereignty to decide on the time, place and nature of their work; benefit from discrimination-free recruitment procedures, performance appraisals and career plans; and ultimately the democratic business counts on the equalization of burdens, the distribution of gains among stakeholders, and the organic interplay of economy and society. According to the self-image of the "democratic business", binding employees' rights are not only superfluous but obstructive, because the employees are elevated to "citizens of the business", which releases them from the immature status in which they are kept by code-termination structures and trade unions, into freedom (Sattelberger et al. 2015).

Nevertheless the model of the "democratic business" can barely conceal the interest politics of its substance. The claim to give primacy to the individual and to collective protection rights is part and parcel of the standard justification of business-oriented deregulation policies. But why should the power-political asymmetry between the employee and employer, which is the basis of collective labour rights, disappear in the digital age? Why should the need for social protection of dependent labour suddenly end? Under these conditions the question of democracy becomes pivotal to the labour and digitalization policy of the trade unions. Within this, the defence and path-dependent expansion of institutional codetermination may well be indispensable, but not sufficient. Correctly positioned, a counter-concept to the "democratic business" needs to align with a version of interest politics that strengthens democratic impulses from the bottom up, but combines these with safeguarded, individual participation rights and the expansion of corporate and trade union codetermination. Should the humanization-policy variant of digitalization prevail, it must go hand in hand with a democratization of labour. It is about having guaranteed institutional channels of influence which enable workplace representations of interests, trade unions and other humanization politicians to mobilize sufficient vigour to assert the interests of labour power effectively.[7]

4.   CONCLUSION AND OUTLOOK

Thus, there is much to suggest that the rationalization and humanization logic in the digitalization process will balance out in line with the particular interests and power resources of the digital actors. Certain steps in the process will always remain contested. And digitalization will not follow a master

---

[7]   In order to be able to regulate the external pressure of competition, a democratized labour policy must be embedded in a concept of economic democracy which involves the social actors in a macroeconomic and social infrastructure policy (Urban 2011 and 2018).

plan. What is more likely is a process of muddling through by trial and error. This applies not only to the world of work. The digital penetration of social relations will change society as a whole. In this regard the warning against "technological totalitarianism" is heavy-handed but justifiable (Schirrmacher 2015). It is probable that the digital networking of society will give rise to new, contested information spaces (Boes et al. 2015). Different scenarios are being discussed (on this, see Dörre 2018). It would be possible for digitalization to proceed like Schumpeter's "creative destruction", initiating a long wave of economic growth ("prosperity scenario"); another conceivable path might lead to technological mass unemployment, which proves too overwhelming for the weakened welfare state to deal with ("downfall scenario"); finally it is not impossible that society might slide into a new social schism, in which mainly the middle class is ground down ("polarization scenario").

But this much is certain: the outlined conflicts about social status, time, health, qualification and influence will be joined by others; mainly conflicts over employment security, for instance, but also over the use of information and data, which takes on an entirely new significance due to the digital penetration of work processes and social relations. In the digital world, large amounts of data are collected, propagated and exploited. Condensed into Big Data they have been interpreted as a new, self-reproducing raw material of a new "platform capitalism". "Just like oil, data are a material to be extracted, refined, and used in a variety of ways. The more data one has, the more uses one can make of them" (Srnicek 2017, p. 23).

From an analytical perspective that follows Polanyi's and Burawoy's paths, here a pressing question arises. The obvious marketization of the new raw material of data prompts speculation that data, as a new fictitious commodity, might set in train a fourth wave of marketization (on this, see also Burawoy 2010, pp. 309 ff.). To be sure, data – certainly Big Data – can be framed as a specific aggregate form of human knowledge, which is subjected to a new quality of marketization and exploitation in digitalized capitalism. But does this alone make knowledge a fictitious commodity in the Polanyian sense? That would necessarily imply that through conversion into an object of exchange it loses its utility value, unleashes destructive dynamics in society and, at the same time, calls forth corresponding countermovements. But more plausible, though, seems to be a viewpoint whereby data-based digitalization, rather than launching a new wave of marketization, might accelerate the processes of the third wave without departing from the paths of these dynamics. This applies to the recommodification of labour, which was analysed here in its industrial form but which is happening with other similarly far reaching consequences in the sectors of formal and informal service sector and care work (on this, see also Aulenbacher and Dammayr 2014). It applies to the recommodification of money, which in financial market capitalism assumes the form of fragile financial transactions outside state controls. And it applies to the market-driven overexploitation of nature, which is destroying the natural resource base on which human life depends.

An answer to the pending questions will not be found without theoretical and empirical research. Be that as it may: in digital capitalism, another Polanyian countermovement for the protection of labour, money and nature is more necessary than ever.

REFERENCES

Ahlers, E. (2018), *Die Digitalisierung der Arbeit: Verbreitung und Einschätzung aus Sicht der Betriebsräte*, Düsseldorf: WSI.

Ahrens, D. and G. Spöttl (2015), 'Industrie 4.0 und Herausforderungen für die Qualifizierung von Fachkräften', in H. Hirsch-Kreinsen, P. Ittermann and J. Niehaus (eds), *Digitalisierung industrieller Arbeit: Die Vision Industrie 4.0 und ihre sozialen Herausforderungen*, Baden-Baden: Nomos, pp. 185–203.

Aulenbacher, B. and M. Dammayr (2014), 'Zwischen Anspruch und Wirklichkeit: Zur Ganzheitlichkeit und Rationalisierung des Sorgens und der Sorgearbeit', in B. Aulenbacher, B. Riegraf and Hildegard Theobald (eds), *Sorge: Arbeit, Verhältnisse, Regime*, Baden-Baden: Nomos, pp. 125–40.

Barthel, G. and J. Rottenbach (2017), 'Reelle Subsumtion und Insubordination im Zeitalter der digitalen Maschinerie. Mit-Untersuchung der Streikenden bei Amazon in Leipzig', *Prokla*, 47 (2), 249–69.

Bauer, W., S. Schlund, D. Marrenbach and O. Ganscher (2014), *Industrie 4.0 – Volkswirtschaftliches Potenzial für Deutschland*, Berlin: BITKOM.

Beyer, J. (2005), 'Pfadabhängigkeit ist nicht gleich Pfadabhängigkeit! Wider den impliziten Konservatismus eines gängigen Konzeptes', *Zeitschrift für Soziologie*, 34, 5–21.

Boes, A., T. Kämpf, B. Langes and T. Lühr (2015), 'Landnahme im Informationsraum: Neukonstituierung gesellschaftlicher Arbeit in der "digitalen Gesellschaft"', *WSI Mitteilungen*, 2, 77–85.

Botthof, A. and E.A. Hartmann (eds) (2015), *Zukunft der Arbeit in Industrie 4.0*, Heidelberg: Springer.

Brynjolfsson, E. and A. McAfee (2014), *The second machine age: Work, progress, and prosperity in a time of brilliant technologies*, New York and London: W. W. Norton.

Brzeski, C. and I. Burk (2015), 'Die Roboter kommen: Folgen der Automatisierung für den deutschen Arbeitsmarkt', *Economic Research* (30 April), Frankfurt: ING-DiBa.

Bundesvereinigung der deutschen Arbeitgeberverbände (2015), *Chancen der Digitalisierung nutzen: Positionspapier der BDA zur Digitalisierung von Wirtschaft und Arbeitswelt*, Berlin: BDA.

Burawoy, M. (2010), 'From Polanyi to Pollyanna: The false optimism of global labour studies', *Global Labour Journal*, 1 (2), 301–13.

Castel, R. (2000), *Die Metamorphose der sozialen Frage: Eine Chronik der Lohnarbeit*, Konstanz: UVK Universitätsverlag.

Crouch, C. (2008), *Postdemokratie*, Frankfurt/Main: Suhrkamp.

Däubler, W. and T. Klebe (2015), 'Crowdwork: Die neue Form der Arbeit – Arbeitgeber auf der Flucht?', *Neue Zeitschrift für Arbeitsrecht*, 17, 1032–41.

Deppe, F. (2013), *Autoritärer Kapitalismus: Demokratie auf dem Prüfstand*, Hamburg: VSA.

Didry, C. and C. Vincensini (2011), 'Beyond the market–institutions dichotomy: The institutionalism of Douglass C. North in response to Karl Polanyi's challenge', accessed 10 September 2018 at https://halshs.archives-ouvertes.fr/halshs-00601544/document.

Dörre, K. (2015), 'The new Landnahme: Dynamics and limits of financial market capitalism', in K. Dörre, S. Lessenich and H. Rosa (eds), *Sociology – capitalism – critique*, London: Verso, pp. 11–66.

Dörre, K. (2018), 'Digitalisierung – neue Prosperität oder Vertiefung gesellschaftlicher Spaltung?', in H. Hirsch-Kreinsen, P. Ittermann and J. Niehaus (eds) (2018), *Digitalisierung industrieller Arbeit: Die Vision Industrie 4.0 und ihre sozialen Herausforderungen*, Baden-Baden: Nomos, pp. 365–81.

European Commission (2017), 'Analysis of national initiatives on digitising industry', accessed 10 November 2018 at https://ec.europa.eu/futurium/en/implementing-digitising-european-industry-actions/national-initiatives-digitising-industry.

Frey, C.B. and M.A. Osborne (2013), *The future of employment: How susceptible are jobs to computerisation?*, Oxford: Oxford University Press.

Häusling, A. and D. von Gloeden (2014), 'Die Relevanz agiler Personal- und Führungsinstrumente: Agile Führung als entscheidende Erfolgskomponente', accessed 3 August 2015 at http://hr-pioneers.com/wp-content/uploads/2014/01/scan0001.pdf.

Hausner, K.H., D. Söhnlein, B. Weber and E. Weber (2015), *Qualifikation und Arbeitsmarkt: Bessere Chancen mit mehr Bildung*, Nürnberg: IAB.

Heng, S. (2014), 'Industrie 4.0: Upgrade des Industriestandorts Deutschland steht bevor', *Deutsche Bank Research* (4 February), Frankfurt/Main: Deutsche Bank.

Hirsch-Kreinsen, H., P. Ittermann and J. Niehaus (eds.) (2018), *Digitalisierung industrieller Arbeit: Die Vision Industrie 4.0 und ihre sozialen Herausforderungen*, Baden-Baden: Nomos.

Hoose, F. (2018), 'Digitale Arbeit: Strukturen eines Forschungsfeldes', accessed 31 July 2018 at www.iaq.uni-due.de/iaq-forschung/2018/fo2018-03.pdf.

Ittermann, P. and J. Niehaus (2018), 'Industrie 4.0 und Wandel von Industriearbeit', in H. Hirsch-Kreinsen, P. Ittermann and J. Niehaus (eds), *Digitalisierung industrieller Arbeit: Die Vision Industrie 4.0 und ihre sozialen Herausforderungen*, Baden-Baden: Nomos, pp. 33–60.

Kagermann, H., W. Wahlster and J. Helbig (eds) (2013), *Securing the future of German manufacturing industry: Recommendations for implementing the strategic initiative INDUSTRIE 4.0: Final report of the Industrie 4.0 Working Group*, Frankfurt/Main: Forschungsunion and Acatech.

Kirchner, S. and M. Wolf (2015), 'Digitale Arbeitswelten im europäischen Vergleich', *WSI-Mitteilungen*, 4, 253–61.

Lutz, B. (1987), 'Das Ende des Technikdeterminismus und die Folgen: Soziologische Technikforschung vor neuen Aufgaben und Problemen', in B. Lutz (ed.), *Technik und sozialer Wandel: Verhandlungen des 23. Deutschen Soziologentages in Hamburg 1986*, Frankfurt/Main: Campus, pp. 34–52.

Maucourant, J. and S. Plociniczak (2013), 'The institution, the economy and the market: Karl Polanyi's institutional thought for economists', *Review of Political Economy*, 25 (3), 512–31.

North, D.C. (2005), *Understanding the process of economic change*, Princeton, NJ: Princeton University Press.

Pfeiffer, S. (2015), 'Industrie 4.0 und die Digitalisierung der Produktion', *Aus Politik und Zeitgeschichte*, 31–32, 6–12.

Polanyi, K. ([1944] 2001), *The great transformation: The political and economic origins of our time*, Boston: Beacon Press.

Sattelberger, T., I. Welpe and A. Boes (2015), *Das demokratische Unternehmen: Neue Arbeits- und Führungskulturen im Zeitalter digitaler Wirtschaft*, Freiburg: Haufe.

Sauer, D. (2013), *Die organisatorische Revolution: Umbrüche in der Arbeitswelt: Ursachen, Auswirkungen und arbeitspolitische Antworten*, Hamburg: VSA.

Schirrmacher, F. (ed.) (2015), *Technologischer Totalitarismus: Eine Debatte*, Berlin: Suhrkamp.

Schmucker, R. (2018), 'Die Digitalisierung der Arbeitswelt aus Sicht der Beschäftigten', in L. Schröder and H.-J. Urban (eds), *Ökologie der Arbeit: Impulse für einen nachhaltigen Umbau*, Frankfurt/Main: Bund, pp. 276–86.

Schröder, L. and H.-J. Urban (eds) (2016), *Gute Arbeit: Digitale Arbeitswelt: Trends und Anforderungen: Ausgabe 2016*, Frankfurt/Main: Bund.

Schwemmle, M. and P. Wedde (2018), *Alles unter Kontrolle? Arbeitspolitik und Arbeitsrecht in digitalen Zeiten*, Bonn: Friedrich-Ebert-Stiftung.

Srnicek, N. (2017), *Platform capitalism*, Cambridge: Polity Press.

Streeck, W. (2016), *How will capitalism end? Essays on a failing system*, London and New York: Verso.

Urban, H.-J. (2011), 'Wirtschaftsdemokratie des 21. Jahrhunderts: Konturen und Realisierungsbedingungen eines gesellschaftlichen Transformationsprojektes', in H. Meine, M. Schumann and H.-J. Urban (eds), *Mehr Wirtschaftsdemokratie wagen!*, Hamburg: VSA, pp. 42–67.

Urban, H.-J. (2013), *Der Tiger und seine Dompteure: Wohlfahrtstaat und Gewerkschaften im Gegenwartskapitalismus*, Hamburg: VSA.

Urban, H.-J. (2016), 'Arbeiten in der Wirtschaft 4.0: Über kapitalistische Rationalisierung und digitale Humanisierung', in L. Schröder and H.-J. Urban (eds), *Gute Arbeit: Digitale Arbeitswelt – Trends und Anforderungen: Ausgabe 2016*, Frankfurt/Main: Bund, pp. 21–45.

Urban, H.-J. (2017), '(Arbeits-)Zeit – Scharnier zwischen Arbeit, Leben und Gesundheit', in L. Schröder and H.-J. Urban (eds), *Gute Arbeit: Streit um Zeit – Arbeitszeit und Gesundheit: Ausgabe 2017*, Frankfurt/Main: Bund, pp. 35–53.

Urban, H.-J. (2018), 'Ausbruch aus dem Gehäuse der European Governance: Überlegungen zu einer Soziologie der Wirtschaftsdemokratie in transformatorischer Absicht', *Berliner Journal für Soziologie*, 28 (1–2), doi: 10.1007/s11609-018-0358-6.

WSI-Mitteilungen (2018), *Industrie 4.0 konkret: Ungleichzeitige Entwicklungen, arbeitspolitische Einordnungen*, Düsseldorf: WSI.

Index